The objective of San Antonio Junior Forum is to create a greater interest among young women in civic, education, and philanthropic fields. All proceeds from the sale of *Celebrate San Antonio* will be returned to the community through San Antonio Junior Forum projects.

Additional copies of *Celebrate San Antonio* may be obtained by writing:

San Antonio Junior Forum Publications
P.O. Box 791186
San Antonio, Texas 78279-1186

Publisher
San Antonio Junior Forum Publications

Book Design
DagenBela Graphics, Inc.
San Antonio, Texas

Art Direction:	Elaine DagenBela
Design & Production:	F. Patricia Denys
Production Editing:	Carl A. Gonzales
Photography:	Oscar Williams
Illustration:	Hobart B. Welsh

Printed by
WIMMER BROTHERS
Memphis/Dallas

First Printing 1986, 15,000
Second Printing 1987, 15,000
Third Printing 1988, 15,000
Library of Congress Catalog Card Number 86-61371
ISBN No. 0-9616917-0-0

Celebrate

SAN ANTONIO

A COOKBOOK

BY THE SAN ANTONIO JUNIOR FORUM

WELCOME

It is my pleasure to share with you this book - a project of San Antonio Junior Forum. We are all proud to take a look at our unique City that captures the flavors of our multi-cultures, enjoys the celebrations that carry us from season to season, and incorporates the best of all cultures into an extraordinary potpourri. We San Antonians appreciate our rich heritage, glory in our climate and savor the lifestyle we work fiercely to protect.

I support the San Antonio Junior Forum and recognize the value of the work done in our community by this group of dedicated volunteers. The volunteers share unselfishly of their time, talents and energy to assist in improving and sustaining the quality of life at the highest possible level for our City. The yearly fund raising events benefit agencies and individuals alike that would otherwise go unnoticed in our community.

Henry G. Cisneros
Mayor of San Antonio
1981-1989

CONTENTS

Entertaining - San Antonio Style 1

    Fiesta Buffet 3
    Barbecue - San Antonio Style ... 8
    Picnic in the Park 15
    KaffeeKlatsch 21
    Mexican Brunch 26
    Folklife Festival 33
    King William Cocktail Buffet ... 39
    Gourmet Celebration 45

Appetizers/Beverages 51

Soups/Salads 87

Main Dishes 131

    Beef & Veal 132
    Lamb 162
    Pork 164
    Game 168
    Poultry 171
    Seafood 195
    Eggs/Cheese 207

Side Dishes 221

    Vegetables 222
    Fruit 238
    Rice/Potatoes 239
    Pasta 248
    Potpourri 251

Breads 257

    Yeast Breads 258
    Quick Breads 264
    Coffee Cakes 280

Sweets 285

    Cakes 286
    Pastries 302
    Cookies 312
    Desserts 324
    Candies 335

Celebrities 341

    Personalities 342
    Caterers 352
    Private Clubs 359
    Hotels 363
    Restaurants 373

Index 393

INTRODUCTION

Unlike many other progressive cities, San Antonio remains true to her varied past. This city is vibrant, exciting and full of surprises. Even native San Antonians are fascinated by the never ending variety of sights and experiences offered by this unique city.

There is a national historic shrine, The Cradle of Texas Liberty, right in the middle of town. A winding river, with a nationally known River-walk, meanders beneath the hustle and bustle of downtown streets in its own peaceful world.

San Antonio is a city of one million people. Its lifestyle is casual, yet cosmopolitan, while the people, not unlike the city's climate, are both warm and pleasant.

Because of its geographic location, San Antonio has always been a meeting place. The contrasts between the fertile hills to the north and east with the arid brush country to the south are as startling as that between the Coastal Plains which stretch to the Gulf of Mexico and the limestone hills of the Texas Hill Country.

The citizens of San Antonio are not of one culture. There are the influences of German settlements and the traditions of the Spanish Village, but also the culture of the Antebellum South and the independence and spirit of the American Frontier. The city has been further influenced by the unlikely influx of Italians, Orientals, Greeks, French, Polish, Lebanese and Irish who have brought to this multi-faceted city a flavor from around the world.

San Antonio is a city of celebrations. San Antonians are festival-happy and are noted for a calendar filled with an endless array of celebrations and fun.

San Antonians are a festive, easy-going and happy people whose history combines with their lifestyles to comprise the surprising mosaic known as San Antonio.

SAN ANTONIO JUNIOR FORUM PUBLICATIONS

Steering Committee

Chairman
Trudy Chance Kinnison
(Mrs. Paul)

Managing Editor/Computer Processing
Tina Carrola Knight-Sheen
(Mrs. Philip)

Recipe Testing Editor
Kathy Leonard Durham
(Mrs. Jody)

Managing Section Editor
Janice Hokanson Wilson
(Mrs. Richard E.)

Cookbook Consultant
Candy Erben Wagner

Treasurer
Ceil Manhoff Barbour
(Mrs. Lou)

Indexing Editor
Ruth Gilpin Thomas
(Mrs. Oren)

Cataloging Editors
Mary Butler Arnold
(Mrs. Robert)
Jan Hill Robertson
(Mrs. Dave)

Business Operations
Barbara Schaffner Austin
(Mrs. Jerry)
Lynda Perry Vine
(Mrs. James B.)

Cultural Editor
Virginia Gregory Van Cleave
(Mrs. Albert W. III)

Proofing Editor
Janet Reinsch Scott
(Mrs. Hugh)

Marketing Chairman
Molly Chance Bailey
(Mrs. David)

Publications Gala Chairman
Sandi Fountain Drummond
(Mrs. Al)

At Large
Lauretta Buschell Manupelli
(Mrs. Frank)
Jane Searcy Hibler
(Mrs. Otis)
Betty Watts Telford
(Mrs. William L.)

At Large
Leona Daniel Maples
(Mrs. Fred E., Jr.)
Mary Denise Reasonover

Margie Morales Weiss
(Mrs. Martin)

Section Editors

Cathy Magavern Blank
(Mrs. Ron)

Mary Ellen Whittredge Mathews
(Mrs. Dan)

Jane Ann Dumm Briscoe
(Mrs. Harry)

Dottie Short Mezzetti
(Mrs. Mike)

Susan Meuth Grohman
(Mrs. Wayne)

Sandy Hairston Reeves
(Mrs. Clint)

Suzanne Pipkin Harrison
(Mrs. Tim)

Kathy Mowrey Roberts
(Mrs. Charles)

Tina Carrola Knight-Sheen
(Mrs. Philip)

Lenore Zarlengo Stehouwer
(Mrs. Ron)

Barbara Greer Laxson
(Mrs. Rick)

Ruth Gilpin Thomas
(Mrs. Oren)

Paula Boyden Leonard
(Mrs. Don)

Judy Blair Treuhaft
(Mrs. Marty)

Jessie Allan Killian
(Mrs. John M.)

Jean Herschede Vickers
(Mrs. Marty)

The contributors whose names are listed in these credits are among the finest cooks, not only in San Antonio, but all of South Texas. The Cookbook Committee of San Antonio Junior Forum expresses appreciation to them for their participation in this project by contributing their favorite recipes, their time and their talents.

The recipes have been tested and carefully edited by our volunteers to insure accuracy and clarity. The selections made by the Steering Committee from the 2,000 recipes submitted targeted regional authenticity, balance in the sections and high scores from testing. Our pride in sharing our city in photography, celebrations and recipes can only be equaled by your delight in using our book.

Trudy Kinnison

Cookbook Committee

Bass, Darlene Hunter
(Mrs. James)

Bates, Ruth
(Mrs. J.D.)

Bevan, Sherry Hill
(Mrs. Norm)

Boyd, Lynnelle Benold
(Mrs. Johnny)

Edgarton, Claudia

Fenn, Pamela Parks
(Mrs. Jerald)

Ferguson, Vicki Cook
(Mrs. Charles)

Forsythe, Donna Chalkley
(Mrs. Allan)

Fry, Jan Hastedt
(Mrs. Steve)

Garland, Mary Sue Schroeder
(Mrs. Edward)

Greiner, Robin Hoch
(Mrs. Donn)

Grogan, Marilyn Rice
(Mrs. Gerald)

Gulledge, Linda Paine
(Mrs. Bill)

Haag, Marsha
(Mrs. Elmer)

Harris, Paula Rutledge
(Mrs. Bill)

Hooks, Rebecca Gaines
(Mrs. Bill)

Hughes, Kathi Strommen
(Mrs. James)

Ingram, Susan Loadman
(Mrs. John Jr.)

Japhet, Gayle

Kierum, Beth Hudson
(Mrs. Michael)

Knibbe, Sharon Hill
(Mrs. Chuck)

Mettler, Sue Ryel
(Mrs. Robert)

Miller, Barbara Poehl

Montgomery, Nancy Smith
(Mrs. Buddy)

Oliver, Mary Ann Maxwell
(Mrs. Leonard)

Reddy, Pam Buffington
(Mrs. Paul)

Rigsby, Dr. Carole Watkins
(Mrs. Richard)

Russell, Neilana

Soules, Marie Fite
(Mrs. Joe)

Stanush, Belinda Mosty
(Mrs. Frank III)

Tollett, Brenda Bridges
(Mrs. J.T. III)

Turner, Sharon Martin
(Mrs. Harvey)

Warren, Marcella Biry
(Mrs. Frank)

Weakly, Terry
(Mrs. Terence)

Woods, Glenda
(Mrs. Gary)

Contributing Membership

Adams, Jerre
(Mrs. Jerry)

Allan, Janelle Dietzmann
(Mrs. Willian N. III)

Allen, Ellen
(Mrs. Andy)

Allen, Freda

Amato, Sherry Woolsey
(Mrs. Charles)

Anderson, Frances Shaw
(Mrs. Thomas H.)

Arnold, Helen

Atkinson, Jeanette
(Mrs. Harold)

Ausburn, Edith
(Mrs. Mack)

Auth, Ruth
(Mrs. Harry)

Bain, Linda Dullye
(Mrs. Cecil)

Bailey, Teri Teague

Banack, Rose Marie Gill
(Mrs. Emerson)

Barnhart, Kathy Small
(Mrs. Clif)

Barton, Sherry Stockett
(Mrs. Ronald)

Bayern, Janice O'Banion
(Mrs. Arthur)

Belsjoe, Fran Winstead
(Mrs. Thomas B.)

Bennett, Kathy
(Mrs. Sam III)

Benninger, Nelda Emmert
(Mrs. Edward)

Bibb, Helen Bramblett
(Mrs. E. Monroe)

Beuhler, Willa Jo Bullard
(Mrs. William)

Bickerton, Pam Weathers
(Mrs. Terry)

Biggs, Carolyn Scroggin
(Mrs. Clark)

Bodnar, Tessa
(Mrs. Emery)

Bonney, Pamela Ashbrook
(Mrs. Jerry)

Boswell, Pat Walker
(Mrs. Steve)

Boyd, Camille Blackburn
(Mrs. Douglass)

Bradford, Kaye Garwood
(Mrs. Brad)

Bridges, Dianne Gotthardt
(Mrs. Ron)

Briggs, Vicki
(Mrs. Kim)

Brockway, Becky
(Mrs. Bruce)

Brotze, Camille Cooper
(Mrs. Wayne)

Brown, Bonnie Boswell
(Mrs. Tom)

Brown, Kathy Guess
(Mrs. Jim)

Brown, Leonora
(Mrs. Walter F.)

Brown, Debra

Buchanan, Linda Temple
(Mrs. Buck)

Burkhart, Sally Fox
(Mrs. David)

Cace, Linda DiQuinzio
(Mrs. John)

Caffery, Jennifer
(Mrs. Gary)

Cage, Sharon Woodhall
(Mrs. Don)

Canady, Charlotte Denny
(Mrs. Don)

Canales, Caro Lozano
(Mrs. Tony)

Carden, Julabeth

Castleberry, Linda Sanders
(Mrs. Larry)

Chamberlain, Dorothy

Chatelle, Jeannine
(Mrs. N.G.)

Childress, Sheryl Stich
(Mrs. Joe)

Chitwood, Cheryl
(Mrs. William)

Christopher, Marjie
(Mrs. Henry)

Closner, Susan
(Mrs. Bennett)

Cooper, Judy La Croix
(Mrs. Robert)

Cooper, Gay Mitchell
(Mrs. Larry)

Copeland, Lucia
(Mrs. Ken)

Copley, Donna Muller
(Mrs. J.Brian)

Corley, Rosemary
(Mrs. Ezra E.)

Covington, Brenda
(Mrs. Ed)

Craighead, Nell Jenschke
(Mrs. Donald)

Cross, Judith Marston
(Mrs. Dennis)

Cunningham, Kathy
(Mrs. Martin)

Curry, Patricia
(Mrs. Mark)

Curtis, Marilyn Hulsey
(Mrs. Jack)

Dalrymple, Judy Wood
(Mrs. Scott)

Dare, Sandy Wesch
(Mrs. Milton)

Dawson, Patti Alexander
(Mrs. E.B.)

Dees, Christine

Doerr, Sharon
(Mrs. Charles J. III)

Dorbandt, Melba
Richardson
(Mrs. Bill)

Dudley, Carolyn Callahan
(Mrs. Gary)

Dufner, Patte Goldbeck
(Mrs. Romie Mark)

Duke, Rosemary Green
(Mrs. Jim)
Easley, Mary Lou Fry
(Mrs. John)
Ebrom, Betty
(Mrs. Charles)
Elliott, Cece Roller
(Mrs. Steve)
Ellis, Carol Emmert
(Mrs. J. Brant)
Ernst, Carol Schilling
(Mrs. Herbert)
Evans, Mary Elizabeth Bell
(Mrs. Dick)
Felty, Marcie NavarroRiera
(Mrs. Steve Alan)
Flynn, Colleen Teague
(Mrs. Peter)
Foster, Iris
(Mrs. John)
Franklin, Lynn Williamson
(Mrs. James)
Fuller, Anita
(Mrs. Paul, Jr.)
Gaddis, Carola Joseph
(Mrs. John M.)
Gale, Beth Cutter
(Mrs. G.G.)
Garrahan, Sarah
(Mrs. Richard)
Gibson, Nancy Young
(Mrs. Larry)
Gideon, Judy McFall
(Mrs. Rhett)
Girardeau, Amy Brown
(Mrs. James)
Goldbeck, Sally Jones
(Mrs. Edward)
Gonzales, Blanca Sanchez
(Mrs. Bernard)
Gragg, Frances
(Mrs. Ernest)
Green, Bettie
(Mrs. Terry C.)
Greenway, Ruth
(Mrs. Charles)
Hall, Carol Barnes
(Mrs. John)
Hallmark, Dianne Huff
(Mrs. Phil)
Haney, Jan Green
(Mrs. Tom)
Hanke, Genie Garrett
(Mrs. Dan H.)
Hardin, Marty Thompson
Harris, Chita Fitzhugh
(Mrs. Lee)
Harris, Linda McClain
(Mrs. Ed)
Harris, Marcia Heinen
(Mrs. Richard W.)
Hatchett, Francille Hollis
(Mrs. Victor)
Heckman, Susan Coleman
(Mrs. James)
Hein, Nancy Tieken
(Mrs. Robert)
Hemmi, Barbara Werner
(Mrs. John U.)
Heyland, Mary Ann Arnette
(Mrs. Gary)
Hibler, Jane Searcy
(Mrs. Otis)
Hill, M'Liss White
(Mrs. Gerald)
Holder, Mary Jo Allie
(Mrs. Bill)
Holzhausen, Barbara Cavazos
(Mrs. Walter)
Hooker, Lucille Quinones
(Mrs. Harry)

Houser, Becky Cannon
(Mrs. C.H.)
Howell, Vilma Puig
(Mrs. Daniel D.)
Hudson, Margaret Nelan
(Mrs. L.H.)
Jauer, Liz
(Mrs. David)
Johnson, Sharon
(Mrs. Jim)
Jonas, Davene Schmidt
(Mrs. William J., Jr.)
Jones, Karen Gass
(Mrs. Thomas)
Jones, Jody Braun
(Mrs. David)
Jones, Kathy Denton
(Mrs. David)
Jopling, Cynthia Thompson
(Mrs. Gene)
Jordan, Melinda
(Mrs. Jerry)
Keeter, Carol Hansen
(Mrs. Jim)
Kenney, Nancy Upton
(Mrs. Jim)
Kern, Mary Sue Viner
(Mrs. Maurie)
Killian, Jessie Allan
(Mrs. John M.)
Kirk, Virginia Eley
(Mrs. James)
Kittrell, Sandy Hinze
(Mrs. John R.)
Landreth, Penny Spicer
(Mrs. George)
Lange, Joyce Robertson
(Mrs. Eric)
Lansdale, Nova
(Mrs. Daryl)
Lemons, Pam Kelley
(Mrs. Bill)
Leonard, Anne Dalton
(Mrs. Dan)
Liberto, Pat Edwards
(Mrs. Frank G.)
Lively, Tudy
(Mrs. Dean)
Lockett, Nikki Clark
(Mrs. Bill)
Lowrey, Deborah Crues
(Mrs. Charles)
Lynch, Judy Gillis
(Mrs. Bernie)
Magness. Camille Tiffany
(Mrs. James)
Malek, Kay Ford
(Mrs. Kenneth)
Marcus, Marsha Albert
(Mrs. Stanley)
Martin, Donna DeRusha
(Mrs. E. Jack)
Martin, Ginger Grabfelder
(Mrs. Cecil)
Mason, Barbara Sutton
(Mrs. William A.)
Mason, Virginia Hollifield
(Mrs. Richard J.)
Maurer, Joan
(Mrs. William T.)
Maurer, Donna
(Mrs. Boone)
McPherson, Winnie Williams
(Mrs. Jean)
Menzies, Sally Morrow
(Mrs. Stephen)
Midkiff, Mary Wall
(Mrs. Charles)
Miller, Nancy Belville
(Mrs. Charles)
Moses, Gaye Lyons
(Mrs. Richard)

Murphy, Sandra Fruits
(Mrs. Richard)
Nauschutz, Kathy Katz
(Mrs. Paul)
Nelson, Ellen Clark
(Mrs. Ronald)
Newman, Carol Soper
(Mrs. Richard)
Nicholas, Virginia Stokes
(Mrs. Anthony)
Nichols, Paula Halford
(Mrs. Bruce)
Nolan, Deanie
(Mrs. Ross)
Nussbaum, Jo Ann Sorenson
(Mrs. Bill)
Ogden, Nancy McMinn
(Mrs. Jack)
Oliver, Karen Lackey
(Mrs. Larry)
Oveland, Debbie
(Mrs. Greg)
Page, Kathleen Corcoran
(Mrs. James)
Pape, Martha Edwards
(Mrs. Patrick J.)
Parker, Sandra Watson
(Mrs. Winn)
Paul, Mary Ann Adler
(Mrs. Hadley)
Pearson, Nancy Mantooth
(Mrs. Park)
Penaloza, Julia Quijano
(Mrs. Paul)
Petitt, Kathy Brown
(Mrs. Richard)
Pfeiffer, Barbara Klar
Phillips, Linda Butz
(Mrs. Stephen)
Polansky, Helenan Halloran
(Mrs. Edward)
Porter, Lauri Komet
(Mrs. Mark)
Powell, Jo Lynn
(Mrs. Lewis)
Radicke, Deborah Spurlock
(Mrs. Lewis)
Ramert, Jan Wechsler
(Mrs. Frank)
Raney, Harriett Van Gundy
(Mrs. Douglas)
Rath, Judy Trevino
(Mrs. Alfred)
Ray, Linnie Livingston
(Mrs. Jon)
Reed, Katie Nowinski
(Mrs. Jim)
Regester, Carol Sullivan
(Mrs. Larry)
Reichert, Nan Keefe
(Mrs. William F., Jr.)
Reneau, Lynne Harris
(Mrs. Randy)
Richardson, Marilyn Jones
Richter, Jerrianne Biry
(Mrs. Tom)
Rountree, Cynthia Quinones
Saidi, Brigitte Bapistella
(Mrs. Mo)
Sanderson, Lynda McGrath
(Mrs. J. Nathaniel)
Saunders, Glenna Pontikes
(Mrs. Douglas)
Schnipper, Lin Connelly
(Mrs. Stephen)
Scoville, Lenetta Lyons
Sheehan, Susan Agee
(Mrs. Patrick)
Shwiff, Sheila Staten
(Mrs. Harold)
Silber, Renee' Rubin
(Mrs. Brent)

Silvia, Carrie Morgan
(Mrs. Steve)
Smith, Cindy Decker
(Mrs. Greg)
Smith, Ann Sauer
(Mrs. Martin)
Smith, Robbie Jennings
(Mrs. Con)
Srp, Kim Lummen
(Mrs. James)
Swinney, Barbara
(Mrs. Boen, Jr.)
Taylor, Susie
(Mrs. Dick)
Tedore, Pamela Varnon
(Mrs. Melvin)
Terrey, Pat Collins
Theis, Janice Carney
(Mrs. Joseph)
Theis, Evelyn Popp
(Mrs. Gerald E.)
Thomas, Elizabeth
(Mrs. Tullis)
Thurmond, Carolyn Garner
(Mrs. Tom)
Tilson, Carol
(Mrs. Hugh B.)
Todd, Jennifer Watson
(Mrs. Bill)
Tomz, Jane
(Mrs. Bob)
Touchstone, Barbara
Buffington
(Mrs. Gaylord)
Trautman, Joyce
(Mrs. Barry)
Trcka, Karen
(Mrs. Chuck)
Trevino, Kathleen O'Connor
(Mrs. Ruben)
Triplett, Sue
(Mrs. Max, Jr.)
Troutz, Barbara Thacker
(Mrs. Herb)
Turner, Helen
Tyra, Connie
(Mrs. John)
Uecker, Ann
(Mrs. Warren W.)
Vance, Vivian Miller
(Mrs. P.J.)
Walker, Debra Coates
(Mrs. Stephen)
Walker, Kay Hartong
Walker, Carmen
(Mrs. Billy C.)
Walling, Amy
(Mrs. Bill)
Watts, Diana Davis
(Mrs. Robert)
Westwood, Barbara Jacoby
(Mrs. Mike)
Wiginton, Kay Freitag
(Mrs. Jay)
Williams, Vicki Veale
(Mrs. Bill)
Willingham, Judy
(Mrs. Jim)
Winkenhower, Angie
(Mrs. Wink)
Woods, Barbara
(Mrs. George)
Wright, Jane Hudson
(Mrs. Tom)
Wright, Yolanda Quinones
(Mrs. Nile)
Wurzbach, Jodie Ross
Zaiontz, Beverly Schwarzer
(Mrs. Milton A.)

Friends of Forum

Bailey, David
Barbour, Mary
 (Mrs. Lou)
Beretta, Mary Austin
Benninger, Bridget
Blankenship, Marilyn
 (Mrs. Don)
Braden, Meredith
Bryant, Judy
Burton, Miriam
 (Mrs. H.L.)
Cantu, Angie
Chance, Frances
 (Mrs. Oscar)
Chance, Opal
 (Mrs. Truett)
Churchill, Virginia
Coghlan, Sandra
 (Mrs. Tom)
Coldewey, Pat
Cole, Lois
Crumley, Neva
Dickson, Gogi Carrola
 (Mrs. John)
Dorsey, Dale Longmoor
 (Mrs. Thad)
Duffin, Myrt
Duke, Gertrude
England, Marcy
Everitt, Bernice
 (Mrs. Bill)
Flores, Alicia
Flores, Tenchita
 (Mrs. Alfredo)
Fountain, Ernestine
 (Mrs. Ross)

Gaines, Barbara
Galvan, Susie
Gardner, Elaine
 (Mrs. Bob)
Grabfelder, Rae E.
Gregory, Gloria
 (Mrs. Joe)
Hammond, Linda
Hardin, Glenda
Hibbetts, Andrea
 (Mrs. Bill)
Hogan, Dorothy
 (Mrs. Woodrow)
Hokanson, Thanet
 (Mrs. Oscar)
Hooks, June
Hubbard, Janice
Hudson, Ann
Ison, Mary
 (Mrs. David)
Jauregi, Kathlin
 (Mrs. Dick)
Joiner, Lorell
Kalinowski, Elaine Lee
 (Mrs. John)
Kalter, Cheryl
Kinnison, Karen
 (Mrs. Bill)
Klar, Joyce
 (Mrs. Edwin M.)
Knight, Hazel
Kruse, Alice
Lemons, Ann
Leonard, Alma Ruth
 (Mrs. Dale)

Leonard, Bette
 (Mrs. Phil)
Leonard, Donna
Leonard, K. Evelyn
Leske, Martha
 (Mrs. Charles)
Lilly, Jeanne
Mangold, Jacque
 (Mrs. Hans)
Manhoff, Charlotte
Marquart, Suzanne
Martin, Esther
McBride, Kathryn
 (Mrs. William B.)
McClellan, Cheryle
McElreath, Virginia
McIntosh, Kathy
Metler, Nancy
Michalski, Valarie
Mireles, Carmen
Mochel, Rene
Monaghan, Louise
 (Mrs. Robert)
Moravec, Cris
Morris, Rhonda
Mueles, Carmen
Mueller, Mary Beth
 (Mrs. Bev)
Myers, Cindy
Nations, Charlotte
 (Mrs. Swanzy)
Nemec, Bobbie
Oholendt, Katherine
Parma, Patty
 (Mrs. Christopher)

Peirce, Jan
Pickard, Mary
Psencik, Patti Stroud
 (Mrs. Rickey)
Ramley, Hazel May
Reeves, Liz
Regente, Carol
Richmond, Laura
 (Mrs. Jack)
Roller, Lyn
Ross, Diane
Simmons, Dee Ann
 (Mrs. Wayland)
Smith, Linda
Staglik, Sue
 (Mrs. Jerry)
Stanford, Louden
Stewart, Kathleen
Stroud, Velma
 (Mrs. Claude)
Tatum, Patsy
Thompson, Mickey
Tollett, Ava
Van Cleave, Albert W. III
Vine, James B. Jr.
Walker, Carmen
Wallace, Glenna
West, Susan
Westwood, Mike
Wille, Shirley
Wilson, Elizabeth
 (Mrs. Wilmer)
Wissler, Louise
Witter, Carla

Special Thanks to:

Hughes, James   Jones, Sheryn   Laxson, Rick   Laxson, Wayne   Turner, Harvey

Thousands of anxious people line the walkways along the San Antonio River in anticipation of the largest river parade in America. The annual Fiesta River parade features magnificently decorated barge floats carrying Kings, Queens, Princesses and Duchesses. It is a spectacular event that captures the imagination of an entire city and surrounding area. The beauty, charm and excitement of San Antonio's Fiesta can be seen and felt at the River Parade.

San Antonio is "One of America's Four Unique Cities." It is worthy of the designation. San Antonio's magnificent past influences its vibrant future. People and places are special here. So are the city's celebrations, its customs and its food. Every season brings new excitement.

FIESTA BUFFET

Fiesta in Spanish means *party*. In San Antonio we fiesta! Our *fiestas* are exciting with casual dress, many good friends, good drink & warm summer nights. Patios decorated with bright flowers add to the festive outdoor ambience. One great thing about fiesta foods is that everyone chooses a meal of his unique taste selecting from among the delicious ethnic dishes.

MENU

CEVICHE WITH TOSTADAS

SAN ANTONIO DIP • CHILE CON QUESO

BEEF AND CHICKEN FAJITAS

CONDIMENT TRAY FOR FAJITAS:
GUACAMOLE, PICO de GALLO
FRESH CILANTRO, SLICED JALAPENOS

SPICY MEXICAN PICKLED VEGETABLES

STUFFED JALAPENOS

FLOUR TORTILLAS

FRIJOLES • BUNUELOS

EL MIRADOR RICE

MEXICAN PRALINES

MEXICAN COOKIES

LIVELY MELON BOAT

TEXAS SUN TEA • BEER

FIESTA MARGARITAS

CEVICHE
(Marinated Fish)

2	cups fresh scallops, cut into bite size pieces
½	cup green onions, chopped
3	small serrano peppers, finely chopped
⅓	cup fresh lime juice
½	cup tomato juice
⅓	cup olive oil (we recommend Bertollis)
2	tomatoes, chopped
1½	cloves garlic, minced
½	teaspoon thyme
1	tablespoon fresh parsley, chopped
1	tablespoon fresh cilantro (coriander), chopped
¼	cup sweet red pepper, chopped
	salt & pepper

Combine ingredients in order given. Mix well. Always use ceramic container for marinating this mixture. Marinate for 24 hours. Drain a little and serve with tostadas or melba toast.

YIELD: 10 servings.

VARIATION: *To serve as a salad, peel and cut avocados in half. Fill with fish mixture and serve on a lettuce leaf.*

GUACAMOLE
(Avocado Mixture)

3	large ripe avocados
1	medium onion, grated
¼	teaspoon garlic powder
1	medium tomato, chopped
2	tablespoons olive oil
	juice of ½ lemon or lime
	salt & pepper

Peel and remove pits from avocados. Using a kitchen fork, coarsely mash avocados. Add remaining ingredients and mix well. Make a few hours ahead to let flavors blend together. Leave the avocado pit in the guacamole and cover tightly with plastic wrap to deter discoloration. Should it turn black on top, fold into mixture at serving time. Serve chilled as a condiment for fajitas, as a dip with tostadas or as a salad on a bed of lettuce and sliced tomato.

YIELD: 8 servings.

FAJITAS
(Marinated Skirt Steak)

One of the most popular tacos in Texas today is **fajitas**. Fajitas means **skirt steak** in Spanish, and it is a flavorful as well as an economical cut of beef. They are great to have outdoors on a ranch, at a campfire or in the backyard.

Fajitas, grilled over mesquite wood, are sliced and served as a taco on a hot flour tortilla with condiments. Some favorite condiments to add to your taco are guacamole, pico de gallo, sliced onions, fresh cilantro, sliced jalapenos, grated monterey jack cheese and sour cream.

San Antonio Marinade

¼ teaspoon rosemary
½ teaspoon thyme
1½ cups corn oil
1 cup lemon juice (or ½ lemon & ½ apple vinegar)
1 tablespoon green onion, chopped
2 teaspoons salt
1 clove garlic (more to taste), pressed
1 tablespoon oregano
pepper to taste
6 pounds fajita meat (skirt, sirloin or flank steak)
20 flour tortillas

Combine all ingredients except meat and mix well. Add meat to marinade and refrigerate for 24 hours. Keep turning mixture for best results at least 4 to 6 times. Barbecue over mesquite coals for best results. Cook for 5 to 8 minutes on each side, being careful not to overcook. For best results, cook to medium rare. Use remaining marinade to baste when cooking.

Remove to a cutting board. Slice in ½x4-inch strips across the grain. Place several strips in the center of the flour tortilla and fold as a taco. Add condiments as desired.

YIELD: 8 to 10 servings.

Everyone has his own secret marinade recipe. A simple marinade consists of: lime or lemon juice, oil and garlic (enough to cover the meat with equal portions of juice and oil; garlic to taste.) Marinate for 24 hours. Barbecue over mesquite. Check index for further information on Fajitas!

Rosita Fernandez, internationally recognized entertainer, is held close to the hearts of San Antonians. "Rosita's Bridge," spanning the River, ties together two sides of the Paseo del Rio, the Riverwalk that winds several miles through downtown San Antonio. This bridge was dedicated to recognize Rosita's devotion to "Entertaining - San Antonio Style."

PICO DE GALLO

1   onion, chopped
3   tomatoes, chopped
1   clove garlic, minced
1-2 fresh serrano peppers,
         minced
2   tablespoons fresh
         lime juice
½   teaspoon salt
¾   cup fresh cilantro
         (coriander), chopped

Combine the ingredients and chill for about 30 minutes. For best results serve immediately.

YIELD: 8 servings.

There are two peppers that work well in a Mexican hot sauce. The serrano pepper, a small, bright green chile about 1½ inches long or the jalapeno pepper, a small bell-pepper like chile. The amount of cilantro is strictly personal preference.

FLOUR TORTILLAS

3   cups flour
3   teaspoons baking powder
1   teaspoon salt
4   tablespoons vegetable oil
1   cup warm water

Sift flour, baking powder and salt into large bowl. Add vegetable oil and water. Mix until well blended. Turn the mixture out on a floured board and knead 3-5 minutes or until the dough is soft and no longer sticky. Cover and set aside for 20 - 30 minutes. Divide the dough into 16 - 18 balls about 1½ inches in diameter. Keep them covered with a damp cloth. Roll out each ball on a floured board with a rolling pin into a circle about 6 inches in diameter and ⅛ to ¼ inch thick. Cook tortillas on a hot, ungreased griddle until lightly browned on each side. As they are done, place them in a cloth-lined basket or bowl and cover to keep warm and moist.

YIELD: 16 - 18 tortillas.

VARIATION: **Using a Packaged Flour Tortilla Mix**
To 1 cup of mix, add ¼ cup of warm water. Knead until well blended to be free of lumps but not sticky. Cover and let stand for 15 minutes, then follow above instructions.

MEXICAN PRALINES

2 cups sugar
1 teaspoon baking soda
1 cup buttermilk
¾ cup butter
1 teaspoon vanilla
2 cups pecan pieces

In large saucepan, combine sugar, soda, salt and buttermilk. Cook over high heat, stirring constantly, to bring mixture to boil. Continue boiling and stirring until mixture begins to thicken and takes on a creamy tinge. (It should be about 210° on a candy thermometer at this time.) Add butter and pecans and continue cooking over medium high heat until it reaches 234° on candy thermometer (soft ball stage). Remove from heat and stir in vanilla. Allow to cool slightly, about 2 minutes. Beat mixture until it begins to lose its gloss and is thick and creamy. Quickly drop into 2-inch mounds on waxed paper and allow to cool. If mixture becomes too hard, immerse pan in hot water for several minutes and resume procedure.

YIELD: 2 dozen.

STUFFED JALAPENO PEPPERS

The fiery hot flavor from jalapeno peppers disappears when the seeds and veins are removed. Even those Texans who cannot tolerate this pepper full strength find stuffed jalapenos a special tasty treat to any appetizer tray!

1 11 to 14-ounce can pickled jalapeno peppers, whole & drained
1 8-ounce package cream cheese, softened
2 eggs, boiled
¼ teaspoon garlic salt
1 tablespoon finely chopped onion
4 tablespoons mayonnaise

Cut each jalapeno pepper in half lengthwise and remove veins and seeds. In a small bowl, blend the cream cheese, eggs and mayonnaise. Stir in onion and garlic salt to taste. Stuff pepper halves with cheese mixture. Chill before serving.

YIELD: Approximately 30 appetizers.

The flamencos play passionately and the dancers swirl. The crowd enjoys. Fiesta Noche del Rio, held at the outdoor Arneson River Theater, is an extravaganza of international music and dance which adds sparkle to San Antonio summer nights.

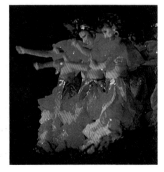

BARBECUE SAN ANTONIO STYLE

Red checkered tablecloths, guests in western attire, the aroma of smoking meats over native hardwoods, sets the stage for a real barbecue - Texas style - perhaps our greatest gift to mankind. Spicy foods produce a casual setting guaranteed to make any evening or afternoon a very festive time.

MENU

ROASTED PECANS

HOT ROASTED PEANUTS

TOSTADAS AND SALSA FRESCA

PICKLED BLACK EYED PEAS

CHOW CHOW

PICKLED EGGS

OLD FASHIONED POTATO SALAD

COLE SLAW

BARBECUED RIBS, SAUSAGE,
BRISKET AND CHICKEN

PAPPY SKRAP'S BARBECUE SAUCE

COWBOY BEANS

JALAPENO CORN BREAD

HOMEMADE VANILLA ICE CREAM

HILL COUNTRY PEACH COBBLER

TEXAS SUN TEA • BEER

San Antonians celebrate in the great outdoors. Families and friends get together and enjoy a western-style barbecue, dancing, horseback riding and good conversation. There are some fabled masters of the open pit at work in San Antonio. If you don't believe it, just ask the next person you see smokin' a brisket.

TOSTADAS
(Toasted Chips)

Tostadas are traditionally used to dip ceviche, guacamole, Mexican salsa or your favorite dip.

12 corn tortillas
oil for frying
salt to taste

Cut tortillas into quarters. Heat 1 inch of oil in a small frying pan over high heat. Fry 3 to 4 pieces of tortillas at a time in oil until crisp and lightly golden. Place on paper towel to drain and salt lightly to taste.

YIELD: 4 dozen tostadas.

Tostadas, or homemade corn chips, have an interesting origin. The first tostadas, or **Fritos** *as we know them today, were invented in San Antonio. The company tried to finance their new enterprise locally, but had to go to Dallas to get business backing. The* **Frito** *is rectangular in shape.*

Tostada means toasted chip. These chips are traditionally triangular in shape and are served with Mexican salsa or sauce, guacamole, dips, refried beans and other Mexican appetizers. Tostadas and salsa accompany meals in most San Antonio Mexican restaurants.

OLD FASHIONED POTATO SALAD

This old-fashioned recipe is a favorite with barbecue. It is mixed warm, therefore, the potatoes have more of a blended texture.

2	**tablespoons green onions, chopped**
1	**tablespoon bell pepper, finely chopped**
2	**tablespoons pimiento, diced**
3	**tablespoons sour pickles, chopped**
1	**stem celery, chopped**
1	**tablespoon prepared mustard**
1	**tablespoon juice from sour pickles**
5	**medium potatoes**
4-5	**tablespoons salad dressing (we recommend Miracle Whip)**

Mix all ingredients in large mixing bowl except potatoes and dressing. Boil potatoes until tender. As soon as potatoes are cool enough to handle, peel and dice. Add potatoes to vegetable mixture, one cup at a time, adding salt and pepper to taste. After each addition, toss lightly. After all potatoes have been added, fold in salad dressing and toss. The potatoes may not remain in cubes through the mixing.

YIELD: 6 servings.

PAPPY SKRAP'S BARBECUE SAUCE

In 1951 Ernest H. Parks wrote a cookbook for a barbecue pit he invented and patented. This is Mr.Parks' original sauce recipe from the book. The word "Skrap" is Parks spelled backwards; and therefore, this delicious sauce has a rather unusual name!!

1	14-ounce bottle catsup
½	cup water
½	cup vinegar
2	tablespoons worcestershire sauce
1	teaspoon salt
4	teaspoons chili powder
1	teaspoon black pepper
	dash red pepper
2	tablespoons lemon juice

Mix all ingredients together and let stand in refrigerator for 1 or 2 days.

Sauce for Beef or Poultry: Add ¼ pound margarine or butter to sauce, heating sufficiently to melt butter.

Sauce for Pork: Omit margarine or butter and add ½ cup white corn syrup.

This sauce can be frozen, but it keeps in refrigerator for at least three months.

YIELD: 1 quart.

February is San Antonio Livestock Show & Rodeo time. Bucking broncos, snorting bulls, Grand Champion Steers, tough cowboys and life-saving clowns share the spotlight with nationally known country and western singing stars. Trailrides and a downtown parade precede the opening of this annual event.

COWBOY BEANS

This is an authentic recipe used by chuck wagon cooks on the open range of Texas. Pinto beans, usually served with beef and cornbread, were a staple for the cowboy on cattle drives.

1	pound dried pinto beans
¼	pound salt pork
1	teaspoon salt
1	onion, diced
1	14½-ounce can whole tomatoes, chopped
3	tablespoons chili powder

Pick beans clean and wash. Place in large pot, at least 4 quarts. Cover with water and soak overnight. When ready to cook, drain beans and add fresh water to cover 1 inch above beans. Add salt pork and salt. Boil for 30 minutes. Add onions, tomatoes and chili powder and continue boiling for 2 to 3 hours or until beans are tender. Add additional water as needed.

YIELD: 4 to 6 servings.

HILL COUNTRY PEACH COBBLER

Orchards of peaches grow in the Hill Country just north of San Antonio near Fredericksburg, Texas. San Antonians prepare many different kinds of peach desserts in the summer when there is an abundance of this wonderful fruit. An all time favorite recipe handed down through generations of Texans is peach cobbler using Hill Country peaches. This is usually served with homemade ice cream.

Filling

8	cups fresh peaches, peeled & sliced
2	cups sugar
2-4	tablespoons all-purpose flour
½	teaspoon ground nutmeg
⅓	cup melted butter or margarine
	pastry for double-crust 9-inch pie

Pastry

2⅔	cups flour
2	teaspoons salt
1	cup shortening
6	tablespoons iced water

Preheat oven to 475°.
Combine peaches, sugar, flour and nutmeg. In a large pan, bring peaches to a boil and cook over low heat 10 minutes or until tender. Remove from heat and add butter.

For Pastry: Mix flour and salt. Cut in shortening. (An electric mixer does a good job.) Add iced water and toss with fork till well blended. Turn out on floured board and knead three or four times. Roll out half of pastry to ⅛ inch thickness on a slightly floured board. Cut pastry into a 9x13-inch rectangle. Spoon half of peaches into a 9x13-inch buttered baking dish and top with pastry. Bake for 12 minutes or until golden brown. Remove from oven and spoon remaining peaches over baked pastry. Roll out remaining pastry and cut into ½-inch strips. Arrange in lattice design over peaches. Brush strips with melted butter and sprinkle with sugar. Return to oven for 10 to 15 minutes.

YIELD: 8 servings.

JALAPENO CORNBREAD

2   eggs
1   8-ounce can cream style corn
1   cup sour cream
1-3 jalapeno peppers, pickled,
     canned & finely chopped
     (or substitute 2 ounces
     mild, canned
     green chiles)
1   cup cheddar cheese, grated
1   cup yellow cornmeal
1   teaspoon baking soda
6   tablespoons butter

Preheat oven to 400°.
In a mixing bowl, beat eggs lightly with wire whisk. Add corn, sour cream, peppers, cheese, cornmeal and soda. Mix all ingredients. Add 3 tablespoons melted butter. In a 9x9-inch pan or 10-inch cast iron skillet, melt 3 tablespoons butter. While pan is still hot, add batter and bake 20 to 25 minutes.

YIELD: 8 servings.

CHOW CHOW

3   pounds green tomatoes,
     chopped
1   cabbage head, shredded
2   large onions, chopped
2   sweet red peppers, chopped
3   cups white vinegar
2   cups sugar
2   tablespoons pickling spice
1   tablespoon mustard seed
1   tablespoon salt

In a large enamel or stainless steel pan, combine vegetables. Add remaining ingredients and toss well. Bring mixture to a boil. Lower heat and simmer 10 to 15 minutes, stirring occasionally. Pour into 4 hot, sterilized pint jars and seal immediately.

YIELD: 4 pint jars.

South Texas is a large beef producing area. On many ranches, the cowboy, or "vaquero," still rides, ropes and works cattle. The vaquero is an independent spirit whose love for the land will endure forever. When not working, many vaqueros enjoy the competition and camaraderie of Mexican rodeos.

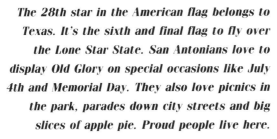

*The 28th star in the American flag belongs to
Texas. It's the sixth and final flag to fly over
the Lone Star State. San Antonians love to
display Old Glory on special occasions like July
4th and Memorial Day. They also love picnics in
the park, parades down city streets and big
slices of apple pie. Proud people live here.*

PICNIC IN THE PARK

Celebrate nature with picnics to remember. Fun, food, friends & family make picnics almost an institution. Whether a tailgate party at the football game or a family reunion, be unique, daring and innovative with this menu. And remember, you don't need great sunshine...try picnicking on a cold, rainy day in front of a blazing fire!

MENU

BLOODY MARYS

ARTICHOKE SOUP

CAVIAR STUFFED EGGS

ALAMO PECAN CHEESE BALL
with crackers

VERMICELLI SALAD

LAYERED GREEN SALAD

SOUR CREAM CUCUMBERS

BEEF AND BREW TAKE ALONG

CHEESE BISCUITS

SKY-HIGH BISCUITS • SWEDISH RYE BREAD

CREME DE MENTHE BROWNIES

STRAWBERRY DIVINITY

CHILLED WHITE WINE

VERMICELLI SALAD

1	10-ounce package dried twisted vermicelli
7	tablespoons lemon juice
7	tablespoons salad oil (or olive oil)
	Accent or MSG to taste
1	cup celery, chopped
1	cup green pepper, chopped
1	cup green onions, sliced
2	4-ounce cans chopped black olives
1	cup mayonnaise
1	4-ounce jar chopped pimientos
	salt & pepper to taste

Cook vermicelli according to package directions. Drain but do not rinse. Toss with lemon juice and oil. Sprinkle generously with Accent or MSG. Cover tightly and refrigerate overnight. When ready to serve, add celery, pepper, onion, olives and pimientos. Add mayonnaise and toss to mix. Add salt and pepper to taste.

YIELD: 6 to 8 servings.

VARIATION: Add 2 cups cubed chicken, small cocktail shrimp or tuna. This is good served in an avocado half for luncheons.

BEEF AND BREW TAKE ALONG

5	pounds sirloin tip roast
1	12-ounce can beer
4	tablespoons flour
½	teaspoon salt
½	teaspoon pepper
½	teaspoon onion salt

Wine Marinade

½	cup salad oil
¼	cup red wine vinegar
½	cup tomato puree
½	cup sherry
¼	cup burgundy
½	teaspoon salt
¼	teaspoon onion salt
¼	teaspoon garlic salt
	pinch of pepper
½	cup prepared marinara sauce

Place roast in large plastic bag and add beer. Close tightly and refrigerate at least 12 hours. When ready to prepare, preheat oven to 325°. Remove roast from plastic bag reserving beer marinade. Rub roast with flour, salt, pepper and onion salt. Place in large roasting pan and add beer marinade to pan. Bake about 1½ hours or until meat thermometer reads 140°.
Baste often with pan drippings.

Combine ingredients for wine marinade. Mix well and set aside. Slice the cooled roast very thin. Place in large casserole and pour wine marinade over meat. Cover and refrigerate about 12 hours. Take to picnic in casserole and serve over pumpernickel bread. If desired, serve warm with wine marinade heated and poured over meat.

YIELD: 12 servings.

SKY-HIGH BISCUITS

Flaky and golden, these biscuits have pleased diners since pioneer days.   Quick and easy to make, they can be mixed and shaped ahead of time, refrigerated and then baked and served hot from the oven.

2	cups all-purpose flour
1	cup whole wheat flour
4½	teaspoons baking powder
2	tablespoons sugar
½	teaspoon salt
¾	teaspoon cream of tartar
¾	cup butter or margarine
1	egg, beaten
1	cup milk

Preheat oven to 450°.
Combine both of the flours, baking powder, sugar, salt and cream of tartar. Cut in the butter until the mixture resembles coarse cornmeal. Add the egg and milk, stirring briefly. Knead lightly on a floured board. Roll or pat to 1-inch thickness and cut with a floured, 2-inch biscuit cutter. Space 2 inches apart on a greased cookie sheet and bake for 12 to 15 minutes.

YIELD: 20 biscuits

ALAMO PECAN CHEESE BALL

4	8-ounce packages cream cheese
1	cup grated sharp cheddar cheese
2	4-ounce bleu cheese packages (we recommend Borden's triangles)
2	tablespoons chives, dried or fresh & chopped
1	tablespoon onion flakes
1	tablespoon worcestershire sauce
	salt to taste
1	cup pecans, chopped

Let cheese soften to room temperature. Mix all ingredients together except pecans. Add salt to taste. Shape into ball in wax paper and roll in chopped pecans. Remove from refrigerator two hours before serving.

YIELD: 12 to 15 servings.

VARIATIONS: Add pimientos and green pepper. Substitute green onions for chives. Substitute walnuts for pecans.

San Antonio provides children and adults alike the opportunity to enjoy outdoor activities virtually year-round. There is a seemingly never-ending array of things to do and places to go. Our sunbelt location and semi-tropical climate make continued outdoor fun a reality.

OVERNIGHT BLOODY MARYS

1   46-ounce can V-8 Juice
1   46-ounce can tomato juice
⅔   cup lemon juice
2   tablespoons worcestershire
      sauce
1   teaspoon salt
½   teaspoon seasoned salt
3   cups vodka
      tabasco to taste

Combine all the ingredients except for the vodka. Mix them well. Cover and chill overnight. Stir in vodka just before serving. Add tabasco if you want it hotter!

YIELD: 12 to 15 servings.

CREME DE MENTHE BROWNIES

Brownies

4   eggs
2   cups sugar
4   1-ounce squares unsweetened
      baking chocolate
1   cup margarine or butter
1   cup flour
      dash of salt
½   teaspoon creme de
      menthe liqueur or
      peppermint extract
½-1 cup pecans, chopped

Topping

4   tablespoons margarine or
      butter, melted
2   tablespoons half-and-half
      cream
1½ teaspoons creme de
      menthe liqueur or
      peppermint extract
2   cups powdered sugar
      a few drops green
      food coloring

Glaze

2   1-ounce squares unsweetened
      baking chocolate
2   tablespoons margarine or
      butter

Preheat oven to 375°.

For Brownies: In a large mixing bowl, beat the eggs and add the sugar. In a sauce pan, melt the 4 squares of chocolate and 1 cup of margarine. Add the chocolate mixture to the egg mixture and mix well. Add the flour, salt, creme de menthe and pecans. Pour into greased 9x13-inch baking pan and bake for 20 to 25 minutes. Allow to cool.

For Topping: In a mixing bowl, combine the 4 tablespoons margarine, half and half cream, creme de menthe and powdered sugar and blend well. Add the green food coloring and spread over cooled brownies. Refrigerate for 15 to 20 minutes.

For Glaze: In a small saucepan, melt the 2 squares of chocolate and 2 tablespoons margarine; dribble mixture over the brownies. Tilt pan to cover. Cool in refrigerator at least 5 minutes. For best results refrigerate for 24 hours before serving.

YIELD: 52 1-inch squares.

STRAWBERRY DIVINITY

This candy is affected by the humidity in the air. Make only on a day when it is dry, high barometric pressure!

3   cups sugar
¾   cup light corn syrup
¾   cup water
2   egg whites
1   3-ounce package
       strawberry gelatin
       (we recommend Jello)
½   teaspoon salt
½   cup coconut, optional
1   cup chopped pecans

In a saucepan, combine sugar, corn syrup and water. Cook, stirring with wooden spoon only until mixture reaches boiling and no sugar crystals cling to sides of pan. Reduce heat and cook to hard ball stage 250° without stirring. In a large mixing bowl, combine egg whites, gelatin and salt. Beat mixture until stiff peaks form. Just when syrup reaches required temperature, pour in a thin stream into egg white mixture beating at high speed constantly. When mixture begins to lose its gloss, quickly add coconut and chopped pecans. Very quickly spoon onto waxed paper.

YIELD: 48 pieces.

Military music is to San Antonio as spice is to great food. The service bands in our city provide parade appearances and many free concerts. An annual favorite is the 5th Army Band's performance of the 1812 Overture with cued cannon & fireworks on the luxurious parade grounds of Ft. Sam Houston.

The diversity of attractions in San Antonio is impressive. A world-class zoo, The Japanese Tea Gardens, river barge rides, art festivals and museums are but a few of the many things that can be enjoyed by the whole family.

KAFFEEKLATSCH

The German words *Kaffee* and *Klatsch* refer to the informal gathering of friends for coffee, pastries & spicy conversation. The German style is to gather with friends & family, usually in the afternoon, as a social occasion with fine linen & china. The San Antonio style, as celebrated by the San Antonio Junior Forum, is a mid- morning gathering of members & friends. And these recipes for KaffeeKlatsch are favorites.

MENU

FANCY LAYERED LOAF

CINNAMON STRAWBERRY CHEESE SPREAD

ELEGANT OVEN OMELET

SAUSAGE CRESCENT NUGGETS

FRESH FRUIT SALAD
WITH COINTREAU MARINADE

CHEESE DATE PASTRY

APRICOT STRUDEL

TOFFEE COFFEE CAKE

ORANGE JUBILEES

MAGNOLIAS

SWEET POTATO, BLUEBERRY & BRAN MUFFINS

COFFEE PUNCH

COFFEE

FANCY LAYERED LOAF

This sandwich loaf is an all-time favorite of Junior Forum Kaffee Klatsch and has been served for 25 years!

Sandwich Loaf

½ cup butter or margarine
1 loaf sandwich bread, unsliced

Frosting

2 8-ounce packages cream
    cheese, softened
2 tablespoons heavy cream
¼ cup mayonnaise
¾ cup heavy cream, whipped

Shrimp Salad Filling

1 hard-boiled egg, chopped
1 7-ounce can shrimp,
    finely chopped or
    ½ pound fresh shrimp,
    cooked & finely chopped
¼ cup celery, finely chopped
¼ cup chili sauce
2 tablespoons lemon juice
¼ teaspoon salt
    dash of pepper

Toasted Pecan Filling

1 3-ounce package
    cream cheese, softened
1 cup pecans, toasted
¾ cup crushed pineapple,
    well drained

Chicken Bacon Filling

8 slices bacon,
    fried crisp & crumbled
1 cup cooked chicken,
    finely chopped
1 tablespoon pimiento,
    finely chopped
¼ cup mayonnaise
¼ teaspoon salt
⅛ teaspoon pepper

For Shrimp Salad Filling: In small bowl, combine egg, shrimp and celery. Toss with chili sauce and lemon juice and season with salt and pepper. Chill until ready to use.

For Toasted Pecan Filling: In small bowl, add pecans and pineapple to softened cream cheese and mix until well blended.

For Chicken Bacon Filling: In small bowl, combine bacon, chicken and pimiento. Add mayonnaise and toss until evenly distributed. Season with salt and pepper and chill until ready to use.

For Sandwich Loaf: Whip the butter on high speed of mixer and set aside. Trim crust from bread loaf. Cut the loaf into 4 equal lengthwise slices (this can be done at the bakery). Flatten each slice with a rolling pin. Spread 1 side of each slice with the whipped butter. Place 1 bread slice, buttered side up, on a serving platter. Spread evenly with Shrimp Salad Filling. Top with second slice and spread with Toasted Pecan Filling. Top with third slice and spread with Chicken Bacon Filling. Top with remaining bread slice.

For Frosting: Beat the cream cheese with 2 tablespoons heavy cream and mayonnaise until fluffy. Fold whipped cream into cream cheese mixture. Frost sides and top of loaf with frosting and refrigerate for a least 1 hour before serving. Garnish with parsley and paprika and serve in slices.

YIELD: 8 servings.

CHEESE DATE PASTRY

Crust

½   cup butter or margarine,
        softened
¼   pound cheddar cheese, grated
1   cup flour

Date Filling

1   9-ounce package pitted dates
½   cup packed brown sugar
¼   cup water
½   cup pecans, chopped

Preheat oven to 350°.
Cream butter and cheese and blend in flour.
Chill for one hour.   On a floured surface, roll
dough into a ⅛-inch thick layer and cut into
small rounds about 2 inches in diameter.   Set
aside.
For Date Filling: Combine all ingredients in
a medium saucepan.   Cook over low heat,
stirring constantly until thick.   Cool.   Place
1 teaspoon of date filling on a round of crust.
Place another pastry round on top of filling.
Press edges together with a damp fork.   Bake
for 15 minutes.   Can be frozen before or after
cooking.

YIELD: 1 dozen.

MAGNOLIAS

4   cups orange juice, chilled
½   cup Grand Marnier
1   fifth champagne, chilled
     maraschino cherries
     orange slices

Combine orange juice, Grand Marnier and
champagne.   Serve over ice.   Garnish with
cherries and orange slices.

YIELD: 15 4-ounce servings.

*Warmed by the style of the buildings
and the style of life - that's the spell
of San Antonio's Market Square.
Whether it's coffee with friends,
business brunching with partners, or
people-watching from a cozy spot,
El Mercado surrounds you with history
as you make history of your own.*

ELEGANT OVEN OMELET

2   cups Canadian bacon, diced
        (may substitute ham)
½   cup onion, chopped
½   cup bell pepper, chopped
12   teaspoons margarine
24   eggs, beaten
1   6-ounce can chopped
        mushrooms, drained
        (we recommend B&B)
4   teaspoons flour
1   teaspoon salt
¼   teaspoon pepper
4   cups milk
2   cups American cheese, grated
4½   cups soft bread crumbs
¼   teaspoon paprika

In a very large skillet or dutch oven, cook bacon, onion and bell pepper in 6 teaspoons margarine until onion and pepper are tender but not brown. Add eggs and scramble until soft set. Fold in mushrooms and set aside. In a large saucepan, over *medium heat,* melt 4 teaspoons margarine and gradually add flour, stirring constantly until well blended. Season with salt and pepper. Gradually add milk, stirring constantly with a wire whisk. When all milk has been added and mixture begins to thicken, lower heat and add grated cheese. Cook only until cheese is melted. Fold cheese sauce into egg mixture and mix well. Pour into two 9x13-inch greased baking dishes. Combine bread crumbs and remaining 2 teaspoons of melted butter and sprinkle top of casserole. Sprinkle with paprika. Cover and chill at least 2 to 3 hours or overnight.
When ready to bake, preheat oven to 350°. Bake for 30 to 45 minutes or until cheese bubbles. Be sure to cook until center feels semi-hard and not soggy. Elegant and delicious!!
YIELD: 12 to 15 servings.

CINNAMON STRAWBERRY CHEESE SPREAD

1½   8-ounce packages cream
        cheese, softened
½   cup butter, softened
½   cup sour cream
⅓   cup sugar
1   ¼-ounce envelope
        unflavored gelatin
¼   cup boiling water
½   teaspoon lemon peel, grated
½   cup white raisins
1   cup slivered almonds, toasted
½   teaspoon almond extract
        cinnamon-flavored crackers
        or cookies
1   pint fresh strawberries

Blend cream cheese, butter and sour cream. Add sugar and mix until well blended. Set aside. Dissolve gelatin in boiling water. Stir dissolved gelatin into cream cheese mixture. Add lemon peel, raisins, almonds and almond extract. Mix well and pour into a lightly greased 1-quart mold. Refrigerate until set, about 2 hours. Unmold and garnish with chopped fresh strawberries. Serve on crackers or cookies.

YIELD: 6 to 7 cups.

TOFFEE COFFEE CAKE

½ cup butter, softened
1 cup packed brown sugar
½ cup white sugar
2 cups flour
1 cup buttermilk
1 teaspoon baking soda
1 egg, slightly beaten
1 teaspoon vanilla

Topping

1½ cups toffee candy bars, chopped (we recommend Heath bars)
¼ cup pecans, chopped

Preheat oven to 350°.

Blend butter, sugars and flour. Set aside ½ cup of this crumb mixture for the topping. To the remaining mixture, add the butter-milk, soda, egg and vanilla. Blend well. Pour into greased and floured 9x13-inch pan.

For the Topping: Mix together the crushed toffee, pecans and reserved ½ cup crumb mixture. Sprinkle on top of cake batter and bake for 25 to 30 minutes. Cool slightly before serving. Delightful!!

YIELD: 10 to 12 servings.

San Fernando Cathedral has been serving parishioners since 1738. As in other churches, certain social occasions in San Antonio begin with religious services in a cathedral or church. The ceremonies are followed by elegant receptions or by simple family gatherings.

MEXICAN BRUNCH

San Antonio brunches are often served with a unique ethnic flair. No other cultures have so greatly influenced San Antonio as did the Spaniards and the Mexicans. From these people, we learned about new foods, tastes and cooking techniques. We borrowed and shared with them. We embraced their customs and have integrated our lifestyles with theirs. Their tasty food lends itself to such occasions and much of it can be easily prepared in advance of a brunch.

MENU

HUEVOS POBLANOS

CHORIZO CON PAPAS

CHICKEN CHILAQUILES

AVOCADO HALVES STUFFED WITH:
CRABMEAT SALAD, CAVIAR, SOUR CREAM,
PICANTE SAUCE, BACON BITS,
CHOPPED TOMATO AND GREEN ONION

SALSA FRESCA

SPICY MEXICAN PICKLED VEGETABLES

TROPICAL MANGO MOUSSE

BOLILLOS

CORN AND FLOUR TORTILLAS

PAN DULCE

MEXICAN COOKIES

BUNUELOS

WHITE SANGRIA

TEQUILA SUNRISE

Market Square, also known as "El Mercado," is located on the original site of San Antonio's first public market. It is made up of over fifty specialty shops, restaurants, street vendors and 'sidewalk' artisans. Pinatas, baskets, pottery and Mexican dresses are favorites with El Mercado shoppers. Today's market retains the flavor and architecture of the original and remains a center for public gatherings and celebrations.

HUEVOS POBLANOS
(Eggs with Poblano Peppers)

6-8	slices bacon, chopped
4-5	green onions, chopped
8	eggs
1	cup milk
1	4-ounce can poblano or green chiles, chopped
¼	teaspoon salt
¼	teaspoon ground cumin
¼	teaspoon pepper
2½	cups monterey jack cheese, grated
1	tablespoon butter

Preheat oven to 325°.

Fry bacon until crisp. Drain and set aside. Remove all but 1 tablespoon bacon drippings from pan. Saute green onions in drippings for 3 to 4 minutes. Whisk eggs in mixing bowl and add bacon, onion, milk, chiles, salt, cumin, pepper and cheese. Mix well and pour mixture into greased 9x9-inch baking dish. Drizzle top with butter. Bake 35 to 40 minutes or until set. Cut into squares and serve hot.

YIELD: 8 servings.

CHICKEN CHILAQUILES
(Chicken and Corn Tortilla Casserole)

"Chilaquiles" is a very familiar word in San Antonio because it is the name of a dish we eat often and enjoy. In Spanish the word means "broken up old sombrero." This expression is used to describe broken pieces of stale corn tortillas in many dishes from scrambled eggs to chicken casseroles.

½	cup butter
1½	cups onions, chopped
2	10-ounce cans tomatoes & chiles (we recommend Ro-Tel)
1	28-ounce can tomatoes, chopped
2	pounds Velveeta Cheese, diced
2-3	cups cooked chicken, chopped
2	cups sour cream
15	stale corn tortillas, broken into small pieces (or 15 fresh tortillas fried until crisp)

Preheat oven to 325°.

In a large skillet, saute onions in butter. Drain all tomatoes and reserve juice. To the onions, add the drained tomatoes and chiles, tomatoes, cheese, chicken and sour cream. Line the bottom of a greased 9x13-inch baking dish with the tortillas pieces. Top with the chicken mixture and bake uncovered for 45 minutes. Add small amounts of tomato liquid if mixture seems too dry.

YIELD: 12 to 15 servings.

SPICY MEXICAN PICKLED VEGETABLES

12   cloves garlic, peeled
1   medium onion, cut in wedges
¾   cup olive oil
4   carrots, peeled & thinly sliced
1   teaspoon whole peppercorns
1½ cups white vinegar
1   3½-ounce can pickled
         jalapeno chiles, drained
2   cups water
3   tablespoons salt
1   head cauliflower,
         separated in flowerets
12   small bay leaves
3   zucchini squash,
         thinly sliced
¾   teaspoon: thyme,
         oregano & marjoram

In dutch oven, saute garlic cloves and onion in olive oil for 3 minutes. Add carrots and peppercorns and saute the mixture for 5 more minutes. Add vinegar and simmer the mixture, covered, for 3 minutes. Add jalapeno chiles and water to the mixture. Cover the pot and bring liquid to a boil. Add salt and cauliflower. Cook mixture, covered, over moderate heat for 12 minutes. Add bay leaves, zucchini, thyme, oregano and marjoram. Simmer covered for 2 minutes. If desired, the following may be added at this time: mushrooms, artichoke hearts, tiny whole ears of corn (available in cans) and black olives. Cover pickled vegetables and cool. Store in refrigerator for up to 2 weeks. Serve as an appetizer, a garnish on a condiment tray or a side salad.

YIELD: 8 cups.

The distinction of being the oldest pharmacy in San Antonio belongs to Botica Guadalupana. For generations it has provided the Hispanic community with herbs, spices and medicines.

CHORIZO CON PAPAS
(Sausage with Potatoes)

½ pound Mexican sausage
   (chorizo) or ½ pound
   bulk pork sausage
   (hot or mild)
6 tablespoons corn oil
1 large potato, diced
1 medium onion, chopped
1 bell pepper, chopped and/or
   1-2 fresh jalapeno
   peppers, finely chopped
2 medium tomatoes, chopped
6 eggs, well beaten
   salt to taste
   picante sauce
6 flour tortillas

Remove casing from sausage. In a small skillet cook sausage, crumbling it with a fork as it cooks. Remove from pan and drain. Set aside. Heat oil in large skillet. Add potato, onions, peppers and tomatoes and cook until potatoes are tender. Add sausage and eggs and cook until eggs are set. Serve on a warm flour tortilla. Add picante sauce.
Yield: 4 to 6 servings.

VARIATION: Add ½ cup chopped pimientos and ½ cup grated cheddar or monterey jack cheese to potato mixture.

MEXICAN COOKIES
(Reposteria)

1 cinnamon stick, broken
   into fine pieces
5 cups flour
2 cups sugar
3 teaspoons baking powder
½ teaspoon baking soda
   pinch of salt
2 eggs, beaten
1 teaspoon vanilla
2 cups shortening, softened
   cinnamon sugar,
      for top of cookies

Preheat oven to 350°.
In a skillet, roast broken cinnamon stick. In a large mixing bowl, combine roasted cinnamon, flour, sugar, baking powder, baking soda and salt and mix thoroughly. Add beaten eggs and vanilla to flour mixture and blend thoroughly. Add softened shortening to flour mixture and mix dough with hands until well blended. Dough should not stick to hands. Shape dough into grape-sized balls. Slash a cross-shaped pattern on top of each cookie and place on cookie sheet. Bake 12 to 15 minutes until golden brown. Let cool partially before removing from cookie sheet. Dip top of cookies into cinnamon sugar while cookies are still warm.
YIELD: 115 cookies.

TEQUILA SUNRISE

This is a dramatic looking drink which resembles a Texas sunrise with yellow and orange hues. It is a favorite mixed drink in the Southwest.

8   ice cubes
1½ ounces tequila
½   ounce grenadine syrup
8   ounces orange juice

Fill a cocktail shaker with ice cubes. Add the tequila and orange juice and shake vigorously. Pour the tequila and orange juice mixture into a glass. Do not use the ice cubes. Layer the grenadine carefully on the top by pouring down the side of a spoon. This creates the effect of a Texas Sunrise!!

YIELD: One 10-ounce serving.

TROPICAL MANGO MOUSSE

1   14¾-ounce can mangos
1   8-ounce package cream
     cheese, softened
2   3-ounce boxes orange-
     flavored gelatin
1   3-ounce box lemon-
     flavored gelatin
2   cups boiling water

Drain mangos, reserving the juice. Blend mangos and softened cream cheese in blender. Dissolve gelatin in boiling water and add to blender mixture along with the juice from the mangos. Continue to blend until smooth. Pour mixture into a 6 cup ring mold pan or bundt pan. Chill until set. To serve for a party, arrange mousse on lettuce leaves and garnish with strawberries or kiwi slices.

YIELD: 8 servings.

Confetti-filled eggs are called "Cascarones." The brightly colored cascaron is made by gently cracking one end of the egg, emptying the contents and later re-filling it with shredded paper. Cascarones are very popular during Fiesta. Tradition has it that if you make a wish before cracking one over a friend's head, the wish will come true. The origin of cascarones dates back to Empress Carlotta of Mexico who introduced them to her people. They are still used today in traditional Mexican Easter celebrations where the eggshell represents the tomb and the confetti the resurrection of joy.

The Texas Folklife Festival, held annually in August on the grounds of The Institute of Texan Cultures, showcases the foods, crafts, dances and traditions of the multi-cultures of San Antonio.

FOLKLIFE FESTIVAL

This party brings together the celebration of all ethnic groups which represent San Antonio. It's a celebration of the state's history under the six flags of Spain, France, Mexico, the Republic of Texas, the Confederacy and the United States of America. The unique culinary influences of the Canary Islanders & Germans are also remembered at this time.

MENU

MARINATED MUSHROOMS

ANTICUCHOS • CHIMICHANGAS

GAZPACHO • SAUERBRATEN

CALDO de POLLO • CHILI • CHALUPAS

MEXICAN ARMY HOT SAUCE

PAELLA • SHY POKE EGGS

CORN ON THE COB • JAMBALAYA

WATERMELON SLICES

PRALINES • CHURROS

BOHEMIAN COFFEE CAKE

CANARY ISLANDER DOUGHNUTS

BEER • SANGRIA

ANTICUCHOS
(Marinated Beef Cubes on a Stick)

Anticuchos are one of San Antonio's favorite casual fiesta foods served on a stick.

¾ cup oil
⅓ cup red wine vinegar
2-3 cloves garlic
2-3 teaspoons cumin (comino)
1-2 jalapeno or serrano
      chiles (optional)
    Accent or MSG to taste
    salt & pepper
2½ pounds lean beef, cut in
      1-2 inch cubes
    wooden skewers

Combine oil, vinegar and spices and mix well. Add beef to marinade and refrigerate for 12 to 24 hours. Skewer about ¼ pound of meat per stick. Cook over very hot coals, two minutes per side, basting often with marinade. Be careful not to overcook. Delicioso!

YIELD: 5 servings.

JAMBALAYA

French and Cajun cooking has been enjoyed in San Antonio since the 1700s when the French Flag flew over Texas and Louisiana during the days of the French exploration. Jambalaya is a perfect example of this influence on our cuisine.

1 pound Italian sausage
2 green onions, chopped
2 large onions, chopped
3 tablespoons parsley, chopped
4 cloves garlic, pressed
2 tablespoons flour
2 tablespoons oil
4 stems celery, sliced
¾ pound uncooked oysters
      & liquid
1 pound uncooked shrimp
1 6-ounce can tomato paste
1 29-ounce can tomatoes,
      chopped
3 bay leaves
½ teaspoon sugar
1 teaspoon Accent or MSG
    tabasco, salt, pepper,
      worcestershire, dried red
      pepper to taste
½ - ¾ cup uncooked rice
2½ cups water

Remove casing from sausage and cut into bite-size pieces. In skillet, cook sausage, onions, parsley and garlic until sausage is done and well browned, about 15 to 20 minutes.

In large soup pot, combine 2 tablespoons of flour and 2 tablespoons of oil and cook over a medium high heat until the flour is cooked and dark brown. Be careful not to burn the flour. Stirring constantly is essential! Add sausage mixture, celery, oysters and liquid, shrimp, tomato paste, tomatoes, bay leaves, and all seasonings to taste. Cook and simmer about 15 minutes. Add rice and water. Cover and cook on low heat for 15 to 20 minutes or until rice is cooked. This is thick Jambalaya. (Thin with tomato juice if desired). Serve with salad and french bread. Men love this recipe!

YIELD: 8 to 10 servings.

SAUERBRATEN
(Haase Family Recipe)

By the 1850's, one-fifth of the population of Texas was German. Their influence in San Antonio has been a strong one. A pioneer German family has contributed this authentic Sauerbraten recipe.

4-5 pound eye of round roast
1 tablespoon dried mustard
3 tablespoons water
1 bay leaf
1 tablespoon whole
    black peppercorns
1½ teaspoons salt
1½ teaspoons poultry seasoning
2 cloves garlic, crushed (or ½
    teaspoon garlic powder)
1 medium onion, chopped (or
    2 tablespoons flakes)
2 tablespoons brown sugar
1 cup water
1 beef bouillon cube
½ cup red wine vinegar
2 tablespoons bacon drippings
    or shortening
    flour for thickening
½ cup sour cream

Place beef in large bowl. Mix water and mustard. Spread over meat and let stand for 10 minutes. In a saucepan combine the bayleaf, peppercorns, salt, poultry seasoning, garlic, onion, sugar, water, bouillon cube, vinegar, and bacon drippings. Bring mixture to a boil and pour over meat. Cool. Cover and refrigerate for 24 - 48 hours, turning occasionally. When ready to cook, preheat oven to 250°. Remove meat from marinade and dry with paper towel, reserving marinade. In dutch oven, brown the roast. Pour in marinade and cover. Cook for 3 - 3½ hours or until tender. Remove meat to warmed serving platter. For gravy, strain marinade and measure. Return to pan. For each cup of marinade blend 1½ tablespoons flour with 2 tablespoons water and add to marinade, cooking until thickened. Stir in sour cream. Do not boil. Serve with potato dumplings or spaetzle.

Yield: 8 to 10 servings.

Enchanting storytellers share tales of past generations while country fiddlers entertain the Folklife Festival crowds.

CANARY ISLANDER DOUGHNUTS

The first permanent settlers in San Antonio came from the Canary Islands in 1731 by royal decree from King Felipe V of Spain who promised them land, a Spanish royal title and all their provisions for one year. The cooking traditions of the original Canary Islanders have influenced San Antonio cuisine. These Canary Islander Doughnuts are related to "empanadas", a savory turnover very popular in San Antonio. The sweet ones are prepared especially for Christmas celebrations.

1	pound sweet potatoes or yams
1	cup sugar
¼	cup water
1½	cups almonds, chopped
	pinch of cinnamon
1	teaspoon grated lemon rind
¼	cup aniseed liqueur
	(we recommend Pernod)

Pastry

8	cups all-purpose flour
3	teaspoons baking powder
1	cup shortening
	(we recommend Crisco)
1	cup sugar
1	teaspoon grated lemon rind
	sunflower oil or vegetable oil for deep frying
	powdered sugar

Peel and boil the sweet potatoes until tender. Drain and push through a sieve. Dissolve sugar in water. In a mixing bowl combine sugar water, sweet potatoes, chopped almonds, cinnamon, grated lemon rind and aniseed liqueur. Cover with cloth and refrigerate for 24 hours.

For Pastry: Thoroughly mix flour with baking powder. Cut in shortening. Add sugar and lemon rind, mixing well, and leave to rest for 30 minutes. Dust pastry board with flour and roll out dough to very thin sheet. Cut out circles with 4-inch pastry cutter. Top each circle with prepared filling. Close them by folding in half and pressing edges with moistened fork so that they will stick together. Deep fry in about 4 inches of hot oil. Drain and sprinkle with powdered sugar.

YIELD: 24 doughnuts.

SANGRIA

2	oranges
1	lemon
1	lime
½	cup sugar
1	fifth burgundy wine
8 - 10	ounces club soda
	ice

Cut one orange, lemon and lime into fourths. Squeeze juices from fruits into a pitcher and add rinds and sugar. Stir, pressing rinds with wooden spoon to mix up. Add burgundy and soda. Pour into tall, ice-filled glasses. Garnish drinks with a slice of orange.

YIELD: 2 quarts.

CALDO de POLLO
(Mexican Chicken Soup)

This is an authentic Mexican recipe very common in Texas. The consistency is stew-like and very hearty.

3-4 pounds chicken pieces

4 medium "calabacitas" (Mexican Squash), cut in chunks (other squash may be substituted)

1 cup fresh corn, cut from cob (or 1 10-ounce package frozen whole kernel corn)

1 large onion, cut in chunks

4 medium tomatoes, cut in chunks (or 14 ounce can tomatoes)

2 teaspoons cumin (comino) seed

½ teaspoon cayenne red pepper

salt & pepper

Stack ingredients in above order in crock pot or dutch oven. Cook on high in a crock pot for 6 hours. If using dutch oven on stove, simmer for 1½ hours. Do not add water. When cooking is completed, remove chicken pieces and allow to cool. Skin and debone chicken and return meat to soup. Mix well and reheat. Serve in soup bowls with corn tortillas.

YIELD: 2 quarts.

Quilting is but one of the many skills showcased at The Texas Folklife Festival to preserve the pioneer heritage of Texas. Others include basket weaving, horseshoeing and sheep shearing.

KING WILLIAM COCKTAIL BUFFET

The community now known as the King William District is a neighborhood of turn-of-the-century mansions near downtown on the San Antonio River. Many of these homes have been passed on for generations, renovated and are now open to the public. In this menu, you'll find recipes from many ethnic groups. We would serve this select formal buffet following one of San Antonio's cultural events such as the symphony, a ballet, or the theater.

MENU

CAPONATA

STUFFED CHERRY TOMATOES

MARINATED GREEK SALAD

STUFFED SNOW PEAS

SHRIMP IN DILL MAYONNAISE

CHICKEN LIVER PATE

BAKED BRIE WITH CRACKERS

FRIED ASPARAGUS PARMESAN

FETTUCINE ALFREDO • CHEESE STICKS

COQUILLES ST. JACQUES

SMOKED TURKEY OR HAM

EYE OF ROUND IN RED WINE

LA VILLITA ROLLS • FRENCH BREAD

MOCHA ANGEL FOOD CAKE

REPUBLIC OF TEXAS TRIFLE

What we now know as The King William Historic District was once the irrigated fields for the Alamo mission. Located just south of downtown, this area was developed by German immigrants in the 1850's. Many of these unique homes have been restored to their original grandeur. A great time to visit is during the King William Fair in the spring.

CAPONATA

Try this eggplant relish as an appetizer served on crackers, or pack it in a decorative jar for a perfect hostess gift.

1½ pound eggplant, unpeeled
salt to taste
⅔ cup vegetable or olive oil
1 medium onion,
    coarsely chopped
1 clove garlic, minced
2 tablespoons vegetable
    or olive oil
1 16-ounce can tomato puree
½ cup water
½ teaspoon dried oregano
½ teaspoon dried basil
¼ teaspoon pepper
1 cup sliced celery
1¼ cups pimiento-stuffed
    green olives
2 tablespoons capers, drained
1 tablespoon sugar
2 tablespoons vinegar
2 tablespoons parsley, minced

Cut eggplant into ½-to-1-inch cubes and sprinkle with salt to taste. Saute in ⅔ cup oil in large skillet and cook until brown and almost tender. Drain and set aside. Saute onion and garlic in 2 tablespoons oil until golden. Stir in tomato puree, water, oregano, basil, pepper and celery. Cover and simmer mixture for 30 minutes. Add eggplant, olives, capers, sugar, vinegar and parsley to mixture and stir well. Cover and simmer an additional 15 minutes. Cool. Cover tightly and refrigerate. Keeps for 3 weeks in refrigerator.

YIELD: 1½ quarts.

FRIED ASPARAGUS PARMESAN

2½ pounds fresh asparagus
1½ cups bread crumbs, toasted
1½ cups parmesan cheese, grated
4 eggs, lightly beaten
½ teaspoon salt
    pepper to taste
½ teaspoon ground nutmeg
3-6 tablespoons butter

Parboil asparagus. Place bread crumbs in shallow dish and parmesan cheese in another shallow dish. In shallow bowl, combine eggs, salt, pepper and nutmeg. Dip stalk of asparagus in egg mixture, roll in cheese, dip in egg again and roll in bread crumbs. Coat remaining stalks in same manner. Chill for 30 minutes. In large skillet, saute asparagus in butter until golden brown.

YIELD: 4 to 6 servings.

COQUILLES ST. JACQUES
(Scallops and Mushrooms in Wine Sauce)

2 cups dry white wine
    (1½ cups dry vermouth
    may be substituted)

1 teaspoon salt
    pinch of pepper

1 bay leaf

4 tablespoons shallots,
    minced (green onions
    may be substituted)

2 pounds scallops (crab,
    shrimp, lobster or redfish
    may be substituted)

1 pound fresh whole
    mushrooms

6 tablespoons butter

8 tablespoons flour

1½ cups milk

4 egg yolks

1 cup whipping cream
    salt & pepper to taste

1 drop of lemon juice

4-6 ounces swiss cheese,
    grated
    butter

VARIATION:

*(As **an appetizer**) Serve in a chafing dish or casserole. Use crusty pieces of fresh French bread to dip into this gourmet mixture. The sauce is terrific with all kinds of seafood.*

In a dutch oven, combine wine, salt, pepper, bay leaf and shallots and simmer for 5 minutes. Add scallops (or other seafood) and mushrooms in enough water to barely cover ingredients. Bring to simmer, cover and simmer for 5 minutes. Remove seafood and mushrooms and set aside. Rapidly boil down cooking liquid until reduced to 2 cups.

In a large saucepan, melt butter and slowly add flour until well blended. Cook slowly, stirring constantly for 2 minutes. Remove from heat and blend in cooking liquid. Gradually add milk and bring to a boil. Boil 1 minute. Blend egg yolks and cream in a large bowl. Beat hot sauce into this mixture by driblets, stirring constantly to keep smooth. Return sauce to pan and boil for 1 minute, stirring vigorously. Thin out with more cream if necessary. Season to taste with salt, pepper and lemon juice.

To Assemble: Cut the scallops into crosswise pieces about ⅛ inch thick. Blend ⅔ of sauce with seafood and mushrooms. Butter serving shell (or individual serving dishes). Spoon mixture into serving dishes and cover with remaining sauce. Sprinkle grated swiss cheese on top. Dot with butter. Arrange serving shells on broiling pan about 6 to 8 inches under broiler to heat thoroughly and to brown top of sauce. Serve immediately. This is a very elegant main course.

YIELD: 6 to 8 servings.

The Commander's House originally served as the residence for the Commanding Officer of the San Antonio Arsenal. Built in 1883 and now totally restored, it has been designated as a national historical landmark. Today, this landmark serves as a center for numerous senior citizen programs.

REPUBLIC OF TEXAS TRIFLE

The Lone Star Flag, the state flag of Texas, honors the period in history when Texas was an independent republic from 1836 to 1846. The spirit of independence inspired the men at the Alamo to defend the principles of freedom and further inspired the settlers, then known as "Texians," to maintain their independence for ten years. In 1846, Texas joined the U.S. when the description of the settlers changed from "Texians" to "Texans" with the loss of the "i" symbolizing the loss of independence. This patriotic trifle is red, white and blue layered with strawberries, blueberries and whipped cream.

Pioneer Sponge Cake

½ cup margarine, softened
½ cup sugar
2 eggs
1 teaspoon baking powder
½ cup self-rising flour

Custard

2 cups prepared custard (use your favorite custard recipe or we recommend Bird's Custard Powder)

Layers

½ cup cherry brandy (or sherry may be substituted)
2 cups fresh strawberries
2 cups fresh blueberries
2 tablespoons sugar
1 cup whipping cream
½ cup slivered almonds

Preheat oven to 375°.

In a mixing bowl, combine margarine, sugar and eggs and beat until fluffy. Stir in baking powder. Add flour and mix until well blended. Pour into a greased and floured 9-inch cake pan. Bake for 20 minutes and allow to cool.

To Assemble: Cut cake into bite-size pieces and place in bottom of trifle bowl or large glass bowl. Pour ¼ cup brandy over cake pieces. Top with strawberries and blueberries, reserving some berries for garnish. Sprinkle 1 tablespoon sugar over fruit and pour remaining brandy over all. Spoon custard over fruit, cover and refrigerate at least 2 hours or overnight.

When Ready to Serve: Combine whipping cream and 1 tablespoon sugar in a small mixing bowl. Whip until stiff peaks form. Spoon over top of cold trifle. Garnish with reserved berries and almonds. This dessert should be prepared one day ahead for the brandy to flavor the cake and fruit. The whipped cream can be layered on top anytime the day of serving. Keep refrigerated until ready to use. For a fancy, formal dinner, serve in champagne crystal glasses with a sprig of mint. This is very elegant and simply delicious!

YIELD: 8 servings.

LA VILLITA ROLLS

2 ¼-ounce packages dry yeast
1½ cups warm water
1 cup instant mashed
    potato flakes
1 cup butter, softened
3 eggs
1½ teaspoons salt
1 cup sugar
8 cups flour

Mix yeast in warm water and let stand for 10 minutes. In a large mixing bowl, combine potatoes, butter, eggs, salt and sugar and mix well. To this mixture, add seven cups of flour, blending well. Add yeast mixture and knead until well blended, about 10 minutes. Place in well greased bowl and cover with damp cloth. Place in refrigerator until ready to use. When ready to use, knead in ½ to 1 cup additional flour. Shape dough into rolls and place on greased cookie sheet or in greased muffin tins. Let stand about 3 hours or until doubled in size. When ready to bake, preheat oven to 450°. Bake for 10 to 12 minutes.

YIELD: 6 dozen rolls.

MOCHA ANGEL FOOD CAKE

A lovely, light, scrumptious cake!

1 tablespoon instant coffee
¼ cup warm water
1 angel food cake mix
    (we recommend
    Duncan Hines)
1 teaspoon maple flavoring

 Frosting

3-4 tablespoons milk
1½ teaspoons instant coffee
¾ cup margarine or butter,
    softened
   dash salt
1½ teaspoons maple flavoring
3½ cups powdered sugar, sifted
½ cup pecans or almonds,
    roasted & chopped

Dissolve coffee in warm water and use this mixture as part of the liquid when preparing cake according to package directions. Fold in maple flavoring. Bake and cool as directed.
For Frosting: Warm milk, add coffee and stir to dissolve. Set aside to cool. In a mixing bowl, cream margarine until fluffy. Add salt and maple flavoring. Beat sugar into margarine gradually along with milk mixture. Continue beating until light and fluffy. Spread on cooled cake and sprinkle with roasted nuts. This cake will be easier to slice on the second day.

YIELD: 10 to 12 servings.

The San Antonio River winds by a little town in the middle of downtown. It's La Villita, one of San Antonio's earliest settlements, and an excellent example of the character of life in San Antonio generations ago.

San Antonio offers its people and its visitors a city filled with varied expressions of the arts. Music, dance and theatre are but a few. The art of preparing culinary master-pieces is one of our finest. San Antonio is brimming with exceptional dining experiences that cross the boundaries of all cultures.

GOURMET CELEBRATION

Much San Antonio dining reflects the wonderful heritage of our diverse community delicately seasoned with our accommodating climate. However, *haute couture avec haute cuisine* are also part of our lifestyle. Our Gourmet Celebration pays tribute to local celebrity recipes and the gourmet chefs that form the culinary artistry of San Antonio. Bon Appetit!

MENU

FRIED AVOCADOS • HOT ARTICHOKE DIP

CHEESE WITH SPINACH PUFFS

RED SNAPPER SOUP

NOISETTES DE PORC AUX PRUNEAUX

SCHNITZEL A LA "SAN ANTONIO"

POACHED SALMON
with Oyster Beurre Blanc and Sorrel

MEDALLIONS AU POIVRE

BROCCOLI CROWN WITH CHERRY TOMATOES

FRESH VEGETABLE MEDLEY WITH
CILANTRO CUMIN BUTTER

PASTA IN CREAM

BAKED FLORENTINE POTATOES

FRENCH APPLE PIE • AMBROSIA CAKE

CANDY CRUNCH CAKE • FRIED ICE CREAM

NOISETTES DE PORC AUX PRUNEAUX
(Pork Tenderloin with Prunes)

2½ pounds pork tenderloin
50 prunes
1 cup dry white wine, preferably Sancerre
flour
butter
⅔ tablespoon red currant jelly
2 cups cream
salt & pepper

Soak the prunes in the wine for 24 hours. Remove pits. Cut the pork into 8 slices about ½ inch thick. Flour and fry to a golden brown in a very hot butter, seasoning with salt and pepper while cooking. Remove slices and arrange on a long platter. Keep warm. In the meantime, boil the prunes for ½ hour in the wine. Arrange on the platter around the slices of pork. Pour the cooking liquor from the prunes into a sauce pan and reduce a little. Add the red currant jelly and blend with the cream. Pour over the pork and serve very hot. Pommard wine is recommended to serve with the pork.

YIELD: 8 servings.

Guillermo, Jacqueline & Miguel Ardid, Chez Ardid

SCHNITZEL A LA 'SAN ANTONIO'

10 2-ounce veal scaloppine
3 ounces butter or margarine for sauteing
½ red bell pepper, julienne
½ green bell pepper, julienne
½ yellow bell pepper, julienne
½ onion, julienne
4 ounces ham, julienne
½ quart demi-glace or brown sauce
6 ounces dry white wine
2 ounces cognac or brandy
white pepper to taste
salt to taste
cayenne pepper to taste

Cut all ingredients "julienne style" the same size, length and thickness. This gives the dish a good appetizing appearance. Melt half the butter in a saute pan over medium heat. Add bell peppers, onion and ham. Saute until onion is glossy. Add brandy or cognac. After 4 minutes, add white wine and let simmer for 5 minutes. Add demi-glace or brown sauce. Simmer for 8 to 10 minutes and adjust seasoning with salt and cayenne pepper. The dish should be spicy. While the sauce is simmering on low heat, saute the seasoned veal with salt and white pepper until tender. Do not overcook or meat gets dry. Place 2 pieces of meat on each plate and put the sauce on top or place the meat on a platter and put the sauce down the middle. Garnish with sprigs of fresh rosemary. Curry rice is excellent to serve with this dish. It adds color and a nice contrast of flavors. Medallions of pork filet or pork chops can be substituted for the veal. Adjust the cooking time accordingly.

YIELD: 5 servings.

Paul Rossmeier, Executive Chef, Oak Hills Country Club

CILANTRO CUMIN BUTTER

Excellent as a sauce on a medley of fresh vegetables, broiled steaks or fish!

5   ounces butter, salted
1   ounce lemon juice
1   tablespoon cumin powder
1   bunch cilantro (coriander),
        fresh and chopped

Place butter at room temperature until soft. In mixing bowl, blend butter with other ingredients.

YIELD: 4 to 6 servings.

Clay Alexander Summers, Executive Chef, La Mansion Hotels

PASTA IN CREAM SAUCE

¼   cup butter
1   small onion, finely chopped
2   cloves garlic, finely minced
½   pound mushrooms,
        cleaned & sliced
1   cup artichoke hearts
1   cup whipping cream
1   tablespoon capers, drained
     salt to taste
     freshly ground black
        pepper to taste
¾   cup freshly grated
        parmesan cheese
5   cups cooked pasta,
        warm & cooked only to
        al dente stage

In a large saute pan, melt butter. Add onion and garlic and saute for 5 minutes. Add mushrooms to pan and cook 2 minutes, then add artichoke hearts and cook for 3 minutes. Remove ingredients to a bowl and return pan to heat, stirring in cream. Gently boil cream in skillet until reduced by half. Return mushroom mixture to pan and stir in capers. Salt and pepper to taste. Add warm pasta to sauce along with parmesan cheese. Toss quickly and serve immediately. This dish can be served as either an entree or side dish.

YIELD: As an entree, it serves 4.

As a side dish, it serves 8.

Karen Haram, Food Editor, San Antonio Express-News

For an open-air ride through historic downtown San Antonio, park the car and hop on an old-fashioned Via Trolley. It's a thrifty trip to any downtown location, including theatres, restaurants, offices and stores.

BAKED FLORENTINE POTATOES

4   large Idaho potatoes
1   10-ounce package
       frozen creamed or
       buttered spinach
2   egg yolks
1   teaspoon salt
¼   teaspoon pepper
¼   teaspoon onion powder
       cheddar cheese, grated

Preheat oven to 450°.

Bake potatoes for 50 minutes until fork tender. Cook spinach as label directs until just thawed, about 8 minutes. Cut baked potato in half lengthwise. Carefully scoop out potato pulp leaving shell intact. With electric mixer at medium speed, combine potato pulp, egg yolks, salt, pepper, onion powder and beat until smooth. Stir in thawed spinach. Place spinach-potato mixture back into potato shells. Top with grated cheese. Sprinkle with paprika. Place on baking sheet and return to oven at 450° for 10 minutes until cheese melts and potatoes are heated thoroughly. Can be prepared earlier in the day and heated for 15 to 20 minutes until potatoes warmed and cheese melted.

YIELD: 8 servings.

Margie Weiss, Beverly Zaiontz & Dana Di Castro, Simply Delicious

AGUACATE FRITOS
(Fried Avocados)

Beer Batter
2   cups flour
2   eggs
1   can of beer
       salt & pepper to taste
4   avocados, slightly firm
       (to avoid mushiness)

Mix the ingredients of the beer batter together to a consistency of a light pancake batter. Do not make too thick. It should be a light, crisp coating when fried. Peel and cut avocados into ⅛ wedges and dip into beer batter. Drop directly into 350° hot oil. When golden brown, place on a platter over shredded lettuce. Accompaniments are sour cream and ranchero sauce.

YIELD: 8 servings.

Thimothy Penn, Executive Chef, Marriott Hotels

AMBROSIA CAKE

2   cups flour
2   cups sugar
2   teaspoons baking soda
1   large can crushed pineapple
2   eggs
½   stick butter, softened
½   box confectioners sugar
1   8-ounce package cream cheese
    coconut
    pecans

Preheat oven 350°.
Sift flour, sugar and soda together. Add pineapple and eggs. Mix well. Bake in a 12x9x2 pan for 30 minutes. Frost cake as soon as it comes out of oven. Mix the softened butter with the confectioners sugar and then add the cream cheese. Top the frosting with coconut and pecans.

YIELD: 10 to 12 servings.

Mrs. Anne Lawton, Cappy's Restaurant, 1776, Inc.

Variety - that's what makes entertaining in San Antonio so exciting. Whether in black ties and formal dresses, in boots and ten-gallon hats, or in sandals and sombreros, San Antonians come together often for festivities and events which draw upon heritage, tradition, patriotism and devotion. Entertainment San Antonio Style is a unique experience in the world today. It continues because of contributions from the past and a dedication to the future of a beautiful way of life.

The King of Spain sent 25 families from the Spanish Canary Islands to begin the first civilian colony in Texas. Only 16 families, comprised of 56 persons, survived the difficult journey. They settled in what is now known as San Antonio in 1731. One of their earliest priorities was to establish a parish church. Seven years after their arrival, they founded, built and named what has become the oldest cathedral sanctuary in the United States which still serves as an active parish. The church was named San Fernando Cathedral in recognition of Fernando III, King of Spain from 1199-1252. In addition to its service to parishioners, San Fernando Cathedral once housed the Spanish Archives of Bexar which documents Spanish military history in the area and contains information about the first civil government of San Antonio. The ashes and remains of the Heroes of the Alamo are buried here.

NACHOS

Toasting corn tortillas has been done in San Antonio for a very long time. Nachos are traditionally round chips, somewhat smaller than a corn tortilla.

Simple *nachos* consist of a corn chip with a slice of monterey jack or cheddar cheese and a slice of jalapeno pepper. They are grilled in the oven or heated in the microwave on high until the cheese is melted.

Nachos are also served with guacamole, ceviche, Mexican salsa or sauce, refried beans, grilled beef, chicken or seafood (crab and shrimp are favorites), and other toppings limited only by your imagination!

MEXICAN MEAT DIP

1	pound ground beef
2	canned jalapeno peppers, chopped
3	cloves garlic, minced
3	green onions, chopped, tops & bottoms
1	2-ounce jar pimientos, chopped
1	6-ounce can tomato paste
1	14½-ounce can tomatoes, chopped
1	teaspoon salt
1	teaspoon black pepper
½	teaspoon oregano
½	teaspoon cumin

In a large skillet, brown beef with chopped onion. Add remaining ingredients and simmer for 1 hour. Serve in chafing dish. Can be made ahead of time and frozen.

YIELD: 3 cups.

ANTICUCHOS

ARTICHOKE DIP

CAPONATA

TOSTADAS
For Recipe Page - See Index.

AVOCADOS

"Cooking San Antonio Style" often means the addition of the delicate flavor of avocados to a dish. The most popular avocado dish, by far, is guacamole, sometimes referred to as "poor man's butter." In San Antonio it is the perfect complement to almost anything. It is served as an appetizer, salad or side dish with meat, fish or poultry.

The secret of the flavor lies in the ripeness of the fruit. It is ready for use when it "gives" a bit when cupped in the hand. To soften an avocado, place it in a paper sack at room temperature in the kitchen for a couple of days. To prolong the life of softened avocados, store in refrigerator.

Avocados wear a green dress in the winter and a black one in the summertime. Inside, they are the same luscious flavor year round.

AVOCADO DIP

8	ounces cream cheese, softened
2	ripe avocados, mashed
½	small onion or 4 green onions
1	clove garlic, minced
1	teaspoon worcestershire sauce
	salt & cayenne pepper to taste
2	tablespoons lemon juice
2	tablespoons mayonnaise

In a food processor using a steel blade, add cream cheese, avocados, onion, garlic, worcestershire sauce, salt and pepper, lemon juice and mayonnaise. Blend until smooth. Chill. Serve with tostadas or Fritos.

YIELD: 2 cups.

Avocados are a native fruit of Mexico, our sister country to the south. South Texans can find this fruit in supermarkets and fruit stands on a year-round basis. They are most commonly used as the main ingredient in guacamole salad.

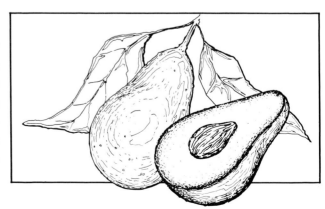

HOT ARTICHOKE DIP

1   4-ounce jar pimientos,
        diced, optional
1   14-ounce can artichoke
        hearts, drained & chopped
1½ cups mayonnaise
2   7-ounce cans green chiles,
        drained & diced
4   ounces monterey jack cheese,
        shredded
½   cup grated parmesan cheese
     additional grated
        parmesan cheese
     corn chips or tortilla chips

Preheat oven to 325°.
Drain pimientos and reserve 2 teaspoons for garnish. In a medium bowl, mix pimientos, artichokes, mayonnaise, green chiles, monterey jack cheese and ½ cup parmesan cheese. Spread mixture into a shallow 1½-quart baking dish. Sprinkle with additional parmesan cheese and 2 teaspoons of pimientos. (Can be made ahead. Cover and refrigerate.) Bake uncovered 30 minutes until bubbly. Serve with corn chips or tortilla chips.

YIELD: 20 appetizer servings.

VARIATION: Add two 6-ounce packages of frozen crabmeat.

SMOKED OYSTER DIP

⅔   cup mayonnaise
1   8-ounce tin whipped
        cream cheese
½   cup finely chopped onion
1   3⅔-ounce tin smoked oysters,
        drained & chopped

In a small mixing bowl, combine all ingredients. Beat at low speed until well blended. Chill before serving. Serve with favorite chips or crackers.

YIELD: 2 cups.

SAN ANTONIO DIP

2	16-ounce cans refried beans
3	large avocados
¼	teaspoon pepper
2	tablespoons lemon juice
½	teaspoon salt
½	cup mayonnaise
1	cup sour cream
2	tablespoons chili powder, more to taste
1	cup chopped green onion, with tops
2-3	tomatoes, chopped
2	4¼-ounce cans pitted, sliced black olives
8	ounces sharp cheddar cheese, grated

In a 9x13-inch ovenproof serving dish, spread refried beans. Heat under broiler until warm. In a small bowl, mash avocados and add lemon juice, salt and pepper. Spread on top of warmed beans. In a separate bowl mix mayonnaise, sour cream and chili powder. Layer carefully on avocado mixture. Sprinkle over sour cream layer: chopped green onions, chopped tomatoes, sliced black olives and grated cheddar cheese. Serve immediately while beans are still warm or refrigerate until ready. May be made ahead. Serve with tostadas.

YIELD: 16 servings.

VARIATIONS:

Taco Meat Filling: *Place a layer of taco meat on the bean layer. Shredded lettuce may also be added. Finely chopped jalapeno pepper can be added for extra tang!*

1½	pounds ground meat
1	teaspoon salt
1½	tablespoons flour
1½	tablespoons chili powder
1½	cups water
½	teaspoon cumin
½	teaspoon garlic powder

In a skillet, saute ground meat until brown and crumbly. Drain grease. Combine salt, flour and chili powder. Sprinkle over meat stirring to distribute evenly. Add water, cumin and garlic powder. Continue cooking over medium heat until thickened. Stir occasionally to prevent sticking.

YIELD: Filling for 1 layer of dip or 12 to 14 tacos.

Mexican Chicken Filling: *Place a layer of cooked, shredded chicken mixed with enough tomato sauce to moisten chicken. Layer as above instructions.*

Tomato Sauce

½	cup onions, sauteed
1	16-ounce can tomatoes
1	clove garlic, minced

Combine onions, tomatoes and garlic. Cook uncovered 30 minutes. Mix with 2 cups cooked, shredded chicken meat.

YIELD: Filling for 1 layer of dip or 4 to 6 tacos.

PRAIRIE FIRE BEAN DIP

2   1-pound cans refried beans
2   cups shredded
        provolone cheese,
        save ¾ cup for topping
1   cup butter or margarine
4   canned jalapenos or whole
        green chiles, drained,
        rinsed, seeded,
        finely chopped
1   teaspoon jalapeno pepper
        juice from can
2   tablespoons minced onion
1   clove garlic, finely minced

In a large mixing bowl, combine refried beans, shredded cheese, butter, chopped jalapeno peppers with 1 teaspoon of juice, onion and garlic. Place in a double boiler over hot water and heat until cheese is melted. Serve hot from chafing dish. Serve with tostadas, corn chips or crisp crackers.

YIELD: 5 cups.

CHIPPED BEEF DIP

1   2½-ounce jar chipped, dried
        beef, rinsed thoroughly
1   clove garlic, minced
1   green serrano pepper,
        chopped
3   green onions, chopped
1   8-ounce package cream
        cheese, softened
½   cup sour cream
        chopped pecans

In a mixing bowl, blend all ingredients together and adjust seasoning to taste. Mold into a ball shape or heat in 1-quart ovenproof dish. Top with pecans to serve. Serve hot or cold as an appetizer with crackers.

YIELD: 10 party servings.

YUCATAN BLACK BEAN DIP

1	pound dried black beans
6	cups water
1	tablespoon salt
1	pound lean ground pork
2	teaspoons oregano
2	tablespoons butter
1	cup chopped onion
5	medium radishes, sliced
1-4	hot green chili peppers, seeded, peeled & minced
6	tablespoons lemon juice
1	cup green chili salsa
8	ounces monterey jack cheese, grated
¼	cup fresh cilantro or coriander, chopped
	taco chips

Soak beans overnight in water. Drain. In a large saucepan, add beans, water and salt. Bring to boil, cover and simmer for 2 hours until beans are tender. Remove beans with a slotted spoon and set aside. Bring bean stock to a boil, add ground pork and oregano and bring to a second boil. Drain and reserve par-boiled pork. In a large, heavy saucepan, melt butter over medium heat. Saute onions, radishes and peppers until limp. Add beans, boiled pork, lemon juice and remaining salt. Lower heat, cover and simmer 10 to 15 minutes until tender. Pour in salsa, add grated cheese and continue simmering until cheese melts. Pour black bean dip into a serving dish, sprinkle with chopped cilantro and surround with taco chips. Serve warm.

YIELD: 10 to 12 servings.

CHORIZO CON QUESO DIP
(Sausage with Cheese Dip)

½	pound Mexican chorizo or regular bulk pork sausage
8	ounces fresh mushrooms, sliced
½	cup chopped onion
2	tablespoons butter
1	pound monterey jack cheese or 1 pound pasteurized cheese (we recommend Velveeta)
1	4-ounce can chopped green chiles

In a large skillet, cook sausage until brown and broken into little pieces. Drain and set aside. Add mushrooms, onion and butter to skillet and saute until soft but not brown. Add cheese, green chiles and reserved sausage to skillet. Heat until cheese has melted and mixture is hot. Serve immediately with tortilla chips or crackers.

YIELD: 8 appetizer servings.

VARIATION: Substitute a 10-ounce can of tomatoes with chiles, chopped, instead of the mushrooms and green chiles.

CHILI CON QUESO
(Peppers with Cheese)

1	2-pound box processed American cheese, cubed
8	ounces monterey jack cheese, grated
8	ounces longhorn cheddar cheese, grated
2	10-ounce cans green chiles, chopped
1	medium tomato, peeled & chopped
½	medium onion, minced
½	teaspoon garlic salt
1	teaspoon chili powder
	jalapeno peppers, fresh or canned, optional

In a double boiler or slow cooker melt cheeses. Stir in green chiles, tomato, onion, garlic salt, chili powder and jalapeno. Heat 30 minutes to 1 hour for flavors to blend. Stir often. Serve in chafing dish with tostadas. Freezes well.

YIELD: 6 cups.

VARIATION: Serve as a side dish with a Mexican dinner by pouring cheese sauce over a bed of tostadas!

CHICKEN PUFFS

¼	cup boiling water
2	tablespoons butter
¼	cup flour
1	egg
¼	cup shredded American cheese
2	cups finely chopped, cooked chicken
¼	cup finely chopped celery
2	tablespoons chopped pimiento
¼	cup mayonnaise
½	teaspoon salt

Preheat oven to 400°.
In a saucepan, add butter and boiling water. Add flour and stir vigorously. Cook and stir until mixture forms a ball that does not separate. Remove from heat and cool slightly. Add egg and beat vigorously until smooth. Stir in cheese. Onto a greased baking sheet, drop dough using a level teaspoon of dough for each puff. Bake about 20 minutes. Remove puffs from oven and cool. Split puffs and set aside. In a bowl, combine chicken, celery, pimiento, mayonnaise and salt. Fill each puff with 2 teaspoons of chicken filling.
YIELD: 20 puffs.

SWEET AND SOUR CHICKEN WINGS

2   dozen chicken wings
1   cup sugar
½   cup soy sauce
½   cup vinegar
1-2 cups all purpose flour or
       potato starch
4-5 eggs, well beaten

Preheat oven to 350°.
For Sauce: Mix sugar, soy sauce and vinegar together very well and set aside. Cut chicken wings in half, throwing away small wing with no meat on it. Dip chicken in beaten egg and flour. In a large skillet, fry chicken in oil until lightly brown. Put on cookie sheet and pour sauce over chicken. Cook for 30 minutes. Turn over and cook another 30 minutes.

YIELD: 24 chicken wings.

PARTY FRIED JALAPENOS

1   gallon canned jalapeno
       peppers, drained
½   cup yellow cornmeal
1   cup flour
1   teaspoon baking powder
½   teaspoon salt
1   tablespoon corn oil
1   cup beer
     oil for frying
4   ounces Muenster cheese or
       cheddar cheese, grated
½   cup flour

Cut each pepper, making a small slit large enough to remove the seeds and veins. Wash carefully, keeping the pepper intact and drain. In a small bowl, mix the cornmeal, 1 cup flour, baking powder and salt. Add the beer and 1 tablespoon corn oil. Mix until well blended. Set aside for 15 minutes. Add 3 inches of corn oil in a skillet and heat to 350° about medium heat. Carefully stuff each pepper with grated cheese. Roll the peppers in ½ cup flour, then dip into batter covering completely. Fry in hot oil 1 to 2 minutes. Turn and brown on all sides. Drain on paper towels. Serve immediately.

YIELD: 24 peppers.

JALAPENO CHEESE SQUARES

6   ounces Swiss cheese, grated
6   ounces American cheese,
       grated
6   ounces cheddar cheese, grated
6   eggs, beaten
3-4 ounces canned pickled
       jalapeno peppers,
       chopped

Preheat oven to 350°.
In a greased 9x13-inch baking dish, place a layer of grated cheeses and a layer of chopped jalapenos. Pour the beaten eggs on top of cheeses and jalapenos. Bake 25 to 30 minutes or until eggs are set. Cut into squares.

YIELD: 12 to 15 squares.

STUFFED JALAPENO PEPPERS
For Recipe Page - See Index.

SHRIMP IN DILL MAYONNAISE

2	tablespoons vegetable oil
2	pounds large shrimp in shell, cleaned
4	tablespoons fresh dill or 2 tablespoons dried
2	tablespoons parsley
½	cup mayonnaise
1	teaspoon dijon mustard
½	teaspoon salt
1	small onion
	bibb lettuce & dill sprigs for garnish

In a wok or large frying pan, stir fry shrimp for 4 minutes in 1 tablespoon oil. Let cool. Peel shrimp and halve lengthwise. Set aside. In a food processor, add dill, parsley and onion and chop until fine. Add mayonnaise, mustard and salt blending for 5 seconds. Pour mixture into plastic bag, add shrimp and coat. Chill 6 hours or overnight. Place on lettuce and garnish with sprigs of dill. Serve as an appetizer or heavy salad.

YIELD: 8 servings.

SALMON MOUSSE

1	¼-ounce envelope unflavored gelatin
¼	cup water
½	cup beef stock, boiling
½	cup mayonnaise
1	tablespoon lemon juice
1	teaspoon tabasco
½	teaspoon paprika
1	teaspoon salt
1	tablespoon capers, minced
½	cup celery, chopped
½	cup green onions, chopped
2	cups flaked salmon
½	cup whipping cream, whipped

In a small bowl, combine gelatin and cold water. Add boiling beef stock and stir. Set aside to cool. Add mayonnaise and spices to cooled mixture. Chill to consistency of egg white in appearance. When chilled, add capers, celery, and green onions and mix with mayonnaise mixture. Add salmon and blend thoroughly. In a separate bowl, whip cream and fold into salmon mixture. In a greased 5½-inch mold or fish-shaped mold, pour salmon mixture and chill until set. Unmold onto a serving platter. Garnish with parsley and serve with crackers or melba rounds.

YIELD: 20 to 25 servings.

SHRIMP CONGIGLIA

½	cup chili sauce
½	cup mayonnaise
¼	teaspoon chili powder
1	tablespoon lemon juice
¼	cup grated parmesan cheese
1	pound medium size shrimp, cooked & shelled

In a large mixing bowl, combine chili sauce, mayonnaise, chili powder, lemon juice, grated parmesan cheese and cooked and shelled shrimp. Mix and fill 6 seashells or an ovenproof casserole and broil 2 minutes until cheese is melted. Serve immediately. Can be served in a chafing dish at a cocktail party.

YIELD: 6 servings.

CAVIAR PIE

1   8-ounce package cream
      cheese, softened
¼   cup mayonnaise
2-3 teaspoons grated onion
1-2 teaspoons worcestershire
      sauce
1-2 teaspoons lemon juice
1   2-ounce jar black caviar
      for garnish
3-6 tablespoons minced parsley
      to cover pie
1   egg, hard-cooked & grated
2   tablespoons finely
      chopped onions

In a small bowl, blend cream cheese, mayonnaise, onion, worcestershire sauce and lemon juice. Spread mixture in center of plate or tray in a circle about 1 inch thick. Cover top with caviar and the sides with minced parsley. Sprinkle hard-cooked eggs and onion on top. Chill.

YIELD: 8 to 12 servings.

CAVIAR STUFFED EGGS

12 eggs, hard cooked
8   tablespoons mayonnaise (we
      recommend Hellman's)
4   tablespoons finely
      chopped onion
      dash of salt
1   2-ounce jar black caviar

Cut eggs in half lengthwise and remove yolks. In a small bowl, mix yolks, mayonnaise, onion and salt until smooth. Fill egg whites with yolk mixture and spoon a small amount of caviar on top of each section. Cover and refrigerate for up to 4 hours.

YIELD: 24 appetizers.

OLIVE TWISTS

10 slices white sandwich bread
½   cup chopped stuffed olives
½   cup chopped pecans
¼   cup butter, melted
8   ounces cheddar cheese,
      grated, optional

Preheat oven to 400°.
Trim crusts from bread and roll slices with rolling pin to flatten. In a bowl, mix olives and pecans and cheese if desired. Spread 1 heaping teaspoon of olive mixture on bread. Roll bread quickly as tightly as possible. Place on buttered cookie sheet with seam down. Brush with melted butter. Bake 10 minutes until golden brown.

YIELD: 10 olive twists.

BAKED BRIE

1   4½-ounce brie cheese
1   sheet frozen puff pastry

Preheat oven to 450°.

Let pastry sheet come to room temperature. Roll pastry out to ⅛-inch thick. Cut out circle 8 to 9 inches in diameter. Place cheese in center of pastry, wrapping pastry around cheese and pinching edges to seal pastry. Decorate pastry case with scraps of pastry cut into various shapes. Place pastry on ungreased baking sheet and immediately reduce temperature to 400°. Bake 25 to 30 minutes until golden brown. Serve with crackers or fresh sliced apples or pears.

YIELD: 8 to 10 servings.

ENGLISH OLIVE APPETIZERS

Great as an accompaniment with soup!

6   English muffins, open
2   4-ounce cans chopped
      black olives
1   cup grated yellow onion
½   cup mayonnaise or
      salad dressing
1½ cups grated sharp
      cheddar cheese
½   teaspoon salt
1   teaspoon curry powder

In a bowl, mix olives, onion, cheese, mayonnaise, salt and curry powder. Spread on English muffin halves. Broil 5 minutes.

YIELD: 12 muffin halves or 48 wedges.

STUFFED CHERRY TOMATOES

1   pint cherry tomatoes
8   ounces cheddar cheese,
      finely grated
2-3 tablespoons mayonnaise
1   teaspoon dijon mustard
2   tablespoons fresh parsley,
      minced
1   teaspoon dried dill or
      2 tablespoons
      fresh dill, minced

Cut top ⅓ from each tomato. Hollow out pulp with spoon or small knife and remove very thin slice from bottom of each tomato so it will sit on serving plate. In food processor, combine cheese, mayonnaise, mustard, parsley and dill. Blend until smooth. Using a spoon or pastry bag, fill tomatoes. Chill until serving time.

YIELD: 20 to 24 stuffed tomatoes.

STUFFED SNOW PEAS

40 snow peas,
        stemmed & blanched
1   8-ounce package
        cream cheese,
        room temperature
¼   cup mayonnaise
1   clove garlic, minced
2   teaspoons chopped chives
1   teaspoon dried basil
½   teaspoon whole caraway seeds
½   teaspoon dillweed
½   teaspoon lemon pepper

Split peas lengthwise on one side. In a small bowl, blend cream cheese, mayonnaise, garlic, chives, basil, caraway seeds, dillweed and lemon pepper. Stuff each pea with mixture. Chill and serve. These lovely appetizers can be made at least 1 day ahead as mixture improves overnight.

YIELD: 40 appetizers.

SWEET PICADILLO

A traditional holiday ground beef dish in South Texas served as a meat dip in a chafing dish with tostadas or served in a hot tortilla as a taco!

½   pound ground beef
½   pound ground pork
1   cup water
1   teaspoon seasoned salt
½   teaspoon pepper
½   teaspoon oregano
¼   teaspoon cumin
2   cloves garlic, minced
1   6-ounce can tomato paste
3   tomatoes, peeled & diced
3-5 green onions, finely sliced
3   small potatoes, diced
¼   cup pimientos, diced
½   cup seedless raisins
3   jalapeno peppers,
        seeded & chopped
½   cup slivered almonds, toasted

In a dutch oven, brown meat and drain excess fat. Cover meat with water. Add salt, pepper, oregano, cumin, garlic and tomato paste. Simmer covered for 30 minutes. Add tomatoes, onions, potatoes, pimientos, raisins and jalapeno peppers and simmer until potatoes are tender, about 30 minutes. Add almonds and simmer another 10 minutes.

YIELD: 8 servings.

SHY POKE EGGS

A San Antonio treat that looks like a fried egg. It is really a crisp corn tortilla with monterey jack and cheddar cheeses and a slice of jalapeno! Delicioso!

12 corn tortillas, cut into 4-inch circles with a cookie cutter or a 1-pound coffee can
12 slices monterey jack cheese, cut into 4-inch circles
3 slices cheddar cheese, cut into 2 inch circles with cookie cutter
12 slices jalapeno peppers
 oil for frying tortillas

In a large skillet on high heat, fry corn tortilla circles until crispy. Drain and set aside. **To Assemble Shy Poke Eggs:** Place a circle of monterey jack cheese over crisp tortilla circle. Place a slice of jalapeno in the center of cheese. Lay cheddar cheese circle on top of jalapeno. On a cookie sheet, place layered appetizers. Broil in oven or toaster oven until cheese begins to melt. Serve immediately.
YIELD: 12 Shy Poke Eggs.

EMPANADAS

½ pound ground beef or ½-pound cooked chicken, cubed
¼ cup chopped onion
6 ounces sharp cheddar cheese, shredded
¼ cup catsup
1 teaspoon chili powder
¼ teaspoon salt
¼ teaspoon tabasco sauce
1 package pie crust mix or four 9-inch crusts

Preheat oven to 450°.
In a large skillet, brown meat and drain. Add onion and cook until tender. Add cheese, catsup and seasonings. Prepare pie crust. Divide dough in half. Roll to ⅛-inch thickness on lightly floured surface. Cut dough in 2½-inch rounds. Spoon 1 teaspoon filling in center of each round. Fold pastry in half and seal. Bake 10 to 12 minutes.
YIELD: 4 dozen appetizers.

CHICKEN LIVER PATE

1½ pounds chicken livers
1 medium onion, sliced
½ teaspoon salt
¼ teaspoon pepper
1 small onion
2 eggs, hard boiled
2-3 tablespoons chicken fat
 olives & pimientos for garnish

In a large skillet, saute chicken livers and onion until cooked using no grease. Add salt and pepper. Put through a food processor with small onion and eggs. Mix in the chicken fat. Mold. Garnish with olives and pimientos. Serve with crackers.
YIELD: 3 cups.

CHEESE STICKS

2 16-ounce packages puff
      pastry, thawed
2 egg whites
1 cup grated parmesan cheese
½ cup grated romano cheese
    dash cayenne pepper,
      more to taste
    caraway, sesame or
      mustard seed
    paprika

Preheat oven to 400°.
In a bowl, combine cheeses and pepper. Roll puff pastry until ⅛-inch thick and brush with egg whites and sprinkle with cheese mixture and one kind of seed. Cut vertically into ½-inch strips. Hold one end of strip and turn other end until twisted. On an ungreased cookie sheet, place cheese sticks. Bake 10 to 14 minutes. Cool and keep in airtight container. May be frozen.
YIELD: 60 appetizers.

HINT: *Keep parmesan cheese in freezer to keep fresh!*

SWISS CHEESE SPREAD

16 ounces swiss cheese, grated
1   bunch green onions, tops
        only, sliced very thin
2½-3 teaspoons Lawry's
        seasoned pepper
1⅓ cups mayonnaise
¼   teaspoon Accent or MSG
¼   teaspoon sugar

In a bowl, combine cheese, onions, pepper, mayonnaise, Accent and sugar. Blend thoroughly. Serve with toasted wheat crackers or club crackers as an appetizer.
YIELD: 5 cups.

BEER CHEESE

16 ounces sharp cheddar
        cheese, grated
16 ounces swiss cheese, grated
1   teaspoon dry mustard
1   small clove garlic, minced or
        ⅛ teaspoon garlic powder
1   teaspoon worcestershire sauce
1   cup beer
    crackers, rye bread or celery

In a large mixing bowl, combine all ingredients and mix thoroughly. Pack into 6-ounce containers. Age for 4 to 5 days in refrigerator. Allow mixture to reach room temperature before serving. Beer cheese also makes a tangy spread to stuff celery.
YIELD: Five 6-ounce containers.

OYSTER STUFFED MUSHROOMS

2	3⅔-ounce cans smoked oysters, drained & chopped
2	pounds fresh mushrooms, washed, stems removed & chopped
4	tablespoons green onions, minced
1	cup sour cream
1	cup fine, dry bread crumbs
	a little milk to add moisture to stuffing

Preheat oven to 375°.
In a large mixing bowl, combine chopped mushroom stems, onions, sour cream, bread crumbs and oysters. Add a little milk if mixture appears to be dry. Fill mushroom caps. In a 9x13-inch baking dish, place stuffed mushrooms. Bake 15 to 20 minutes.

YIELD: 40 to 50 appetizers.

VARIATION: **For Crab Stuffed Mushrooms:** *substitute a 7½-ounce can of crabmeat for oysters.*

STUFFED MUSHROOMS

3	tablespoons finely chopped shallots
½	pound fresh mushrooms
4	tablespoons butter or margarine
2	tablespoons flour
1	cup cream
½	teaspoon salt
⅛	teaspoon cayenne or less
1	tablespoon chives
½	teaspoon lemon juice
2	tablespoons parmesan cheese

Clean mushrooms, remove and chop stems. Reserve caps for stuffing. In a large skillet, saute shallots in butter over moderate heat about 4 minutes. Stir in chopped mushroom stems and cook until moisture is evaporated, about 10 to 15 minutes. Remove from heat. Sprinkle flour over mixture and stir. Add cream and return to heat. Bring to boil. Mixture will thicken heavily. Stir in salt, pepper, chives and lemon juice. Pour into bowl and let cool. Refrigerate until ready to use.
Preheat oven to 350°.
Before guests arrive, fill mushrooms, heaping slightly. Sprinkle with parmesan cheese. Bake 10 minutes.

YIELD: Approximately 16.

MARINATED MUSHROOMS

¾	cup salad oil
¼	cup vinegar
½	teaspoon salt
¼	teaspoon pepper
½	teaspoon dry thyme
½	teaspoon marjoram
½	teaspoon rosemary
1	clove garlic
1	pound mushrooms

Wash and remove stems from mushrooms. In a large mixing bowl, combine all ingredients. Refrigerate overnight. Drain. Serve at room temperature.

YIELD: 1 pound marinated mushrooms.

STUFFED MUSHROOMS PARMIGIANA

12- 15 large mushrooms
2 tablespoons butter
1 medium onion,
    chopped finely
2 ounces pepperoni, diced
¼ cup finely chopped
    green pepper
1 small clove garlic, minced
½ cup finely crushed Ritz
    crackers, about
    12 crackers
3 tablespoons grated parmesan
1 tablespoon chopped parsley
½ teaspoon seasoned salt
¼ teaspoon dried oregano
    dash of pepper
⅓ cup chicken broth

Preheat oven to 325°.
Wash mushrooms and remove stems. Finely chop stems and reserve. Drain caps on paper towels. In a large skillet, melt butter and cook onion, pepperoni, green pepper, garlic and chopped mushroom stems until tender but not brown. Add crackers, cheese, parsley, salt, oregano, pepper and mix well. Stir in broth. Spoon mixture into mushroom caps, heaping tops. In a shallow baking pan with ¼-inch water covering bottom of pan, place stuffed mushrooms. Bake uncovered about 25 minutes until heated thoroughly. Can be made the day before.

YIELD: 12 to 15 mushrooms.

SPINACH DIP IN PUMPERNICKEL

1 10-ounce package frozen,
    chopped spinach, drained
1 package Knorr's Swiss
    Vegetable Soup
1 cup mayonnaise
2 cups sour cream
1 8-ounce can water
    chestnuts, chopped
1 small onion, chopped
1 round pumpernickel loaf,
    hollowed

In a bowl, mix all ingredients except bread. Chill 6 hours before serving. May be refrigerated for 1 week. Spoon into hollowed pumpernickel round loaf. Reserve remaining bread and cut into squares to be used for dipping.

YIELD: 5 cups.

CHEESE WITH SPINACH PUFFS
For Recipe Page - See Index.

CORNED BEEF IN RYE

A hollowed loaf of rye is used to serve this corned beef dip. Use the pieces of rye from the hollowed center to dip into the spread.

1⅓ cups sour cream
1½ cups mayonnaise
6   ounces corned beef, chopped
2   tablespoons minced onion
2   tablespoons chopped parsley
2   teaspoons whole dill seed
1-2 teaspoons Beau Monde
        seasoning
1   small rye loaf, hollowed
        cocktail rye slices for serving

In a bowl, combine sour cream, mayonnaise, corned beef, onion, parsley, dill and Beau Monde seasoning. Mix and refrigerate overnight. Spoon into hollowed loaf. Serve with cocktail rye slices.

YIELD: 3 cups.

CRABBIES

1   7½-ounce can flaked
        crabmeat
8   tablespoons butter,
        room temperature
1   8-ounce jar Kraft
        Old English Cheese
1   tablespoon mayonnaise
½   teaspoon seasoned salt
½   teaspoon garlic salt
6-8 English muffins

Preheat oven to broil.
In a mixing bowl, combine crabmeat, butter, cheese, mayonnaise and salts and mix thoroughly. Split muffins and spread mixture. Place on a cookie sheet and freeze for at least 8 minutes. Cut into eights. Broil 5 minutes and serve immediately.

YIELD: 8 to 10 servings.

COASTAL CRAB DIP

2   8-ounce packages cream
      cheese, softened
⅓   cup mayonnaise
1½ teaspoons dried mustard
3   tablespoons sauterne
      white wine
4   tablespoons powdered sugar
1   tablespoon worcestershire
      sauce
½   teaspoon salt
½   teaspoon garlic salt
½   teaspoon onion juice,
      fresh is best
2   6½-ounce cans crabmeat or
      16 ounces fresh crabmeat

In a mixing bowl, combine cream cheese, mayonnaise, mustard, wine, sugar, worcestershire, salt, garlic salt and onion juice. Blend thoroughly. Fold in crabmeat and refrigerate. Serve with crackers.

YIELD: 5 cups.

SEAFOOD COCKTAIL SPREAD

1   10¾-ounce can cream of
      mushroom soup or cream
      of celery soup
2   ¼-ounce envelopes
      unflavored gelatin
      (we recommend Knox)
3   tablespoons water
1   cup mayonnaise
1   8-ounce package cream
      cheese, softened
1   cup finely chopped celery
1   small onion, finely chopped
14 ounces cooked,
      flaked crabmeat
14 ounces cooked shrimp,
      chopped

In saucepan, heat mushroom soup adding gelatin and water. Bring to boil. Set aside and let cool completely. In a large bowl, mix mayonnaise and cream cheese. Stir in celery, onion, crabmeat and shrimp. To the seafood mixture, add mushroom soup and stir thoroughly. In a 2 quart mold or fish-shaped mold, pour seafood mixture. Chill until firm. Serve with fancy crackers.

YIELD: 2 quarts.

CEVICHE

SHRIMP CEVICHE
For Recipe Page - See Index.

SHRIMP MOLD

1   10¾-ounce can tomato soup
6   ounces cream cheese,
       softened
1   ¼-ounce envelope unflavored
       gelatin
¼   cup milk
1   cup mayonnaise (we
       recommend Hellman's)
1   cup chopped celery
1   4½-ounce can
       shrimp, chopped
2   scallions, chopped
½   cup bell pepper, chopped
1   tablespoon lemon juice

In a saucepan, heat soup with cream cheese. In a bowl, dissolve gelatin in milk. Pour gelatin mixture into soup mixture and add shrimp, mayonnaise, celery, scallions, bell pepper and lemon juice. Stir well. Pour into a 1 quart mold. Chill until set. Serve with crackers.

YIELD: 4 cups.

SHRIMP PATE

⅓   cup mayonnaise
1   3-ounce package cream
       cheese, cut in cubes
3   tablespoons chopped onion
¾   pound cooked small shrimp,
       well drained
1   tablespoon white horseradish
1   teaspoon dijon style mustard
1   teaspoon dry dill
½   teaspoon sugar
½   teaspoon salt
1   tablespoon lemon juice
¼   teaspoon tabasco sauce
     crackers or bread rounds

In a food processor with steel blade, combine mayonnaise and cream cheese. Add remaining ingredients and mix until blended. Shape mixture into a ball or spoon into a crock. Refrigerate several hours or overnight for flavors to blend. Can be refrigerated up to 2 days. Do not freeze. Serve with crackers or bread rounds.

YIELD: 2 cups.

CHEESY POTATO SKINS

3   medium baking potatoes
     vegetable oil
     seasoned salt
1   cup shredded cheddar cheese
6   bacon slices,
          cooked & crumbled
     sour cream, jalapenos
          & picante sauce,
          optional

Preheat oven to 400°.
Scrub potatoes thoroughly and rub skin with oil. Bake for 1 hour or until done. Allow potatoes to cool to touch. Cut in half lengthwise. Carefully scoop out pulp, leaving ¼- to ⅛-inch shells. (Save pulp for another recipe.) Cut skins in half crosswise and deep fry in hot oil for 2 minutes until lightly browned. Drain on paper towels. Place skins on a baking sheet. Sprinkle with salt, cheese and bacon. Place under broiler until cheese melts. Serve with sour cream, jalapenos and picante sauce.

YIELD: 1 dozen small servings.

FLAUTAS DE POLLO
(Chicken Flutes)

8   ounces chicken breasts,
          cooked & shredded
½   cup minced onion
2   cloves garlic, minced
¼   cup butter
2   teaspoons picante sauce
8   2-inch long chile
          poblano strips
8   corn tortillas
1   cup sour cream
1   cup guacamole

In a large skillet, saute onion and garlic in butter. Add shredded chicken and picante sauce. Mix well. Salt and pepper to taste. (Be sure mixture is very moist.) Dip each tortilla in hot oil to soften. Roll approximately 2 tablespoons of mixture and one 2-inch poblano strip in each tortilla. (It should be rolled up to resemble a flute.) Secure with toothpicks. Refrigerate until ready to serve. May be frozen. To serve, fry in deep fat fryer until crisp. Garnish each chicken flute with 3 tablespoons sour cream and 3 tablespoons guacamole. Dust with paprika.

YIELD: 8 chicken flutes.

A molcajete is the Mexican version of a mortar and pestle. It is used in the Mexican kitchen to grind all sorts of ingredients such as chili peppers, garlic, onions, comino (cumin), cilantro and avocados. A molcajete is made from volcanic rock.

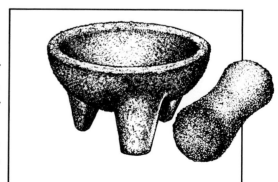

SALMON BALL

1	16-ounce can red salmon
1	teaspoon horseradish
4	teaspoons finely chopped onion
	juice of lemon or lime
1	teaspoon Liquid Smoke
1	16-ounce package cream cheese, softened
	fresh chopped parsley and/or chili powder for garnish
	sliced olives for decoration

In a bowl, combine salmon, horseradish, onion, lemon juice and Liquid Smoke. Add the softened cream cheese and blend. Roll into a ball. Roll cheese ball into parsley and/or chili powder. Decorate with sliced olives. Serve with crackers.

YIELD: 10 servings.

CHEDDAR LOG

1	pound New York aged cheddar, grated
¼	pound roquefort or 6 ounces bleu cheese
2	5-ounce glasses Old English Cheese Spread
1	8-ounce package cream cheese, softened
4	cloves garlic, pressed
	cayenne pepper to taste
	chili powder

In a large bowl, mix all cheeses together and add garlic and cayenne pepper. Knead with hands to assure a complete mixture for 10 to 15 minutes. Divide mixture into 4 portions. Roll each portion into a log about 8 inches long. Roll each log in chili powder. Wrap in foil and refrigerate. Can be frozen. Stays fresh up to 10 days when refrigerated. Slice and serve with cocktail crackers.

YIELD: 4 cheese logs.

ALAMO PECAN CHEESE BALL

CINNAMON STRAWBERRY CHEESE SPREAD
For Recipe Page - See Index.

MEXICAN CORN BASKETS

An attractive, bite-size appetizer with a distinct Mexican-basket look filled with all sorts of spicy goodies!

6	tablespoons unsalted butter or margarine, softened
3	ounces cream cheese, softened
1	cup all purpose flour
½	cup yellow cornmeal pinch of salt

Preheat oven to 350°.

In a medium bowl, combine softened butter and cream cheese and blend thoroughly. In a separate bowl, combine flour, cornmeal and salt. Add small amounts of cornmeal mixture to butter mixture, stirring until well mixed. Knead dough and divide into 1-inch balls. In small muffin tins, press dough balls with thumbs to form cups inside the mold. Dough should come up to top of tin. Bake 20 minutes until golden brown.

YIELD: 30 corn baskets.

Fillings: Beef chili, guacamole, refried beans, grated monterey and cheddar cheese, green onions, chopped jalapenos, pimientos, black olives, Salsa Fresca, shredded lettuce, chopped tomatoes, etc.

QUESADILLAS
(Cheese Filled Tortillas)

Fried flour or corn tortillas served with Salsa Fresca, Guacamole, refried beans, sliced onion rings and other condiments.

16	corn or flour tortillas
8	ounces mild cheddar or monterey jack cheese, grated
1	onion, sliced in rings
1	jalapeno chile, chopped oil for frying, optional

Heat a griddle or heavy frying pan until it sizzles when a few drops of water are sprinkled on it. Lay a tortilla on the hot griddle and place 1 ounce of grated cheese, 1 onion ring and a few pieces of jalapeno pepper on it. Place another tortilla on top to cover cheese or fold first tortilla in half. Cook on medium heat until cheese starts to melt. Turn on other side and cook for 1 more minute. When the cheese is completely melted, remove from heat and serve immediately. The quesadillas can be cut into pie-shaped eights.

YIELD: 64 pie-shaped appetizers.

SAUSAGE CRESCENT NUGGETS

These nuggets can be made ahead and frozen. Can be reheated in oven with great success. An ideal appetizer for brunches.

1   **pound highly seasoned sausage (we recommend Jimmy Dean)**
1   **8-ounce package cream cheese**
2   **packages crescent rolls (we recommend Pillsbury)**
     poppy seeds
1   **egg white, slightly beaten**

Preheat oven to 350°.

In a medium sized skillet, lightly brown sausage and drain. While sausage is still hot, add cream cheese and stir until cheese is melted and mixture is creamy. Cool completely. Separate crescent rolls into two rectangles. Form log of sausage mixture lengthwise down center of each rectangle. Fold over the long sides of pastry to cover sausage log. Place on ungreased cookie sheet, seam down. Brush with egg whites. Sprinkle with poppy seeds. Bake 20 minutes until crust is golden. When completely cooled slice into 1½-inch slices.

YIELD: 4 dozen.

VARIATION: Substitute 2 cans of chopped mushrooms for sausage.

BACON TURKEY BITES

1   **recipe Beer Puffs (See Bread Section)**
1   **pound smoked turkey tidbits**
½   **pound bacon, cooked & crumbled**
½   **pound Swiss cheese, grated**
¼   **cup pickle relish**
¼   **cup chopped celery**
½   **cup mayonnaise, more to taste**

In a large mixing bowl, combine all ingredients. Spoon into Beer Puffs. This appetizer is best made several hours before serving.

YIELD: 60 puffs.

PICANTE SAUCE

San Antonians add their favorite bottled or fresh picante sauce to give extra zest to almost every dish imaginable. Bottled picante sauce, now sold nationwide, was born in San Antonio in 1947 when a localite experimented with various combinations of old family recipes. When just the right ingredients were perfected, the picante sauce was marketed for all the world to enjoy. Picante has found its way from coast to coast to add its distinctive zest to everything from scrambled eggs to hamburgers and most Mexican cuisine!

MEXICAN ARMY HOT SAUCE

This recipe was a favorite of Pancho Villa. Thus the name Mexican Army Hot Sauce. It is so hot it can actually be used as a paint stripper!

9   large fresh or canned jalapeno peppers, diced
1   large onion, diced
1   large clove garlic, minced
2   tablespoons bacon grease
1   tablespoon salt
2   16-ounce cans tomatoes, slice & quartered

In a large skillet with bacon grease, saute peppers, onion and garlic until golden not brown. Add salt. Add quartered tomatoes and cook over low heat for 30 minutes. Remove from heat and allow to stand 1 hour. Serve either warm or cold with chips. Sauce can be used as an accompaniment to Mexican food. A little bit goes a long way!

YIELD: 4 cups.

SALSA FRESCA
(Fresh Sauce)

3   large tomatoes (very ripe), diced
1   fresh jalapeno pepper, diced
3   4½-ounce cans green chiles, chopped
1   bunch green onions, chopped, tip to tip
1   tablespoon salt
1½ tablespoons pepper
½   cup oil (we recommend Wesson)
1   teaspoon chili powder
1½ tablespoons garlic salt
    pinch of oregano
3-4 tablespoons chopped cilantro, optional

In a large mixing bowl, combine all ingredients and refrigerate. Serve immediately or will keep for 3 days. Salsa Fresca will become hotter the longer it sits. Add more chopped tomato to cut the spice. Serve whenever a Mexican sauce is needed. Great with tacos, fajitas or as a dip with tostadas.

YIELD: 1 pint.

CRANBERRY HOLIDAY PUNCH

1   32-ounce bottle
        cranberry juice
1   18-ounce can pineapple juice
1   cup orange juice
½   cup lemon juice
8   ounces bourbon or more to
        taste, optional
2   18-ounce bottles ginger ale

In a large punch bowl, combine ingredients and add crushed ice.

YIELD: 18 punch cup servings.

HOLIDAY HOT PUNCH

1½ 48-ounce bottles
        cranberry juice
1   cup water
1   46-ounce can pineapple juice
¼   cup lemon juice
½   cup brown sugar,
        firmly packed
½   teaspoon ground cloves
½   teaspoon ground allspice
½   teaspoon ground cinnamon
¼   teaspoon ground nutmeg

In a 30-cup percolator, combine all ingredients. Simmer for at least 30 minutes before serving. Serve warm.

YIELD: 1 gallon or
20 to 30 punch cup servings.

HOT CIDER FOR A CROWD

1   gallon apple cider
1   3-ounce can frozen lemonade
        concentrate
1   3-ounce can frozen orange
        juice concentrate
3   whole cinnamon sticks
1   teaspoon nutmeg or
        1 whole nutmeg
1   teaspoon whole cloves
1   teaspoon whole allspice

In a cheese cloth bag or tea ball, place spices. Drop spice ball in 30-cup coffee pot. Add juices and cider and simmer for 20 minutes. Serve hot. Can be served in a punch bowl. Float 3 oranges studded with whole cloves in bowl.

YIELD: 30 punch cup servings.

VARIATION: *Spiced Tea*
Follow cider directions, substituting 8 tea bags and 1 gallon water for 1 gallon apple cider.

BIG RED PUNCH

2 6-ounce cans lemonade
concentrate
6 6-ounce cans water
2 cups pineapple juice
1 32-ounce bottle carbonated
strawberry soda (we
recommend Big Red)
1 10-ounce package frozen
strawberries, thawed,
sliced

In a large punch bowl, combine all ingredients. Mix and chill. Make an ice ring ahead of time of Big Red to serve in punch.

YIELD: 20 punch cup servings.

CHAMPAGNE PUNCH

This punch is great for receptions and parties. It looks really festive around the holidays with a red ice ring floating in the punch bowl!

1 quart sauterne wine, chilled
1 quart club soda, chilled
2 ounces orange liqueur
6-8 ounces brandy
1 fifth champagne or sparkling
white wine, chilled
(we recommend
Asti Spumanti)

In a large punch bowl, mix all ingredients. Serve chilled or with an ice ring in bowl.

YIELD: 16 champagne glass servings.

COFFEE PUNCH

A very rich, cold coffee drink with creme de cacao and ice cream!

4 cups water
¼ cup instant coffee granules
3½ cups vanilla ice cream,
softened
½ cup whipped cream (can
substitute Cool Whip)
½ cup creme de cacao
½ teaspoon vanilla
pinch of salt

Mix all ingredients. Serve cold in a chilled punch bowl.

YIELD: 16 punch cup servings.

*VARIATIONS: Substitute Amaretto or Kahlua
for creme de cacao.*

ALMOND TEA

3   cups sugar
9   pints water
1   lemon rind, grated
6   cups strong tea
3½ teaspoons almond extract
3   teaspoons vanilla

Combine ingredients and serve hot or cold.
YIELD: 24 cup servings.

LULING WATERMELON WINE PUNCH

Luling is 56 miles east of San Antonio on the road to Houston. Its annual **"Watermelon Thump"** celebrates the area's 80,000 acres of watermelons. Top watermelons are auctioned as a highlight bringing up to $2,000 for the best. Texans especially enjoy eating juicy watermelon in the summer at barbecues.

½   medium watermelon,
        cut lengthwise
½   cup sugar
½   cup water
⅓   cup frozen lemonade
        concentrate, thawed
1   fifth dry white wine, chilled
2   cups small melon balls
        from watermelon
1   28-ounce bottle ginger ale

Using the rim of a cup as a guide, trace scallops around cut edge of melon. Carve out scalloped edges. With a melon ball scoop, cut out 2 cups of melon balls. In a saucepan, combine sugar and water. Boil for 5 minutes. Remove from heat. Add lemonade concentrate and wine. Chill 2 hours. To steady melon on serving table, cut a thin slice from bottom of melon for better balance. Pour chilled wine mixture into melon half. Add reserved melon balls. Carefully add ginger ale. Serve in champagne glasses.
YIELD: 2 quarts.

YULETIDE EGGNOG

1   quart commercial eggnog
1   cup bourbon
½   cup brandy
½   cup rum
2   cups heavy cream
        nutmeg

Prepare several days before serving. Combine eggnog, bourbon, brandy and rum. Early preparation allows flavors to mellow. When ready to serve, whip cream and fold into eggnog mixture. Blend well. Pour into punch bowl and sprinkle with freshly grated nutmeg.
YIELD: 2 quarts.

VARIATION: For a thicker, creamier eggnog, add 1 pint softened vanilla ice cream to eggnog mixture.

CHOCOLATE EGGNOG

3   quarts eggnog, chilled
1¼ cups Hershey's
      Chocolate Syrup
1½ cups whipping cream
1   tablespoon granulated sugar
1   ounce grated semi-sweet
      chocolate for garnish
      rum flavoring to taste

Prepare about 20 minutes before serving. In a large punch bowl, combine eggnog, chocolate syrup and rum flavoring. In a small bowl whip cream with 1 tablespoon granulated sugar to form peaks. Spoon whipped cream into eggnog and grate chocolate over whipped cream.

YIELD: 24 punch cup servings.

VARIATION: ¾ cup rum may be substituted for rum flavoring. Ice cream may be substituted for whipping cream.

YELLOW ROSE PUNCH

Great for weddings, teas, showers or other special occasions. Men love this punch because it is not too sweet.

2   6-ounce cans frozen orange
      juice concentrate
2   6-ounce cans frozen
      lemonade concentrate
1   46-ounce can pineapple juice
2   quarts water
1   28-ounce bottle ginger ale
      maraschino cherries

Combine all juices and water. Add ginger ale and maraschino cherries when ready to serve. Chill.

YIELD: 35 punch cup servings.

TEXAS SUN TEA

This is the most popular drink in San Antonio. A refreshing, thirst-quenching, year-round drink brewed with real Texas Sun!

9   tea bags (or 3 family-sized
      bags) or flavored tea bags
1   gallon water
      sweetener to taste
      lemon or mint to taste

Fill a glass or plastic gallon jar with cold water. Place the tea bags on the top with the tags hanging on the outside of the jar. Loosely cap the jar. Place in the hot sun for 3 to 4 hours. Do not leave out in sun more than a day because the tea will sour. Remove tea bags. Refrigerate. When ready to serve, add sweetener, sliced lemons and/or mint leaves. Serve over ice.

YIELD: 1 gallon iced tea.

IRISH CREAM LIQUEUR

A unique liqueur made with Irish whiskey which takes 3 weeks to ferment but worth the time.   Scrumptious!

3	eggs
1	cup whiskey
½	pint cream
1	can Eagle Brand Condensed Milk
2	tablespoons instant coffee granules
1	tablespoon chocolate syrup
½	teaspoon vanilla

In a blender, add all ingredients and blend thoroughly. Pour into bottles and allow to ferment in refrigerator for 3 weeks.

YIELD: 1 quart.

COFFEE LIQUEUR

Make this homemade liqueur from scratch.   Great to give as gifts.   Use in coffee or serve over ice cream as a dessert!

3	cups sugar
12	rounded teaspoons instant coffee
4	cups water
1	quart vodka
3	teaspoons vanilla

In a large saucepan, combine sugar, coffee and water. Bring to a boil. Reduce heat and simmer gently for 1 hour. Remove from heat and cool. Add vodka and vanilla. Pour into bottle and seal tightly. This recipe will keep indefinitely. To serve, pour 2 ounces over crushed ice.

YIELD: 3 quarts.

VARIATIONS:
For Mexican Coffee: Add 1½ ounces coffee liqueur to a cup of hot coffee.   Top with 1 tablespoon whipped cream.

OVERNIGHT BLOODY MARYS

CHOCOLATE MEXICANO

SANGRIA

MAGNOLIAS

TEQUILA SUNRISE
For Recipe Page - See Index.

CHABLIS SURPRISE

3	ounces club soda
3	ounces chablis
1	tablespoon black currant liqueur (we recommend Creme de Cassis)
1	cup ice cubes
1	fresh strawberry

Chill all ingredients. In a 10-ounce wine glass, pour club soda and chablis. Stir. Carefully trickle liqueur into glass, creating layers of color as it sinks. Add ice and float a strawberry on the surface.

YIELD: 1 10-ounce wine glass.

MARGARITA

1	ounce fresh lime juice
1½	ounces tequila
½	ounce Triple Sec
4	ice cubes
½	fresh lime
	salt

In a cocktail shaker, combine lime juice, tequila, Triple Sec and ice. Shake until well blended and chilled. Rub rim of champagne glass with lime half and dip in salt to coat rim. Strain mixture into glass and serve.

YIELD: 1 champagne glass serving.

FROZEN MARGARITAS

6	ounces frozen limeade concentrate
3	ounces Triple Sec
6	ounces tequila
2	cups crushed ice
½	fresh lime
	salt

In a blender, combine limeade concentrate, Triple Sec, tequila and ice and blend until smooth. Rub rims of 6 champagne glasses with lime half and dip in salt to coat. Scoop mixture into glasses and serve.

YIELD: 6 champagne glass servings.

TEXAS SUNSHINE

1	pint orange sherbet
2	ounces liqueur Galliano

In a blender, combine ingredients and mix until blended. Pour into champagne goblets and serve. This drink makes a nice, light dessert and is delicious served with your favorite homemade cookies.

YIELD: 3 to 4 champagne goblet servings.

PINA COLADA A LA ALAMO

This is a tropical, refreshing San Antonio favorite.   In some restaurants ice cream is added to make the drink more delicious!   Young people can order a "Virgin Pina Colada" without the rum and have a thirst quenching drink on a hot summer's day!

2   ounces cream of coconut
      (we recommend
      Coco Lopez)
4   ounces pineapple juice
3   ounces rum
2   cups ice cubes
      shredded coconut, cherries,
         pineapple and/or
         orange slices

In a blender, combine cream of coconut, pineapple juice, rum and ice cubes and mix well.   This makes a very thick drink.   Serve in red wine glasses.   Sprinkle with toasted, shredded coconut on top.   Garnish with a slice of fresh pineapple or orange and insert a maraschino cherry with a toothpick to the slice.   Serve with a straw.

YIELD: 3 red wine glass servings.

ORANGE JUBILEES

6   ounces frozen orange juice
      concentrate
1   cup milk
1   cup water
¼   cup sugar or to taste
1   teaspoon vanilla extract
7 - 10 ice cubes
      orange slices & mint leaves
         for garnish

In a blender, place orange concentrate, milk, water, sugar and vanilla and blend for 15 to 20 seconds.   Slowly add ice cubes, a few at a time, until slushy.   Refrigerate until ready to serve.   Good for morning meetings or before a brunch.

YIELD: 3 to 4 servings.

BOURBON CLOUD

A unique marshmallow and whipped cream topping for after dinner coffee.   An exciting way to impress special dinner guests.   Can be made ahead.

½   cup milk
20 large marshmallows
½   pint whipping cream
¼   cup bourbon
      coffee
      nutmeg

In a double boiler, melt marshmallows in milk. Remove from heat and cool. Whip cream until stiff peaks form.   Fold bourbon and whipped cream into marshmallow mixture.   Refrigerate until ready to serve.   Pour steaming hot coffee into large mugs.   Add two generous dollops to coffee.   Sprinkle with freshly grated nutmeg.   Marshmallow mixture can be stored for 2 to 3 days in refrigerator.

YIELD: 8 servings with coffee.

GREEN LIZARDS

1 6-ounce can lime juice
    concentrate
4-5 ounces vodka
20 fresh mint leaves
4 cups ice cubes

Add all ingredients in a blender and process. Serve in tall glasses with a garnish of kiwi slices or mint leaves.

YIELD: 4 to 6 servings.

STRAWBERRY DAIQUIRIS

Prepare these daiquiris the night before a small dinner party.

8 strawberries
12 ounces lime soda
    (we recommend 7-Up)
6 ounces frozen lemonade
    concentrate
6 ounces light rum

In a blender, place the strawberries and lime soda and blend thoroughly. Pour into a large pitcher or quart plastic container. Add the lemonade and rum. Stir until mixed. Freeze overnight. When ready to serve, stir several times to the consistency of a slush.

YIELD: 4 servings.

VARIATION: **Banana Daiquiris**
Substitute 2 bananas or more if desired instead of the strawberries.

JUNGLE JULEP

2 ounces water
½ teaspoon powdered sugar
    ice to fill glass
2 ounces dark rum
2 ounces light rum
    dash apricot brandy
6 sprigs fresh mint

In a 6-ounce glass, add the water and sugar stirring to dissolve sugar. Add mint and ice cubes and stir until glass is frosted. Add dark rum, light rum and apricot brandy. Stir and garnish with a sprig of mint.

YIELD: 1 6-ounce serving.

WHISKEY SOUR PUNCH

A popular, budget stretcher party punch.

1	12-ounce can orange juice concentrate
1	6-ounce can pink lemonade concentrate
12	ounces whiskey
48	ounces water
12	ounces lime juice

Mix all ingredients together in a large container and chill. Garnish with cherries and orange slices.

YIELD: 15 to 20 6-ounce servings.

TEXAS TUMBLEWEEDS

Use the homemade coffee liqueur recipe for Tumbleweeds. Serve as an after dinner dessert drink.

½	cup vanilla ice cream
1	ounce creme de cacao
1	ounce coffee liqueur

In a blender, combine ice cream, creme de cacao and coffee liqueur and blend for 8 to 10 seconds.

YIELD: 1 6-ounce serving.

VARIATION: **Tumbleweed Dessert**

½	gallon vanilla ice cream
6	ounces coffee liqueur
6	ounces creme de cacao chocolate syrup
4	maraschino cherries

Mix all ingredients together and freeze. When ready to serve dessert, spoon into dessert cups. Drizzle chocolate syrup on each cup of dessert. Garnish with half of a cherry.

YIELD: 8 servings.

HOT BUTTERED RUM MIX

¼	pound butter
1	pound dark brown sugar
¼	teaspoon cinnamon
¼	teaspoon nutmeg
¼	teaspoon ground cloves dark rum

For Mix: Cream butter and sugar. Sprinkle spices and mix thoroughly. Store in refrigerator in covered container.
For Drink: Place 1 heaping tablespoon of mix in a mug. Add 1½ ounces of dark rum. Fill with boiling water. Stir and serve.

YIELD: 1 8-ounce serving.

HOT CHOCOLATE MIX

1   2-pound box chocolate drink
    mix (we recommend
    Nestle's Quik)
1   15-ounce jar chocolate malted
    milk drink mix
½   cup cocoa
1   16-ounce jar coffee creamer
1   1-pound box powdered sugar
1   15-ounce box powdered milk
2   teaspoons cinnamon

In a large container, mix all ingredients. Pour mix into festive airtight containers for gift giving during the holidays!

2   heaping tablespoons hot
    chocolate mix,
    more to taste
8   ounces boiling water

To Prepare Hot Cocoa: Place hot chocolate mix into mug and add boiling water. Stir and serve.

The Battle of Flowers Parade, a major event of San Antonio's annual Fiesta Week, spotlights the military influence in the city with many decorated floats and marching units. San Antonio is extremely proud of its military heritage. Five important installations are located here including Randolph Air Force Base, known as "The West Point of the Air;" Lackland Air Force Base, the home of all Air Force basic training; Fort Sam Houston, Headquarters of 5th Army; Brooks Field; and Kelly Air Force Base, a large equipment maintenance facility with military and civil service personnel. San Antonio's military prominence began as early as 1836 when a small, volunteer army fought courageously at the Battle Of The Alamo.

ARTICHOKE SOUP

4	14-ounce cans artichoke hearts, drained
1½	10¾-ounce cans cream of mushroom soup
¼	cup chablis wine
5	cups half & half cream
1	cup strong chicken stock salt & pepper to taste

In a food processor, puree artichokes. Place artichokes in a large double boiler or large saucepan and add mushroom soup, wine, half and half cream and chicken stock. Stir and heat until well blended. Do not boil. Add salt and pepper to taste.

YIELD: 8 servings.

ARTICHOKE SOUP WITH LEMON AND DILL

A gourmet soup for artichoke lovers with fresh lemon juice, sour cream and snipped dill for garnish!

1	14-ounce can artichoke hearts, drained & chopped
½	cup fresh lemon juice
2	small boiling potatoes, diced
2	cups thinly sliced onion
4	cups canned chicken broth
4	tablespoons snipped fresh dill, chopped
4	tablespoons sour cream

In a food processor using a steel blade, add the artichokes, lemon juice and potatoes and blend completely. In a large saucepan, combine the artichoke mixture with the onion and chicken broth. Bring to a boil and simmer, covered, for 25 to 30 minutes, stirring occasionally until vegetables are tender. When ready to serve, stir in the sour cream and 2 tablespoons of dill to the soup and heat, stirring until completely blended. Garnish with the remaining dill on top.

YIELD: 4 servings.

SHERRIED AVOCADO CREAM SOUP

2   large ripe avocados
1   clove garlic, crushed
1   cup half & half cream
¼   cup lemon juice
2   cups chicken broth
1   bunch scallions,
        coarsely chopped
     salt & pepper to taste
8   tablespoons dry sherry
        to taste
     avocado balls for garnish

In a blender, combine avocado, garlic and ½ cup cream and add 1 tablespoon lemon juice, 1½ cups chicken broth and scallions. Blend at high speed for 30 seconds. In a mixing bowl, combine avocado mixture and add remaining chicken broth, lemon juice and cream. Add salt and pepper to taste. Final consistency should be a thin cream. Chill several hours. Add 1 tablespoon sherry per soup cup or 2 tablespoons per soup bowl. Garnish with avocado balls.

YIELD: 8 cups or 4 bowls of soup.

CABBAGE CHOWDER

3   tablespoons butter or
        margarine, melted
2½ cups finely chopped cabbage
1   large potato, finely chopped
1½ cups water, divided
2   chicken bouillon cubes
2   cups half & half cream
     salt & white pepper to taste
1   cup swiss cheese, shredded

In a 3-quart saucepan, combine butter, cabbage, potato and half a cup water. Cover and cook over low heat for 20 minutes. Slightly mash potatoes. Add remaining water, bouillon cubes and half and half cream. Cover and simmer over low heat 15 minutes. Add salt, pepper and cheese. Stir until cheese melts.

YIELD: 8 servings.

CALDO DE POLLO

CALDO XOCHITL
For Recipe Page - See Index.

Cilantro is a native herb used in many Southwestern culinary creations. Its distinctive flavor complements and cools off hot Texas chiles. Cilantro should be used fresh for maximum flavor and can be purchased in bunches in supermarkets.

1886 CHEESE SOUP

This soup recipe comes from the Driskill Hotel in Austin, Texas!

¼   cup butter
½   cup finely diced onion
½   cup finely diced carrot
½   cup finely diced celery
¼   cup flour
1½ tablespoons cornstarch
4   cups milk, room temperature
4   cups chicken stock,
        room temperature
⅛   teaspoon baking soda
1   pound processed Old English
        Cheese, cut in pieces
1   teaspoon salt
    white pepper to taste
1   tablespoon dried parsley
    dash cayenne pepper,
        optional
    paprika to garnish

In a heavy saucepan, melt butter and saute vegetables until tender. Stir in flour and cornstarch. Cook until bubbly. Add stock and milk gradually, blending into a smooth sauce. Add soda and cheese pieces. Stir until thickened. Season with salt and pepper and add parsley and cayenne, if desired. Before serving, heat thoroughly in a double boiler. Do not let boil. Garnish with paprika.

YIELD: 6 to 8 servings.

CHEESY CHICKEN SOUP

4   tablespoons butter
¼   cup chopped onion
½   cup sliced carrot
½   cup sliced celery
4   cups chicken stock
1   cup whipping cream
1   pound American processed
        cheese, diced
2   cups cooked chopped chicken
    salt & white pepper to taste
    chopped parsley for garnish

In a large saucepan, melt butter and saute onion, carrot and celery for 10 minutes. Add chicken stock and simmer for 15 minutes until vegetables are tender. Add cream and cook another 5 minutes. Add cheese and chicken and simmer until cheese melts, stir constantly. Season with salt and pepper to taste and garnish with parsley.

YIELD: 6 servings.

EASY CORN CHOWDER

6	bacon slices, cooked crisp, drained & crumbled
1	small white onion, diced
2	8-ounce cans whole kernel corn
2	8-ounce cans cream-style corn
2	10¾-ounce cans cream of potato soup
4	cups half & half cream cayenne pepper to taste

In a large skillet cook bacon and reserve bacon drippings. Set bacon aside. In 2 tablespoons of bacon drippings, brown onion and add whole kernel and cream style corn, potato soup and half and half cream, stirring constantly to prevent sticking. Heat completely and carefully. Before serving, add cayenne pepper and garnish with bacon on top.

YIELD: 6 to 8 servings.

CORN CHOWDER WITH HAM AND THYME

3	tablespoons bacon drippings or oil
8	ounces smoked ham, diced
3	onions, chopped
2	celery stalks, coarsely chopped
3	carrots, sliced
2	thyme sprigs or ¼ teaspoon dried
1	small bay leaf
1	pound boiling potatoes, diced
2	cups chicken broth
¾	teaspoon salt
⅔	cup heavy cream
1½	cups milk
5	cups corn, fresh or canned fresh thyme leaves, diced raw red bell pepper for garnish

In a large skillet with bacon drippings, saute ham and set aside. In remaining drippings over medium heat, saute celery, carrots, thyme and bay leaf turning constantly until vegetables are tender but not brown. To the skillet, add the potatoes and chicken broth to cover and simmer vegetables for 20 to 25 minutes until potatoes are tender. Discard thyme and bay leaf. Skim any remaining drippings from skillet and discard. In a large saucepan, bring cream and milk just to a boil. Add the corn and potato mixture stirring constantly and simmer 5 minutes. Remove the solids to a food processor and puree. To assemble the corn chowder, add the pureed vegetables to the milk and cream mixture along with the sauteed ham stirring constantly. Thin with more milk if necessary. Chowder should be a medium-thick consistency. Season with salt and pepper and garnish with thyme leaves and bell pepper. Serve with crackers.

YIELD: 6 to 8 servings.

CRAB SOUP

4	tablespoons butter
1	medium yellow onion, diced
1½	cup diced celery
⅓	cup diced red bell pepper
½	cup diced green bell pepper
½	cup flour
4	cups chicken stock or fish stock
4	cups milk
1½	cups half & half cream
⅓	cup sherry (we recommend Harvey's Bristol Cream), optional
	salt and pepper to taste
16	ounces lump crabmeat or 2 7½-ounce cans crabmeat
4	tablespoons chopped fresh parsley

In a large skillet over medium heat, melt butter and add onion, celery, red and green peppers cooking slowly, stirring occasionally until vegetables are tender but not brown. Remove skillet from heat and sprinkle vegetables with flour and blend. Return skillet to medium-high heat and cook 6 to 8 minutes, stirring constantly with a wooden spoon until flour is golden brown. In a 4-quart saucepan, transfer vegetable mixture and gradually add chicken or fish stock, stirring with a whisk to eliminate lumps. Blend in milk, cream and sherry. Bring to a quick boil and continue boiling for 1 minute. Season with salt and pepper to taste. Add crabmeat and parsley simmering for 5 minutes. Soup should be creamy but not thick. Add a little more stock if thinning is desired. Serve hot.

YIELD: 6 to 8 servings.

CUCUMBER/SHRIMP BISQUE

LOBSTER BISQUE

RED SNAPPER SOUP

For Recipe Page - See Index.

EASY CREAM OF CUCUMBER SOUP

2	cups cucumbers, peeled, seeded & coarsely chopped
1	cup chicken broth
1	cup half & half cream
¼	cup chives
¼	cup chopped celery leaves
3	sprigs parsley
3	tablespoons butter, soft
2	tablespoons flour
	salt & pepper
	dillweed

In a blender, combine cucumbers, chicken broth, cream, chives, celery, parsley, butter and flour. Blend until smooth. Season with salt and pepper. Serve either hot or cold. Garnish with a dash of dillweed.

YIELD: 4 to 5 servings.

LEMON SOUP

4	14½-ounce cans chicken broth, undiluted
1	small onion, chopped
½	cup uncooked rice
2	egg yolks, beaten
¼	cup lemon juice
1	cup whipping cream
2	tablespoons grated lemon rind
1	tablespoon grated parmesan cheese

In a dutch oven, combine chicken broth and onion. Bring to a boil. Add rice and reduce heat, cooking 15 minutes. In a bowl, combine egg yolks and lemon juice, mixing well. Gradually stir about 1 cup hot mixture into yolk mixture. Add remaining hot mixture, stirring constantly. Stir in cream, lemon rind and parmesan cheese. Cook until thoroughly blended and heated.

YIELD: 4 to 6 servings or 7½ cups.

LENTIL SOUP

1	pound lentils
¼	cup olive oil
2	celery ribs, diced
2	small to medium carrots, diced
1	medium onion, diced
1	medium potato, diced
2	small cloves garlic, minced
6	cups chicken stock
¼	teaspoon dry basil
¼	teaspoon dry oregano
¼	teaspoon white pepper
1	tablespoon lemon juice

Soak lentils 5 hours in a pot of water. Drain and set aside. In a large pot, pour olive oil and heat. Add diced vegetables including garlic and stir until lightly browned. Add lentils and chicken stock. Place on high heat and boil for 20 minutes. Add basil, oregano, pepper and lemon juice reducing heat to low to medium for 40 minutes until lentils are soft.

YIELD:6 servings.

VARIATION: *Cream of Lentil Soup*
After vegetables are lightly browned, reserve ½ cup each of celery, carrots, onions and set aside. In a blender, add small amounts of soup and blend. Slowly add 1 cup heavy cream. Return to large pot and add reserved vegetables and boil slowly for 8 minutes. Serve steaming.

NAVY BEAN SOUP

1½ pounds dried navy beans or
   3 cups dried beans
1 16-ounce can tomatoes,
   undrained
1 large onion, finely chopped
1 clove garlic, minced
1 pound ham hock
2 cups chicken broth
½ cup white wine
   salt & pepper to taste

In a large pot, wash beans and cover with water soaking overnight. Drain beans and place in a large dutch oven. Add tomatoes and liquid, onion, garlic, ham hock, chicken broth and wine, salt and pepper to beans. Add enough water to cover beans and bring to a boil. Reduce heat and simmer 1½ hours until beans are tender. Add more water, if necessary, to keep beans covered during cooking. When done, remove ham hock and half of beans. Remove meat from hock, shred with fork and set aside. Place beans in blender and puree. Return meat and pureed beans to dutch oven, heating thoroughly.

YIELD: 12 servings.

MUSHROOM SOUP

½ cup butter
2 cups sliced mushrooms or
   more to taste
4 tablespoons flour
¼ teaspoon dry mustard
1 teaspoon salt
2 cups chicken broth
2 cups half & half cream
¼ cup sherry
¼ cup chopped chives

In a dutch oven or large soup pot, melt butter and saute mushrooms until soft. Add flour, mustard and salt. Cook 1 minute. Add broth and cook until thick. (Stop here and refrigerate if serving later.) Add cream, sherry and chives. Heat until thoroughly warmed. Do not boil. For real mushroom lovers, more mushrooms can be used.

YIELD: 6 servings.

FRENCH ONION SOUP

2	pounds onions, thinly sliced
4	tablespoons butter
4	14½-ounce cans beef broth (we recommend Swanson's)
2	tablespoons flour
1	loaf french bread, sliced in 2-inch pieces
8	tablespoons butter, melted
1	clove garlic
12	ounces gruyere or swiss cheese, grated

In a large dutch oven or soup pot, saute onions in butter until translucent, about 10 minutes. Add flour and stir until blended. Pour in broth and stir. Simmer for 15 minutes.

For Croutons: Slice loaf of French bread crosswise into 2-inch pieces. Brush with melted butter and rub each side with fresh garlic clove. Place in 250° oven for 15 minutes on one side and then turn and heat 15 minutes on other side until bread is toasted.

To Serve French Onion Soup: Place crouton in bowl, pour soup over and top with grated gruyere or Swiss cheese. Place under broiler and melt cheese until bubbly.

YIELD: 6 to 8 servings.

LOCRO DE PAPAS
(Ecuadorian Potato Soup)

This festive and colorful soup from Ecuador is garnished with avocado, monterey jack cheese, corn, parsley and hot sauce.

2	tablespoons oil
2	tablespoons butter
2	medium onions, chopped
1	bell pepper, chopped
2	medium tomatoes, peeled & chopped
8-10	large red potatoes, peeled & cubed
1	pound monterey jack cheese, grated
1	cup milk or ½ cup cream
	salt & pepper to taste

Optional ingredients include:

	hot sauce
	parsley
2	10-ounce packages frozen whole kernel corn, cooked
3	medium avocados, chopped

In a large pot, heat the butter and oil. Saute onions, bell pepper and tomatoes until tender but not brown. Add cubed potatoes and saute, stirring constantly with a wooden spoon for 5 minutes. Add water to cover potatoes adding salt and pepper. Cook on low heat for 30 minutes. Uncover and continue cooking on high heat until soup thickens. Mash some of the potato pieces to help thicken soup. Lower heat and add milk or cream and ¼ pound of grated cheese and stir until completely blended. Serve with side dishes of corn, grated cheese, avocado pieces, parsley and favorite hot sauce. Use as garnishes on the top of each bowl of soup.

YIELD: 10 servings.

SPINACH BISQUE

1   10-ounce package frozen chopped spinach, cooked
2   tablespoons butter or margarine
2   tablespoons grated onion
2   tablespoons flour
2   cups half & half cream
1   10-ounce can chicken broth
¾   teaspoon salt
½   teaspoon paprika
     egg yolk for garnish

In a medium saucepan, saute onion in butter. Stir in flour and blend. Add cream, chicken broth, spinach and seasonings. Heat thoroughly. Do not boil. Serve steaming, garnished with sieved egg yolk.

YIELD: 6 servings.

COLD SQUASH SOUP

¼   cup margarine
1½   cups finely chopped onion
1¼   pounds small yellow squash, sliced
2   cups chicken broth
¼   teaspoon sugar
2   cups half & half cream
     salt & white pepper to taste
     chopped parsley or chives to garnish

In a large soup pot or dutch oven, saute onion in butter and cook over low heat until soft but not brown. Add squash and chicken broth and stir. Cook until squash is tender. Add sugar. Put mixture through a sieve or puree in blender and cool. Add cream and salt and pepper and chill again. Serve very cold sprinkled with either parsley or chives.

YIELD: 6 servings.

CATTLEMEN'S STEAK SOUP

A hearty soup that is excellent served on a cold day.

1½ pounds ground round steak or other steak meat
2 tablespoons vegetable oil
8 tablespoons butter
1 cup flour
8 cups water
2 cups sliced carrots
1½ cups sliced celery
1 large onion, chopped
1 16-ounce package frozen mixed vegetables
1 16-ounce can tomatoes, chopped
1 teaspoon Accent or MSG
4 tablespoons Kitchen Bouquet
3 teaspoons beef stock base
   salt & pepper to taste

In a large skillet, brown steak well in oil, drain and set aside. In a soup pot or dutch oven, melt butter and stir in flour stirring constantly. **Very slowly add water, one cup at a time** to prevent mixture from becoming lumpy. Add carrots, celery and onion. Add frozen mixed vegetables and tomatoes. Add Accent, Kitchen Bouquet, beef stock base, salt and pepper to taste. Add browned meat, cover and simmer on low 3 to 4 hours, stirring occasionally. Uncover after 2 hours of cooking to thicken. Serve hot with cornbread and green salad.

YIELD: 8 servings.

VEGETABLE BEEF SOUP

2 pounds stew meat or leftover beef
2 beef bouillon cubes
1 medium onion, chopped
1 16-ounce can tomatoes, chopped & juice reserved
1 10-ounce package frozen mixed vegetables
2 teaspoons salt
1 teaspoon pepper
1 teaspoon worcestershire sauce

In a large dutch oven, place stew meat and add enough water to fill almost to top of pan. Cook over medium heat for 2 to 3 hours until meat is tender, occasionally adding water to keep pot full. Add remaining vegetables, cover and simmer for 3 to 4 more hours. This is a great time to add leftover vegetables, rice noodles and/or potatoes. Add salt, pepper and worcestershire.

YIELD: 8 servings or 3 quarts.

ZUCCHINI SOUP

A low calorie, rich tasting soup spiced with curry and lemon juice.

1	pound zucchini squash or other squash
1	small onion, minced
1	tablespoon margarine
2	cups chicken broth
½	teaspoon curry powder
½	teaspoon lemon juice
½	teaspoon salt
1	clove garlic, minced, optional
	dash of tabasco, optional

Wash and scrub zucchini. Trim off edges and slice thinly. In a large skillet over moderately low heat, melt margarine and saute zucchini, garlic and onion. Cook covered for 10 minutes until vegetables are softened but not brown. In a dutch oven or soup pot, heat chicken broth but do not boil. Add curry powder,lemon juice and salt. Add zucchini, garlic and onion and stir.In small batches, add mixture to blender (or food processor with a steel blade) and blend until smooth about 1 minute. Transfer blended soup back to soup pot. Heat over moderate heat until thoroughly heated and blended. Garnish each bowl of hot soup with chopped chives. Add a dash of tabasco for the San Antonio flair! Serve with pita bread drizzled with melted margarine and grated parmesan cheese toasted under the broiler.

YIELD: 4 servings.

CHUNKY GAZPACHO

A perfect appetizer for a warm evening barbecue!

1   46-ounce can tomato juice
1   clove garlic, pressed
1   tablespoon sugar, heaping
1   teaspoon salt
1   teaspoon seasoned salt
¼   cup olive oil
3   tablespoons lemon juice
1½ teaspoons worcestershire
      sauce
½   teaspoon liquid hot sauce
1   cucumber, peeled & diced
1   green pepper, diced
2   carrots, diced
3   celery stalks, diced
3-5 green onions, diced
3   tomatoes, diced

In a large mixing bowl, mix tomato juice, garlic, sugar, salt, seasoned salt, olive oil, lemon juice, worcestershire sauce and hot sauce. Mix until oil and seasonings are dissolved. Pour into a large refrigerator pitcher. Stir chunky vegetables into juice mixture and add diced fresh tomatoes. Chill overnight or 4 hours. Serve cold with seasoned croutons on top.

YIELD:12 servings.

SMOOTH AND EASY GAZPACHO

1   28-ounce can tomatoes,
      undrained
1   cup tomato juice or V-8 Juice
1   cup buttermilk
1   small onion, coarsely chopped
1   small cucumber, peeled &
      coarsely chopped
1   small green pepper,
      coarsely chopped
1   clove garlic
2   tablespoons olive oil
½   teaspoon chili powder,
      more to taste
½   teaspoon salt
½   teaspoon cumin seeds
½   teaspoon Pickapeppa Sauce

In a large mixing bowl, combine all ingredients and mix. Place half of mixture in blender or food processor and blend until smooth. Remove and repeat with remaining mixture. Return to mixing bowl, cover and chill.

YIELD: 6 to 8 servings, 7½ cups.

EASY TORTILLA SOUP

The first course of a casual Mexican meal!

1	14½-ounce can tomatoes, undrained
1	medium onion, diced
1	clove garlic, minced
2	tablespoons cilantro or parsley
¼	teaspoon sugar
	salt & pepper
5	cups chicken broth
2	cups monterey jack cheese, cubed
2	medium avocados, cubed
8	ounces fried corn tortilla chips

In blender, combine undrained tomatoes, onion, garlic, cilantro, and sugar. Blend until chunky. In a large saucepan, add vegetable mixture and chicken broth. Simmer 20 minutes. Season with salt and pepper to taste. To serve, place cubed cheese, avocado and broken tortilla chips in bottom of bowl. Pour hot soup in bowl. Serve immediately.

YIELD: 4 to 6 servings.

TORTILLA SOUP
For Recipe Page - See Index.

MEXICAN CHOWDER

½	pound bulk pork sausage
2	cups pinto beans, cooked or canned
1½	cups chopped tomatoes
2	cups water
1	small onion, chopped
1	bay leaf
¾	teaspoon salt
¼	teaspoon garlic salt
¼	teaspoon thyme
⅛	teaspoon pepper
½	cup diced potatoes
¼	cup chopped green pepper

In a large skillet, brown sausage and drain grease. In a large dutch oven or soup pot, add sausage, pinto beans, tomatoes, water, onion, bay leaf, salt, garlic salt, thyme and pepper. Simmer for 1 hour. Add potatoes and green pepper, cooking 15 minutes more. Remove bay leaf and serve.

YIELD: 4 to 6 servings.

MEXICAN TAMALE SOUP

An easy crock pot favorite for a busy day! This thick soup is the consistency of a stew with a Mexican flavor.

1   pound ground beef or
      ground venison
1   onion, chopped
1   green pepper, chopped
2   tablespoons oil
1   cup frozen corn
2   cups water
2   beef bouillon cubes or
      beef stock base
1   16-ounce can pinto beans
1   tablespoon chili powder
1   teaspoon comino seed or
      powder
    salt & pepper to taste
10 tamales, shucked & quartered

In a skillet, brown beef, onion and green pepper in oil until browned. In a crock pot, combine beef mixture, corn, water and bouillon cubes. Add pinto beans, chili powder, comino, salt and pepper to taste. Cook on low in crock pot for 6 to 8 hours. About 30 minutes prior to serving, add tamale chunks and heat thoroughly. Do not cook tamales too long as they will cook apart. Serve with salad and jalapeno cornbread.

YIELD: 4 to 6 servings.

LIME POPPY SEED DRESSING

Use on fresh fruit, sliced avocados, melon and bananas!

⅔ cup cider vinegar
1½ cups honey
2 teaspoons dry mustard
2 teaspoons salt
3 tablespoons grated onion
⅓ cup frozen limeade
   concentrate
2 cups oil
3 tablespoons poppy seeds

In a blender, combine vinegar, honey, mustard, salt, onion and limeade and blend. Add oil slowly, beating until thick. Stir in poppy seeds until ingredients are well blended. Refrigerate and shake before using.

YIELD: 1 quart.

SPINACH SALAD
For Recipe Page - See Index.

SWEET & SOUR SPINACH SALAD DRESSING

1 cup oil
¾ cup wine vinegar
1 tablespoon soy sauce
½ cup sugar
¾ cup chili sauce
1 tablespoon worcestershire
   sauce

In a blender, combine all ingredients and blend completely. Dressing can be served hot or cold with spinach salad. Keeps well in refrigerator.

YIELD: 1½ pints.

HONEY LEMON DRESSING

1 cup sugar
½ cup honey
⅓ cup lemon juice
⅓ cup water
2 cups oil
1½ cups apple cider vinegar
2 tablespoons dry mustard
3 teaspoons ground ginger
¼ teaspoon basil
¼ teaspoon fine herbs

In blender, combine all ingredients and blend completely. Chill. Keeps well in refrigerator.

YIELD: 1½ quarts.

REINEE DRESSING

Wonderful with any green salad.   An heirloom recipe passed down from generation to generation.

1⅜ cups oil (we recommend
    Wesson Oil)
⅛ cup olive oil
2   tablespoons chopped onion
1   teaspoon chives or parsley
2   teaspoons sugar
3   teaspoons salt
1   teaspoon dry mustard
1   teaspoon celery salt
1½ teaspoons thyme
1   clove garlic, chopped
½ cup tarragon vinegar
1   cup whipping cream or
     1 cup buttermilk

Mix all ingredients in order given and shake well. Add whipping cream and mix thoroughly.

YIELD: 3½ cups.

TOMATO VINAIGRETTE MARINADE

1   cup olive oil
⅓ cup red wine vinegar
2   teaspoons crushed oregano
1   teaspoon salt
½ teaspoon pepper
½ teaspoon dry mustard
2   cloves garlic, crushed

Mix all ingredients together. Pour over sliced tomatoes or halved cherry tomatoes. Marinade should cover tomatoes. Put in refrigerator at least 2 to 3 hours or overnight. Serve on a relish tray or as a salad on a lettuce leaf. Also delicious on cucumbers.

YIELD: 1 pint.

HERB SALAD DRESSING
For Recipe Page - See Index.

FRESH VEGETABLE MARINADE

Marinade

1 bottle Italian dressing
1 tablespoon dill
½ cup lemon juice
1 teaspoon garlic salt
½ teaspoon lemon pepper

Vegetables (Use any or all of the following)

green & red pepper,
    cut in strips
cauliflowerets
zucchini, sliced & scored
broccoli flowerets
cherry tomatoes
cucumbers, sliced & scored
radishes
stuffed green olives, whole
artichoke hearts,
    halved or quartered
mushrooms, whole if small or
    sliced if large
avocados, sliced

Mix marinade ingredients together. If using mushrooms or avocados, add an hour before serving only. Olives are a must for this marinated vegetable salad. Make a single layer of vegetables and pour marinade over. Cover and refrigerate overnight, spooning marinade over vegetables several times. Drain and serve. Makes a colorful combination of vegetables.

YIELD: 10 to 12 servings.

SUPER SALAD SEASONING MIX

A great seasoning mix for vegetables, salads and baked potatoes!

2	cups grated parmesan cheese
2	teaspoons salt
½	cup sesame seeds
2	teaspoons paprika
½	teaspoon pepper
½	teaspoon garlic salt
1	tablespoon instant minced onion
2	tablespoons parsley flakes
½	teaspoon dried dill seed
2	tablespoons poppy seeds
3	tablespoons celery seeds

Mix all ingredients thoroughly. Store in cool, dry place in airtight container.

YIELD: 3 cups.

Serving Suggestions:
As a Vegetable Dip: Mix 3 tablespoons mix with 1 cup sour cream or plain yogurt and a little seasoned salt.
As a Crust for Baked Chicken: Skin chicken breasts, dip in egg or melted butter and coat with mix and bread crumbs. Bake 1 to 1½ hours at 350°.
For Croutons: Cut buttered bread slices into cubes and sprinkle with mix. Place on ungreased cookie sheet in 225° oven for 2 to 3 hours or until crisp. Store in airtight container. Great with soups and salads. Freezes beautifully.
For Cauliflower or Broccoli Appetizers: Dip vegetables in butter and then dip in mix combined with bread crumbs. Microwave until crisp tender. Serve with toothpicks.

OLD-FASHIONED POTATO SALAD
For Recipe Page - See Index.

POTATO SALAD WITH SOUR CREAM

7	medium potatoes, cooked in jackets, peeled & sliced
⅓	cup clear Italian or French dressing
¾	cup sliced green onions, tops included
4	hard-boiled eggs, chopped
½	cup mayonnaise
1	cup sour cream
1½	teaspoons prepared horseradish mustard
	salt & celery seed to taste
	garnish with crumbled bacon & chopped celery

In a large saucepan, boil potatoes until tender. While still warm, peel, slice and pour dressing over potatoes. Chill 2 hours. Add onion and chopped eggs. In a bowl, mix mayonnaise, sour cream, mustard, salt and celery seed until well blended. Gently fold into potato mixture.

YIELD: 6 to 8 servings.

MANDARIN LETTUCE SALAD

Caramelized Almonds

2 tablespoons sugar
⅓ cup chopped almonds

Dressing

½ teaspoon salt
   dash pepper
2 tablespoons sugar
2 tablespoons vinegar
¼ cup salad oil
   dash tabasco

Salad

½ head iceberg lettuce,
   shredded or torn thinly
1 cup chopped celery
1 tablespoon parsley
2 green onions, chopped
1 11-ounce can mandarin
   oranges, drained

To Prepare Caramelized Almonds: In a heavy skillet, place the sugar and almonds. Over medium heat, stir until the sugar melts and coats the almonds. Cool and break apart.

To Prepare Dressing: Mix all of dressing ingredients together and shake very well.

To Prepare Mandarin Lettuce Salad: In a large mixing bowl, place lettuce, celery, parsley, onions and oranges. Toss gently. Add caramelized almonds and dressing just before serving.

YIELD: 4 to 6 servings.

ON THE GO FRIENDLY FRUIT SALAD

This nutritious salad will last for days in the refrigerator!

1 21-ounce can peach pie filling
1 20-ounce can pineapple
   tidbits, drained
1 11-ounce can mandarin
   oranges
1 10-ounce carton frozen
   strawberries, with juice
2 bananas

Thaw strawberries. In a bowl, mix the peaches, pineapple, oranges and strawberries. Just before serving, slice and add the bananas.

YIELD: 8 to 10 servings.

FRESH FRUIT SALAD
WITH COINTREAU MARINADE

A very colorful tropical fruit salad especially appropriate for a ladies brunch.

½ cup sugar
¾ cup water
¾ cup Cointreau liqueur
3 apples, peeled,
      quartered & sliced
½ pound grapes, halved
4 peaches, quartered & sliced
1 pound cherries,
      pitted & halved
3 bananas, sliced
3 oranges, peeled & sliced
4 kiwis, peeled & sliced
1 pint strawberries, halved
1 pint blueberries

In a saucepan, combine sugar and water, mixing well. Bring to the boil. Cool to lukewarm and add Cointreau. In a large, deep, glass bowl, such as an English trifle bowl, arrange fruit in layers in this suggested order:

> apples
> grapes
> peaches
> cherries
> bananas
> oranges
> kiwis
> strawberries
> blueberries

Pour the syrup over the fruit and refrigerate for at least 3 hours.

YIELD: 12 to 15 servings.

YOGURT FRUIT LOW-CAL SALAD

3 apples, cut in ½ inch portions
1 20-ounce can sliced
      pineapple, cut in
      1-inch portions
2 bananas, cut in
      ½-inch portions
1 20-ounce package frozen
      strawberries, unsweetened
½ cup unsweetened coconut
½ cup chopped pecans
1 8-ounce carton
      strawberry yogurt
   sugar substitute (we
      recommend Sweet & Low)

Thaw strawberries. In a large mixing bowl, combine the apples, pineapple, bananas, strawberries, coconut, pecans and yogurt. Sweeten to taste.

YIELD: 8 servings.

SPICY MELON BOAT

1   large watermelon, carved
2   cantaloupes
2   15-ounce cans pineapple
        chunks, drained
    grapes
    cherries
    blueberries
    other fruit in season

Tequila Sauce

1   cup tequila
½   cup orange juice
½   cup powdered sugar
¼   cup grenadine

Shape fruit in cubes, balls or slices. In a large mixing bowl, combine all fruit. In a separate bowl, mix thoroughly tequila, orange juice, powdered sugar and grenadine. Pour Tequila Sauce over fruit and mix. Fill the watermelon shell with the fruit mixture. Refrigerate overnight. This attractive fruit boat will liven up any shower or casual dinner party!

YIELD: 20 servings.

LIVELY MELON BOAT

1   cantaloupe
1   honeydew melon
1   small watermelon
    fresh blueberries (canned or
        frozen berries are not
        recommended because
        the color 'bleeds')

Rum Sauce

⅔   cup sugar
⅓   cup water
1   rind of lime, grated
6   tablespoons lime juice
½   cup rum

In a small saucepan, combine sugar and water, bringing to a boil. Remove from heat and add grated rind, lime juice and rum. Allow to cool completely. With a melon scoop, take out the insides of all 3 melons, carefully removing all seeds. Add blueberries. Pour rum sauce over the fruit and toss lightly. Place in container with tight lid. Every 3 or 4 hours, turn container upside down, allowing sauce to coat fruit. Chill at least 12 hours before serving. Fruit will remain good for about 3 days before it gets too soggy. Serve as a fruit salad. The juice is delicious and could be served over ice cream as a dessert sauce.

YIELD: 18 to 20 servings.

VARIATION: Tequila Sauce instead of Rum Sauce.

HOT FRUIT SALAD WITH VARIATIONS

1   17-ounce can unpeeled
     apricot halves, save liquid
1   20-ounce can cling peach
     halves, drained
     & quartered
1   20-ounce can pineapple
     chunks, drained
1   17-ounce can dark sweet
     pitted cherries, drained
1   17-ounce can pear halves,
     drained

Rum Sauce

1   cup brown sugar, packed
1⅓ cups light rum (1 cup during
     baking, ⅓ at serving)
1   pint sour cream for garnish
     with spoonful on fruit

Spicy Sauce

¾   cup brown sugar
⅓   cup butter
1   teaspoon ground ginger
1   teaspoon cinnamon

**Curried Sauce (Refrigerate over-
     night; reheat at 350° until warm)**

⅓   cup butter
¾   cup brown sugar
3   teaspoons curry powder

Garnish

2   bananas, cut in chunks
⅔   cup slivered almonds
1   cup pecans, halves
     or chopped

Preheat oven to 350°.

In a large bowl, combine all fruit and place in a 3-quart greased baking dish. Prepare one of the special sauces and pour over the fruit. Bake uncovered 1 hour.

YIELD: 8 to 10 servings.

Sweet, juicy peaches are raised in the nearby Texas Hill Country. Many San Antonians are more than willing to take the short trip to cities like Fredericksburg and Stonewall to pick their own peaches - a great family outing with tasty results.

RASPBERRY SALAD

1   3-ounce package raspberry gelatin
1¼ cups boiling water
1   16-ounce package frozen raspberries
1   8½-ounce can crushed pineapple, drained
1   banana, sliced
½   cup chopped pecans
1   cup sour cream
1½ cups marshmallows
1   tablespoon sugar
3   tablespoons lemon juice

In a saucepan, boil the water and add the raspberry gelatin. To mixture, add frozen raspberries, pineapple, banana and pecans and mix carefully. Pour in favorite mold and refrigerate. For the topping, combine the sour cream, marshmallows, sugar and lemon juice and mix. Refrigerate until ready to serve. Unmold gelatin and add topping. Keep refrigerated until ready to serve.

YIELD: 8 to 10 servings.

ORANGE PINEAPPLE CONGEALED SALAD

1   6-ounce package orange gelatin
1½ cups boiling water
2   cups orange juice
1   20-ounce can crushed pineapple, undrained
1   11-ounce can mandarin oranges, drained
1   10-ounce package miniature marshmallows
1   8-ounce carton sour cream
1   cup grated American cheese

In a saucepan, boil water and dissolve orange gelatin. Pour into a 9x13-inch dish and add orange juice, crushed pineapple, mandarin oranges and marshmallows. Refrigerate. Top with sour cream and sprinkle with grated American cheese.

YIELD: 12 servings.

TROPICAL MANGO MOUSSE
For Recipe Page - See Index.

PURPLE PLUM SALAD

Great for a Christmas buffet!

2   eggs, beaten
2   tablespoons sugar
1   tablespoon unflavored gelatin
⅓   cup fresh lemon juice
      dash salt
¼   cup butter or margarine
1   cup miniature marshmallows
1   15¼-ounce can pineapple
      chunks, drained & halved
1   16-ounce can purple plums,
      drained, pitted, quartered
1   cup chopped pecans
1   cup whipping cream,
      whipped

In the top of a double boiler, combine eggs, sugar, gelatin, lemon juice and salt. Cook over boiling water until mixture thickens and gelatin dissolves, stirring constantly. Remove from heat, add butter and marshmallows. Stir until marshmallows are almost melted. Cool until partially thickened. Fold in fruits, nuts and whipped cream. Pour into greased 7x10-inch pan. Chill until firm, cut into squares and serve.

YIELD:8 to 10 servings.

BOOBERRY SALAD

1   15-ounce can blueberries,
      reserve liquid
1   8½-ounce can crushed
      pineapple, reserve liquid
2   3-ounce packages black
      raspberry gelatin
1   cup boiling water
1   8-ounce package cream
      cheese, softened
1   8-ounce carton sour cream
½   cup sugar
1   teaspoon vanilla extract
1   cup chopped pecans

Drain fruit and reserve liquid. In a saucepan, boil water and dissolve gelatin. Add enough water to reserved liquid to make 1¾ cups and add to dissolved gelatin. Pour into a 9x13-inch baking dish. When gelatin is slightly thickened, fold in fruit. Chill until firm. In a bowl, combine cream cheese, sour cream, sugar and vanilla and beat well. Spread over gelatin and sprinkle with pecans. Chill until set. Cut into squares and serve.

YIELD: 12 servings.

STRAWBERRY NUT SALAD

2	3-ounce packages strawberry gelatin
1	cup boiling water
2	10-ounce packages frozen strawberries, thawed
1	8-ounce can crushed pineapple, drained
3	medium bananas, mashed
1	cup chopped nuts
1	pint sour cream

In a large saucepan, combine gelatin and boiling water, stirring until dissolved. Fold in strawberries and juice, pineapple, bananas and nuts. Pour half of mixture into dish and let set until firm. Gently spread sour cream on surface. Gently spoon on rest of gelatin mixture. After salad becomes firm, cut into squares and serve on lettuce leaves.

YIELD: 10 to 12 servings.

CONGEALED APRICOT SALAD

2	3-ounce packages orange or apricot gelatin
2	16-ounce cans apricots, drained & finely cut, reserve juice
1	20-ounce can crushed pineapple, reserve 1 cup juice
2	cups boiling water
¾	cup miniature marshmallows
¾	cup chopped pecans
½	cup sugar
3	tablespoons flour
1	egg, slightly beaten
1	cup reserved apricot juice
2	tablespoons butter
2	cups whipped topping (we recommend Cool Whip)

Dissolve gelatin in boiling water. Add pineapple juice and chill until slightly thickened. Add fruit, marshmallows and pecans. Pour into a 9x13-inch dish and chill until firm. In a saucepan, combine sugar, flour, egg and apricot juice. Add butter and cool. Fold in whipped topping and spread on gelatin.

YIELD: 15 servings.

CRANBERRY CREAM CHEESE SALAD

A beautiful and tasty gelatin salad especially for Christmas and Thanksgiving!

1   4-ounce package cream
      cheese, softened
1   cup whipping cream
18 large marshmallows,
      quartered
1   pound fresh or
      frozen cranberries
1   medium apple, cored
      & quartered
1   cup plus 2 tablespoons sugar
2   3-ounce packages
      cherry gelatin
2   cups boiling water
½   cup chopped pecans
      green & red candied cherries
        (or maraschino)
        for decoration

In a mixing bowl, whip cream cheese with electric mixer. At low speed, gradually add cream. Do not whip. Stir in marshmallows. Cover and chill overnight to soften marshmallows. In a food processor, blend together cranberries and apple. Add sugar and set aside. In a saucepan, boil water and dissolve gelatin. Pour into a bowl and chill until thick and syrupy. Fold in cranberry mixture and nuts. Pour into 9x13-inch glass baking dish. Cover and chill overnight. Recipe should be prepared one day ahead. In a mixing bowl, whip chilled marshmallow mixture at high speed until thick and creamy. Spread over gelatin. Cut red cherries in half. Cut green cherries in small slices resembling stems and leaves. Place halves on top of cream layer to look like cherries. Arrange green stems and leaves under cherries to make decorative design.

YIELD: 20 to 30 servings.

FANCY SPECIAL SUNDAY SANDWICH

1   rye bread slice
1   ham slice
1   swiss cheese slice
      mustard
      Thousand Island dressing
      shredded lettuce & tomato
        slice for garnish
      bacon bits or crumbled bacon

On a slice of rye bread, spread a thin layer of mustard. Place a slice of lean ham on the rye. Place a slice of Swiss cheese on top and melt in broiler. Top with tomato, lettuce and a spoonful of Thousand Island Dressing. Garnish with bacon bits or crumbled bacon.

YIELD: 1 serving.

FANCY LAYERED LOAF

For Recipe Page - See Index.

WESTERN SALAD

Dressing

1	cup salad oil
½	cup vinegar
¼	cup catsup
½	cup sugar
1	tablespoon grated onion
1	teaspoon salt
1	teaspoon dry mustard
1	teaspoon celery seed
1	teaspoon paprika
1	clove garlic, cut in half, remove before serving

Salad

1	23-ounce can ranch style beans, drained
1	purple onion, sliced in rings
4	tomatoes, cubed
8	ounces American cheese, grated
2	2¼-ounce cans pitted ripe olives
6	avocados, cubed
½	10-ounce package regular corn chips (we recommend Fritos)

In a small mixing bowl, combine all dressing ingredients and mix well. In a salad bowl, combine all salad ingredients except chips and refrigerate. Add chips, pour dressing over salad and toss just before serving. Men love this salad. Great with grilled steaks or chicken.

YIELD: 6 to 8 servings.

TACO SALAD

1	onion, chopped
4	tomatoes, chopped
1	lettuce head, chopped
4	ounces grated cheddar cheese
8	ounces 1000 Island dressing, French dressing or Western Salad dressing
	hot sauce to taste
1	10-ounce bag tortilla chips (we recommend Doritos)
1	large avocado, sliced
1	pound ground beef, seasoned
1	15-ounce can kidney beans, drained
¼	teaspoon salt
	Tortilla chips, sliced tomato & avocado for garnish

In a large salad bowl, toss together onion, tomatoes, lettuce, grated cheese, salad dressing and hot sauce to taste. Lightly crush and add tortilla chips on top. Layer avocado on top. In a skillet, brown and season ground beef. Add kidney beans and salt, simmer 10 minutes. Drain and mix into cold salad. Garnish with tortilla chips, avocado and tomato slices. Serve *pronto!*

YIELD: 6 to 8 servings.

GUACAMOLE

PICO DE GALLO
For Recipe Page - See Index.

MARINATED GREEK SALAD

1   pound fresh mushrooms, sliced
2   bunches green onions, chopped
½   pound Swiss cheese, cubed
½   cup red wine vinegar
½   cup oil
1   teaspoon sugar
3   tablespoons Cavenders Greek seasoning

In a large bowl, toss the mushrooms, green onions and cheese. In another bowl, combine vinegar, oil, sugar and Greek seasoning and blend thoroughly. Pour over vegetable mixture. Refrigerate 8 hours before serving.
YIELD: 8 servings.

FIESTA MACARONI SALAD

¾   cup salad dressing (we recommend Miracle Whip)
1   teaspoon salt
½   teaspoon basil
1½ teaspoons parsley, snipped
1   8-ounce package macaroni twirls, cooked & drained(substitute another macaroni pasta)
1   cup sliced celery
2   tablespoons diced green pepper
2   tablespoons sliced scallions (or green onions)
2   tomatoes, diced
   pimientos for garnish

In a bowl, stir together the salad dressing, salt, basil and parsley. Add the other ingredients and mix gently. Add the pimientos for garnish. Cover and chill.
YIELD: 8 servings.

VARIATION: Add tuna, chicken or ham to make this a main dish salad.

VERMICELLI SALAD
For Recipe Page - See Index.

LAYERED GREEN SALAD

1   head iceberg lettuce,
     coarsely chopped
¼   cup chopped red onions
½   cup chopped green peppers
½   cup chopped celery
1   10-ounce package frozen
     peas, thawed
2   cups mayonnaise
1   cup grated cheddar cheese
8   bacon slices, fried
     crisp & crumbled

The following ingredients can
be added to make this
'your' favorite salad:

1   cup sliced water chestnuts
1   cup diced cauliflower tips
4   hard-boiled eggs, sliced
1   cup fresh sliced mushrooms

In a 9x13-inch dish, layer the lettuce, onions, peppers, celery and peas. Spread mayonnaise on top until it completely covers all the salad ingredients and seals the edges. Garnish with cheese and bacon. Cover tightly and refrigerate overnight.

YIELD: 15 to 20 servings.

VARIATIONS: Substitute swiss cheese for cheddar cheese. Substitute a pint of sour cream or one package prepared Hidden Valley Ranch Dressing for the mayonnaise.

GARDEN PASTA SALAD

1½ cups mostaccioli, rigatoni
     or other pasta
     salted, boiling water
3   tablespoons wine vinegar
2   tablespoons olive oil
1   teaspoon dried tarragon
1   teaspoon dried dill weed
½   teaspoon salt
¼   teaspoon dry mustard
⅛   teaspoon ground black pepper
1   large clove garlic,
     chopped finely
1   cup coarsely chopped tomato
1   cup sliced zucchini
1   cup pitted ripe olives
¼   cup sliced green onions

In a large pot, cook pasta to al dente in salted boiling water. Drain and rinse under cold water and set aside. In a small bowl, combine vinegar, oil, tarragon, dill, salt, mustard, pepper and garlic. Mix well. In a large bowl, combine the cooked pasta, tomato, zucchini, olives and green onions. Pour dressing over salad mixture and toss well to combine ingredients. Cover and refrigerate at least 1 hour; however, overnight is better for the flavors to blend. Serve on leaves of Romaine lettuce.

YIELD: 4 to 6 servings.

COLE SLAW

5	cups shredded cabbage
1	cup shredded carrots
¼	cup shredded red cabbage
¼	cup sour cream
½	cup mayonnaise
1	tablespoon vinegar
1	teaspoon sugar
½	teaspoon salt
⅛	teaspoon celery seed
¼	cup French dressing, bottled creamy style

In a large bowl, mix cabbage and carrots together. In a separate bowl, cream the remainder of the ingredients and add to cabbage. Refrigerate 3 to 4 hours before serving.
YIELD: 6 to 8 servings.

VARIATION: **Low Calorie Dressing:** *Substitute light mayonnaise, light sour cream or light French dressing in the recipe.*

24 HOUR COLE SLAW

1	large cabbage, shredded
1	small onion, grated
1	small green pepper, finely chopped (optional)
1	cup sugar
¾	cup vegetable oil
1	cup vinegar
1	teaspoon salt
1	teaspoon celery seed
1	teaspoon dry mustard
	pimiento

In a large bowl, combine cabbage, onion, green pepper and sprinkle with sugar. In a medium saucepan, combine remaining ingredients and boil for 3 minutes. Pour over vegetables, stirring well. Chill overnight. Garnish with pimiento for color.
YIELD: 10 servings.

SOUR CREAM CUCUMBERS

An excellent side dish or salad of crisp cucumbers and onions with flavors that meld deliciously with sour cream dressing.

3	large cucumbers, peeled & sliced
1	onion, thinly sliced
1	cup sour cream
½	cup white vinegar
1	teaspoon salt
½	teaspoon sugar

In a large glass or ceramic bowl, layer cucumbers and onion slices, separated into rings. In a small bowl, combine sour cream, vinegar, salt, pepper and sugar. Stir until blended and smooth. Pour over cucumbers and onion rings. Cover and refrigerate 4 to 6 hours or overnight, tossing once or twice.
YIELD: 4 to 6 servings.

VARIATION: *Add snipped fresh dill.*

MARINATED VEGETABLE SALAD

1	14-ounce can artichoke hearts, quartered & drained
1	7¼-ounce can black olives, pitted & drained
1	pint cherry tomatoes, quartered
1	bottle Italian salad dressing
2	ripe avocados

In a bowl, combine the artichokes, olives and tomatoes and marinate in the Italian dressing overnight. Slice the avocados and serve with the marinated vegetables on a bed of lettuce.

YIELD: 6 servings.

VARIATIONS: Add mushrooms, bell pepper and/or squash.

AUNT DIXIE'S PEA SALAD

½	lettuce head, chopped
1	cup sliced water chestnuts
1	10-ounce package frozen peas, thawed
	assorted vegetables: green peppers, green onions, celery & radishes, chopped or sliced
3	ounces cream cheese
1	cup mayonnaise
½	cup parmesan cheese
	bacon bits for garnish

In a large mixing bowl, combine the chopped and sliced vegetables and toss. In a small bowl, blend the cream cheese, mayonnaise and parmesan cheese. Add the cream cheese dressing to the assorted vegetables and mix. Sprinkle top with bacon bits. Let stand at least 8 hours in the refrigerator. Serve chilled in a flat casserole dish.

YIELD: 10 servings.

HILLY DILLY SALAD

3	large stalks fresh broccoli
1	medium head cauliflower
1	pound fresh mushrooms, sliced
1	7¼-ounce can large pitted black olives, drained
1	14-ounce can artichoke hearts, cut in half & drained
1	tablespoon sugar
1	tablespoon dillweed
1	tablespoon MSG or Accent
1	teaspoon salt
1	teaspoon pepper
1	clove garlic, pressed
½	cup vegetable oil

Wash and clean vegetables. Cut cauliflower and broccoli into bite sized flowerets. In a separate bowl, combine spices and oil. Put all vegetables in a large bowl and pour dressing over vegetables, mixing carefully. Cover and marinate 24 hours. Keeps for several days and improves with age!

YIELD: 12 servings.

BROCCOLI SALAD SUPREME

1	3-ounce package cream cheese, softened
1	egg
2	tablespoons vinegar
2	tablespoons sugar
2	tablespoons vegetable oil
1	tablespoon prepared mustard
¼	teaspoon salt
⅛	teaspoon garlic salt
	dash pepper
6	cups fresh broccoli, cut into bite sized flowerets
⅓	cup raisins
2	tablespoons chopped onion
½	pound bacon, cooked & crumbled
	chopped pimiento (optional)
	lettuce leaves (optional)

In a mixing bowl, combine the cream cheese, egg, vinegar, sugar, vegetable oil, mustard, salt, garlic salt and pepper. Blend with an electric blender until smooth. In a large bowl, combine broccoli, raisins and onion. Add the cream cheese mixture to the vegetables and toss gently. Cover and chill at least 3 hours. Place salad in a lettuce lined bowl. Sprinkle with bacon and garnish with pimiento.

YIELD: 8 to 10 servings.

BROCCOLI MOLDED SALAD

1	¼-ounce package unflavored gelatin
1	10-ounce can consomme
¾	cup mayonnaise
1	teaspoon seasoned salt
2	tablespoons lemon juice
2	10-ounce packages cut broccoli, cooked, drained
3	eggs, hard-cooked & chopped
2	tablespoons chopped green onions

In a bowl, dissolve gelatin in ¼ can of consomme. Pour into a small saucepan and heat ¾ can consomme and add to gelatin mixture. In a mixing bowl, combine mayonnaise, salt and lemon juice. Add broccoli, eggs, green onions and gelatin mixture and mix thoroughly. Into an ungreased 1 quart mold or 9x9-inch pan, pour mixture. Chill until set. Unmold and serve immediately.

YIELD: 12 servings.

CAULIFLOWER AND BACON SALAD

½ lettuce head, shredded
½ cauliflower head, cut
    into flowerets
8 bacon slices,
    cooked & crumbled
¾ tablespoon chopped onion
1¼ cups mayonnaise
½ cup parmesan cheese

Wash and clean vegetables. In a bowl, combine bacon, onion, mayonnaise and parmesan cheese, mixing well. In a 9x13 dish, layer the vegetables and place the dressing on top. Refrigerate overnight. Mix before serving.

YIELD: 10 to 12 servings.

CAULIFLOWER AND BROCCOLI SALAD

1 medium cauliflower head, cut
    into flowerets
1 broccoli bunch, stemmed &
    cut into flowerets
1 small onion, finely chopped
2 tablespoons sugar
2 tablespoons vinegar
1 8-ounce carton sour cream
1 cup salad dressing

Wash and clean vegetables. In a small bowl, combine sugar, vinegar, sour cream and salad dressing mixing thoroughly. In a large bowl, toss the cauliflower, broccoli and onion. Add the dressing and toss. Cover and chill overnight.

YIELD: 8 servings.

CORN SALAD

2 17-ounce cans whole
    corn, drained
½ cup chopped onions
1 cup diced,
    unpeeled cucumbers
1 cup diced celery
2 tomatoes, diced
1 cup sour cream
1 teaspoon salt, or more to taste
¾ cup salad dressing
2 tablespoons sugar
¼ cup vinegar
1 teaspoon prepared mustard

Wash and clean vegetables. In a large mixing bowl, toss the vegetables. In a small bowl, combine the sour cream, salt, salad dressing, sugar, vinegar and mustard. Pour the dressing over the vegetables and refrigerate overnight. The flavor improves overnight.

YIELD: 12 servings.

RICE SALAD WITH EGGPLANT & PEPPERS

1 pound eggplant, peeled &
    diced into ½-inch cubes
    salt
2-3 tablespoons olive oil
2 small green peppers,
    seeded & diced
6 cups cooked rice
1 clove garlic, crushed
    salt & freshly ground pepper
2 tablespoons chopped basil
    romaine lettuce leaves
    garnish with chopped parsley

Wash and cut eggplant. Sprinkle with salt and let drain in a colander for 30 minutes. Cook rice. Place the eggplant on paper towels and pat dry. In a large skillet, heat oil and cook eggplant over medium high heat for a few minutes, scraping bottom of pan frequently. Reduce heat, cover pan and cook eggplant for 15 minutes until well softened. Add peppers and garlic to skillet, mixing well. Cook 10 minutes more until eggplant is very soft and peppers are cooked but still firm. Season with salt. Mix the vegetables into the hot, cooked rice and add seasonings. Serve on romaine lettuce leaves garnished with parsley.

YIELD: 6 to 8 servings.

HOT CHICKEN PASTA SALAD

2 cups rotini (spiral pasta),
    uncooked
2 cups broccoli flowerets,
    cooked crisp-tender
    & drained
1 medium red pepper, cut
    into 1x¼-inch strips
2 cups cooked diced chicken
⅔ cup vinaigrette
    (we recommend La
    Martinique True French)
1 teaspoon dried basil
    leaves, crushed
½ cup snipped parsley
    salt & black pepper to taste

In a large pot of salted boiling water, cook pasta al dente and drain. Transfer to large bowl. Add broccoli and red pepper to hot pasta. In saucepan, combine chicken, vinaigrette and basil and heat thoroughly. Pour over hot pasta and vegetables. Toss lightly. Add parsley, salt and pepper to taste. Toss again.

YIELD: 6 servings.

HOT CHICKEN SALAD

4   cups cold, diced chicken
2   tablespoons lemon juice
1   teaspoon salt
¾   cup mayonnaise
2   cups diced celery
4   hard-cooked eggs, diced
¾   cup cream of chicken
      soup concentrate
1   teaspoon finely minced onion
4   ounces pimientos
1   cup grated cheddar or
      longhorn cheese
1½ cups crushed potato chips
⅔   cup slivered almonds

In a large mixing bowl, combine chicken, lemon juice, salt, mayonnaise, celery, eggs, soup, onion and pimientos and mix thoroughly. Place in a 2- to 3-quart casserole and refrigerate overnight. Preheat oven to 400°. When ready to serve, add topping of cheese, chips and almonds. Bake for 25 minutes.

YIELD: 10 servings.

VARIATIONS: Add sliced water chestnuts, ½ cup olives or substitute ⅔ cup chopped pecans for slivered almonds.

PICANTE CHICKEN SALAD

2   whole chicken breasts, boned,
      skinned & cut in half
3   tablespoons soy sauce
⅓   cup vinaigrette (we
      recommend La Martinique
      True French)
¼   cup picante sauce (we
      recommend Pace)
½   teaspoon sugar
¼   teaspoon ground ginger
4   cups shredded
      Romaine lettuce
1   cup fresh or canned
      bean sprouts,
      rinsed & drained
½   cup shredded carrot
½   cup thinly sliced celery
½   cup coarsely chopped dry
      roasted peanuts

In a medium saucepan, combine chicken, 2 tablespoons soy sauce and enough water to cover chicken. Simmer about 10 minutes until cooked and tender. Drain and set aside. In a small saucepan, combine vinaigrette, picante sauce, 1 tablespoon soy sauce, sugar and ginger. Heat thoroughly, stirring frequently. On a large platter, arrange lettuce, sprouts, carrot and celery. Slice the chicken meat into thin slices and arrange over vegetables. Sprinkle with peanuts. Drizzle with warm vinaigrette.

YIELD: 4 servings.

ALOHA CHICKEN SALAD

1   20-ounce can pineapple chunks, drained but reserving 3 tablespoons heavy syrup
3   cups diced, cooked chicken
1   cup chopped celery
1   cup seedless grapes
½   cup toasted slivered almonds
½   teaspoon lemon juice
½   teaspoon salt
½   teaspoon pepper
1   teaspoon sesame seeds
¾   cup mayonnaise
½   cup whipping cream, whipped
     flaked coconut, optional

In a large bowl, combine pineapple, chicken, celery, grapes, almonds, lemon juice, salt, pepper and sesame seeds. In a small bowl, whip whipping cream and add mayonnaise and reserved syrup. Mix thoroughly. Fold into pineapple mixture and sprinkle with coconut.

YIELD: 6 to 8 servings.

CHINESE CHICKEN SALAD

4   cups diced, cooked chicken
1   15-ounce can pineapple chunks, drained
1   cup chopped celery
1   11-ounce can mandarin oranges, drained
½   cup sliced black olives
½   cup chopped green pepper
2   tablespoons grated onion
     lettuce leaves

Dressing

1   cup mayonnaise
1   tablespoon prepared mustard
1   5-ounce can chow mein noodles

In a large bowl, combine cooked chicken, pineapple, celery, oranges, olives, green pepper and onion. In a small bowl, blend mayonnaise and mustard. Toss gently into chicken mixture. Cover and chill several hours. Just before serving, mix in chow mein noodles. Turn salad into a lettuce-lined serving bowl.

YIELD: 8 servings.

VARIATION: Substitute Sesame Dressing

2 tablespoons sugar
1 teaspoon salt
½ teaspoon Accent or MSG
¼ cup salad oil
½ teaspoon cracked pepper
1 tablespoon sesame oil
2 tablespoons vinegar
1 tablespoon sesame seeds, toasted
2 tablespoons chopped almonds, toasted

CHICKEN CANTONESE

5   cups diced, cooked chicken
1   cup chopped water chestnuts
2   cups pineapple tidbits,
        drained
½   cup chopped celery
¼   cup sliced green onions

Dressing

4   tablespoons chutney
        (we recommend
        Major Gray's)
½   teaspoon curry powder
¾   cup sour cream
¾   cup mayonnaise

In a large mixing bowl, toss chicken, chestnuts, pineapple, celery and green onions. In a separate bowl, combine chutney, curry powder, sour cream and mayonnaise. Pour dressing over chicken mixture. Refrigerate. For the best results, make this salad at least 8 hours ahead. Serve on a lettuce leaf, garnish with radishes and/or cherry tomatoes. Serve with bran muffins.

YIELD: 8 to 10 servings.

MOLDED CHICKEN ASPIC

2   8-ounce packages cream
        cheese, softened
1   10¾-ounce can cream
        of celery soup
1   10¾-ounce can cream
        of chicken soup
1½ cups cold water
5   ¼-ounce envelopes
        unflavored gelatin
¾   cup warm water
½   cup minced green onions
¼   cup chopped green pepper
2   cups chopped celery
¼   cup diced pimiento
4   cups diced, cooked chicken
        (Do not add
        extra chicken)
2   cups mayonnaise
4   tablespoons lemon juice
½   teaspoon salt

In a large mixing bowl, combine softened cream cheese, soups and water. Set aside. In a double boiler, add gelatin to ¾ cup warm water and soften. Do not cool. Stir warm gelatin into soup mixture. Add vegetables and stir. Add mayonnaise, lemon juice, pimiento and finally the chicken. Pour into large ring mold and refrigerate until set.

YIELD: 18 to 20 servings.

RICE AND ARTICHOKE SALAD

1	8-ounce package chicken flavored rice, cooked
4	green onions, thinly sliced
½	green pepper, chopped
12	stuffed olives, sliced
2	6-ounce jars marinated artichoke hearts, drained & chopped, reserving liquid
½	teaspoon curry powder
⅓	cup mayonnaise

Cook rice and cool in large bowl. To rice add onions, pepper, olives and artichokes. In a small bowl, add the artichoke liquid, curry powder and mayonnaise. Add dressing to vegetables and mix well. Chill 24 hours before serving.

YIELD: 8 servings.

VARIATION: **Oriental Chicken Rice-A-Roni**

1 box Chicken Rice-A-Roni, cooked
1½ cups cooked cubed chicken
1 6-ounce jar marinated artichokes, drained
1 10-ounce box frozen snow peas, thawed & drained
1 6-ounce jar marinated mushrooms, drained
1 cup mayonnaise
1½ teaspoons curry powder
salt & pepper to taste
1 3-ounce jar chopped pimientos
¾ cup chopped pecans

Add cooked, diced chicken for a great main dish. Follow above instructions. Garnish with chopped pecans and pimientos.

CURRIED RICE AND CHICKEN SALAD

A great luncheon or summer supper dish. Make early in the day and chill.

½	teaspoon salt
1	teaspoon curry powder
1½	cups water
1⅓	cups instant rice (we recommend Minute Rice)
1	10-ounce package frozen green peas, cooked
1	apple, unpeeled and cut in thin strips
1	teaspoon grated onion
⅛	teaspoon ground black pepper
1½	cups cubed, cooked chicken
½	cup diced celery
¾	cup mayonnaise or ½ cup mayonnaise and ¼ cup French dressing
2	tomatoes, cut in wedges salad greens

In a saucepan, combine salt, curry powder and water. Bring to boil and add rice. Cover and remove from heat. Let stand 5 minutes until all water is absorbed. Add peas, apple, onion and pepper. Toss lightly with fork and chill. Just before serving, add chicken, celery and mayonnaise. Toss lightly in a large bowl. Serve on crisp salad greens and garnish with tomato wedges. Excellent with white wine and crackers.

YIELD: 6 servings.

SHRIMP SALAD MOLD

1½ ¼-ounce envelopes
    unflavored gelatin
⅓ cup water
1 8-ounce package cream
    cheese, softened
1 10¾-ounce can tomato soup
2 7-ounce cans shrimp
¾ cup chopped celery
    salt & pepper to taste
1 cup mayonnaise
½ cup choppped onion,
    add more if desired
    cayenne pepper

In a small bowl, dissolve gelatin in water and set aside. In a double boiler, melt cream cheese in tomato soup. Add gelatin and blend until dissolved and very smooth. Cool. Add shrimp, celery, salt, pepper, mayonnaise, onion and cayenne pepper and mix until blended. In a greased mold, pour shrimp mixture and refrigerate until set. Serve as a salad on a bed of lettuce or as an appetizer.

YIELD: 3 cups.

SHRIMP SALAD
For Recipe Page - See Index.

MEXICAN SHRIMP SALAD

1 pound cooked diced shrimp
½ cup chopped celery
3 tablespoons finely
    chopped onion
¾ cup mayonnaise
½ teaspoon chili powder
    garnish with tomato wedges
    and ripe olives
    lettuce leaves

In a large bowl, mix shrimp, celery, onion, mayonnaise and chili powder. Chill several hours or overnight. Serve on on a bed of lettuce with tomato wedges and olives for garnish.

YIELD: 4 servings.

SHRIMP SOUFFLE SALAD

1   3-ounce package lemon
       gelatin
⅔   cup boiling water
1   10¾-ounce can tomato soup
2   3-ounce packages
       cream cheese
¼   cup minced onion
¼   cup chopped green pepper
1   cup chopped celery
⅔   cup mayonnaise
1-2 cans shrimp

Dissolve gelatin in boiling water. In a saucepan, heat tomato soup and melt cream cheese. This mixture will be lumpy. Stir in dissolved jello. Add the onion, green pepper, celery, mayonnaise and ¾ of the shrimp, reserving some for garnish. Pour mixture into a 8½x11-inch dish, sprinkle reserved shrimp on top and refrigerate until firm. A copper mold in a fish shape could also be used.

YIELD: 5 cups.

CRABMEAT SALAD

2   tablespoons unflavored
       gelatin
1   cup boiling water
1   8-ounce can tomato sauce
1   8-ounce package cream
       cheese, softened
1½ cups diced celery
1   large green pepper,
       finely chopped
1   onion, finely chopped
1   6½-ounce can crabmeat,
       flaked
1   cup mayonnaise

In a large bowl, add boiling water to gelatin and stir until dissolved. Add tomato sauce and softened cream cheese and blend thoroughly. Add celery, green pepper and onion and chill until slightly thickened. Fold in crabmeat and mayonnaise. In a greased mold, place crabmeat mixture and chill until set.

YIELD: 6 to 8 servings.

MOLDED TUNA-AVOCADO SALAD

First Layer

2-3	avocados
1	8-ounce package cream cheese
1	3-ounce package lime gelatin
1	3-ounce package lemon gelatin
2	cups boiling water
1	cup mayonnaise
	salt to taste
2	cups diced celery
	juice of ½ onion
	tabasco to taste

Second Layer

2	¼-ounce envelopes unflavored gelatin
2½	cups water
6	tablespoons lemon juice
2	7-ounce cans tuna
⅔	cup diced pimiento
1	teaspoon salt

For First Layer: In a small bowl, cream avocados and cream cheese together and set aside. In a large bowl, add hot water to lime and lemon gelatins and dissolve completely. Add mayonnaise to the gelatins and mix. Slowly add avocado mixture to gelatins. Add salt, celery, onion juice and tabasco sauce. In a 9x13-inch glass baking dish, pour the mixture and chill.

For second layer: in a small saucepan, soften gelatin in ½ cup cold water and stir over low heat until dissolved. Stir in 2 cups water, lemon juice and salt. Chill slightly. Fold in tuna and pimiento. Pour over first layer and chill.

YIELD: 15 servings.

BEEF AND MUSHROOM SALAD

1-	1½ pounds leftover roast or steak, thinly sliced
12	small fresh mushrooms, sliced
12	cherry tomatoes, halved
1	14-ounce can artichoke hearts, drained & halved
10-	12 stuffed green olives
½	cauliflower head, cut into flowerets
1	lettuce head, shredded
2	tablespoons parsley, chopped
1	avocado, sliced

Dressing

½	cup olive oil
¼	cup red wine vinegar
2	teaspoons dijon mustard
1	clove garlic, crushed
½	teaspoon sugar
1	teaspoon salt
	freshly ground pepper to taste

In a large bowl, combine beef, mushrooms, tomatoes, artichoke hearts, olives and cauliflower flowerets. In a separate bowl, combine olive oil, vinegar, mustard, garlic, sugar, salt and pepper and mix thoroughly. Pour dressing over beef and vegetables. Marinate several hours or overnight. Line salad bowl with shredded lettuce. Add avocado to beef mixture and arrange on lettuce. Sprinkle with parsley.

YIELD: 4 to 6 servings.

PASTA TIMBALE

"Timbale" is a creamy mixture of ham, lobster, cheese or fish cooked in a drum-shaped mold or small pastry shell filled with a gourmet Italian mixture. This is truly a show stopper recipe. It is much simpler than it seems and worth the effort. Serve as a salad for a gourmet Italian meal or any festive occasion.

4	large or 8 small leeks, trimmed
¼	cup olive oil
½	pound mushrooms, finely chopped
2	cloves garlic, chopped
4	large tomatoes, seeded & chopped
¼	cup all-purpose flour
1	5½-ounce jar oil-cured Greek olives, coarsely chopped
⅓	cup capers, rinsed & drained salt
1½	pounds mozzarella cheese, shredded
½	teaspoon dried oregano, crumbled
8	jumbo round cheese ravioli or square ravioli
½	pound mortadella, thinly sliced (about 15 slices) or Italian ham, thinly sliced

Chianti Vinaigrette

⅓	cup Chianti
¼	cup red wine vinegar
1	cup olive oil
2	tablespoons fresh basil leaves, minced
2	teaspoons salt
1	teaspoon sugar
¼	teaspoon freshly ground pepper

Generously grease a 10-inch springform pan. Cut white part of leeks into slices along with green leaves. In a saucepan, simmer leeks for 5 minutes. Drain well. Arrange leek slices in single layer in bottom of springform pan. Cover with layer of leaves. Drape remaining leaves around edges of springform, allowing ends to hang over top and down sides temporarily.

In a heavy large skillet, over medium high heat warm the olive oil and add mushrooms and garlic and saute 5 minutes. Add tomatoes. Sprinkle with flour and blend well. Simmer about 20 minutes until a thick sauce is made. Stir in olives and capers. Season with salt. Set aside. In a separate bowl, combine mozzarella cheese and oregano and set aside. In a large pot, bring salted water to boil. Add ravioli and cook 10 minutes stirring frequently. Drain and rinse under cold water. Pat dry. (If using canned ravioli, it is unnecessary to cook. Gently rinse away the sauce in a colander.)

Preheat oven to 350°.

Sprinkle 1½ cups cheese mixture over leeks in springform pan. Layer one third mortadella slices (about 5) over cheese. Arrange 6 ravioli over top. Pour ⅓ of vegetable sauce over ravioli. Repeat layering, ending with cheese. Fold leek ends over top, pressing gently to flatten layers. Set springform pan on baking sheet. Cover top of pan with foil. Bake 1 hour. Cool in pan 30 minutes.

For Vinaigrette: In a small bowl, mix wine and vinegar. Whisk in oil 1 drop at a time. Add basil, salt, sugar and pepper.

To serve: Refrigerate overnight in pan. Arrange platter over top of springform pan and invert mold. Carefully remove sides of pan, then gently lift off bottom. Cut timbale into wedges. Pass Chianti Vinaigrette separately.

YIELD: 12 servings.

San Antonio is a city of many meetings. It is a favorite destination for businesses conducting small seminars and for organizations having large conventions. The charm of the Riverwalk and the rich Spanish heritage of the city attract many business visitors. However, The Henry B. Gonzalez Convention Center makes many meetings possible. This outstanding complex was originally built to coincide with the opening of HemisFair '68. Due to unparalleled success, it has been recently expanded to accommodate even more simultaneous activities. Adjacent to the Convention Center is the Lila B. Cockrell Theatre For The Performing Arts and HemisFair Arena, home of the San Antonio Spurs.

BARBECUE

Barbecuing has been a Texas tradition since early pioneer days. Cowboys drove cattle to market on long trail drives. The chuck wagon and cook followed the herd. Using dried staples, cooks prepared beans, corn bread, fruit cobbler and delicious barbecued beef on the open range. Mesquite logs found on the way were used to cook the meat, giving it a flavorful, smoked taste.

Cattle raising has been one of Texas' major industries since the 1820's. Although trail drives are a thing of the past, barbecuing is still very much alive. The word *barbecue* originated from the Spanish word *"barbacoa"* and now has many definitions: a method of cooking, a cooking pit, a social gathering and/or a place where the meat is sold.

TECHNIQUES FOR BARBECUING

Using Barbecue Sauces. Helpful hints about barbecuing include knowing about the different sauces and how they can be used. Sauces with tomato or sugar will burn if used for basting over a long period of time. Such sauces are used on the meat a few minutes before serving and are referred to as *Barbecue Sauce.* The sauce used to baste the meat during long, slow barbequing is referred to as *Basting Sauce* (See recipes).

Using Charcoal Briquets. Soak the briquets in a plastic container with liquid charcoal starter for 5 minutes. Place in barbecue pit in a pyramid shape. Carefully light charcoal. It takes about 15 to 20 minutes for the coals to turn white. Carefully disperse coals evenly over cooking area with long handled barbecuing tool. (If coals are still red, this will cause fat from meat to ignite and burn, giving the meat a bitter taste along with being discolored.) When the coals are white, they are ready for barbecuing. (If mesquite chips are available, sprinkle over coals at this point.)

Using Mesquite or Hickory. Put lots of kindling down first and then stack the logs in pyramid shape. This method takes longer than using briquets. Light the kindling with matches. Wait until the logs are white (about 30 minutes) then proceed with barbecuing.

Using the oven to barbecue. Put Liquid Smoke and seasonings on the meat and marinate overnight in refrigerator. Bake for 5 to 6 hours in oven at 250° slowly. See index for recipe on **Oven Baked Barbecued Brisket.**

BARBECUED BRISKET, RIBS AND CHICKEN:

Meat	Pounds	Time
Brisket	12	4 to 5 hours
Beef Ribs	12	2½ to 3 hours
Spare Ribs (Pork)	8	1½ to 2 hours
Chicken (4 2½-lb. fryers)	10	1½ to 2 hours

Trim all excess fat off the meat. Rinse well and season with salt and pepper. Baste with marinade. Adjust coals to be 8 inches from the meat. Cook slowly. Turn and baste every 30 minutes. Use above chart for approximate time to barbecue. When cooked as desired, serve with a favorite barbecue sauce.

BARBECUED SAUSAGE:

Using Cased Sausage. Prick sausage to prevent bursting and wrap links in aluminium foil. Place package on a cool area of the pit and allow to cook slowly until done (approximately 1 hour). Remove foil and brown for 5 to 10 minutes. Be aware that the fat from the sausage will cause the fire to flare during browning process and should be watched closely. If using precooked sausage, only browning is needed.

BARBECUED STEAKS:

Using 1-inch Thick Steaks (T-bone, sirloin, New York strip or ribeyes). Adjust the grill 4 to 6 inches from the meat. Use the basting sauce if desired. A simple method is to use butter, salt and pepper on the steaks. Here are the times for barbecuing steaks:

	First Side (minutes)	Second Side (minutes)
For rare steaks	9	6
For medium steaks	12	6

(If a charred outside and warm pink middle is desired, adjust grill to 3 inches from the meat for 1 minute on each side. This can only be done if grill is adjustable. Use above directions, subtracting 1 minute from each side.)

Serve the steaks with baked potatoes stuffed with grated cheese, bacon bits, chopped green onions, sour cream and butter. A tossed green salad with ranch dressing completes a real Texas barbecue. Strawberry shortcake would be an ideal dessert.

Longhorn cattle are synonymous with Texas. This breed is a descendent of Spanish cattle brought to the new world by Christopher Columbus. Many a Longhorn traveled The Chisholm Trail from South Texas to the railroad towns of Kansas City and Abilene. Longhorns adapted well to the rugged, dry conditions of early Texas.

BASTING SAUCE

1   cup oil, butter or margarine
1   teaspoon salt & pepper
1   clove garlic, minced
2   cups water
2   teaspoons chili powder
2-4 tablespoons lemon juice
      (or apple vinegar)

Combine all ingredients. Bring to a boil and cook for 10 minutes.

YIELD: 4 cups.

CHUCKWAGON BARBECUE SAUCE

2   cups catsup
3   cups water
2   tablespoons flour
6   tablespoons cider vinegar
1   teaspoon tarragon
2   tablespoons worcestershire
      sauce
½   teaspoon oregano
½   teaspoon marjoram
¼   teaspoon thyme
1   clove garlic, minced

In a saucepan, combine ingredients and mix thoroughly. Simmer for 10 minutes until mixture is heated and blended. Use as a barbecue sauce on beef, pork and chicken. The tarragon gives a unique country flavor. This recipe can be halved.

YIELD: 5 cups.

BARBECUE SAUCES

PAPPY SKRAP'S BARBECUE SAUCE
For Recipe Page - See Index.

BARBECUED BRISKET
For Recipe Page - See Index.

OVEN BAKED BARBECUED BRISKET

If you have a busy day planned, this is an easy way to prepare the evening meal. Place brisket in oven around 1:00 p.m. and it will be ready by 6:00 p.m.

4-6 pound beef brisket, trimmed
½ teaspoon garlic salt
½ teaspoon onion salt
½ teaspoon celery salt
1 4-ounce bottle Liquid Smoke, reserve 3 teaspoons

Sauce

2 cups catsup
½ cup vinegar
½ cup sugar
3 teaspoons liquid smoke
½ cup worcestershire sauce

In a large dutch oven, place brisket, sprinkle with spices and coat generously with Liquid Smoke. Cover with foil and refrigerate overnight.
The next day, preheat oven to 250°.
In a saucepan, bring all ingredients for sauce to a boil and simmer until sugar is dissolved. Discard any remaining marinade. Generously coat brisket with sauce. Cover with foil. Bake 5 to 6 hours. Slice and serve.
YIELD: 6 to 8 servings.

BRISKET IN BEER

4 6-pound beef brisket, trimmed
salt & pepper to taste
2 12-ounce cans beer

Preheat oven to 325°.
Salt and pepper brisket. Pour beer around brisket and cover pan tightly with aluminum foil. Bake 6 hours or overnight. Remove meat and strain off grease from pan. Add enough water or beer to pan drippings to make a rich gravy. Cut meat in thin slices against grain and serve with pan gravy. Serve as a main course meat or for cocktails with small split rolls, pan gravy on the side and a relish tray.
YIELD: 8 to 12 servings.

BRISKET IN SOY SAUCE

6	pounds brisket
½	cup soy sauce
½	cup red wine
1	tablespoon brown sugar
2	cloves garlic, minced
2	tablespoons coarsely ground pepper

In a large dutch oven, place brisket. Mix remaining ingredients. Pour over meat and cover. Marinate all day or overnight. Preheat oven to 300°.
Bake uncovered, fat side up, for 4 hours, basting several times. Slice and serve hot.

YIELD: 8 to 12 servings.

BRISKET SAUCE

Delicious as a sauce over sliced brisket and polish sausage!

½	cup margarine
1	cup chopped onion
1	cup chopped bell pepper
¼	cup worcestershire sauce
2	tablespoons mustard
2	heaping tablespoons sweet pickle relish
2	tablespoons vinegar
1	cup brown sugar
½	teaspoon salt
1	29-ounce can tomato puree

In a large saucepan, saute onion and pepper in margarine until tender. Mix in remaining ingredients. Bring to boil and simmer 5 minutes.

YIELD: Sauce for 14 to 16 sandwiches.

CREME DIJON

⅓	cup dijon mustard (we recommend Grey Poupon)
2	eggs, beaten
1	cup whipping cream
1	tablespoon vinegar
¼	teaspoon tarragon

In a small saucepan, combine all ingredients blend until smooth. Cook over low heat, stirring constantly just until mixture begins to thicken. Serve over steaks, chicken or vegetables.

YIELD: 1⅔ cups.

BEARNAISE SAUCE
For Recipe Page - See Index.

PEPPER STEAK

1½ pounds round steak, cut into
    1-inch squares
1   clove garlic, minced
¼   cup butter
1½ teaspoons salt
½   teaspoon pepper
1   teaspoon oregano
½   cup cooking sherry
1   pound mushrooms, sliced
¼   cup oil
3   green peppers, diced
    1-inch thick
3   tomatoes, cut into quarters

In a large skillet, saute garlic in butter. Add meat and brown. Add ½ teaspoon salt, ¼ teaspoon pepper, ½ teaspoon oregano and sherry. Simmer. In another pan, cook mushrooms in oil for 5 minutes. To the mushrooms, add 1 teaspoon salt, ¼ teaspoon pepper, ½ teaspoon oregano and green peppers. Cover and cook for 10 minutes. Add to meat mixture along with tomatoes and heat thoroughly. Serve over white rice.

YIELD: 4 servings.

CHILI CHEESE STEAKS

2   pounds round steak,
    cut 1-inch thick
3   tablespoons flour
2   teaspoons salt
2   teaspoons chili powder
¼   teaspoon pepper
¼   cup shortening
2   cups chopped onion
1   16-ounce can whole tomatoes
1   4-ounce package
    cheddar cheese

Preheat oven to 350°.
In a large skillet, brown meat in shortening and place in a 9x13-inch baking dish. Brown onions until tender and stir in remaining ingredients except cheese. Add to meat. Bake 2 hours. Add grated cheese on top and bake 5 minutes longer.

YIELD: 4 to 6 servings.

CHICKEN FRIED STEAKS

This method of preparing round steak continues to be an all-time favorite of most men in Texas. Here's an authentic cowboy recipe served with rich cream gravy!

2　pounds round steak, pounded to tenderize & cut into serving-size pieces
2　teaspoons salt
2　teaspoons apple vinegar
2　cups water
　　salt & pepper
　　flour
　　cooking oil

Cream Gravy
2　tablespoons grease from frying pan
2　tablespoons flour
2　cups milk or cream

After tenderizing round steak, soak in mixture of 2 teaspoons salt, vinegar and water for 2 hours. Dredge meat in salt and peppered flour. In a large cast iron skillet with hot cooking oil, brown meat until tender. Drain on paper towels and keep warm.

For Cream Gravy: Pour off all but 2 tablespoons of grease from skillet. In a bowl or jar combine the milk and flour and mix thoroughly. (If flour is not completely dissolved in milk, gravy will be lumpy.) Pour into skillet and stir constantly until thickened and heated. Mouth watering!

Serve Chicken Fried Steaks with lots of Cream Gravy real hot!

YIELD: 4 to 6 servings.

24 HOUR MEAT MARINADE

2　cups olive oil
½　cup tarragon vinegar
1　clove garlic, chopped
1½ teaspoons salt
1½ teaspoons pepper
½　teaspoon curry powder
2　bay leaves
½　teaspoon lemon juice
3　dashes tabasco

In a large mixing bowl, combine olive oil, vinegar, garlic, salt, pepper, curry powder, bay leaves, lemon juice and tabasco. Mix well and use as a 24 hour marinade on beef. Barbecue, stir fry or oven bake as desired.

YIELD: 4 cups.

BEEF JERKY

1   flank steak
    Accent or MSG
    pepper
    onion salt
    garlic salt
    Pam or vegetable spray

Slightly freeze a flank steak, trim off fat, slice with grain of meat, bacon thin. Season both sides of meat with each seasoning, one at a time, patting each into meat with hand forcing seasonings into meat. The salt crystals must dissolve in meat juices. Spray Pam on oven racks and hang meat strips over bars of rack. Turn oven to its coolest temperature, usually 140°. Prop oven open about 2 inches at top. Leave overnight.

YIELD: 25 pieces.

ROCK SALT ROAST
(For Prime Rib or Standing Rib Roasts)

1   standing rib or prime rib
    roast, room temperature
1   teaspoon Accent or MSG
2   tablespoons worcestershire
    sauce
1   teaspoon paprika
    salt & pepper to taste
1   box ice cream salt
1   cup water

Preheat oven to 500°.

In a bowl, combine Accent, worcestershire sauce, paprika, salt and pepper. Rub seasonings into meat. Put ice cream salt in bottom of large roasting pan. Put meat on top of salt. Cover roast with ice cream salt completely. Lightly dampen salt with water until it moistens bottom of pan and roast. Place roast in oven.

For a *medium* roast,
    cook 15 minutes per pound.
For a *rare* roast,
    cook 12 to 13 minutes per pound.

Remove roast from oven. Salt will be extremely hard. Hammer away salt until all is away from meat. Slice and serve.

STEAK TARTARE A LA JOSEF

MEDALLIONS AU POIVRE
(Tenderloins on Pepper Sauce)

BEEF AND BREW TAKE ALONG

BEEF WELLINGTON WITH PUFF PASTRY
For Recipe Page - See Index.

CORNED BEEF

Make your own Corned Beef in 18 to 21 days. Add potatoes, onions and carrots and have wonderful meal in one pan.

5 -10 pound beef brisket
3-5 tablespoons salt
    water to cover
1 onion, chopped
1 clove garlic, minced
1 bay leaf
1 teaspoon peppercorns
1 teaspoon cloves
1 pickle, chopped
1 14½-ounce can beef stock
1 teaspoon chili powder,
    optional

Sauce (optional)
1 stick butter, melted
3 teaspoons flour
3 cups milk
1 teaspoon salt
1 teaspoon white pepper
1 cup fresh horseradish

In a large pan, add beef brisket, salt, water, onions, cloves, bay leaf, peppercorns, garlic and pickle chips. Marinate for 18 to 21 days in refrigerator turning at least once a week. Preheat oven to 250°

After marinating, drain and put in fresh cold water. Bring to a boil. Drain again and place in a roasting pan with a lid. Add beef stock and chili powder, if desired. Cook 3 to 5 hours, depending on size of brisket. About midway through cooking, vegetables can be added such as potatoes, onions and carrots. Serve with cole slaw.

        YIELD: 10 to 20 servings.

For Sauce: In a small saucepan, mix butter, flour and milk. Cook until smooth and thick. Add horseradish and stir until smooth. Serve with corned beef.

FAJITAS COOKING TECHNIQUES

The popular way to prepare beef or chicken fajitas is to barbecue the meat over mesquite or charcoal briquets. The recipe for Fajitas, San Antonio Marinade, Pico de Gallo and Guacamole are found in the Entertaining - San Antonio Style Section. Use this handy guideline for preparing fajitas for a party:

Guests	Beef	Chicken	Pico de Gallo	Guacamole
8-12	6 lbs.	12 breasts	2 recipes	2 recipes
13-l6	8 lbs.	16 breasts	3 recipes	3 recipes
17-20	12 lbs.	20 breasts	4 recipes	4 recipes

Use "SAN ANTONIO MARINADE" *(For Recipe Page - Check Index.)*

For Chicken Fajitas: Marinate chicken breasts for 24 hours. It will take longer to barbecue chicken, about 10 to 15 minutes on the flesh side and 5 to 7 minutes on the back side. When cooked, slice chicken breasts into strips and serve with beef fajita condiments.

For Shishkebobs: Thread meat (flank steak or lamb cut into cubes), cherry tomatoes, bell peppers, mushrooms, and wedged onions on skewers. Alternate meat, vegetable, etc. on skewers. Marinate. Barbecue for 2 minutes on each of 4 sides.

For Marinated Vegetables: Use fresh vegetables in season such as: cherry tomatoes, bell pepper, cauliflower, carrots, green onions, broccoli, zucchini, yellow squash and mushrooms. Marinate for 24 hours. Do not cook vegetables. Serve as a vegetable salad or as appetizers. The vegetables will be crisp but delicious!

ADDITIONAL FAJITA MARINADES

Use picante and sangria.
Italian dressing.

SERVING FAJITAS

Use a sizzling hot *comal* (a heavy iron skillet). For serving the Pico de Gallo, use a *molcajete* (a triangular footed bowl made from volcanic rock).

FAJITAS

FAJITAS AND FRESH MEXICAN SALSA
from 'Cooking Texas Style' by Candy Wagner

CHICKEN FAJITAS
For Recipe Page - See Index.

CHIMICHANGAS
(A Deep Fried Burrito)

"A Night in Old San Antonio"

Chimichangas, anticuchos, chalupas, churros and bunuelos are some of the favorite treats served at A Night in Old San Antonio, an annual festival commonly referred to by the natives as "NIOSA!" Each year the San Antonio Conservation Society sponsors this festival of food, song and dance in historic and old La Villita, the original Spanish village of San Antonio. During NIOSA, food booths representing Mexican, German, Greek, Spanish, French, English and Texas cuisines are decorated and offer their unique flavors, decorations and costumes.

This festival coincides with Fiesta Week in celebration of Texas Independence from Mexico. The Battle of San Jacinto fought on April 21, 1836, marks the week designated as Fiesta Week. San Antonio spends the entire week in many unique celebrations: The River Parade, The Pilgrimage to the Alamo, the Battle of Flowers Parade, the Flambeau Parade (Night Parade), the King William Fair, the Coronation of Fiesta kings and queens, carnivals, band concerts and fireworks!! The Spanish word *"fiesta"* means party and San Antonians party during Fiesta Week!

1   pound ground meat, browned & drained
1   medium onion, chopped
½   cup red chile sauce or enchilada sauce
12 flour tortillas
   oil for frying
2   cups cheddar cheese
2   cups shredded lettuce
2   cups chopped green onions

In a large skillet, brown meat and drain. Add onion and chile or enchilada sauce. Spoon about 3 tablespoons of meat filling in center of each tortilla. Fold tortilla, tucking in ends, and fasten with wooden toothpicks. Only assemble 2 or 3 at a time as tortilla will absorb liquid from sauce. In a large frying pan, with 1 inch of oil over medium heat, fry folded tortilla, turning until golden about 1 to 2 minutes. Drain on paper towels and keep warm. Garnish with cheese, lettuce and onion.

YIELD: 12 Chimichangas or fried burritos.

BEEF CHALUPAS

Chalupa means *"little boat"* in Spanish. It is a *"Tex-Mex"* version of an open-faced sandwich with a variety of toppings - grated cheese, avocado, chicken and beef! Be creative and make your own!

12   corn tortillas
      oil for frying
2   cups refried beans, canned
      or homemade
½   pound ground beef,
      cooked & drained and
      seasoned with chili
      & garlic powder,
      salt & pepper
2   cups cheddar cheese, grated
3   cups lettuce, shredded
1½ tomatoes, chopped
1   cup chopped onion
      picante sauce, optional
      guacamole, optional

Preheat oven to 350°.
In a large skillet, fry tortillas flat in cooking oil until crisp. Spread each tortilla with beans, ground beef and cheese. Place on a cookie sheet. Bake until cheese melts. While hot, sprinkle each chalupa with a little salt and pepper. Layer lettuce, tomato and onion and serve immediately.

YIELD: 12 beef chalupas.

VARIATIONS:
For "Chalupas Compuestas": Add guacamole on top of chalupas!
For "Chicken Chalupas": Substitute chopped chicken for beef.

CHILI

A *"bowl of red"* commonly known as *"chili"* has been a part of San Antonio's past since the 1800's. Most historians agree that the first pot of chili was prepared in the quaint little village of La Villita in the shadow of the Alamo.

Local women selling chili from downtown stands became a common practice. The chili was cooked at home and brought to the downtown streets in the evening. These *"Chili Queens"* spread red tablecloths on the ground and served chili from large washtubs which they had used earlier in the day for washing soldiers' uniforms from the nearby garrison.

Selling chili from downtown stands continued into the next century. By that time the legacy was well established and chili found its place as a favorite in South Texas and all over the world. When Lyndon B. Johnson was President of the United States, he served many world figures his Pedernales River Chili at the L.B.J. Ranch near San Antonio.

2	16-ounce cans tomatoes, undrained
4	cups water
5	pounds coarsely ground lean beef
2	large onions, diced
5	tablespoons shortening
3	cloves garlic, minced
4	bay leaves, broken
2	teaspoons oregano
4	teaspoons ground cumin
2	teaspoons salt, more or less to taste
6	tablespoons chili powder
	cayenne or black pepper
3	tablespoons fresh cilantro or 1 teaspoon coriander
3-5	tablespoons flour
	cold water or tomato juice

In a blender, puree tomatoes. In a 2-gallon kettle, pour water, and tomatoes and begin cooking over medium heat. In a skillet, brown beef and onion in shortening. In kettle with tomatoes, add beef, onions, garlic, bay leaves, oregano, cumin, salt, chili powder and pepper. Bring to a boil and reduce heat to simmer for 2½ to 3 hours. Add water if chili gets too thick during cooking. Add cilantro 30 minutes before chili is ready. Mix flour with cold water or tomato juice to form a paste and add to chili to thicken. Stir thoroughly. Chili is best made at least 1 day before serving.

YIELD: 1 gallon chili.

VARIATION:
For Chili Beans: *Cook 2 pounds of Frijoles (Pinto Beans) recipe. (Check index for page.) Add approximately 4 cups of leftover Chili recipe to Frijoles. Simmer about 30 minutes before serving. Serve with jalapeno cornbread and tossed green salad.*

YIELD: *Approximately 15 to 20 servings.*

CARNE GUISADA
(Stewed Meat)

1   cup oil
2-3 pounds round steak,
        cut in pieces
⅓   bell pepper, chopped
1- 1½ tablespoons flour
⅓   onion, chopped
¾   teaspoon garlic powder
½   tablespoon pepper
¾   tablespoon comino (cumin)
1   8-ounce can tomato sauce
     salt to taste
2   cups water
     flour tortillas

In a large skillet or dutch oven, heat oil and brown meat. Add onions and bell pepper and cook 3 more minutes. Add flour and brown. Add garlic, pepper and comino. Stir in tomato sauce, salt and water. Simmer 10 to 15 minutes. Serve with hot flour tortillas.
YIELD: 6 to 8 servings.

TACO AVOCADO PIE

1   pound ground beef,
        cooked & drained
½   cup diced onions
1   package taco seasoning
        (we recommend Lawry's)
1   8-ounce can tomato sauce
1½ cups crushed corn chips (we
        recommend Doritos)
1   cup sour cream
1   cup shredded cheddar cheese
2   cups guacamole
     garnish with shredded lettuce

Preheat oven to 350°.
In a large mixing bowl, combine cooked beef, taco seasoning, onions and tomato sauce. In a 2-quart baking dish, layer crushed corn chips, cooked beef mixture, a layer of sour cream and top with grated cheese. Bake in oven for 15 to 20 minutes. Serve on shredded lettuce and top with guacamole!
YIELD: 4 servings.

ENCHILADA CASSEROLE

2   pounds ground beef
1   large onion, chopped
2   cloves garlic, chopped
1   package taco seasoning mix
1   package enchilada
      seasoning mix
1   12-ounce can tomato paste
1   10½-ounce can cream of
      mushroom soup
2-3 jalapeno peppers, less to
      taste, chopped
4-5 cups water
1   pound sharp cheddar cheese,
      grated or substitute
      ½ American & ½ Velveeta
      cheese
15 corn tortillas

Preheat oven to 350°.
In a large skillet, brown beef and drain. Add onions and garlic, mixing thoroughly. Stir in taco and enchilada seasonings. Add tomato paste, soup and jalapenos. Add water slowly. Cover and simmer about 45 minutes. In a greased 9x13-inch baking dish, layer meat sauce, tortillas and grated cheese. Repeat layers. Bake, covered, for 45 minutes. Uncover and bake an additional 12 minutes.
YIELD: 8 servings.

2   pounds ground beef
1   large onion, chopped
1   10½-ounce can cream
      chicken soup
1   10½-ounce can
      cream mushroom soup
1   10½-ounce can
      enchilada sauce
1   pound Velveeta cheese, cubed
15 corn tortillas, quartered

VARIATION:
Very Easy Enchilada Casserole
Preheat oven to 350°.
In a skillet, brown meat and onion. Add soups and enchilada sauce. In a greased baking dish, layer meat, tortillas and cheese. Repeat layers until all used. Bake 30 minutes.
YIELD: 8 servings.

EASY TORTILLA BAKE

A true *"Tex-Mex"* dish served with guacamole salad, tortilla chips and Mexican rice!

1   pound ground beef
2   tablespoons chili powder
1   12-ounce can tomato sauce
12 corn tortillas, quartered
1   16-ounce carton sour cream
1   medium onion, diced
2   cups grated cheddar or
      Monterey jack cheese

Preheat oven to 350°.
In a large skillet, brown ground beef and drain grease. Add chili powder and tomato sauce. Simmer 10 minutes. Dip quartered corn tortillas in sour cream. In a greased 8x12-inch baking dish, place half of tortillas to line bottom of dish. Top with half of meat mixture, half of diced onion and half of grated cheese. Repeat layers. Bake 30 minutes.

YIELD: 8 to 10 servings.

VARIATION: Add a layer of refried beans in between meat and cheese layers!

TORTILLA CASSEROLE

Sauce
8- 10 fresh jalapenos
2   cloves garlic
1   14½-ounce can tomatoes
1   small onion
      salt & pepper to taste
¼   teaspoon oregano,
        adjust to taste
1   bay leaf

Picadillo
1¼ pounds ground round steak
½   pound ground pork
2   medium onions, chopped
3   large cloves garlic
3   medium tomatoes, peeled,
        seeded & chopped
¼   cup slivered almonds
½   cup raisins
2   jalapeno peppers, seeded
1½ teaspoons oregano
      salt & pepper
¼   cup chopped parsley
¼   cup instant flour
        (we recommend
        Wondra Flour)
10 corn tortillas
2   cups Mexican white cheese,
        crumbled
¼   cup oil for dipping tortillas

For Sauce: Boil jalapenos in a small amount of water 10 to 15 minutes. Drain. Cut off stems. In a food processor, combine jalapenos, 2 cloves garlic and tomatoes. Blend until mixed. In a small saucepan, saute small onion until wilted and add tomato mixture. Season with salt, pepper, oregano and bay leaf. Simmer 30 minutes.

For Filling: In a large skillet, brown beef and pork. When thoroughly cooked, add onions and reduce heat, cooking until onions are soft. Add garlic, tomatoes, almonds, raisins, peppers, oregano, salt and pepper. Simmer until tomatoes are fork tender. (If very juicy, thicken with ¼ cup instant flour.) Add parsley last. This filling can be frozen. Preheat oven to 350°.

To Assemble Tortilla Casserole: Dip corn tortillas in warm oil and then sauce. Layer in a 9x13-inch baking dish, tortillas on bottom, meat filling, crumbled cheese and 2 tablespoons sauce. Repeat this procedure two times. Top with additional cheese. Bake uncovered 30 minutes.

YIELD: 12 to 15 servings.

TAMALE CASSEROLE

1   dozen tamales, with corn
       shucks removed
1   10½-ounce can chicken
       a la king
1   12-ounce can evaporated milk
½   cup tomatoes with green
       chiles, chopped
       (we recommend Ro-Tel)
¼   pound cheddar cheese, grated
½   2-ounce jar pimientos
¼   cup finely chopped bell
       pepper, more to taste
¼   cup finely chopped onion,
       more to taste
       crushed potato chips

Preheat oven to 350°.

In a large greased, ovenproof casserole, place tamales in bottom of dish. In a mixing bowl, combine chicken a la king, milk, tomatoes with green chiles, cheese, pimientos, bell pepper and onion and mix together. Pour over tamales. Sprinkle top with crushed potato chips. Bake 35 to 40 minutes.

YIELD: 4 to 6 servings.

ROAST BEEF FLAUTAS

12   corn tortillas
1   cup roast beef, shaved
       (great for leftovers)
1   cup shredded longhorn cheese
1   cup cooking oil
1   cup guacamole
½   cup salsa or picante sauce
1   cup chopped lettuce
½   cup chopped tomato

In a skillet with hot oil, dip tortillas to soften. Place a small amount of roast beef and cheese across each tortilla. Roll tightly and secure with toothpicks. Fry in hot oil until tortillas are browned and crisp. Drain on paper towels. Serve 2 to a person with guacamole and salsa. Garnish with lettuce and tomato.

YIELD: 6 servings.

MACHACADO

(A Mexican Mashed Beef Filling for Flour Tortillas)

3	large skirt steaks, cut into 2-inch wide strips and long enough to fit in skillet lengthwise, scored at 2-inch intervals
2	tablespoons oil
6	bell peppers, cut in half & seeded
8	large tomatoes, cut in half
13	cloves garlic
	salt

In a deep skillet, brown meat in oil, a few pieces at a time. When all meat is browned, return to pan. Add peppers, tomatoes with skin side up and garlic. Season with salt. Cover pan and cook over low heat about 1 hour or until meat is fork tender. Let cool. When cool enough to handle, shred beef and put in bowl. Take remaining ingredients in pan and puree in blender or food processor a little at a time. Return pureed mixture and meat to skillet. Heat until mixture is bubbling, reduce heat and simmer approximately 30 minutes more. Test for any seasoning adjustments. Should have a good garlic flavor. Add more fresh, pressed garlic if necessary. Serve with hot flour tortillas. Can be scrambled with eggs for breakfast tacos. Can be frozen.

YIELD: 10 to 12 servings.

VARIATION: **To Serve 100 Guests:** *Adjust portions and follow same directions:*

16 skirt steaks
25 tomatoes
17 bell peppers
33 cloves garlic

A Tree Of Life is a commonly seen Mexican art form which carries with it rich, religious significance. It is an earthenware art object that honors the dead. Mexican families remember friends and family members on All Souls Day.

STEAK DIANE

4	tablespoons chopped green onions or scallions
4	tablespoons butter
4	6-8 ounce beef filets, tenderloin or filet mignons
8	tablespoons butter
3	tablespoons worcestershire sauce
3	dashes tabasco
1	cup fresh snipped parsley salt & pepper to taste

In a large skillet, melt 4 tablespoons butter and saute green onions until tender but not brown. Remove from pan with slotted spoon and set aside. Slice filets into 3 or 4 strips against the grain. Place meat in 8 tablespoons melted butter at medium heat. Let beef brown for 3 minutes on each side and remove from pan. Add worcestershire, tabasco and parsley to butter. Return meat and green onions to pan and cook 3 more minutes per side. Salt and pepper to taste. This is a wonderful recipe to serve with noodles for a dinner party. It makes a colorful plate served with a green vegetable.

YIELD: 4 servings.

EYE OF ROUND IN RED WINE

1	5-pound eye of round roast
1	clove garlic, cut in 8 slices
1	teaspoon salt
½	teaspoon pepper
1	teaspoon dried thyme leaves

Marinade

½	cup bottled Italian dressing
1	cup dry red wine
1	bay leaf, crumbled

Sauce

2	tablespoons roast drippings
2	tablespoons flour
1	cup dry red wine
¼	teaspoon salt
¼	teaspoon pepper

Prepare roast 24 hours before serving. Wipe roast and make 8 slices, 1-inch deep across top of meat. Insert sliver of garlic in each slit. Rub surface of meat with salt, pepper and thyme.

For Marinade: In a bowl, combine Italian dressing, wine and bay leaf. Place roast in a dutch oven and pour marinade over roast. Cover tightly, refrigerate overnight and turn twice.

Preheat oven to 450°.

In a shallow roasting pan, place meat and roast 25 minutes. Pour marinade over meat and roast 25 minutes longer. Remove meat.

For Sauce: In a small saucepan combine roast drippings, flour, wine, salt and pepper. Bring to a boil and simmer 3 minutes. Add a little water if sauce is too thick. Slice meat thinly on diagonal.

YIELD: 8 servings.

BEEF AND DUMPLINGS

Beef

¼   cup flour
½   teaspoon salt
2   pounds round steak,
        cut in cubes
½   pound mushrooms, sliced
1   tablespoon oil
1   large onion, sliced
1   clove garlic, crushed
1   12-ounce can light beer
1   tablespoon soy sauce
1   tablespoon worcestershire
        sauce
1   tablespoon steak sauce

Dumplings

1½ cups flour
2   teaspoons baking powder
¾   teaspoon salt
3   tablespoons shortening
¾   cup milk

In a large bowl, combine flour and salt. Add round steak cubes tossing to coat. In a large skillet, saute mushrooms in oil until golden brown and set aside. Saute onions and garlic until tender. Add meat and remaining ingredients. Cover and simmer for 1½ to 2 hours until meat is tender. Add mushrooms.

For Dumplings: In a medium size bowl, blend flour, baking powder and salt. Cut in shortening and add milk. Stir until well mixed. Drop by spoonfuls onto simmering beef mixture in skillet and cook 10 minutes uncovered. Cover tightly and cook an additional 10 minutes.

YIELD: 6 to 8 servings.

QUICK ORIENTAL BEEF WITH SNOW PEAS

1   pound round steak, cut into
        1-inch diagonals
1   8-ounce bottle French
        dressing
     garlic salt to taste
1   tablespoon soy sauce
1   16-ounce jar white onions
½   pound fresh snow peas
1   bell pepper, sliced
1   tomato, cut into ⅛'s

Thickening agent

1   tablespoon cornstarch
        mixed with
1   tablespoon cold water

In a large bowl, marinate sliced, uncooked beef for at least 1 hour in French dressing with garlic salt to taste. Remove meat from marinade and brown in a skillet. Add remainder of marinade, soy sauce and onions and heat. Add thickening agent and cook until clear. Add snow peas, bell pepper and tomato. Stir for a couple of minutes only. Do not overcook vegetables. Serve with steamed white rice.

YIELD: 4 servings.

MARINATED TENDERLOIN

2   carrots, sliced
2   onions, sliced
10   black peppercorns
1   whole clove
2   bay leaves
     fresh parsley
¼   teaspoon thyme
4   cloves garlic
½   cup wine vinegar,
        red or white
2   tablespoons oil
2   shallots, chopped
2   tablespoons lemon juice
2   cups sherry
1   tablespoon worcestershire
        sauce
3-5 pounds tenderloin of beef
     butter

In a large dutch oven, combine carrots, onions, peppercorns, clove, bay leaves, parsley, thyme, garlic, wine vinegar, oil, shallots, lemon juice, sherry and worcestershire sauce. Mix thoroughly. Puncture meat with a meat fork. Place in marinade and refrigerate for at least 24 hours.
Preheat oven to 450°.
Drain and dot with butter. Baste with 2 cups of marinade. Roast for 30 to 45 minutes depending on degree of doneness desired. This can be served as a cocktail buffet dish when sliced thinly. Serve with flaky biscuits or rolls.

YIELD: 8 servings.

PIQUANT HERB SAUCE

Try this Bearnaise-like sauce for red meats or fish!

½   cup dry white wine
½   cup parsley sprigs
¼   cup white vinegar
1   small onion, quartered
2   large cloves garlic
2½   teaspoons dried tarragon
        leaves, crushed
¼   teaspoon dried chervil
        leaves, crushed
⅛   teaspoon pepper
1   cup mayonnaise (we
        recommend Hellman's)
     chopped parsley

In a blender, combine wine, parsley sprigs, vinegar, onion, garlic, tarragon, chervil and pepper. Blend on high until uniform. In a small saucepan heat blender mixture on medium heat until reduced to ⅓ cup. Strain and return to saucepan. Stir in mayonnaise. Stir over medium heat until just warm. Garnish with chopped parsley.

YIELD: 1¼ cups.

BEEF BURGUNDY

⅓ cup flour
2 teaspoons salt
½ teaspoon pepper
2 pounds round steak, cut in 1-inch cubes
2 cloves garlic, minced
⅓ cup cooking oil
2 cups burgundy
2 cans condensed beef broth
½ teaspoon dillweed, crushed
½ teaspoon dried marjoram, crushed
2 14-ounce cans artichoke hearts, drained & quartered
3 cups fresh mushrooms, sliced
⅓ cup flour
½ cup water

In a bowl, combine flour, salt and pepper. Toss meat in mixture to coat. In a dutch oven with hot oil, brown meat and garlic. Add broth, burgundy, dillweed and marjoram. Simmer covered 1½ hours, stirring occasionally. Add artichoke hearts and mushrooms. Cook 10 minutes. In a separate bowl, combine remaining flour and water and mix well. Stir into beef mixture. (Freeze or refrigerate at this point, if desired.) Preheat oven to 400°.

Place beef burgundy in oven and bake 30 to 40 minutes until heated thoroughly. Serve over buttered noodles.

YIELD: 10 servings.

BEEF STROGANOV

1 tablespoon dry mustard
1 tablespoon sugar
2 teaspoons salt
1 teaspoon ground black pepper
4-5 tablespoons vegetable oil
4 cups onions, sliced in rings
1 pound fresh mushrooms, sliced
2 pounds filet of beef
1 cup sour cream

In a bowl, combine mustard, 1½ teaspoons sugar, pinch of salt and 1 teaspoon hot water and form a thick paste. Let mixture rest at room temperature. In a large skillet, heat 2 tablespoons of oil, saute onions and mushrooms and cover pan and cook on low heat. Stir occasionally simmering for 30 to 40 minutes until vegetables are soft. Drain in colander and discard liquid. Return vegetables to skillet and set aside. Cut beef to make 1-inch cubes. In a separate skillet with 2 tablespoons of hot oil, fry meat until lightly browned. When cooked, remove with a slotted spoon and add to vegetables. Stir in salt, pepper and mustard mixture. Stir in sour cream, one tablespoon at a time and remaining 1½ teaspoons of sugar. Cover and simmer 2 to 3 minutes or until sauce is heated thoroughly. Serve immediately. This recipe is very similar to an original Russian recipe!

YIELD: 4 to 6 servings.

KONIGSBERGER KLOPSE
(German Meatballs)

1   pound lean ground beef
½   pound lean ground pork
1   cup soft bread crumbs
2   eggs, well beaten
1   medium onion, chopped
1   tablespoon parsley
1   teaspoon salt
2   tablespoons vegetable oil
2   8-ounce cans tomato sauce
         with mushrooms
1   cup water
½   teaspoon dillweed
½   teaspoon sugar
1   cup sour cream
6   servings noodles,
         hot & buttered

In a large mixing bowl, combine beef, pork, bread crumbs, eggs, onion, parsley and salt and mix well. Shape into 1½-inch balls. In a large skillet, brown meatballs in vegetable oil. Pour off fat. In a bowl, combine tomato sauce, water and dillweed. Add sugar and mix. Pour over meatballs. Simmer 20 minutes. Remove from heat and blend in sour cream. Continue cooking only until heated thoroughly. Do not boil. Serve over hot buttered noodles.

YIELD: 6 servings.

VARIATION: Serve without noodles by using a little less tomato sauce or thicken sauce slightly with flour or cornstarch. Make meatballs bite size. The authentic version of this old German recipe is seasoned with lemon, capers, cloves and anchovies!

SAUERBRATEN
(German Marinated Roast)
For Recipe Page - See Index.

ALAMO CITY STEW

2   pounds boneless stew meat,
        cut into 1-inch pieces
2   tablespoons vegetable oil
1   10½-ounce can condensed
        beef broth
1   cup hot water
1   8-ounce jar picante sauce
        (we recommend Pace)
1   medium onion, cut
        into ½-inch wedges
¼   cup chopped parsley
1   teaspoon salt
1   teaspoon ground cumin
2   cloves garlic, minced
1   16-ounce can tomatoes
3   medium carrots, cut
        into 1-inch pieces
2   ears fresh corn, cut
        into 1-inch pieces
2   medium zucchini, cut
        into 1-inch pieces
½   cup cold water
2   tablespoons flour

In a large dutch oven with hot oil, brown meat, one half at a time. Return all meat to dutch oven and add broth, hot water, picante sauce, onion, parsley, salt, cumin and garlic. Bring to a boil and reduce heat. Cover and simmer 1 hour or until meat is tender. Drain and coarsely chop tomatoes, reserving juice. Add tomatoes and juice to dutch oven with carrots, corn and zucchini. Cover and simmer 25 minutes longer until vegetables are tender. In a bowl or jar, gradually add cold water to flour and mix until smooth. Gradually stir into stew. Heat to boiling, stirring constantly. Boil and stir 1 minute until thickened.

YIELD: 8 servings.

EASY OVEN MEAT STEW

2   pounds beef, cubed
3   tablespoons cooking oil
1   onion, sliced
3   carrots
1-2 celery ribs
3   potatoes
2   cans tomato sauce
        with mushrooms
1   cup water
     seasoned flour
     garlic salt to taste
     salt, pepper & paprika
        to taste

Preheat oven to 400°.
Place in a paper bag, flour seasoned with salt, pepper, paprika and garlic salt. Shake cubed beef in bag to coat meat. In a dutch oven with hot oil, brown beef cubes. Bake beef, uncovered, for 30 minutes stirring once. Drain oil. To dutch oven add onion, potatoes, carrots, celery, water and tomato sauce with mushrooms. Put lid on dutch oven and reduce heat to 350°. Bake for 2½ hours.

YIELD: 4 to 8 servings.

BEEF STEW WITH WINE

A simply delicious stew with lots of fresh vegetables. Feel free to adjust the vegetables according to your family's taste buds!

6	tablespoons shortening
3	pounds beef, round or rump, cut in 1½-inch cubes
2	medium onions, coarsely chopped
4	cups water
1	cup red wine
2	beef bouillon cubes
1	clove garlic, finely chopped
2	tablespoons finely chopped parsley
1	bay leaf
⅛	teaspoon dried thyme leaves
1½	tablespoons salt
¼	teaspoon pepper
6	medium potatoes, cut in halves
6	medium carrots, cut in halves
10	small white onions or 2 large quartered onions
3	stalks celery, cut in 3-inch pieces
2	medium bell peppers, seeded, ribs removed, cut in chunks
2	medium tomatoes, quartered or 1 8-ounce can tomatoes, undrained & quartered

In a dutch oven slowly heat shortening over medium heat. Brown meat cubes well, turning on all sides. Remove meat cubes and set aside. Saute coarsely chopped onions in dutch oven until tender. Return meat to pan and add water, wine, bouillon cubes, garlic, parsley, bay leaf, thyme, salt and pepper. Cover and simmer 1½ hours until meat is tender. Add potatoes, carrots, onions and celery. Cook 1½ hours until vegetables are tender. Add bell peppers and tomatoes and cook 20 more minutes. Gravy in the stew will be thin. If a thicker gravy is preferred, in a bowl or jar add ¼ cup flour and ¼ cup water and mix thoroughly to avoid lumps. Stir quickly into stew. Bring to a boil and stir until gravy thickens.

YIELD: 6 servings.

LASAGNA WITH TINY MEATBALLS

1   box lasagna noodles
2   pounds ricotta cheese
2   eggs, beaten
½   cup provolone cheese, diced
¼   cup fresh parsley, snipped
     salt, pepper & paprika
          to taste
½   cup prosciutto Italian ham,
          chopped
1   pound ground beef
1   teaspoon garlic powder
     salt & pepper to taste
     marinara sauce
1   cup grated Parmesan
1   pound mozzarella cheese

Marinara Sauce

8   tablespoons olive oil
2   large cloves garlic
1   large onion, chopped
2   28-ounce cans Italian
          style tomatoes
2   6-ounce cans tomato paste
1   8-ounce can sliced
          mushrooms
2   teaspoons dried basil
2   teaspoons dried oregano
     salt & pepper to taste
     mushrooms

In a large pot of boiling water, boil noodles al dente. Blanch in cold water, drain, dry and set aside. In a large bowl, mix ricotta, eggs, provolone, prosciutto, parsley, salt, pepper and paprika. In a separate bowl, mix ground beef and garlic powder, salt and pepper to taste. Form meat into tiny balls and bake for 10 minutes. Add meatballs to marinara sauce.

For Marinara Sauce: In a large pot, heat olive oil on moderate heat and add garlic and onion. Saute until onions look clear. Add remaining ingredients and reduce heat to low and simmer partly covered for 90 minutes until sauce is thickened.

Preheat oven to 350°.

To Assemble Lasagna: In a large, greased oblong baking dish, place a layer of noodles, layer of mozzarella, layer of ricotta mixture, layer of Parmesan, layer of sauce and meatballs. Alternate layers until all ingredients are used and ending with layer of noodles and Parmesan. Bake for 90 minutes. May be frozen.

YIELD: 10 to 12 servings.

Bluebonnets, the State Flower of Texas, cover the countryside in early spring with a sea of blue. They received their name from the sun bonnets worn by early Texas pioneer women.

ITALIAN MEATBALLS WITH SAUSAGE SAUCE

Sauce

¾ pound Italian sausage, cut
    into 1½-inch slices
2 pounds lean ground beef,
    divided in half
2 tablespoons olive oil or
    corn oil
1 medium onion, finely
    chopped
3 cloves garlic, mashed slightly
1 28-ounce can tomatoes,
    mashed, Italian
    plum recommended
2 28-ounce cans tomato puree

Meatballs

    remaining 1 pound
        ground meat
2 large eggs, beaten
½ cup minced dry onion
½ cup Italian bread crumbs
2 tablespoons minced
    fresh parsley
¼ cup grated parmesan cheese
½ teaspoon salt
½ teaspoon pepper

For Sauce: In a large skillet, fry Italian sausage browning on all sides. Remove from pan, drain and set aside. Fry 1 pound of ground beef in sausage pan. Drain and set aside. In a large dutch oven, saute onion and garlic in oil, cooking until tender and clear. Add mashed tomatoes, tomato puree, browned sausage and beef. Cover pot leaving a slight opening to allow steam to escape. Simmer 3 hours.
Preheat oven to 350°.

For Meatballs: In a large mixing bowl, with the remaining 1 pound of ground beef, combine eggs, onion, bread crumbs, parsley, parmesan cheese, salt and pepper. Roll into meatballs approximately 2 inches in diameter. Place on a cookie sheet. Bake 15 minutes. Turn once and cook another 5 minutes. Add to sauce. Serve with lots of spaghetti, garlic bread and antipasto salad!

YIELD: About 24 meatballs with sauce.

EASY ITALIAN SPAGHETTI SAUCE

½ cup onion slices
2 tablespoons olive oil or
    salad oil
1 pound ground beef
2 cloves garlic, minced
2 14½-ounce cans tomatoes,
    chopped
1 3-ounce can sliced
    mushrooms
1½ teaspoons oregano
½ teaspoon Accent or MSG
1 bay leaf
2 8-ounce cans seasoned
    tomato sauce
¼ cup chopped parsley
1 teaspoon salt
¼ teaspoon thyme
1 cup water

In a large skillet, cook onion in hot oil until golden. Add meat and garlic browning lightly. Add remaining ingredients. Simmer uncovered 2 to 2½ hours until thick. Remove bay leaf and serve.

YIELD: 5 cups.

BEEFY PASTA FLORENTINE

1	10-ounce package chopped spinach
1	pound ground beef
1	medium onion
1-2	cloves garlic
1	15½-ounce jar spaghetti sauce with mushrooms
1	8-ounce can tomato sauce
1	6-ounce can tomato paste
1	8-ounce package shell macaroni, cooked & drained
8	ounces sharp cheddar cheese, grated
2	eggs, beaten
1	cup bread crumbs
½	cup oil

Preheat oven to 350°.

Cook spinach according to package directions. Drain and reserve liquid. Add enough water to spinach liquid to make 1 cup. Set aside.

For Meat Sauce: In a large skillet, brown ground beef with onion and garlic. Stir to crumble meat. Drain grease from pan. Stir in spinach liquid, spaghetti sauce, tomato sauce, tomato paste. Salt and pepper to taste. Simmer 10 minutes. Set aside.

For Pasta Layer: In a large mixing bowl, combine cooked macaroni shells, spinach, cheese, bread crumbs, eggs and oil. Stir gently to mix well. In a lightly greased 9x13-inch baking dish, spread pasta layer. Top with meat sauce. Bake 30 minutes.

YIELD: 8 servings.

BEEF SPAGHETTI CASSEROLE

1	tablespoon fat, bacon grease or Crisco
2	onions, chopped
1	celery stalk, chopped
1	green pepper, chopped
3	cloves garlic, slivered
1	pound ground beef
1	14½-ounce can tomatoes, chopped
3	tablespoons chili powder
1	cup water
1	4-ounce can mushrooms, pieces & stems
1	10-ounce package frozen peas, cooked
1	16½-ounce can whole kernel corn
	salt & pepper to taste
1	8-ounce package spaghetti, cooked
2	cups grated sharp cheese

In a skillet, melt fat and saute onions, pepper, celery and garlic until tender but not brown. Add ground meat and cook until browned. Add tomatoes, chili powder and water. Cover and cook over very slow heat 30 minutes. Add mushrooms, peas, corn, salt and pepper. Adjust seasoning to taste.

Preheat oven to 350°.

Cook spaghetti as directed on package. Add cooked spaghetti to sauce and blend well. In a large greased baking dish, place half of spaghetti mixture. Cover with half of cheese. Add remaining mixture. Cover with remaining cheese. Bake 20 to 25 minutes. (Can prepare casserole in morning and refrigerate until ready for baking. Add 10 to 15 minutes to baking time using this method.)

YIELD: 10 to 12 servings.

EASY VEAL SCALOPPINE

2	pounds veal cutlets
½	teaspoon garlic salt
¼	teaspoon pepper
	flour
¼	cup butter or oleo
1	medium onion, thinly sliced
1	6-ounce can sliced mushrooms
1	teaspoon parsley flakes
½	teaspoon salt
½	teaspoon oregano
7	ounces 7-Up soft drink

Season cutlets with garlic salt and pepper. Dredge in flour and pound lightly. In skillet, brown veal in butter. Remove veal and set aside. Add mushrooms and onions to skillet and cook until lightly browned, adding more butter if necessary. Stir in parsley flakes, oregano, salt and 7-Up. Blend well. Set veal on top and cover. Simmer until meat is tender about 45 minutes to 1 hour. When ready to serve, remove veal to warmed serving platter and place vegetable mixture on top.

YIELD: 6 servings.

APPLE BRANDY VEAL CHOPS

4	veal chops (or pork chops can be substituted)
	salt & pepper to taste
	flour
3	tablespoons butter, more if needed
2	ounces apple brandy
2	ounces white wine
½	cup sliced mushrooms
½	cup whipping cream

Salt and pepper chops. Dredge in flour. In a large skillet, saute chops in hot butter until brown. Pour apple brandy over chops and flame. Remove chops from pan and keep warm. Add wine and mushrooms to the drippings. Cook for only 2 to 3 seconds. Add cream and cook until gravy is thick. Serve wine and mushroom gravy over veal. Delicious!

YIELD: 4 servings.

LEMON VEAL WITH PAPRIKA

1	tablespoon oil
8	bacon slices, chopped
1	onion, sliced
10	ounces lean veal, cubed
7	ounces chicken stock
2	teaspoons paprika
1	tablespoon lemon juice & grated rind
	salt
	freshly ground black pepper
4	tablespoons sour cream
1	ounce flaked almonds, toasted to garnish

Preheat oven to 350°.
In a frying pan, heat oil and fry bacon and onion until lightly browned. Drain and place in ovenproof casserole. In pan add veal cubes and brown on all sides. Add to casserole. In a saucepan, heat stock, paprika, lemon rind and juice, salt and pepper. Pour into casserole. Cover tightly and bake 1 hour until veal is tender. Stir in sour cream and adjust seasonings to taste and reheat gently. Serve sprinkled with almonds.

YIELD: 6 servings.

SAUTEED VEAL CHOPS PALERMO

ITALIAN VEAL ROLLS

SALTIMBOCCA ALLA LUIGI

SCHNITZEL A LA "SAN ANTONIO"
For Recipe Page - See Index.

ROAST LEG OF LAMB
WITH GRANDAD'S MINT SAUCE

The English consider this dish one of their favorites. This authentic recipe came from an English gentleman from Chester, England, who came to Texas to visit his relatives! Lamb has been a favorite in San Antonio since 12 Englishmen died in the Battle of the Alamo in 1836. Leg of lamb can be spiced with garlic and rosemary for a Texas flavor. The mint sauce is a must. Leftovers make a wonderful lamb stew with carrots, potatoes and green peas!

Lamb

5-6 pound leg of lamb
1 clove garlic
¼ teaspoon rosemary
    salt & pepper to taste
1½ cups hot water
1 tablespoon flour (mixed with
    a little cold water)

**Grandad's Mint Sauce (Serve also
    with lamb chops)**

1 teaspoon vinegar
1 tablespoon mint, FRESH,
    finely chopped
1 tablespoon boiling water
1 teaspoon sugar
    (add more to taste)

Preheat oven to 475°.
Take the leg of lamb and puncture slits in 5-6 places and insert strips of garlic. Sprinkle with rosemary, salt and pepper. Bake the lamb for 30 minutes at 475°. Reduce heat to 325° and continue roasting. (Allow 20 minutes per pound). Baste occasionally with drippings. Remove leg of lamb to a hot platter when roasted to desired doneness. Take the garlic strips and rosemary off of the lamb and discard.

For the Gravy: Pour all of the fat off except for 2 tablespoons left in the roasting pan. Add 1½ cups of water and stir, scraping the bottom of the roasting pan. Thicken with the flour and water. Bring to a boil and cook for a few minutes. Strain gravy into a gravy dish. Slice the lamb and serve with gravy. Use mint sauce as a condiment. Other condiments include mint jelly, chutney and/or fruit such as peaches. Roast potatoes, green peas and popovers or Yorkshire pudding make this a feast fit for a king!

For the Mint Sauce: Mix the ingredients together and add more sugar to taste.

YIELD: 6 servings.

PEG'S YORKSHIRE PUDDING

This recipe was brought over from England and has been in the Bickerton family for centuries.   There is a small town in the County of Cheshire, near Chester, named Bickerton.   Some of their descendents now live in Texas.

4	tablespoons fat drippings
8	tablespoons flour
1½	teaspoons salt in enough water to make a smooth paste
3	eggs
1½	cups milk
2½	quart stainless steel mixing bowl or 9x12 ovenproof casserole

Preheat oven to 475°.
Place fat in stainless steel mixing bowl and heat in oven until sizzling. (This is best but an ovenproof casserole can be substituted.) Mix flour and salt with enough water to make a smooth paste.   Add eggs and beat with egg beater. Stir in milk. Take hot, sizzling fat out of oven and immediately pour batter into hot bowl or casserole. Bake until brown and puffy for about 20-30 minutes. Serve at once with Roast Leg of Lamb or Roast Beef.
YIELD: 6 to 8 servings.

*VARIATION: This recipe can also be used to make **popovers**.   Simply use a muffin tin instead of the bowl or casserole.   Place one spoonful of fat in each muffin tin and heat.   It will take less time to bake popovers.   Pour the batter in the hot fat and bake for about 15 minutes.   Popovers can be served with honey or gravy.*

LAMB KEBOBS SAN ANTONIO STYLE

5	pounds lamb, cubed
5	pounds vegetables, cubed: cherry tomatoes, bell peppers, mushrooms, onions
	San Antonio Marinade (Check Index for page)

Mix all of the marinade ingredients together. Add the lamb and vegetables.   Marinate for 12-24 hours. **KEEP REFRIGERATED.** Turn the mixture for best results. To make the Lamb Kebobs, thread the meat and vegetables on skewers, alternating: lamb, onion cube, lamb, cherry tomato, lamb, bell pepper, lamb, mushroom, etc. Barbecue on outdoor grill for 5-l0 minutes on each side until done. These lamb kebobs can also be broiled in the oven for 5-l0 minutes on each side but barbecuing will provide an unique flavor. Remember that the lemon juice partially cooks the meat and vegetables so very little grilling is needed. Serve on a hot bed of rice pilaf with a tossed green salad and fresh french bread.
YIELD: 10 to 12 servings.

VARIATIONS: The marinade is excellent for fajitas (skirt steak), flank steak, and chicken.   It will make a wonderful marinated vegetable dish to serve as appetizers or a side dish.   Do not cook the vegetables.   The lemon juice makes them crisp and delicious.

HAM CARVONARA

2 cups chopped ham
1 bunch parsley, chopped
2 bunches green onions, thinly chopped
3 cloves garlic, pressed
¼ cup olive oil
1 quart half & half cream
1 quart whipping cream
8 egg yolks
16 ounces fresh parmesan cheese, grated
2 pounds uncooked thin spaghetti (we recommend authentic Italian pasta)
   parsley for garnish

In a dutch oven, saute ham, parsley, onions and garlic in olive oil until onions are tender. In a large mixing bowl, mix half and half cream, whipping cream and egg yolks just to blend. In a large pot, bring water, oil and salt to a boil. Add spaghetti and cook al dente. Drain and add to ham mixture in dutch oven. Pour egg mixture on top of ham and spaghetti. Stir until thickened. Add grated cheese and keep stirring. Sprinkle with reserved parsley on top and serve immediately on warmed plates.

YIELD: 10 servings.

CREOLE PORK CHOPS

6 pork chops
6 lemon slices, thin
6 onion slices, thin
6 teaspoons dark brown sugar
½ cup catsup
½ cup water

In a large skillet, brown pork chops on both sides. On each chop place a lemon slice, an onion slice and 1 teaspoon brown sugar. In a small bowl, combine catsup and water and mix. Pour over chops. Cook covered 1 hour over low heat until chops are cooked.

YIELD: 6 servings.

ITALIAN PORK CHOPS

1½-2 pounds pork chops
   salt & pepper
1 28-ounce can tomatoes
2 tablespoons brown sugar
1 package Italian spaghetti sauce mix with mushrooms
1 large onion, sliced
1 bell pepper, sliced

Preheat oven to 375°.
Wash pork chops, salt and pepper. In a skillet, slightly brown pork chops on both sides. Place in an ovenproof casserole. In a medium bowl, combine tomatoes, brown sugar and spaghetti sauce mix. Pour over pork chops. Top with sliced onions and bell pepper. Cover with aluminum foil. Cook 1 hour to 1 hour and 15 minutes. Serve over rice.

YIELD: 6 to 8 servings.

SAUSAGE AND KRAUT

1   pound smoked pork sausage,
        cut in 1-inch pieces
1   27-ounce can sauerkraut,
        drained
1   cup chopped apples
¼   cup brown sugar
¼   cup water
½   teaspoon caraway seeds

In a large frying pan, combine all ingredients. Cover and simmer 30 minutes.
YIELD: 6 servings.

ITALIAN SPICED PORK CHOPS

1   envelope Italian salad
        dressing mix
1   cup water
¼   cup rose wine
6   pork loin chops,
        cut 1-inch thick

In a bowl, combine Italian dressing mix, water and wine. Mix well. In a shallow dish, pour dressing mixture over chops. Marinate 2 hours at room temperature or overnight in refrigerator, turning occasionally. Drain chops, reserving marinade. Grill over medium low coals about 15 minutes on each side, brushing with marinade occasionally.
YIELD: 6 servings.

BARBECUED SPARERIBS

3-4 pounds spareribs,
        cut individually
1   teaspoon salt
1   large onion, sliced
1   lemon, sliced
1   cup catsup
⅓   cup worcestershire sauce
1   teaspoon chili powder
2   dashes tabasco sauce
1½   cups water

Preheat oven to 450°.
Salt ribs and place in a shallow roasting pan, meat-side up. Roast in hot oven for 30 minutes. Drain fat from pan. Top each sparerib with a slice of onion and lemon. In a saucepan, combine catsup, worcestershire sauce, chili powder, tabasco and water. Bring to a boil and pour over ribs. Lower temperature to 350°. Bake an additional 1½ hours. Baste ribs with sauce.
YIELD: 4 servings.

PORK ROAST IN VERMOUTH

3   pounds boneless pork loin
    salt
    black pepper, freshly ground
1   teaspoon sugar
    pinch cayenne pepper
    crushed rosemary
½   cup dry vermouth,
        more to taste
4   tablespoons flour

Preheat oven to 450°.
Remove pork from refrigerator 1 hour prior to cooking. Rub pork with salt, pepper, sugar and cayenne pepper. Place meat in a roasting pan or glass baking dish in oven for 10 minutes. Reduce heat to 325°. Pour dry vermouth over meat and sprinkle with rosemary. Insert meat thermometer in center of roast and bake to 170°. Baking time is approximately 40 minutes per pound. Baste several times with more vermouth.

For Gravy: Pour drippings from pan into a measuring cup. Use 4 tablespoons drippings and 4 tablespoons flour to make a roux over low heat. Add 1 cup warm water to baking pan and scrape remaining particles from pan. Add pan drippings and water to roux. Stir constantly. Cook over medium heat until slightly thickened. Add more water or vermouth if needed to make a total of 2 cups of gravy.

YIELD: 6 to 8 servings.

BAKED PORK ROLL-UPS

12 -14 pork steaks
    salt & pepper
    prepared mustard
4   cups soft bread crumbs
½   cup raisins
½   cup celery, chopped
½   cup chopped apple
1   teaspoon salt
2   teaspoons sage
    flour
1   cup hot water
    oil for browning

Preheat oven to 350°.
Remove bone and trim fat from pork. Pound steaks to ¼-inch thick. Salt and pepper. Spread lightly with mustard. In a bowl, combine bread crumbs, raisins, celery, apple, salt and sage. Spread on meat, roll up and fasten with toothpicks. Dust with flour and brown in oil. Place in 3-quart casserole or a glass 9x13-inch baking dish. Bake for 1 hour. Serve on sauerkraut.

YIELD: 6 to 10 servings.

STUFFED HAM SLICES

2   slices ham, cut ½-inch thick

Stuffing

2   cups soft bread crumbs
½   cup raisins
½   cup chopped peanuts
2   tablespoons dark corn syrup
½   teaspoon dry mustard
¼   cup butter
10   whole cloves
1   can raisin pie filling
     fresh orange slices

Preheat oven to 300°.
In a bowl, combine bread crumbs, raisins, peanuts, syrup, mustard and butter. Place one slice ham in shallow baking dish and spread stuffing over ham. Top with second slice of ham. Stick whole cloves on top. Bake 1 hour. Before serving ham slices, spread with raisin pie filling and heat in oven 10 minutes. Garnish with fresh orange slices.
YIELD: 4 to 6 servings.

BOURBON CASHEW STUDDED HAM

PORK LOIN WITH TANGY SAUCE

PORK TENDERLOIN WITH PRUNES
For Recipe Page - See Index.

TIM'S GRILLED DOVE OR QUAIL

8   quail or dove breasts,
        cleaned & skinned
8   pieces of bacon, ½ slice each
     poultry seasoning
     salt & pepper
     lemon pepper
     jalapeno pepper slices,
     optional

Special Sauce

1   tablespoon bottled
        barbecue sauce
1   tablespoon melted butter
2   tablespoons dry sherry
½   teaspoon lemon pepper

Prepare birds by sprinkling with poultry seasoning, salt, pepper and lemon pepper. If desired, make small cut in each side of breast meat and slip in a slice of jalapeno. Wrap birds in pieces of bacon and secure with toothpicks.

Mix sauce ingredients together. (Make extra sauce as recipe doubles easily.) Grill birds over hot coals, basting continually with sauce and turning often. Cook until bacon is done, about 15 to 20 minutes.

YIELD: 3 to 4 servings.

SMOTHERED QUAIL

DUCK BREAST WITH HONEY PORT SAUCE
For Recipe Page - See Index.

QUAIL IN SHERRY

6-8 quail or doves
6   tablespoons butter
3   tablespoons flour
2   cups chicken broth
½   cup sherry
     salt & pepper to taste

Wash and pat dry the quail or doves. Brown in heavy skillet in butter. Remove birds when brown. Add flour to pan and stir well. Slowly add chicken broth, sherry, salt and pepper. Blend well. Return birds to pan and cook over low heat until birds are cooked, about 45 minutes to an hour. Serve over rice.

YIELD: 3 to 4 servings.

VENISON GUISADA

¼   cup oil
1   pound venison, cut in
        1-inch strips or chunks
2   tablespoons flour
½   cup water
1   14¾-ounce can peeled
        tomatoes, mashed,
        reserve juice
1   clove garlic, minced
2   teaspoons fresh ground
        comino or cumin
    salt & pepper to taste

Brown venison in oil. Remove from pan. Add flour and water to pan drippings to make thick gravy. Thin with juice from tomatoes. Add meat, tomatoes, garlic, comino, salt and pepper to gravy. Simmer until meat is tender. May be served alone, over rice or with flour tortillas.

YIELD: 6 servings

VENISON STROGANOFF

2   pounds venison backstrap
        or tenderloin
⅓   cup flour
    salt & pepper to taste
2   tablespoons paprika
3   tablespoons vegetable oil
1   cup chopped onions
2   cloves garlic, minced
1   7-ounce can mushrooms,
        drained
1   10-ounce can cream of
        mushroom soup
1½ cups sour cream

Cut tenderloin in ½-inch strips across grain. Combine flour and seasonings. Roll strips in mixture. Brown meat in oil and remove from pan when browned. Add onions, garlic and mushrooms to pan. Cook over low heat until onions are golden brown. Add soup and cook until thick, stirring frequently. Add meat and cook over low heat 45 minutes or until meat is tender. Stir frequently. Add sour cream 15 minutes before serving. Heat but do not boil. Serve with wild rice.

YIELD: 6 servings.

VENISON BACKSTRAP

4   tablespoons butter
2   tablespoons vegetable oil
8   slices backstrap, 1-inch thick
8   large mushrooms
8   shallots (or 4 green onions),
        chopped
    salt & ground pepper
½   cup burgundy
½   10¾-ounce can consomme

In a large skillet, heat butter and oil. Cook meat about 4 minutes. Add mushrooms and onions. Season with salt and ground pepper. Cook meat about 4 minutes longer. While cooking, add wine and consomme. Heat thoroughly. Venison should be pink and juicy inside. It only takes about 8 minutes to cook the venison. Overcooking makes game dry and stringy. Cook at the last minute and serve immediately.

YIELD: 4 servings.

DOVES A LA SAN ANTONIO

12	doves or quail
	flour for dusting birds
2	tablespoons butter
2	tablespoons oil
2	10¾-ounce cans chicken stock
2	cloves garlic, minced
2	tablespoons finely
	chopped jalapenos or
2	ounces green chiles, chopped
1	onion, chopped
2	tomatoes, chopped
½	cup white wine
8	ounces fresh mushrooms

Preheat oven 325°.
Dust birds with flour and brown in dutch oven in butter and oil. Add chicken stock, garlic, jalapenos and onions. Bake in oven for about 1½ hours. Remove from oven. Add tomatoes, wine and mushrooms. Simmer on top of stove until blended and heated thoroughly. This makes a medium thick gravy. Delicious over wild rice. Birds are very tender.

YIELD: 6 servings.

ROCK CORNISH HENS WITH HERBS

4	1-pound frozen rock
	cornish hens, thawed
4	cloves garlic, split
4	teaspoons dried thyme leaves
1	teaspoon seasoned salt
1	teaspoon salt
½	teaspoon pepper

Basting Sauce

¾-1	cup butter or
	margarine, melted
½	cup lemon juice
¼	teaspoon paprika

Preheat oven 450°.
In each hen, place 1 clove garlic, ½ teaspoon thyme, ¼ teaspoon seasoned salt, ¼ teaspoon salt and ⅛ teaspoon pepper. Truss hens by bringing skin over neck opening and fastening to back with wooden picks. Tie legs together with string. Bend wings under bird. Close cavity with wooden picks.
To Make Basting Sauce: Combine ½ cup butter, lemon juice, paprika and 2 teaspoons of remaining thyme. Stir well. In a skillet, heat remaining butter and brown hens, turning to brown well on all sides and adding more butter as needed. Arrange hens in large roasting pan without rack. Brush well with basting sauce. Roast, basting several times with sauce, about 40 minutes or until nicely browned and tender.

YIELD: 4 servings.

CHICKEN OLE

6   chicken breasts,
         boneless & skinned
¾   cup grated monterey
         jack cheese
¾   cup grated sharp
         cheddar cheese
1   4-ounce can sliced
         black olives
1   4-ounce can chopped
         green chiles
2   tablespoons dehydrated
         onions
½   cup butter
1   teaspoon cumin
1   teaspoon chili powder
         or more to taste
     crushed tortilla chips

Preheat oven to 350°.
Pound chicken breasts flat. In a bowl, mix cheeses, olives, chiles and onions. Place a few tablespoons of cheese mixture on each chicken breast and roll placing seam side down. Place chicken in large ovenproof casserole. In a saucepan melt butter and add cumin and chilipowder. Pour over chicken. Top with crushed tortilla chips and bake 45 minutes.

YIELD: 4 to 6 servings.

CHICKEN MEXICANA

2   2½- to 3-pound broiler fryers,
         cut in serving pieces
2   8-ounce cans tomato sauce
1   13¾-ounce can chicken broth
2   tablespoons dry onion
         soup mix
¾   cup sliced onion
1   clove garlic, minced
6   tablespoons peanut butter,
         chunky or crunchy style
½   cup half & half cream
½   teaspoon chili powder,
         more to taste
¼   cup dry sherry

In large skillet, brown chicken pieces. In saucepan combine tomato sauce, 1 cup chicken broth, soup mix, onion and garlic. Heat thoroughly, stirring constantly. Pour over chicken in skillet. Simmer covered 30 to 40 minutes or until tender. In a separate bowl, combine the cream, remaining chicken broth and add the peanut butter gradually. When blended, stir peanut butter mixture into skillet with chili powder and sherry. Heat completely. Serve with white rice.

YIELD: 6 to 8 servings.

FIESTA CHICKEN KIEV

4   whole chicken breasts,
      split, skinned & boned
3   tablespoons butter, softened
3   tablespoons Old English
      sharp cheese spread
2   teaspoons instant
      minced onion
1   teaspoon salt
1   teaspoon Accent or MSG
2   tablespoons chopped
      green chiles

Coating

¼   cup butter, melted
1   cup cheddar cheese
      crackers, crushed
1½ tablespoons taco
      seasoning mix

Pound chicken breasts with mallet to flatten and set aside. In a bowl, beat butter and cheese spread until well blended. Add minced onion, salt, Accent and green chiles. Place portion of mixture on one end of each chicken piece. Roll up each piece, tucking ends to completely enclose filling. Fasten rolls with toothpicks. In a bowl, mix crushed crackers and taco seasoning. Dip each chicken roll in melted butter to cover, then coat with mixture of crackers and taco mix. Arrange chicken rolls in glass 12x8x2-inch baking dish. Cover with wax paper. Microwave on High for 10 to 12 minutes, rotating dish after the first 5 minutes. Let stand for 5 minutes before serving.

YIELD: 8 servings.

CHICKEN WITH AVOCADO SAUCE

2   tablespoons clarified butter
1   2½- to 3-pound chicken
      broiler, cut in pieces
⅔   cup sherry
2   tablespoons flour
¾   teaspoon salt
      dash of paprika
1¼ cups half & half cream
1   large avocado, sliced
      watercress for garnish

In a 12-inch skillet, over medium heat, warm the clarified butter and cook chicken until browned on all sides. Stir in sherry and heat to boiling. Reduce heat to low; cover and simmer 25 minutes until fork tender. Remove chicken to warm platter. Into liquid in skillet, stir in flour, salt and paprika until well blended. Gradually stir in half and half cream. Cook until thickened, stirring constantly. Gently add sliced avocado and heat completely. Spoon over chicken. Garnish with watercress.

YIELD: 4 servings.

ARROZ CON POLLO ESPANOLA
(Spanish Rice with Chicken)

¼ cup olive oil
1 frying chicken, cut in pieces
1 small onion, chopped
1 clove garlic, minced
¼ cup tomato sauce
⅛ teaspoon powdered saffron
2½ cups chicken broth
    salt & pepper
1 cup rice, uncooked

In a large skillet, heat oil and brown chicken on both sides. Add onion and garlic and fry a few minutes, then add tomato sauce, saffron dissolved in chicken broth, salt and pepper. Cover and cook 20 minutes. Add rice and stir well. Cover again and simmer 30 minutes longer until all liquid has been absorbed and chicken is tender.

YIELD: 4 to 6 servings.

CHICKEN CHILAQUILES

GREEN ENCHILADAS
For Recipe Page - See Index.

CHICKEN TACO FILLING

3 tablespoons oil
1 medium onion, chopped
1 large clove garlic, minced
2 cups chicken
1½ cups canned tomatoes &
      green chiles with juice
½ teaspoon cumin (comino)
    salt & pepper to taste

In a large, heavy skillet, heat oil and saute onion, garlic and chicken. Use 2 forks to stir and pull chicken apart as it cooks. Cook over medium heat until chicken starts to brown and gets crisp around edges. Add tomatoes and green chiles with juice, breaking tomatoes into small pieces as you add them. Add cumin, salt and pepper. Continue cooking over medium heat until all liquid has cooked down, about 10 minutes. Scrape bottom of pan frequently to prevent sticking. Use as a filling for tacos or soft tacos serving with corn or flour tortillas and condiments of grated monterey jack cheese, shredded lettuce and guacamole.

YIELD: 6 servings.

CHICKEN FAJITAS
(Marinated Chicken Strips)

For the ultimate chicken fajita, serve the grilled chicken bite-size pieces on a hot Flour Tortilla with sour cream, Guacamole and Pico de Gallo! Check Index for recipe pages.

2 pounds boneless
    chicken breasts
1 8-ounce bottle Italian
    Dressing (we recommend
    Kraft Zesty Italian)
½ cup white wine
12 flour tortillas, warmed
1 onion, thinly sliced & sauteed
    fajita seasoning to taste
    (we recommend Bolner's
    Fiesta Fajita Seasoning
    with Salt)

Sprinkle chicken breasts thoroughly with fajita seasoning. In a large bowl, combine Italian dressing, white wine and chicken. Marinate overnight. Prepare charcoal. Grill chicken over hot coals for 5 to 8 minutes per side, depending on thickness of breasts. Baste with marinade. Do not overcook. Slice into lengthwise strips. Place chicken on hot platter and scatter sauteed onion slices on top.

YIELD: 6 servings.

VARIATION: If barbecuing is not possible, cut the marinated breasts into strips and cook in a large skillet until chicken is tender. Of course, the chicken fajitas will not have the barbecued flavor but will still be delicious!

Check Index for Fajitas Cooking Techniques.

PERUVIAN BAKED CHICKEN

4 chicken breasts
1 clove garlic, minced
2 tablespoons vinegar
1 teaspoon salt
1 teaspoon pepper
1 teaspoon cumin
1 teaspoon oregano
1 tablespoon paprika
1 tablespoon vegetable oil

Preheat oven to 350°.

In a small bowl, combine minced garlic, vinegar, salt, pepper, cumin, oregano, paprika and oil. Mix thoroughly and pour over the chicken breasts. Bake in shallow baking dish for 1 hour. Baste occasionally while baking.

YIELD: 4 servings.

CHICKEN STUFFED WITH CRAB

6 chicken breasts
½ cup chopped onion
½ cup chopped celery
3 tablespoons butter
3 tablespoons dry white wine
1 7½-ounce package crabmeat, drained & flaked
½ cup herb-seasoned stuffing mix
2 tablespoons flour
½ teaspoon paprika
2 tablespoons butter
1 10¾-ounce can mushroom soup
¾ cup milk
2 tablespoons dry white wine
½ cup shredded swiss cheese

Preheat oven to 325°.

Pound chicken breasts until flattened. Sprinkle with salt and pepper. In a skillet, saute onion and celery in 3 tablespoons butter until tender. Remove skillet from heat and add wine, crab and stuffing mix and toss. Divide mixture among the six breasts equally. Spoon onto chicken breast, roll and secure with toothpicks. Combine flour and paprika and dust over chicken. Place the rolled chicken breasts into a greased 9x13-inch ovenproof baking dish and drizzle with 2 tablespoons melted butter. Cover and bake for 1 hour. Uncover and bake an additional 15 minutes. In a saucepan, blend the soup and milk cooking until thick, stirring constantly. Add remaining wine and cheese stirring until all cheese melts. Transfer chicken to a heated platter and pour sauce over chicken. Serve remaining sauce as gravy.

YIELD: 6 servings.

EL RANCHO CHICKEN

2	2½-pound chickens

Sauce

4	tablespoons butter
4	tablespoons flour
1	cup milk
¼	teaspoon pepper
½	teaspoon salt
½	teaspoon garlic powder
2	cups canned tomatoes, chopped
½	cup green chiles, chopped

Layers

1	onion, chopped
12	corn tortillas
2	cups grated cheddar cheese
	Optional ingredients include: 1 diced bell pepper, 2 ounces chopped pimientos and/or ½-pound fresh sliced mushrooms.

In a large pot, place chicken and cover with water. Simmer for 45 to 60 minutes until tender. Allow to cool. Remove skin and bone. Reserve stock.

Preheat oven to 350°.

In a saucepan, over low heat, melt butter, add flour and blend until smooth. Combine 1 cup reserved stock with milk and gradually add to flour mixture, stirring constantly until thickened to make cream sauce. Remove from heat and season with salt and garlic powder. Stir in tomatoes, chiles and onion and set aside. Bring remaining chicken stock to a boil. Dip each tortilla in stock to soften and cut into 2-inch strips.

To Assemble Casserole: Cover bottom of a 9x13-inch ovenproof casserole with ⅓ of tortilla strips. Layer half of chicken over tortillas and top with ½ of creamed tomato mixture. Sprinkle 1 cup of cheese over sauce. Add another layer of tortillas, top with remaining chicken, spoon over remaining sauce, top with remaining tortillas. Sprinkle with cheese on top. Bake 30 to 40 minutes or until sauce is bubbly and cheese has melted.

YIELD: 8 servings.

*VARIATION: **Busy Day El Rancho Chicken***

1	large fryer, stewed, boned & cut in bite size pieces
1	large onion, chopped
1	large green pepper, chopped
12	corn tortillas, dipped in hot stock
½	pound cheddar cheese, grated
¼	teaspoon pepper
1½	teaspoons chili powder
1	can cream of mushroom soup
1	can cream of chicken soup
1	can tomatoes with chiles (we recommend Ro-Tel)

Follow the El Rancho Chicken recipe for assembling and baking instructions.

YIELD: 4 to 6 servings.

PRAIRIE CHILI CHICKEN

1   tablespoon oil
1   pound chicken breasts,
        boned, skinned & cut
        into strips
¼   cup chopped green pepper
¼   cup chopped onion
1   40-ounce can chili
        without beans

In a large skillet over medium heat, brown chicken strips in oil. Add green pepper and onion cooking until vegetables are tender. Stir in chili and lower heat simmering until thoroughly heated about 15 minutes.

YIELD: 4 to 6 servings.

VARIATION: **For Mexican Chili Chicken:** *Substitute 2 14-ounce cans of tomatoes instead of the canned chili. Add chili powder to taste.*

HEALTHY CHICKEN

4   chicken breasts, skinned
        & boned, cut in
        ½-inch cubes
2   tablespoons oil
1   cup thinly sliced onions
2   cups sliced mushrooms
2   tablespoons minced garlic
1   cup chopped celery
1   tablespoon oregano
1   tablespoon basil
2   cups sliced green peppers
2   cups chopped tomatoes,
        peeled
½   cup dry white wine
2   tablespoons lemon juice
¼   teaspoon cayenne pepper
        or to taste
1   tablespoon margarine
        fresh ground pepper
2   tablespoons fresh finely
        chopped parsley

In a large skillet, heat oil and saute onion. Add mushrooms, garlic, celery, oregano and basil cooking for 1 minute. Add pepper and cook 2 minutes. Stir in tomatoes and cook for 5 minutes. Add wine, lemon juice, cayenne pepper and mix. Set aside. In another skillet, heat half margarine and add half the chicken and sprinkle with black pepper. Cook over high heat, stirring until pieces are lightly browned. Do not overcook. Set aside and repeat with remaining chicken. Place all chicken in skillet and pour sauce over chicken stirring gently to blend. Simmer 1 minute. Served over rice and garnish with parsley.

YIELD: 8 servings.

LEMON-GARLIC CHICKEN BARBECUE

1 cup salad oil
¾ cup lemon juice
3 teaspoons salt
1 teaspoon dried oregano
2 medium size garlic
   cloves, peeled
   fresh ground pepper to taste
3-4 pounds chicken pieces

In a blender, add oil, lemon juice, salt, oregano, garlic and pepper. Blend until smooth. Place chicken pieces in large bowl and pour marinade over chicken and marinate overnight in refrigerator. Drain chicken and reserve marinade for basting. Prepare charcoals for barbecuing. Grill over medium coals until tender, brushing occasionally with marinade.

YIELD: 6 servings.

APRICOT CHICKEN

Elegant enough for a special dinner party, this recipe is so simple to prepare and is a great tasting recipe!

8 ounces apricot preserves
1 8-ounce bottle Russian
   dressing
1 package onion soup mix
   (we recommend Lipton's)
6 chicken breasts

Preheat oven to 300°.
In a bowl, mix apricot preserves, dressing and soup mix. Place the chicken breasts in a large ovenproof baking dish and pour apricot mixture over chicken. Bake uncovered for 2 hours.

YIELD: 6 servings.

CHICKEN PAPRIKA

A fool-proof recipe that is excellent for beginners!

1	chicken, cut in parts
2	tablespoons peanut oil
¾	cup sliced green onions with tops
1	tablespoon paprika
½	teaspoon garlic salt
	black pepper to taste
1	pint sour cream

In a large, heavy skillet with lid, swish oil around to cover surface of pan. Place chicken pieces, skin side down and sprinkle with onions and seasonings. Cook covered over medium to low heat 30 minutes being careful not to burn onions. Turn pieces over and cook 30 minutes more. Remove from heat and spread pieces with sour cream. Let stand 5 minutes and serve over rice.

YIELD: 4 servings.

ARTICHOKE CHICKEN

8	boneless chicken breasts
	salt, pepper & paprika to taste
6	tablespoons butter or margarine
1	pound fresh mushrooms, sliced in large pieces
1	12- to 15-ounce can artichoke hearts
2	tablespoons flour
⅔	cup chicken bouillon (use 2 cubes in ⅔ cup water)
3	tablespoons sherry, more to taste

Preheat oven to 350°.

In a large skillet, melt 4 tablespoons butter and brown seasoned chicken. Place the chicken in a large baking casserole. In another skillet, melt 2 tablespoons of butter and saute sliced mushrooms for 2 minutes. Sprinkle with flour and stir in bouillon and sherry. Cook 5 minutes and arrange artichokes between chicken in casserole. Pour mushroom mixture over all and bake 30 to 40 minutes. Baste while cooking for moistness.

YIELD: 6 servings.

CHICKEN WELLINGTON

1   package 15-minute chicken or meat marinade

⅔   cup water

      sauterne or other white wine

6   small, whole chicken breasts, skinned & boned

1   10-ounce package frozen patty shells, thawed

1   2¼-ounce canned deviled ham

7-8 green onions including tops, chopped

½   pound fresh mushrooms, sliced

2   tablespoons butter

¼   teaspoon tarragon, crushed

Preheat oven to 425°.

In shallow 9x13-inch glass baking dish, thoroughly blend chicken marinade, water and ⅓ cup wine. Place rinsed and well-drained chicken pieces in marinade and thoroughly coat. Pierce all surfaces of chicken deeply with fork. Marinate for 15 minutes turning several times. Remove chicken from marinade and place on un-greased 10x15-inch jelly roll pan or cookie sheet with sides. Reserve remaining marinade for mushroom sauce. Bake for 20 minutes. Cool. On a floured board, careful-ly roll out each patty shell into rectangles large enough to wrap around each individual breast. Spread each rectangle with 1/6 of the deviled ham. Place 1 whole chicken breast (which has been split in half, one on top of the other for ease in wrapping) on each pat-ty shell. Bring dough up over chicken, over-lapping edges and pressing together. Place seam side down in 9x13-inch greased, glass baking dish. Bake uncovered 15 to 18 minutes until golden.

For The Mushroom Sauce: In a skillet, saute onions and mushrooms in butter a few min-utes, stirring constantly. Add tarragon and the reserved marinade which has been com-bined with an equal amount of white wine. Heat to boiling, stirring constantly. Reduce heat and simmer for 5 minutes uncovered. Serve Chicken Wellington immediately from oven with hot mushroom sauce.

YIELD: 6 servings.

CHICKEN WASHINGTON

12 chicken cutlets or ½ breasts,
        boned & skinned
1   cup finely chopped,
        fresh mushrooms
¼   cup butter or margarine
¼   cup flour
1   cup half & half cream
½   teaspoon salt
2   dashes cayenne
2½ cups shredded sharp
        cheddar cheese
¼   cup finely diced cooked ham
¼   cup half & half cream, for
        thinning cheese sauce
3   eggs, beaten
2   cups fine bread crumbs

In a large skillet, saute mushrooms in butter for 5 minutes. Blend in flour and stir in 1 cup cream. Add salt and cayenne. Cook until very thick and smooth, stirring constantly. Stir in cheese over low heat until cheese melts. Add diced ham. Spread mixture in a shallow pan or dish to cool for 1 hour or so. On a cutting board or butcher block, pound the chicken cutlets carefully into thin, flat pieces. Sprinkle with salt. Put a finger of cooled, cheese mixture in center of cutlet and roll up, sealing well. Dust each with flour, then dip in slightly beaten eggs and roll in bread crumbs. Cover rolls and chill approximately 4 hours.
Preheat oven to 300°.
One hour before serving, deep fry rolls at 375° for 5 minutes until golden. Place in shallow baking dish and bake 45 minutes. In a saucepan, put leftover cheese mixture and heat, thinning with ¼ cup cream. Use this as a sauce for the chicken rolls.
                    YIELD: 8 to 12 servings.

IMPERIAL CHICKEN ROLL-UPS

¾   cup melted butter
2   cloves garlic, pressed
1   cup fine dry bread crumbs
⅔   cup grated parmesan cheese
¼   cup fresh minced parsley
1   teaspoon salt
¼   teaspoon pepper
4   whole chicken breasts,
        deboned & skinned
    juice from 2 lemons
    paprika, to taste

Preheat oven to 350°.
In a small bowl, combine butter and garlic and set aside. In another bowl, combine bread crumbs, cheese, parsley, salt and pepper and stir well. Dip chicken in butter mixture first and then coat with bread crumb mixture. Fold long sides of chicken breasts together, bringing short ends over and secure with toothpicks. Place chicken roll-ups seam side down in a greased 9x13-inch baking dish. Sprinkle with lemon juice and paprika. Bake 1 hour until done.
                    YIELD: 4 servings.

CHICKEN POT PIE

1   cup chopped onion
1   cup chopped celery
1   cup chopped carrots
½   cup frozen green peas,
       optional
⅓   cup butter, melted
½   cup flour
2   cups chicken broth
1   cup half & half cream
1   teaspoon salt
¼   teaspoon pepper
4   cups chopped cooked
       chicken, reserve
       chicken broth

Pie Crust for 2 Crusts

2   cups flour
⅔   cup shortening (we
       recommend Crisco)
     dash of salt
6-7 tablespoons cold water

Preheat oven to 400°.

In a skillet, saute onion, celery, carrots and peas in butter for 10 minutes. Add flour and cook 1 minute stirring constantly. In a bowl, combine chicken broth and half and half cream mixing well. Gradually stir broth mixture into vegetable mixture. Cook over medium heat stirring constantly until thickened and bubbly. Season with salt and pepper. Add chicken and stir well.

For Pie Crust: Cut in shortening, salt and flour and add cold water to form a ball. Divide in half. Roll out half of pie crust on a floured cutting board and line bottom of 2-quart baking dish. Pour chicken mixture in dish. Roll out other half of crust and put on top of chicken mixture. Bake 40 minutes until crust is golden brown. Serve with vegetable or gelatin salad.

YIELD: 6 servings.

*VARIATION: **For An Easy Version:*** Make a soft dough of:

2   cups flour
3   tablespoons shortening
2   tablespoons baking powder
1   teaspoon salt
     milk, enough to mix dough

Place chicken mixture in greased 2-quart casserole and drop dough by tablespoons over mixture. Bake 30 minutes until golden brown.

CLASSIC CHICKEN DIVAN

2   bunches fresh broccoli,
      cooked until tender
¼   cup butter
¼   cup flour
2   cups chicken broth
½   cup whipping cream
3   tablespoons sherry
½   teaspoon salt
     pepper to taste
3   chicken breasts,
      cooked & deboned
½   cup shredded parmesan
      cheese

Preheat oven to 350°.
In a greased 9x13-inch baking dish, place the cooked broccoli. In a saucepan, melt butter and blend in flour. Add chicken broth and cook until thick. Stir in cream, sherry, salt and pepper. Pour half sauce over broccoli and add ¼ cup cheese to remaining sauce. Add chicken to broccoli. Pour sauce over chicken and sprinkle more cheese. Bake 20 minutes then broil until top is golden brown.
YIELD: 8 servings.

*VARIATION: **Easy Chicken Divan***

2   chicken breasts
1   10-ounce package
      frozen broccoli,
      cooked & drained
1   10¾-ounce can cream
      of chicken soup
½   cup mayonnaise
1   teaspoon lemon juice
½   teaspoon curry powder
     salt & pepper
¼   cup parmesan cheese

Preheat oven to 350°.
Combine the sauce ingredients and mix. Layer broccoli in a greased 11x14-inch baking dish and pour half soup mixture over broccoli. Layer chicken breasts and pour remaining sauce. Sprinkle with parmesan cheese. Bake 30 to 45 minutes.
YIELD: 4 servings.

CHICKEN STRIPS

This recipe has to be prepared one day ahead or can be cooked early in the day and reheated in the evening!

6   whole chicken breasts,
        boned & skinned,
        cut into ½ inch strips
1½ cups buttermilk
2   tablespoons lemon juice
2   teaspoons worcestershire
        sauce
1   teaspoon soy sauce
1   teaspoon paprika
1   tablespoon Cavender's
        Greek seasoning
1   teaspoon salt
1   teaspoon pepper
2   cloves garlic, minced
4   cups soft bread crumbs
½   cup sesame seeds
¼   cup butter
¼   cup shortening

In a bowl, combine buttermilk, lemon juice, sauces and seasonings. Add chicken strips to buttermilk mixture and mix until well coated. Cover and refrigerate overnight.
Preheat oven to 350°.
Drain chicken thoroughly in a colander. In a bowl, combine bread crumbs and sesame seeds mixing well. Add chicken and toss in a plastic bag (Ziploc) until coated. In a saucepan, melt butter and shortening. Dip chicken in butter mixture and place in two greased 9x13-inch baking dishes. Bake uncovered 35 to 40 minutes until crisp. Serve with Plum Sauce.

YIELD: 6 to 12 servings.

Plum Sauce

1½ cups plum jam
1½ tablespoons prepared mustard
1½ tablespoons horseradish
1½ tablespoons lemon juice

In a small saucepan, combine all ingredients and mix well. Cook over low heat until just warm, stirring constantly. Do not boil.

POLLO ALLA FIORENTINA
(Chicken Fiorentina)

This original recipe came from an Italian Count's family. It is very easy to prepare in large quantities one day ahead of time. Served with Milanese Risotto, a fresh Bibb lettuce salad, Zabaglione and Espresso Coffee would make a truly authentic Italian meal. Buon appetito!

3½-4 pound chicken, cut into serving pieces
½ cup olive oil
1 clove garlic, crushed
2 bacon slices, finely chopped
1 cup finely chopped onion
½ cup Marsala or dry white wine
salt & pepper to taste
¼ pound fresh mushrooms, cut into thick slices
1 28-ounce can peeled Italian tomatoes, coarsely chopped
2 tablespoons chopped parsley

In a large skillet, heat the oil and gently brown the chicken with garlic, bacon and onions. Remove the garlic and add the wine. Season with salt and pepper. Add mushrooms, tomatoes and parsley. Cook gently about 30 minutes until chicken is tender. If necessary, moisten with a little hot chicken stock. Sauce is fairly thick. Serve with pasta or rice.

YIELD: 4 servings.

FORTY CLOVE GARLIC CHICKEN

Do not be fooled by all of the garlic. The secret is not to peel the garlic. This recipe is easy, delicious and low calorie!

3 pounds chicken pieces
40 cloves garlic, unpeeled
⅔ cup white wine

Preheat oven to 350°.
In a large ovenproof baking dish, place the chicken skin side up and sprinkle **unpeeled garlic** over the chicken. Bake uncovered for 20 minutes. Pour wine over chicken and continue to bake 1 more hour, basting every 20 minutes and turning the last 20 minutes.
YIELD: 4 to 6 servings.

CHICKEN SPAGHETTI

1 chicken fryer
1 12-ounce box spaghetti
1 tablespoon bacon drippings
1 bell pepper, chopped
1 cup chopped celery
1 large onion, chopped
1 8-ounce package
  mushrooms, sliced
1 2-ounce jar chopped
  pimientos
1 10¾-ounce can chicken broth
1 13-ounce can evaporated milk
1 10¾-ounce can cream of
  chicken &
  mushroom soup
1 10¾-ounce can cream of
  chicken soup
8 ounces grated cheddar cheese

In a large pot, boil chicken in seasoned water until cooked. Debone and chop chicken and set aside. In another large pot, cook the spaghetti al dente in salted boiling water with a teaspoon of oil to prevent pasta from sticking. Drain and place in a greased 9x13-inch baking dish and set aside. In a skillet, heat the bacon drippings and saute the pepper, celery, onion, pimiento and mushrooms until crisp and tender. Stir in chicken pieces until blended. Pour chicken-vegetable mixture over spaghetti. In a bowl, mix the broth, soups and milk to make a sauce and pour over spaghetti. Top with grated cheese and bake for 20 to 30 minutes until heated thoroughly and cheese is melted. Can be frozen.

YIELD: 8 to 10 servings.

HINT: The secret to this recipe is keeping the ingredients crisp to prevent getting mushy in the baking.

CHICKEN CANNELONI WITH BOLOGNESE SAUCE

1 pound manicotti
4 10½-ounce cans chicken broth
¾ cup butter, divided
3 shallots or green onions, chopped
3 cloves garlic, minced
3 whole chicken breasts, boned, cooked & diced
5 stalks celery, chopped
2 small onions, chopped
¾ cup chopped raw spinach
3 bay leaves
¾ teaspoon oregano
½ teaspoon thyme
4 egg yolks, beaten
Bolognese Sauce
shredded cheddar cheese

Preheat oven to 350°.

In a large pot, cook manicotti with broth and ¼ cup butter. Cool. In a skillet, saute shallots and garlic in remaining butter. Add the diced chicken, celery, onions, spinach and seasonings. Simmer covered until tender. Quickly stir in egg yolks. Remove from heat. Discard bay leaves. Chop vegetables finely and stuff into manicotti. In a 3-quart greased ovenproof casserole, place the stuffed manicotti and top with Bolognese Sauce. Sprinkle with cheese. Bake 30 minutes until bubbly.

YIELD: 14 stuffed manicotti shells.

Bolognese Sauce

¼ cup diced ham
¼ cup grated raw carrot
6 tablespoons butter
¼ pound ground beef
2 cups beef bouillon
⅛ teaspoon ground nutmeg
2 tablespoons tomato paste
1 lemon rind, cut in fine slivers
¼ cup whipping cream
salt & white pepper to taste

In a skillet, saute the ham, carrot, butter and ground beef until beef is brown. Add beef bouillon, nutmeg, tomato paste and lemon rind and simmer covered for 1 hour. Remove lemon rind and add cream, salt and pepper. Simmer 2 minutes.

YIELD: 4 cups.

CHAPEAU ROUGE
(Red Hat)

This very French chicken recipe has a rather descriptive name which means **red hat.** When cooked with red wine vinegar, the red color makes the chicken look like red hats!

4	boneless chicken breasts
4	tablespoons butter
½	pound mushrooms, sliced
2	shallots or green onions, chopped
¼	cup red wine vinegar
1	cup whipping or heavy cream
3	tablespoons dijon mustard
1	tablespoon reduced veal or beef stock (1 beef bouillon cube dissolved in 1 tablespoon hot water), consistency of soft butter
2	tablespoons chopped parsley
	salt & pepper to taste

Wash chicken and dry well with paper towels. In a large skillet, sear chicken in butter. Lower heat and saute mushrooms and shallots. Stir in vinegar and let simmer for several minutes. Blend in cream. Let simmer until chicken is cooked and cream is reduced and thickened about 15 to 20 minutes. Add salt and pepper to taste. Remove chicken to heated platter and keep warm. Stir dijon mustard, reduced stock and parsley into sauce mixture. Let simmer again for a few minutes. Spoon sauce over chicken and serve.

YIELD: 4 servings.

FRICASSEE DE POULET AU PAPRIKA
(Chicken Fricassee with Paprika)

¼	pound slab bacon
1	3-pound chicken
1½	cups minced onions
1½	tablespoons flour
2	tablespoons sweet Hungarian paprika
1½	cups chicken stock or broth
1	cup dry white wine
½	teaspoon marjoram
½	teaspoon chervil
½	cup sour cream
½	cup whipping cream

Remove rind from bacon and dice meat into ¼-inch pieces. In a skillet, fry bacon until browned and crisp. Transfer with a slotted spoon to a dutch oven or flameproof dish with a cover. Cut chicken into 8 pieces and pat dry. Saute chicken in remaining bacon fat until lightly golden. Transfer pieces to dutch oven. In same skillet, add onions and cook over moderately low heat for 10 minutes. Stir in flour and cook mixture, covered, over low heat for 5 minutes. Stir in paprika and add chicken stock, white wine, marjoram and chervil. Bring to a simmer cooking over moderate heat, stirring for 2 minutes. Pour sauce over chicken and bring to a simmer. Cover chicken and cook over very low heat for 25 minutes. Transfer pieces to hot platter and keep warm. Simmer sauce until reduced to 2 cups. In a bowl, combine 1 cup of sauce with sour cream and cream. Stir mixture into sauce and simmer 3 minutes. Spoon some of sauce over chicken and serve remainder separately as a gravy.

YIELD: 4 servings.

CHAMPAGNE CHICKEN WITH SHRIMP

2   pounds medium shrimp or
2   12-ounce packages
     frozen, shelled,
     deveined, thawed
2   green onions, cut
     into 1-inch pieces
3   tablespoons lemon juice
1½ teaspoons salt
3   tablespoons butter
     or margarine
3   whole medium chicken
     breasts, boned &
     cut in half
¾   pound mushrooms,
     thinly sliced
1⅓ cups water
⅓   cup flour
1   chicken flavored
     bouillon cube
1½ cups half & half cream
¾   cup champagne or sparkling
     dry white wine

If using fresh shrimp, shell and devein. In a bowl, combine shrimp, green onions, lemon juice and salt and set aside. In a large skillet over medium to high heat, cook chicken breasts in hot butter until well browned and fork tender about 10 minutes. Remove chicken to heated platter and keep warm. In same skillet, cook mushrooms until tender about 5 minutes. With slotted spoon, remove mushrooms to small bowl and keep warm. Add shrimp mixture to skillet over high heat and cook until shrimp turn pink about 5 to 7 minutes. With slotted spoon, remove shrimp to heated platter with chicken. In small bowl, combine water, flour and bouillon. Stir flour mixture into hot liquid in skillet until blended. Gradually add half and half cream and champagne. Cook stirring constantly until mixture thickens and boils. Stir in mushrooms and heat thoroughly. Pour sauce over chicken and shrimp on platter.

YIELD: 6 servings.

CHICKEN ALMOND CREPES

Crepe Batter

1	cup plus 2 tablespoons flour
¼	teaspoon salt
3	eggs
1½	cups milk
1	tablespoon butter, melted
1½	tablespoons brandy

Chicken Almond Filling

4	tablespoons butter
4	tablespoons flour
2	cups chicken stock
1	teaspoon tarragon
1	teaspoon salt
2	tablespoons brandy, optional
1	cup whipping cream
3	egg yolks
3	cups diced chicken
¾	cup toasted almonds
½	cup grated swiss cheese

For Crepe Batter: Blend ingredients in blender until smooth. Wait 2 hours before making crepes. In a crepe pan or hot skillet, pour batter into a well greased pan. Cook crepes until lightly browned and stack between sheets of wax paper. These freeze well. Makes 20 crepes.

For Chicken Almond Filling: In a saucepan, make a roux with flour, butter and chicken stock, stirring constantly until smooth. Add tarragon, salt and brandy and stir. Slowly add cream and egg yolks. Do not allow to boil. Divide sauce in half. To the first portion, add chicken and almonds.
Preheat oven to 425°.
Roll crepes with filling and cover with remaining sauce. Sprinkle with swiss cheese. Bake 10 minutes until bubbly.

YIELD: 20 crepes.

CHICKEN A LA KING AND CREPE FILLING

A public favorite at church luncheons. It also makes a wonderful filling for chicken crepes.

¼	cup chopped onion
3	cups sliced mushrooms
1	cup butter or margarine
2	cups flour
2	cups milk
1½	quarts chicken broth
2	cups half & half cream
1	cup sliced pimientos
8	cups diced chicken
1	tablespoon salt
1	teaspoon pepper
½	teaspoon cayenne pepper
½	cup dry sherry

In a large skillet, saute onions and mushrooms in butter until tender and lightly browned. Stir in flour blending well. Take skillet from heat and gradually add milk stirring constantly until thick and smooth. Add chicken and remaining ingredients and heat thoroughly. Add sherry just before serving. The recipe fills two 9x13-inch baking dishes. It is easy to cut recipe in half to serve a family. Serve over rice or biscuits.

YIELD: 20 to 25 servings.

MOO GOO GAI PAN

1	pound chicken breasts, deboned
	salt & pepper to taste
3	teaspoons sherry
4	tablespoons oil (we recommend peanut oil)
1	clove garlic, sliced
3	ribs celery, sliced
2	green onions & 1 inch of green tops, sliced thinly
1	4-ounce can sliced mushrooms, drained
1	4-ounce can water chestnuts, drained & sliced
24	snow peas, stringed
3	teaspoons soy sauce
¾	teaspoon sugar
3	teaspoons cornstarch in ½ cup cold water

Remove skin from chicken breasts and cut into 1-inch pieces. In a bowl, place chicken pieces and mix with salt, pepper and sherry. In a wok or large skillet, quickly fry garlic in hot oil but do not brown. Add chicken and stir fry for 3 to 5 minutes until almost cooked. Add celery and onion sauteing 2 or 3 minutes. Add mushrooms, water chestnuts and snow peas. After stirring, add sugar and soy sauce. Heat thoroughly and thicken with cornstarch and water mixture. Serve immediately over rice.

YIELD: 6 servings.

EAST INDIAN CHICKEN DELIGHT

1	pound bulk sausage
2	chicken breasts, cooked, boned & cubed or substitute one canned chicken
1	package slivered almonds, toasted to light brown
1	package wild & long grain rice with seasoning, cooked (we recommend Uncle Ben's)
	raisins to taste, optional

Preheat oven to 350°.
In a large skillet, brown sausage, drain and set aside. Toast almonds in oven or toaster oven. Cook chicken in microwave or boil. Cut into cubes. In a mixing bowl, combine sausage, chicken, cooked rice, almonds and raisins. In a greased 9x13-inch baking dish, place the mixture and heat in oven until heated thoroughly about 30 minutes. May be frozen after cooking.

YIELD: 8 servings.

JAPANESE MANDARIN CHICKEN BREASTS

1	11-ounce can mandarin oranges, drained, reserving syrup
6	chicken breasts, boned
6	teaspoons butter or margarine, softened
6	teaspoons minced onion
¼	cup fine dry bread crumbs
¼	cup flour
	salt & pepper to taste
¼	cup margarine or butter
1	tablespoon chopped onion
2	tablespoons flour
½	cup sherry
1	cup white grapes, halved

Preheat oven to 500°.
Lay each chicken breast flat and spread 1 teaspoon butter and several orange sections, 1 teaspoon minced onion and sprinkle with salt and pepper. Roll up and secure with toothpick. Repeat with the other chicken breasts. In a bowl, combine bread crumbs, flour, salt and pepper and mix. Roll breasts in mixture. In a roasting pan, place the 6 rolled chicken breasts. Brush with melted butter. Bake 15 minutes basting often. Add remaining onion and bake 10 additional minutes. Remove chicken to a heated platter. Stir 2 tablespoons flour into drippings and add sherry, orange syrup and grapes. Pour over chicken. Serve with white rice.

YIELD: 6 servings.

SZECHWAN CHICKEN

1	tablespoon cornstarch
3	tablespoons soy sauce
2	chicken breasts, boned, skinned, cut in ½-inch cubes
1	tablespoon sherry
2	teaspoons sugar
1	teaspoon white vinegar
¼	cup peanut oil
2	scallions, sliced
¼	teaspoon crushed red pepper
½	teaspoon ground ginger
½	cup salted peanuts

In a bowl, blend cornstarch and 1 tablespoon soy sauce. Mix in chicken and set aside. In another bowl, combine 2 tablespoons soy sauce, sherry, sugar and vinegar and set aside. In a wok or large skillet, heat peanut oil over high heat and add red pepper. Cook until black. Add chicken and stir fry for 3 minutes. Remove chicken and set aside. Stir fry scallions and ginger for 1 minute. Mix in chicken and cook 2 minutes, stirring constantly. Add soy mixture and stir 1 minute. Mix in salted peanuts. Serve hot with fried rice and stir-fried vegetables such as broccoli or snow peas.

YIELD: 4 servings.

HOT CHICKEN AMANDINE

4	cups chicken, cooked & diced
4	cups chopped celery
1	teaspoon salt
1¼	cups sliced almonds
2	teaspoons grated onion
2	tablespoons lemon juice
2	cups cooked rice, long grain brown rice recommended
2	cups mayonnaise
	salt & pepper to taste
2	cups grated cheddar cheese

Preheat oven to 350°.

In a large mixing bowl, combine chicken, celery, salt, almonds, onion, lemon juice, rice and mayonnaise. Season with salt and pepper. In a greased 9x13-inch baking dish, place mixture. Sprinkle with grated cheese. Bake 25 minutes.

YIELD: 6 servings.

GINGER NECTARINE CHICKEN

¼	cup flour
1½	teaspoons seasoned salt
1	teaspoon paprika
1	large frying chicken
¼	cup butter or margarine
1	teaspoon brown sugar
2	teaspoons soy sauce
2	teaspoons chopped candied ginger
⅓	cup water
3	large fresh nectarines, cut in slices
1	green pepper, cut in rings

Preheat oven to 425°.

In a mixing bowl, combine flour, salt and paprika. Coat chicken in mixture. In a large skillet, heat butter and add chicken and brown on all sides. Cut one 22x18-inch piece of heavy duty foil or 6 squares 12 inches each. Place all chicken side by side on large piece of foil or 1 serving on each square. Add to butter in skillet brown sugar, soy sauce, ginger and water. Bring to a boil, stirring constantly until slightly thickened. Spoon sauce over chicken. Fold ends of foil over chicken envelope style to form high seal, leaving a little room for steam to expand in baking. Place in shallow pan. Bake for 35 to 45 minutes. Open foil and arrange nectarine slices and green pepper rings over chicken. Close foil and bake an additional 5 minutes.

YIELD: 6 servings.

TURKEY CREOLE

½   cup chopped green pepper
½   cup chopped celery
¼   cup chopped onion
1   tablespoon margarine
1   tablespoon flour
1   16-ounce can tomatoes,
        chopped
1   teaspoon sugar
½   teaspoon salt
¼   teaspoon garlic powder
1   bay leaf
    dash of pepper
    dash of bottled hot pepper
        sauce, optional
1½ cups diced cooked turkey
    cooked rice, enough for
        6 servings

In a large skillet, saute green pepper, celery and onion in margarine until tender. Add flour and stir. Add tomatoes, sugar, salt, garlic powder, bay leaf, pepper and hot pepper sauce, if desired. Cook until thickened and bubbly. Add turkey and cover simmering for 5 to 10 minutes. Serve over hot rice.
YIELD: 6 servings.

TURKEY IN SWISS CHEESE SAUCE

⅓   cup margarine
1   onion, chopped
½   cup chopped celery
4   tablespoons flour
1   cup chicken broth
½   cup dry white wine
½   cup milk
½   cup swiss cheese, cubed
¼   teaspoon nutmeg
    dash of black pepper
2   cups cubed turkey
    cooked rice, enough for
        4 servings

In a large skillet, melt margarine and saute onion and celery until lightly golden. In a bowl, blend flour into chicken broth and stir well. Add to skillet and also add wine. Stirring constantly, cook until mixture thickens. Add milk, cheese, nutmeg, pepper and turkey. Continue to cook over low heat stirring constantly until cheese melts and turkey is heated thoroughly. Serve over rice.
YIELD: 4 servings.

"TEJAS" GARLIC SHRIMP

1   pound fresh jumbo shrimp
1   pint half & half or
       light cream or milk
      flour
1   cup olive oil
1   cup vegetable oil
1   egg yolk
      juice of ½ lemon
½   cup butter
1-2 cloves garlic, minced
      parsley & chives, chopped

Preheat oven to broil.

Clean and devein shrimp and soak in cream for 10 minutes. Drain and dredge in flour. Saute in oils over medium heat for five minutes. Do not turn over. Remove shrimp and place on baking sheet in preheated oven and broil for 5 minutes.

For Sauce: Mix egg yolk and lemon juice in heavy saucepan. Add half of butter and stir over low heat until melted. Add garlic and remaining butter. Stir briskly until butter melts and sauce thickens. Add chives and parsley. Pour over shrimp and serve.

YIELD: 4 servings.

Windmills of varying shapes and sizes can be seen throughout the rural areas of South Texas. They stand as visual reminders of a glorious past. Farmers and ranchers drilled their own wells, put up a windmill and prayed for a strong, continuous breeze. Today, many windmills still serve the everyday function of pumping water for family consumption and agricultural use.

SHRIMP STEAMED IN BEER

1   can beer
2   pounds shrimp in shells
½   teaspoon thyme
½   teaspoon dry mustard
1   bay leaf
1   clove garlic, chopped
1   tablespoon salt
1   tablespoon chopped parsley
¼   teaspoon pepper
½   teaspoon chopped chives

 Sauce

4   tablespoons butter
2   tablespoons lemon juice
1   tablespoon chopped parsley
1   tablespoon chopped chives
1   teaspoon salt

For Sauce: Melt butter in a saucepan and add other sauce ingredients.

For the Shrimp Mixture: Combine beer, shrimp and spices. Cover tightly and bring to boil. Reduce heat and start timing. Simmer shrimp for **3 minutes until pink, no longer!** Add sauce to shrimp mixture. Peel and eat. This is fun to serve at a football party with corn on the cob, salad and french bread.

YIELD: 4 servings.

TROUT AMANDINE

2   pounds trout fillets
¼   cup flour
1   teaspoon salt
1   teaspoon paprika
½   cup butter, melted
¼   cup slivered almonds
3   tablespoons lemon juice
¼   teaspoon tabasco
2   tablespoons parsley, chopped

Preheat oven to broil.
Combine flour, salt and paprika. Roll fillets in flour mixture and arrange in greased pan. Pour half of butter over fillets. Broil for 10 to 15 minutes or until fillets flake easily. Saute almonds in remaining butter. Mix in lemon juice, tabasco and parsley with almonds. Pour over fillets. Garnish with sprigs of parsley.

YIELD: 4 to 6 servings.

SALMON SOUFFLE TORTE

Souffle Layers

4   tablespoons butter
        or margarine
½   cup all-purpose flour
2   cups milk
4   egg yolks
1   teaspoon sugar
        dash of salt
4   egg whites
        dash cream of Tartar

Smoked Salmon Filling

½   cup sour cream
8   ounces cream cheese,
        room temperature
2   tablespoons lemon juice
4   tablespoons chopped
        green onions
¼   pound smoked salmon,
        shredded (lox)
4   tablespoons peeled &
        chopped cucumber
¼   teaspoon dried dill (or 1
        tablespoon fresh dill)

Sour Cream Frosting

1   cup sour cream
1   teaspoon onion powder
1   tablespoon lemon juice

Garnish

1   slice smoked salmon, (reserve
        from ¼ pound)
        black olives, pitted & sliced
        chives or green onion
            tops for leaves
        fresh sprigs of dill or parsley

Preheat oven to 350°.

For Souffle Layers: Make by melting butter in a small saucepan. Stir in flour and cook over low heat until well blended about 2 minutes. **Do not brown.** Whisk in milk and continue cooking and stirring until sauce comes to a boil and thickens. In small bowl, lightly whisk egg yolks, sugar and salt. Stir a small amount of hot mixture into the yolks; return to saucepan. Cook for 1 minute, stirring constantly. Remove from heat. Meanwhile beat egg whites until frothy. Add cream of tartar and beat until mixture forms stiff but not dry peaks. Fold sauce into whites. Line bottoms of two 9-inch layer cake pans with rounds of parchment or wax paper. Grease the paper and the sides of the pan. Turn souffle mixture into 2 pans, dividing evenly. Bake for 35 to 40 minutes or until lightly browned and top springs back when lightly pressed. Cool in pans for 10 minutes. Invert layers onto cake racks and pull off paper. Cool completely. May be refrigerated overnight wrapped in foil. May also be frozen for 1 month. Wrap individually. Defrost in refrigerator.

For Smoked Salmon Filling: Beat cream cheese, sour cream and lemon juice in bowl with electric mixer until smooth. Mix in remaining filling ingredients until blended. Place 1 souffle layer on serving platter. Spread with filling. Place second layer on filling. May be covered with plastic wrap and refrigerated 2 days. Several hours before serving, make sour cream frosting by mixing all frosting ingredients together in a small bowl. Frost torte and decorate top with flowers from smoked salmon and olives. Make stems and leaves from green onion stems. Garnish with fresh dill. Serve in cut wedges.

YIELD: 12 servings.

IMPERIAL SAUCE FOR SEAFOOD

Delicious with red snapper, sea trout or sole, but this sauce can also be served with shrimp, lobster or crabmeat in individual casseroles for a luncheon dish. It makes a very pretty topping!

Thick Cream Sauce

3-4 tablespoons butter

3-4 tablespoons flour

1   cup milk or cream

Imperial Sauce

2   tablespoons finely
       chopped onion

¼   cup finely diced mushrooms

1   tablespoon butter

1   cup Thick Cream Sauce

1   cup mayonnaise

1   teaspoon lemon juice

2   tablespoons finely chopped
       sweet mustard pickles

1   tablespoon finely
       chopped pimientos

¼   teaspoon worcestershire sauce

Preheat oven to 300°.

For Thick Cream Sauce: Combine ingredients and blend. In a saucepan, cook over low heat, stirring constantly until thick.

For Imperial Sauce: Saute onion and mushrooms in butter. Add cream sauce, mayonnaise, lemon juice, pickles, pimientos and worcestershire sauce. Completely cover any boned fish and bake for 45 minutes. Part of the sauce cooks into the fish and part stays on top.

YIELD: 2½ cups or 6 to 8 servings.

SENORITAS' SOLE

Use this delicious Spanish recipe for other fish fillets such as flounder, red snapper or red fish. It is an elegant dish for impressing special dinner guests!

8   sole fillets
1   teaspoon salt
1   teaspoon pepper
1   teaspoon paprika
     juice of ½ lemon
     flour
1   large egg, lightly beaten
2   tablespoons whipping cream
¼   cup butter

  Sauce

½   cup butter
¼   cup sliced mushrooms
¼   cup chopped tomatoes
¼   cup finely chopped onion
2   teaspoons chopped
        fresh parsley
½   clove garlic, minced
1   teaspoon paprika
1   lemon, cut into wedges
2   teaspoons capers

For The Sauce: Melt butter in medium skillet. Add mushrooms, tomatoes, onion, parsley, garlic, paprika, lemon and capers and saute for 3 to 4 minutes. Remove lemon wedges.

For The Sole Fillets: Sprinkle with seasonings, drizzle with lemon juice and dust with flour. Combine egg and cream in flat dish and coat fillets. Heat butter in large skillet and brown fish over medium heat on both sides. Keep warm. Pour sauce over sole and serve immediately. Try this method with other fish fillets. It is quite delicious!

YIELD: 6 to 8 servings.

The Texas Coast is noted for its outstanding annual crab catch. This abundant crustacean is quite tasty and is enjoyed by the people of the Alamo City. Succulent crabmeat can be prepared in a wide variety of delicious recipes or eaten directly from the claws.

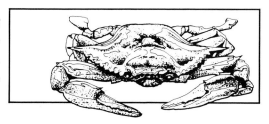

OYSTER STEW A LA BURT

(with Smelts on the Side)

3 pints oysters
½ cup butter
1 pint half & half cream
½ pint whipping cream
    salt & pepper to taste
    dried parsley
12 -16 smelts, fresh or canned
    salt water
    flour
    cornmeal

Clean oysters under running water and make sure all shell fragments are out. Discard juice from container. Heat butter in frying pan until butter melts and sizzles. Add oysters. Cook only until edges curl and sauce is just on verge of boiling. **Do not boil.** Add half and half and whipping cream. Salt to taste and add coarse ground pepper. For added oyster flavor, cut a few oysters through the fatty center while cooking. Heat this mixture only until thoroughly hot. **Do not boil.** Garnish with dried parsley and serve a few fried smelts with this dish. This oyster stew can be served without the smelts if desired.

For Smelts: Take whole headless smelts and marinate in salt water for 1 hour. Batter in a mixture of 50% flour and 50% cornmeal with salt and garlic to taste. Shake in a bag. Add to hot fat 1 inch deep and fry until very crisp. All of the smelt is eaten including the bones.

YIELD: 4 servings.

PAELLA

"Paella" is a traditional Spanish rice dish which contains seafood and usually chicken. It originated in Valencia, Spain, where a combination of crops of rice and saffron were harvested and blended to create one of the most unique tasting cuisines in the world. Saffron is the secret ingredient which gives paella its yellow color and special aroma. It is the world's most expensive spice and is grown mainly in Spain and the Canary Islands. Paella was brought to San Antonio by the Canary Islanders in the early 1700's. The San Antonio River was rich in fresh water fish and crayfish. Paella can contain local ingredients in season such as shrimp, crayfish, lobster, clams, snails, rabbit, quail and vegetables.

Chicken Stock

4½	cups boiling water
4	cubes chicken bouillon
⅛	teaspoon saffron powder (or a large pinch saffron soaked in 2-3 tablespoons hot water for 30 minutes)
3	teaspoons salt
1	teaspoon Accent or MSG
¼	teaspoon pepper

Paella

12	large raw shrimp, cleaned & shelled
¾	pound scallops
¾	pound fish fillets (flounder or perch), bite sizes
2	cups wine
2	teaspoons lemon spices or seafood marinade
12	tablespoons olive oil
6	pieces chicken, cut in half & deboned
1½	medium onions, chopped
2	tomatoes, peeled, seeded & chopped
1	green pepper, cut in strips
1	clove garlic, crushed
2	cups long grain rice
¾	pound ham, cut in strips
5	ounces pepperoni, sliced
1	small package frozen peas

For Chicken Stock: Dissolve 4 cubes chicken bouillon in boiling water and then add saffron, salt, Accent and pepper. Have this liquid very hot and ready to pour over rice.

In a large skillet with 3 tablespoons hot olive oil, saute the shrimp and scallops for 1 to 2 minutes and reserve. Marinate the fish in wine and lemon spices for 30 minutes. In a paella pan or large skillet, heat 9 tablespoons oil and saute chicken pieces gently until golden on all sides. Remove chicken and add onions and fry until transparent. Add tomatoes and cook until soft. Blanch the green peppers in salted, boiling water for 1 minute and drain. Add to skillet with garlic. Cook for 2½ to 3 minutes. Stir in rice. Cook over medium heat until grains are transparent. Lay chicken pieces in bottom of pan and also arrange the rest of the meats and seafood in pan. Pour in hot chicken stock with saffron and other seasoning. Bring to a quick boil. Turn down heat and sprinkle frozen peas in pan. Simmer uncovered until rice is tender, liquid absorbed, and all ingredients cooked, approximately 1 hour. Let stand for 8 minutes before serving.

YIELD: 12 servings.

ENGLISH FISH BATTER

English crispy fried fish is known the world over.   It can also be used for shellfish like shrimp, scallops and oysters if a crispy batter is preferred.   Try with vegetables also.   Serve with french fries or "chips" as the British call them for authentic "Fish and Chips!!"

⅔	cup beer
⅓	cup lemon juice
1	egg
½	cup self-rising flour
	salt & pepper to taste
3	pounds fish fillets or shrimp
1	cup all-purpose flour
	oil for frying

Mix the beer, lemon juice, egg and self-rising flour in a large mixing bowl with a wire whisk.   Whip the mixture until completely mixed.   Let stand at room temperature for 10 minutes before using.   Take the fish fillets and moisten with water then flour lightly with all-purpose flour.   Let the fillets dry on a wire rack.   When fillets are dry, dip one piece into the batter at a time.   Fry in 385° oil for 4 minutes on each side.   Remove the fillet with a slotted spoon or tongs.

YIELD: 4 to 6 servings.

REDFISH IN LEMON-CAPER-DILL BUTTER

COQUILLES ST. JACQUES
(Scallops in Wine)

CRAB AND AVOCADO ENCHILADAS

CRAYFISH BIENVILLE

SEAFOOD CREPES

POACHED SALMON WITH SORREL

SHRIMP AND ZUCCHINI BROCHETTES

BLACKENED RIVER TROUT
For Recipe Page - See Index.

CAJUN COO BEE YON
(Court Bouillon)

Court Bouillon is a French phrase for aromatic broth of water, oil, herbs and seasonings. The Cajuns of Louisiana changed its original pronunciation to Coo Bee Yon and used it as a fish broth to serve over rice. This is an ideal dish for a large casual gathering such as a football party so common in Texas.

4	pounds red snapper or redfish, cubed
1	cup water with salt & pepper
1	cup bacon drippings
1	large onion, chopped
6	stalks celery, chopped with leaves included
1	large bell pepper, chopped
8	ounces tomato paste
1	14½-ounce can tomato sauce
1	lemon, juice & grated peel only
1	cup water
1	cup white or red wine
3	cloves garlic, minced
1	teaspoon tabasco
1	cup worcestershire sauce
1	pound shrimp
1	pound scallops (other seafood combinations can be used such as oysters or crab)
	small bunch green onions, chopped
	small bunch parsley, chopped
6	bay leaves
¼	teaspoon basil
¼	teaspoon oregano
	salt & pepper to taste
	rice (enough for 12-15 servings)

For Fish Stock: Filet fish and set aside for later. Cook fish heads and bone in 1 cup of water seasoned with salt and pepper for approximately 45 minutes. Remove the heads and bones and set aside to cool. In a large pot, saute onion, celery and bell pepper in bacon drippings - do not brown. Add tomato paste and sauce, lemon, water and fish stock. Add wine and remaining seasonings such as garlic and herbs. Simmer for 2 hours. Later add the cubed fish and other seafood and cook only 20 minutes. Serve over hot rice with a salad and hot french bread.

YIELD: 12 to 15 servings.

SEAFOOD CASSEROLE

Any combination of seafood can be used such as lobster with shrimp and crab or just shrimp alone.

2 tablespoons butter
2 tablespoons flour
¼ teaspoon salt
1 cup milk
24 medium-large shrimp,
    cooked, deveined & split
1½ cups fresh lump crabmeat or
6 - 12 ounces frozen crab
1 3-ounce can sliced
    mushrooms, drained
2 tablespoons sherry
1 tablespoon lemon juice
    dash tabasco
¼ teaspoon worcestershire sauce
½ cup sharp cheddar or
    longhorn cheese, grated
1 cup soft bread crumbs,
    in pieces
2 tablespoons melted butter

Preheat oven 375°.
In a large 2-quart saucepan, melt butter over low heat. Blend in flour and salt. Add milk all at once. Cook quickly, stirring constantly until sauce thickens and bubbles. Remove from heat. Next add the shrimp, crab, mushrooms, sherry, lemon juice, tabasco, and worcestershire sauce and mix well. Place mixture in greased 9x13-inch casserole. Sprinkle cheese over top. Combine bread crumbs with melted butter and sprinkle over cheese. Bake for 40 minutes or until heated thoroughly. Serve with broccoli, a crisp green salad and croissants.

YIELD: 4 to 6 servings.

SHRIMP VICTORIA GOURMET

1 pound raw shrimp,
    peeled & deveined
½ cup finely chopped onion
¼ cup margarine or butter
1 6-ounce can mushrooms
1 tablespoon flour
¼ teaspoon salt
    dash cayenne red pepper
1 cup sour cream
1½ cups cooked rice

Saute shrimp and onion in margarine for 10 minutes or until shrimp is tender. Add mushrooms and cook for 5 minutes more. Sprinkle in flour, salt and pepper. Stir in sour cream and cook gently for 10 minutes. **Do not boil.** Serve over rice.

YIELD: 4 to 6 servings.

CRAB, SHRIMP AND ARTICHOKES AU GRATIN

1   pound shrimp, shelled
      & deveined

2   6-ounce cans crabmeat
      (fresh can be used)

1   9-ounce package artichoke
      hearts, frozen

¼   cup butter

½   pound fresh mushrooms

1   clove garlic, crushed

2   tablespoons shallots,
      finely chopped

¼   cup flour

½   teaspoon pepper

1   tablespoon fresh dill (or
      1 teaspoon dry dill)

¾   cup half & half cream

10 ounces sharp cheddar
      cheese, grated

⅔   cup dry white wine

2   tablespoons corn flakes
      or bread crumbs, dried

½   tablespoon butter.

Preheat oven 375°.

Cook shrimp in salted boiling water until pink. Cook artichoke hearts according to directions on the package and drain. In a skillet, saute mushrooms, shallots and garlic in 2 tablespoons butter for 5 minutes. Remove from heat and put into casserole. Stir in flour, pepper and dill to butter and add 2 more tablespoons butter. Add cream and stir. Bring to boil while stirring and remove from heat. Add ½ grated cheese and stir until melted. Add wine. Drain crab before adding to 2-quart casserole. Combine sauce, shrimp, crab, artichokes and mushrooms. Add the rest of the cheese and mix lightly. Sprinkle corn flakes on top. Dot with remaining butter. **Bake for 30 minutes.** Serve over rice with vegetables such as asparagus or broccoli.

YIELD: 8 servings.

San Antonio is located only 150 miles from one of the largest shrimping areas in the country. Shrimp boats leave Corpus Christi, Aransas Pass, Rockport and other Texas coastal cities each morning and return in the evening loaded with plentiful catches.

SHELLFISH IN PAPRIKA

Due to the richness and high seasoning, this Greek and Creole dish is very good in the fall and winter.

3	pounds of shellfish (crayfish, scallops and/or shrimp)
1	pound butter
3	large tomatoes
	paprika (Hungarian)
	garlic
	gumbo file
	salt to taste
9	ounces Greek salted or parmesan cheese, finely minced
¼	cup brandy or metaxa

Preheat oven 350°.

Take the cleaned shellfish and arrange raw in a greased shallow baking dish. Dot with butter and cover lightly with tomato slices which have been skinned and seeded. Put paprika and garlic over this mixture and add a bit of gumbo file for flavor and salt to taste. Put Greek or parmesan cheese over the top and a dash of brandy. Bake until the mixture bubbles, approximately 20 to 30 minutes. This is a beautiful dish and can be prepared ahead and baked at the last minute.

YIELD: 4 to 6 servings.

THE PERFECT OMELET

2   eggs, room temperature
½   teaspoon tap water
    dash of tabasco
    salt & ground black pepper
1   teaspoon butter

Tips for the Perfect Omelet
Use 2 eggs per omelet for effective cooking and texture. Invest in a good pan such as one with a layer of metal alloy and **never** cook anything in it but omelets. Clean by scouring with salt and a paper towel. Drain all fillings well and do not overfill. Learn to work the pan quickly and firmly. Practice makes perfect especially with omelets. Use a long metal spatula about 1½ inches wide.

In a small bowl, combine eggs, water, tabasco, salt and pepper and beat well with a wire whisk. In an omelet pan over high heat, melt the butter. When drops of water flicked into the hot butter sputter and sizzle, pour egg mixture into pan. Using a spatula, lift the edges of the omelet as they cook, working quickly in a circular motion, tilting pan slightly to allow seepage under firmer parts. Keep over heat no longer than 2 minutes. Center may be runny, but it will cook when filling is added and the omelet is folded in the pan. Quickly add filling and roll either in half or in rug style onto a heated plate. Serve immediately.

YIELD: 1 omelet.

Suggested Fillings:

Swiss and Mushroom: Grated swiss cheese and chopped, sauteed mushrooms.

Spanish: Sauteed, chopped ripe tomatoes, green peppers, green onions and ripe olives.

Chicken Livers: Sauteed, chopped chicken livers sprinkled with strips of mozzarella cheese.

Potato: Chopped, cooked potato with chopped green onions and pimiento sauteed together in butter.

Cheddar: Grated cheddar cheese mixed with crisp bacon bits or cooked, chopped ham.

Tips For Parties: Set up an electric burner on serving table surrounded with tempting bowls of fillings for personalized omelets.

ELEGANT OVEN OMELET
For Recipe Page - See Index.

FLORENTINE CHICKEN OMELET

Filling

2 tablespoons butter
½ cup chopped onion
¼ pound mushrooms, chopped
2 10-ounce packages frozen
    spinach, thawed,
    squeezed dry
1 cup diced, cooked chicken
1 3-ounce package cream cheese
½ cup sour cream
2 tablespoons dijon mustard
    salt & pepper to taste

Omelet

4 tablespoons butter
4 tablespoons flour
1½ cups milk
½ cup parmesan cheese
½ cup grated cheddar cheese
¼ teaspoon salt
4 eggs yolks
4 egg whites, beaten to
    soft peak stage

Preheat oven to 325°.

For Filling: In a large skillet, melt butter and saute onion and mushrooms until tender. Add spinach, chicken, cream cheese, sour cream and mustard mixing thoroughly until well heated. Season with salt and pepper to taste and set aside. Grease a 15x10x1-inch jelly roll pan and line with aluminium foil that has been sprayed with vegetable oil or Pam and set aside.

For Omelet: In a saucepan, melt butter and add flour to make a roux. Add milk and stir until mixture thickens. Stir in cheeses, salt and add yolks one at a time. Fold in beaten egg whites into the warm cheese mixture. Pour batter onto prepared jelly roll pan and spread evenly. Bake in lower third of oven 25 to 35 minutes until golden brown and springy to the touch.

For Assembly: Remove omelet from oven. Carefully loosen edges of foil. Place another piece of foil over omelet and invert. Carefully remove pan from top and peel off foil. Spread filling over top of omelet and roll up lengthwise, using foil to help roll. Slide seam side down onto prepared pan. May be covered and refrigerated overnight. Preheat oven to 375°. Sprinkle with additional cheese and dots of butter on top. Bake for 20 minutes until hot. Broil a few minutes if necessary to brown cheese.

YIELD: 10 to 12 servings.

MIGAS

"Migas" in Spanish means "fried crumbs." This delicious breakfast is made with corn tortillas and eggs.

8	corn tortillas, cut in 8 wedges each
12	eggs, slightly beaten
8	bacon slices
4	green onions, sliced thin including tops
12	cherry tomatoes, cut in halves
2	fresh jalapeno peppers, sliced thin with seeds removed
1	cup shredded cheddar cheese

In a skillet, brown bacon, remove from pan and cut in small bits and set aside. Fry tortilla strips in bacon fat (or corn oil) until slightly crisp (about 30 seconds). Add remaining ingredients and bacon all at once. Scramble until eggs are firm. Serve with hot flour tortillas and refried beans.

YIELD: 8 to 10 servings.

CHORIZO CON PAPAS
For Recipe Page - See Index.

MEXICAN BREAKFAST CASSEROLE

Try this delicious and easy Mexican breakfast served with picante sauce, refried beans with cheese and hot flour tortillas!

9	eggs, beaten
4	tablespoons chopped onion
1	cup shredded cheddar cheese or monterey jack cheese
1	cup buttermilk
1	cup diced ham or bulk sausage, browned & drained
5	corn tortillas, cut into quarters
	jalapeno peppers, optional

Preheat oven to 350°.
In a 12x8-inch greased baking dish, line the bottom with tortillas. In a bowl, add the beaten eggs and buttermilk and beat again. Add cheese, ham and onion and mix thoroughly. Pour mixture over tortillas. Bake 35 to 40 minutes until firm. Cut into serving squares. Garnish with jalapeno peppers.

YIELD: 6 to 8 servings.

ASPARAGUS BRUNCH CON QUESO
(Asparagus Brunch with Cheese)

1   pound colby cheese, grated
1   pound Velveeta cheese, melted
1   10-ounce can tomatoes & green chilies (we recommend Ro-Tel)
2   15-ounce cans asparagus
1   dozen medium eggs, beaten garnish with hard boiled eggs & paprika

Preheat oven to 325°.

In a greased 9x13-inch baking dish, place the grated cheese and cover with beaten eggs. Bake 45 minutes to 1 hour until eggs are set. Remove from oven and arrange drained asparagus on top. In a saucepan, combine tomatoes and melted Velveeta cheese heating until warm. Pour over top of cooked cheese and egg mixture. Return to oven and bake for 5 to 8 minutes. Garnish with sliced hard boiled eggs. Sprinkle with paprika.

YIELD: 8 servings.

PRAIRIE CASSEROLE

This old time cowboy recipe is still a favorite today using canned milk and staple ingredients carried by the chuck wagons!

1   2¼-ounce can pickled jalapeno peppers, chopped
1   pound monterey jack cheese, coarsely grated
1   pound cheddar cheese, coarsely grated
4   egg whites, beaten until stiff
4   egg yolks
1   5-ounce can evaporated milk
1   tablespoon flour
½   teaspoon salt
⅛   teaspoon pepper
2   medium tomatoes, sliced

Preheat oven to 325°.

In a large bowl, combine cheeses and peppers. In a greased 2-quart baking dish, pour the cheese and pepper mixture. In a separate bowl, blend together the yolks, milk, flour, salt and pepper. Using a rubber scraper, fold egg whites into yolk mixture. Pour egg mixture on top of cheeses. Bake 30 minutes. Remove from oven and place sliced tomatoes on top and return to oven for 30 more minutes until eggs are set and knife comes out clean.

YIELD: 8 servings.

VARIATION: Substitute green chiles for jalapenos.

HAM STRATA

20 slices sandwich bread
     (we recommend
     Pepperidge Farm)
3 cups cooked ham,
     chopped bite size
10 ounces sharp cheddar
     cheese, grated
10 ounces swiss cheese, grated
6 eggs, slightly beaten
½ teaspoon dry mustard
3 cups milk
3 cups corn flakes
½ teaspoon onion salt
½ cup melted butter or
     margarine

On a cutting board, remove the edges of the bread slices and cut in half. Grease two 9x13-inch baking dishes with butter and arrange a layer of bread in the bottom. Layer half of the ham and sprinkle with half of the cheeses. Repeat again with bread layer, ham and cheese layers. In a bowl, combine eggs, milk and seasonings. Pour over layers. Cover with wax paper and foil, refrigerating overnight.

Preheat oven to 375°.

Make sure all liquid has been absorbed by bread. Sprinkle corn flakes over baking dishes and pour melted butter over casserole. Bake 50 to 60 minutes. Allow casseroles to stand for 10 minutes before serving.

YIELD: 10 to 12 servings for each casserole.

EGG AND ARTICHOKE CASSEROLE

7-8 green onions, finely minced
     using half of tops
1 6½-ounce jar marinated
     artichoke hearts, drained
1 14-ounce can water packed
     artichoke hearts, drained
7 eggs, beaten
1 clove garlic, minced
8 ounces medium cheddar
     cheese, grated
6 saltine crackers,
     rolled to crumbs

Preheat oven to 350°.

Cut artichokes into thirds. In a large skillet with oil from marinated artichokes, saute onions and garlic. In a greased 9x13-inch baking dish, combine the green onions, artichokes, beaten eggs, garlic, cheese and cracker crumbs. Bake 40 minutes. Can be prepared a day ahead. Also freezes well.

YIELD: 6 to 8 servings.

SAUSAGE BRUNCH SQUARES

1½ pounds pork sausage
(we recommend Owens)
1 8-ounce can refrigerator
crescent rolls
8 ounces mozzarella
cheese, grated
4 eggs, beaten
¾ cup milk
⅓ teaspoon salt
⅛ teaspoon pepper

Preheat oven to 425°.
In a medium skillet, crumble sausage and cook over medium heat until brown stirring once. Drain well. In a buttered 9x13-inch baking dish, line the bottom with crescent rolls firmly pressing perforations to seal. Sprinkle with sausage and cheese. In a mixing bowl, combine eggs, milk, salt and pepper and beat well. Pour over sausage mixture. Bake 15 minutes until eggs are set. Let stand 5 minutes. Cut into squares and serve immediately.

YIELD: 6 to 8 servings

HERBED EGG AND CHEESE CASSEROLE

This dish is a rich and tasty way to serve hard boiled eggs. May be served with cornmeal biscuits, toast points or English muffins.

¼ cup butter
¼ cup flour
1 cup half & half cream
or evaporated milk
1 cup milk
¼ teaspoon thyme
¼ teaspoon basil
¼ teaspoon marjoram
1 pound very sharp cheddar
cheese, grated
1½ dozen eggs, hard boiled,
sliced thin
1 pound bacon, fried,
drained & crumbled
¼ cup finely chopped parsley
1 cup bread crumbs, buttered

Preheat oven to 350°.
In a saucepan, melt butter and blend in flour. Add cream and milk gradually. Cook stirring with wire whisk until thick. Add thyme, basil and marjoram. To white sauce, add cheese gradually and stir until all cheese is melted. In a greased 9x13-inch baking dish, place a layer of sliced eggs, sprinkle bacon then parsley over eggs. Pour cheese sauce over eggs and repeat two more layers. Top with buttered bread crumbs. Bake 30 minutes or until bubbly.

YIELD: 12 servings.

VARIATION: Substitute diced ham for bacon.

QUICK BRUNCH PIE

1 9-inch unbaked pie shell
½ cup mayonnaise
2 tablespoons flour
2 eggs, beaten
½ cup milk
1 8-ounce package swiss
    cheese, diced
1 7½-ounce can crabmeat or
    1 cup chicken or
    1 cup ham
½ pound bacon, fried,
    drained & crumbled

Preheat oven to 350°.
In a mixing bowl, combine mayonnaise, flour, eggs and milk blending until creamy and smooth. Stir in swiss cheese and crabmeat, chicken or ham. Pour mixture into unbaked pie shell. Sprinkle crumbled bacon over mixture. Bake 40 to 45 minutes. Serve immediately. Can be frozen before cooking.
YIELD: 6 servings.

JALAPENO QUICHE

1 pound monterey jack
    cheese, shredded
1 cup milk
1 cup flour
1 pint cottage cheese
6 eggs, lightly beaten
¼ cup margarine or butter,
    melted
1 4-ounce can jalapeno
    peppers, sliced

Preheat oven to 375°.
In a large bowl, combine monterey jack cheese, milk, flour, cottage cheese, beaten eggs, melted margarine and jalapenos mixing well. In a 9x13-inch greased baking dish, pour egg mixture. Bake 40 minutes until eggs are set.

For Appetizers: Cut into small pieces and serve warm. May be prepared ahead of time and frozen. Reheat in microwave 2 to 3 minutes or in 400° oven 10 minutes.
YIELD: 12 to 15 servings.

SAUSAGE QUICHE

1   9-inch deep dish pie
      crust, baked
1   pound hot or spicy
      bulk sausage
3   eggs
⅔   cup milk
¼   teaspoon salt
      dash of pepper
      dash of cayenne pepper
1½ cups shredded sharp cheddar
      cheese, divided

Preheat oven to 375°.
In a large skillet, cook sausage until lightly browned. Drain and crumble and set aside. In a medium mixing bowl, combine eggs, milk and seasonings beating lightly. Sprinkle ¾ cup cheese over pie crust and top with sausage. Carefully pour egg mixture on top of sausage. Sprinkle with remaining ¾ cup cheese. Bake 50 minutes until eggs set.

YIELD: 6 servings.

MAKE AHEAD BAKED EGGS

1   dozen eggs, beaten
½   cup milk
½   teaspoon salt
¼   teaspoon pepper
1   tablespoon butter
1   8-ounce container sour cream
12 bacon slices, cooked
      & crumbled
4   ounces sharp cheddar
      cheese, shredded

In a medium bowl, combine beaten eggs, milk, salt and pepper and set aside. In a large skillet, over medium-low heat, melt butter and pour in egg mixture. Cook stirring occasionally until eggs are set but still moist. Remove from heat to cool. Stir in sour cream. In a greased 2-quart baking dish, pour egg mixture and top with bacon and cheese. Cover with foil and refrigerate overnight.

Preheat oven to 300°.
Uncover eggs and bake 20 to 25 minutes until hot and cheese has melted.

YIELD: 8 servings.

MAGIC CRUSTLESS QUICHE

10 eggs, beaten well

12 ounces small curd
    cottage cheese or
    8 ounces cream cheese

1 pound monterey jack
    cheese, grated

1 4-ounce jar or can
    sliced mushrooms

4 tablespoons margarine

⅛ teaspoon celery salt

⅛ teaspoon chervil

¼ teaspoon medium grind
    black pepper

1 small onion, chopped
    & sauteed

1 teaspoon salt

1 cup unsifted flour

½ teaspoon baking powder

2 4-ounce cans chopped
    green chiles

1 4-ounce can sliced
    black olives

Optional: 10 ounces frozen
    chopped broccoli,
    thawed; 8 ounces break-
    fast sausage or 8 ounces
    peeled shrimp.

Note: Reduce flour to ½ cup
    when vegetable, sausage
    or shrimp are added!

Preheat oven to 350°.

In a large mixing bowl, combine beaten eggs, cottage cheese, grated cheese, mushrooms, spices, onion, flour, baking powder, green chiles, black olives and optional ingredients. Blend carefully and pour into a greased 9x13-inch baking dish or 8-cup quiche pan sprayed with non-stick vegetable cooking spray. Bake 35 to 45 minutes. Let stand 5 minutes before cutting and serving. Recipe may be halved and poured into a 10x6-inch pan or 9-inch quiche pan.

YIELD: 8 to 10 servings.

QUICHE LORRAINE TARTS

1   package pie crust mix
1   tablespoon poppy seeds
1⅓ cups coarsely shredded
       swiss cheese
⅔   cup chopped salami or
       cubed ham
⅓   cup sliced green onions
4   eggs, slightly beaten
1⅓ cups sour cream
1   teaspoon salt
1   teaspoon worcestershire sauce

Preheat oven to 375°.
Prepare pastry for 2 crust pie as directed on package stirring in poppy seeds. Roll pastry 1/16-inch thick on lightly floured board and cut into 3-inch rounds. Fit rounds into 2½-inch muffin pans. In a bowl, combine cheese, salami and onion. Spoon cheese mixture into pastry shells. In another bowl, combine eggs, sour cream, salt and worcestershire sauce. Into each pastry shell, pour about 1 tablespoon of sour cream mixture. Bake 20 to 25 minutes until lightly browned. Cool in pan 5 minutes. May be cooled, wrapped in foil and then frozen. To serve, reheat in 350° oven for 10 minutes.

YIELD: 36 tarts.

BREAKFAST PIZZA

¾   pound bulk pork sausage (we
       recommend Owens Hot)
2   8-ounce packages refrigerated
       crescent rolls (we
       recommend Pillsbury)
2   8-ounce packages loose
       pack hash brown
       potatoes, thawed
4   ounces sharp cheddar
       cheese, grated
5   eggs, beaten
¼   cup milk
½   teaspoon seasoned salt
¼   teaspoon pepper
2   tablespoons grated
       Parmesan cheese
       pimiento for garnish

Preheat oven to 375°.
In a medium skillet, cook sausage until brown and crumbly. Drain and set aside. Separate dough into 12 triangles (4 triangles will be unused). Place triangles with elongated point toward center in a greased 12-inch pizza pan.
Press bottoms and sides to form crust. Seal perforations with dampened fingers. Bake for 10 minutes. Spoon sausage over partially baked crust. Sprinkle with hash browns and cheese. In a medium bowl, whisk eggs, milk, salt and pepper. Pour over sausage mixture. Bake for 25 minutes until eggs are set. Sprinkle with parmesan cheese. Bake 3 to 4 more minutes. Garnish with pimiento. Serve in pizza slices.

YIELD: 6 to 8 servings.

CHEESE ENCHILADAS

20 corn tortillas, red or plain
2-3 tablespoons oil
¼ - ½ cup chili powder
1 teaspoon salt
2 15-ounce cans tomato sauce
½ cup water
1 medium onion,
     finely chopped
2 8-ounce packages monterey
     jack cheese or queso
     fresco ranchero,
     grated or crumbled
½ cup oil

Preheat oven to 400°.

In a large skillet with 2 to 3 tablespoons oil, add chili powder and fry for 3 or 4 minutes over low heat. Add salt and tomato sauce and simmer for 10 to 15 minutes. Add water. Sauce should not be too thick.

For Filling: In a small bowl, mix cheese and chopped onions together and set aside. In a small skillet, heat ½ cup oil to warm. Have a small shallow dish with lukewarm water and chili sauce in another bowl warmed side by side. Dip tortillas very quickly in water, put in oil briefly to soften and transfer to sauce. Remove with spatula to plate. Do only about 6 at a time. In a 9x13-inch baking dish, place about 2 tablespoons of onion and cheese mixture on tortilla and roll up. After assembling the first 6 tortillas, dip 6 more and fill until each batch of 6 enchiladas are finished. If sauce becomes too thick, add small amount of water and stir. Spoon remaining sauce over enchiladas. Cover with remaining cheese. (Should you run out of cheese, grate more. Do not hesitate to mix cheeses). Bake for 15 minutes. These can be prepared early in the day and covered with plastic wrap, refrigerated until ready for serving. Allow to come to room temperature before baking.

YIELD: 10 servings or 20 cheese enchiladas.

GREEN ENCHILADAS
For Recipe Page - See Index.

GOURMET CRAB QUICHE

Crab Filling

2 tablespoons minced shallots
  or green onions
3 tablespoons butter
1 cup cooked fresh or
  canned crab
  salt & pepper to taste
2 tablespoons dry vermouth
3 eggs
1 cup whipping cream
1 tablespoon tomato paste
¼ teaspoon salt
  pinch of pepper
¼ cup sliced almonds
  for garnish

Short Pastry

2 cups all purpose flour
½ teaspoon salt
2 pinches sugar
½ cup butter, chilled & cut
  into ½-inch bits
3 tablespoons chilled
  vegetable shortening
5-6 tablespoons cold water

For Crab Filling: In a large saucepan over moderate heat, cook shallots in butter until tender. Add cooked crab and cook for 2 minutes. Sprinkle with salt and pepper. Add vermouth and boil 1 to 2 minutes. Set aside and allow to cool slightly. In a bowl, beat eggs and add whipping cream, tomato paste, salt and pepper. Pour egg mixture into crab mixture and blend. Set aside.

For Short Pastry: In a mixing bowl, add flour, salt, sugar, ½ cup butter and vegetable shortening. Rub flour, butter and shortening together rapidly with finger tips until broken into pieces the size of oatmeal flakes. Do not overdo this step as the butter and shortening will be blended more thoroughly later. Add water and blend quickly. Gather dough into a mass and place on a floured surface. Knead thoroughly until all butter and shortening are blended. Knead into a smooth ball. Wrap in waxed paper and chill for at least 1 hour or overnight.
Preheat oven to 400°.
Roll dough into a 10-inch circle to fit a standard quiche pan. Place dough into quiche pan being careful not to stretch dough. Prick bottom of dough being careful not to go through the pastry to the quiche pan. To keep sides of pastry from collapsing and the bottom from puffing up, butter one side of a piece of foil and lay on top of pastry. Weight down the foil with dry beans or another pie pan. Bake in middle level of oven for 8 to 9 minutes until the pastry is set. Remove the beans and foil. Bake 2 to 3 more minutes. Preheat oven to 375°.
To Assemble Crab Quiche: Pour crab mixture into baked pastry shell. Sprinkle with almonds on top. Bake for 25 to 30 minutes.
YIELD: 8 to 10 servings.

VARIATION: *Substitute lobster, shrimp or scallops for crab.*

SWISS PIE

1   cup cracker crumbs,
        finely crushed
¼   cup butter, melted
6   bacon slices, fried,
        drained, and crumbled
        retaining drippings
1   cup chopped onion
8   ounces natural swiss
        cheese, shredded
2   eggs, slightly beaten
¾   cup sour cream
½   teaspoon salt
      dash of pepper
½   cup shredded sharp processed
        cheddar cheese

Preheat oven to 375°.

In a bowl, combine cracker crumbs and melted butter. In an 8-inch pie plate, press the buttered cracker crumbs mixture on the bottom and sides. In a skillet, saute onion in bacon drippings until tender but not brown. In a bowl, combine crumbled bacon, onion, swiss cheese, eggs, sour cream, salt and dash of pepper. Into cracker crumbs pie plate, pour egg mixture and sprinkle with cheddar cheese on top. Bake 25 to 30 minutes or until knife inserted in center comes out clean. Let stand 5 to 10 minutes before cutting.

YIELD: 4 to 6 servings.

Ever since the first gusher came in at Spindletop, the Lone Star State has been oil country. South Texas has been blessed with its fair share of black gold. Pump jacks dot the country- side and are nicknamed "Texas Grasshoppers."

Something incredible happens in La Villita on four consecutive nights in April. We call it "A Night In Old San Antonio," or NIOSA. Native San Antonians and visitors to our beautiful city come to this party in unbelievable numbers. La Villita, which means "little town," is filled to overflowing. Food, drink, music and dancing from the rich blend of San Antonio cultures highlight each evening. "A Night In Old San Antonio" is a most memorable occasion.

ARTICHOKE SPINACH DELIGHT

3-4 10-ounce packages frozen,
    chopped spinach
8   tablespoons butter or
    margarine
1   medium onion, finely
    chopped
1   pint sour cream
½   cup grated parmesan cheese
1   teaspoon salt
2   14-ounce cans artichoke
    hearts, well drained
1   6-ounce can french
    fried onion rings

Preheat oven to 375°.
Cook spinach and drain very well. In a skillet, melt butter and saute onion. In a mixing bowl, combine sour cream, parmesan cheese, onion and salt. To this add the spinach and mix well. In a 9x13-inch oven-proof casserole, line the bottom with the artichokes. Pour the spinach mixture over the artichokes. Top with french fried onion rings. Bake for 30 minutes.

YIELD: 8 to 10 servings.

VARIATION: Put an artichoke in a ramekin or custard cup and add spinach mixture topped with onion rings and bake for about 15 minutes.

ARTICHOKE MUSHROOM VELVET

2   9-ounce packages frozen
    artichoke hearts or
    2 14-ounce cans,
    cooked & drained
1   6-ounce can broiled, sliced
    mushrooms, drained
1   envelope chicken gravy mix
¼   teaspoon crushed thyme
¼   teaspoon crushed marjoram
4   ounces processed
    swiss cheese, diced,
    about 1 cup
1   tablespoon dry white wine
1   cup soft bread
    crumbs, buttered

Preheat oven to 350°.
Combine artichokes and mushrooms and divide among 6 ramekins or place in a 2-quart casserole. In a small saucepan, prepare chicken gravy mix according to package directions. Remove from heat; add thyme, marjoram and cheese; stir just till cheese melts. Add wine; pour over vegetables. Top with a wreath of buttered crumbs. Bake uncovered 25 to 30 minutes. This is an elegant side dish for a dinner party or for a ladies luncheon. It is better prepared a day ahead and stored in refrigerator until cooked at party time.

YIELD: 6 servings.

FRIED AVOCADOS
For Recipe Page - See Index.

SWEET AND SOUR ASPARAGUS

⅔ cup white vinegar
½ cup sugar
½ teaspoon salt
1 teaspoon whole cloves
3 sticks cinnamon
1 tablespoon celery seed
½ cup water
2 large cans asparagus
     spears, drained
1 egg, hard boiled,
     sliced or crumbled

In a saucepan, mix and bring to a boil vinegar, sugar, salt, cloves, cinnamon, celery seed and water. Place the asparagus in a flat baking dish and pour the boiling hot liquid over it. Cover and store in refrigerator for 24 hours. To serve, pour off liquid and garnish with hard-cooked egg.

YIELD: 8 servings.

FRIED ASPARAGUS PARMESAN
For Recipe Page - See Index.

HOLIDAY ASPARAGUS

2 10-ounce packages frozen
     asparagus spears
½ teaspoon seasoned salt
¼ teaspoon pepper
1 8-ounce can water chestnuts,
     sliced & drained
1 4-ounce can sliced
     mushrooms, drained
1 2-ounce jar diced pimiento
1 egg, hard-cooked & sliced
2 cups medium white sauce
1 teaspoon worcestershire sauce

Preheat oven to 350°.
Thaw asparagus and drain well. Cut spears in 1-inch lengths. Place asparagus in a buttered 8x12-inch baking dish. Sprinkle with salt and pepper to taste. Layer water chestnuts, mushrooms, pimiento and egg over asparagus. To medium white sauce add worcestershire, salt and pepper. Pour white sauce over vegetables. Dish may be refrigerated for convenience. Remove from refrigerator and let stand 30 minutes. Bake uncovered for 25 minutes.

YIELD: 6 to 8 servings.

ORANGE BUTTER FOR ASPARAGUS

⅓ cup butter
2 tablespoons grated orange rind
¼ cup orange juice
1½ pounds fresh asparagus
     mandarin orange sections
       for garnish

Combine butter, orange rind and juice in a saucepan. Bring to a boil. Reduce heat and simmer until mixture is reduced by half and slightly thickened. Stir occasionally. Set aside and keep warm. Cook asparagus in small amount of water 6 to 8 minutes until crisp and tender. Drain and arrange on serving dish. Pour orange sauce over asparagus. Garnish with mandarin orange sections.

YIELD: 6 servings.

CHINESE STIR-FRY BROCCOLI WITH MUSHROOMS

5   slices ginger
4   tablespoons oil (peanut
      or corn oil)
1¼ pounds fresh broccoli
1   7-ounce can mushrooms,
      drained
1   teaspoon garlic powder
1   tablespoon sherry
1½ tablespoons bottled
      oyster sauce
1   tablespoon cornstarch &
      enough water
      to make a paste

Rub bottom of wok with ginger and then add oil which prevents sticking. Peel off hard scales of broccoli and cut into ½-inch stalks with flowerets and slice ¼-inch thick. Heat oil in wok or large frying pan. Add ginger. Stir fry broccoli for two minutes. Add garlic and sherry. Stir and pour in oyster sauce and mushrooms. Stir and lower heat. Cover wok and cook (not simmer) for 5 minutes. Add cornstarch paste and stir another minute. Serve immediately.

YIELD: 4 to 6 servings.

BROCCOLI CROWN WITH CHERRY TOMATOES
For Recipe Page - See Index.

RITZ CHEESE BROCCOLI

¾   cup mayonnaise
1   8-ounce package sharp
      cheddar cheese, grated
1   egg
1   medium onion, chopped
1   7-ounce can mushrooms,
      drained (optional)
1   16-ounce package frozen
      chopped broccoli,
      thawed & undrained
36 Ritz crackers, crushed
¼   cup butter or margarine,
      melted

Preheat oven to 350°.
In a bowl, mix mayonnaise, cheese, egg, onion and mushrooms. Add broccoli and place in 2-quart casserole dish. Top with crushed Ritz crackers and pour melted butter over top. Bake for 45 minutes. This can be frozen for several days in advance until ready to bake. Thaw at room temperature then bake.

YIELD: 8 servings.

AUNT BESSIE'S SWEET AND SOUR BAKED BEANS

¾ cup brown sugar, packed
1 teaspoon dry mustard
   garlic powder to taste
½ teaspoon salt
½ cup vinegar
4 large onions, cut in rings
8 bacon slices, fried
      crisp & crumbled
2 15-ounce cans cooked dry
      butter beans, drained
1 16-ounce can baby green
      lima beans, drained
1 16-ounce can red kidney
      beans, drained
1 16-ounce can baked beans,
      undrained (we
      recommend B&M)
4 bacon slices, uncooked

Preheat oven to 350°.

In a bowl, combine sugar, mustard, garlic powder, salt and vinegar. In a skillet, add this mixture and the onion rings. Cover and simmer for 20 minutes. Add beans, crumbled bacon and mix well. Pour into 3-quart casserole and arrange 4 uncooked strips of bacon on top. Bake 1 hour.

YIELD: 12 to 16 servings.

COWBOY BEANS
For Recipe Page - See Index.

FRIJOLES
(Pinto Beans)

1 pound dried pinto beans
¼ pound salt pork, cubed
1 clove garlic, minced
1 teaspoon fresh cilantro or
      1 teaspoon dried
      coriander
1 teaspoon cumin
1 onion, chopped
1 tomato, chopped
   picante sauce

Check beans for little rocks, cover with water and soak overnight. Rinse and cover with about 4 inches of water in a large pot. Add salt pork, garlic, cilantro and cumin. Cook slowly in a covered pot for 3 hours or until beans are cooked to taste. Check from time to time to see if additional water is needed. Top with onion, tomato and picante sauce just before serving if desired.

YIELD: 4 to 6 servings.

*VARIATION: **Using Ham Hocks.***
Two or 3 ham hocks may be substituted for salt pork. Add ham hocks to beans and cook. Before serving, remove ham hocks to a cutting board. Dice ham, discard bone and return ham to bean pot.

STUFFED TOMATOES

6	fresh tomatoes, cut in halves
⅛	teaspoon salt
⅛	teaspoon pepper
2	cloves garlic, minced
3	tablespoons minced green onions
4	tablespoons minced parsley
½	cup dry bread crumbs, finely crushed
¼	cup olive oil

Preheat oven to 400°.
Wash and clean tomatoes removing stems. Clean out juice and seeds. Sprinkle with salt and pepper. In a bowl, blend garlic, green onion, parsley and bread crumbs. Fill each tomato half with 1 to 2 teaspoons of mixture. Sprinkle a few drops olive oil on each tomato. Arrange in a large ovenproof casserole. Bake 10 to 15 minutes.

YIELD: 8 to 10 servings.

VARIATION: Sprinkle parmesan cheese and bread crumbs on top.

RED CABBAGE AND APPLES

3	tablespoons bacon drippings
4	cups shredded red cabbage
2	cups cubed, unpeeled apples
¼	cup brown sugar
¼	cup vinegar
1¼	teaspoons salt
	pepper to taste
¼	cup water

In a large skillet, heat bacon drippings. Add the cabbage, apples, brown sugar, vinegar, salt and pepper. Add water and cover tightly to steam for 5 minutes. Simmer until cabbage and apples are crisp and tender.

YIELD: 6 servings.

LAYERED CABBAGE CASSEROLE

1	medium size head cabbage
¼	cup butter
¼	cup all-purpose flour
½	teaspoon salt
¼	teaspoon pepper
2	cups evaporated milk
¼	cup chopped green pepper
¼	cup chopped onion
⅔	cup shredded cheddar cheese
½	cup mayonnaise
3	tablespoons chili sauce

Preheat oven to 350°.
Cut cabbage into small wedges. Cook in boiling water until tender. Drain and place cabbage in a 13x9x2-inch dish and set aside. In a small saucepan, melt butter and stir in flour, salt and pepper. Gradually stir in milk. Cook over medium heat until thickened, stirring constantly. Pour sauce over cabbage. Bake for 20 minutes. In a mixing bowl, combine green pepper, onion, cheese, mayonnaise and chili sauce and mix well. Spoon over cabbage. Return to oven and bake an additional 20 minutes.

YIELD: 8 servings.

CASTROVILLE STUFFED CABBAGE

In 1843, Henri Castro, an empresario of the Republic of Texas, received contracts and land grants to establish 600 families in two communities. He recruited colonists from France of Alsatian origin who spoke German. They settled Castroville which today is a thriving community 25 miles west of San Antonio. Cabbage dishes were favorites among early Texas pioneers. Often in the winter months, it was the only vegetable available.

1	large cabbage head
1	egg, beaten
1	8-ounce package saltine crackers, finely crushed
	salt & pepper to taste
¼	cup chopped onion
3	tablespoons butter
1	cheese cloth

In a colander, wash the cabbage head removing the outer leaves carefully for stuffing later. Drain and set aside. Shred remainder of cabbage head. Cook in water until tender and drain. In a large bowl, combine the cooked cabbage, egg, crackers, onion, salt and pepper. Take a cheese cloth and cover bottom of bowl. Put the big outer leaves in the bowl to form a cup. Fill the leaves with the prepared stuffing. Put another leaf or two on top and tie the cheese cloth together. Put in steamer, cover and steam approximately 20 to 30 minutes until soft. Remove from pan and put in bowl. Pour melted butter on top. Serve immediately.

YIELD: 4 to 6 servings.

CARROTS WITH HORSERADISH GLAZE

2	pounds carrots, scraped & diagonally cut into ½-inch slices
¼	cup butter or margarine
⅓	cup honey
2	tablespoons prepared horseradish

In a saucepan with a small amount of salted water, cook carrots covered for 18 to 20 minutes or until tender. Drain. In a large saucepan, melt butter over low heat and stir in honey and horseradish. Gently stir in carrots. Cook until thoroughly heated.

YIELD: 6 to 8 servings.

CARROTS LYONNAISE

1   chicken bouillon cube
½   cup boiling water
6   medium carrots, cut into
        3-inch strips
3   medium onions, sliced
4   tablespoons butter or
        margarine
¾   cup water
1   tablespoon all-purpose flour
¼   teaspoon salt
    dash of pepper

Dissolve bouillon cube in boiling water. Add carrots, cover and cook 10 minutes. Saute onion in butter and add ¾ cup water. Cook covered 15 minutes stirring occasionally. Add the carrots. Combine flour, salt and pepper. Add enough liquid from vegetables to dissolve flour and add to vegetables. Simmer uncovered about 10 minutes or until carrots are tender.

YIELD: 6 servings.

LEMON BASIL CARROTS

1   pound carrots, cleaned
        & sliced
2   tablespoons butter
1   tablespoon lemon juice
½   teaspoon garlic salt
½   teaspoon basil, crushed
⅛   teaspoon pepper

Partially cook the carrots in either boiling water or microwave. In a saucepan, melt butter and stir in the lemon juice, garlic salt, basil and pepper. Add the carrots and cook until tender.

YIELD: 4 servings.

CELERY AND CORN

¼   cup butter
2   cups celery, diagonally sliced
2   tablespoons pimiento
1   10-ounce package frozen
        sweet corn, cooked
½   teaspoon salt

In a saucepan, melt butter and add celery. Cover and cook for 5 minutes. Add corn, pimiento and salt and heat thoroughly. This recipe freezes well after cooking.

YIELD: 4 servings.

CHILES EN FRIO
(Cold Peppers)

Stuffed poblano peppers are very popular in San Antonio. They can be served hot or cold as a side dish, appetizer, main dish or salad. No *"fiesta"* would be complete without stuffed peppers to enjoy. Ole!

6	poblano peppers, roasted, peeled & deveined
	white vinegar for soaking
1	large onion, thinly sliced
2	6½-ounce cans tuna, drained & flaked
1	small tomato, seeds removed, juiced & diced
2	scallions, finely chopped
1	diced avocado, optional
	salt & pepper to taste
1	tablespoon mayonnaise
	shredded lettuce, marinated onion & sour cream for garnish

In a bowl, soak peppers in vinegar several hours or overnight with onion.

For Filling: Mix together tuna, tomato, scallions, avocado, salt, pepper and mayonnaise. Remove peppers from vinegar and dry on paper towels. Stuff with tuna mixture. Serve on a bed of shredded lettuce. Top with marinated onion and sour cream. Serve for lunch with cold gazpacho soup and hot bolillos.

YIELD: 6 servings.

CHILES RELLENOS
(Stuffed Peppers)

SPICY MEXICAN PICKLED VEGETABLES
For Recipe Page - See Index.

MEXICAN CORN PUDDING

1	cup yellow cornmeal
1	cup grated cheddar cheese
1	teaspoon baking powder
1	teaspoon salt
5	tablespoons melted butter or bacon drippings
1	16-ounce can cream style corn, undrained
2	eggs, beaten
2	cups milk
1	cup chopped green chiles, adjust to taste
	garlic salt to taste

Preheat oven to 350°.

In a large mixing bowl, combine cornmeal, cheese, baking powder, salt, butter, cream corn, eggs, milk, green chiles and garlic salt. In a greased 9x13-inch baking dish, pour batter. Bake 1 hour uncovered.

YIELD: 12 to 15 servings.

HONDO CORN CASSEROLE

"Hondo" in Spanish means *"deep."* In 1689, Spanish Commander Alonzo de Leon, on an expedition sent by the King of Spain to name the territory, came to a deep valley filled with water and named it "Hondo." Later in 1840 a permanent settlement was established. Located 41 miles west of San Antonio, Hondo's main industries include corn, cattle and the national weather service for all of South Texas.

1   16-ounce can cream-style corn
1   cup grated sharp cheddar cheese
1   16-ounce can whole kernel corn, drained
1   cup Ritz crackers, crushed
1   onion, chopped
1   egg
3   tablespoons sugar
⅔   cup evaporated milk
¼   pound butter or margarine
     salt & pepper to taste
     tabasco to taste

Preheat oven to 350°.
In a mixing bowl, mix all ingredients together. Bake in a 3-quart ovenproof casserole for 50 to 60 minutes.

YIELD: 6 servings.

VARIATIONS: Add green chiles or bell pepper to taste.

CREAMED CHEESE CORN

1   8-ounce package cream cheese, softened
⅔   cup milk
2   tablespoons butter or margarine
1   teaspoon onion salt
2   17-ounce cans whole kernel corn, drained

In a saucepan, combine cream cheese, milk, butter and onion salt. Cook over low heat, stirring often until cheese melts completely. Add corn and stir constantly until thoroughly heated.

YIELD: 8 to 10 servings.

SAVORY GREEN BEANS

1½ pounds fresh green beans
¼   cup cooking oil
1   clove garlic, minced
1   tablespoon chopped onion
¾   cup diced green pepper
¼   cup boiling water
½   teaspoon salt
1   teaspoon basil
½   cup parmesan cheese, grated

Wash and trim ends off beans and cut into 1½-inch pieces. In a saucepan, heat oil and garlic. Add onion and green pepper. Cook for 3 minutes. Add beans, water, salt and basil. Cover and simmer for 15 minutes or longer until beans are tender. Stir in ¼ cup parmesan cheese. Turn into serving dish and sprinkle with remaining cheese.

YIELD: 6 servings.

GREEN BEAN BUNDLES

1   16-ounce can whole
        green beans (we
        recommend Blue Lake)
8 - 10 slices bacon, cut in half
        French dressing

Place 7 or 8 green beans into a bundle and wrap with half slice of bacon. Secure ends with a toothpick. Place bundles into a baking dish and pour French dressing over bundles to marinate. Cover and refrigerate overnight.
Preheat oven to 350°.
Bake until bacon is cooked. Lift onto platter with slotted spoon. Serve warm.

YIELD: 6 servings.

BACON FRIED GREEN BEANS

6   bacon strips
1-2 medium onions, sliced
1   pound green beans, snapped

In a skillet, fry bacon until crisp. Remove bacon and crumble. Stir fry onion in remaining bacon drippings until tender. Add green beans to skillet and stir fry until tender. Do not overcook. Remove beans and onions from skillet and serve with crumbled bacon.

YIELD: 6 servings.

VARIATION: Add ¼ cup sliced almonds and stir fry.

EGGPLANT PARMIGIANA
For Recipe Page - See Index.

EGGPLANT PIE

This is a great side dish for spaghetti or any pasta dish!

1   eggplant
4   bacon strips
1   medium onion, chopped
3-4 cloves garlic, chopped
1   egg
        salt & pepper to taste
⅛   cup fresh grated parmesan
        cheese (use more if
        eggplant is large)

Preheat oven to 350°.
Peel eggplant. Cut up and boil until tender. While eggplant is cooking, cut up bacon and fry in a skillet with onion and garlic until done. Drain eggplant. Put in mixing bowl and mash. Add bacon, onion, garlic and egg. Mix thoroughly. Add salt, pepper and parmesan cheese. The eggplant mixture should be the consistency of thick paste, but still have plenty of moisture. Pour into a greased 9-inch pie plate. Bake for 10 to 15 minutes.

YIELD: 8 servings.

VARIATION: Chop fresh hot pepper and add to casserole or top with cheddar cheese strips.

BAKED MUSHROOMS IN SOUR CREAM

1	pound fresh large mushrooms, remove stems & slice
2	tablespoons butter
1	cup sour cream
2	tablespoons flour
	salt & pepper to taste
½	cup grated cheddar cheese
½	cup grated monterey jack cheese

Preheat oven to 325°.

In a skillet, saute mushrooms in butter and drain. Place in a small baking dish. In a small saucepan, combine sour cream, flour, salt and pepper. Heat but do not boil, stirring until sauce is smooth. Pour sauce over mushrooms and top with cheeses. Bake for 15 minutes.

YIELD: 4 servings.

GLAZED ONIONS

A delicious side dish when served with baked ham.

1½	pounds very small white onions (substitute canned or large onions, cut into 4-6 pieces each)
	salted water
⅓	cup butter
⅓	cup brown sugar, packed
¼	cup maple flavored syrup
¼	cup slivered almonds

In a saucepan, boil onions in salted water until tender about 20 to 25 minutes. Drain well. (Canned onions do not need cooking; just drain well.) In a skillet, melt butter and sugar together. Stir in maple flavored syrup and almonds. Add onions and let simmer 15 minutes.

YIELD: 6 servings.

BAKED ONIONS

12	medium to large onions, cut crosswise into halves
4	tablespoons butter
4	teaspoons sugar
1	teaspoon dry mustard
½	teaspoon salt
	paprika

Preheat oven to 350°.

In a saucepan, boil onions gently for 15 minutes and drain. Arrange cut side down in a greased 3-quart ovenproof casserole. Melt butter and blend with other ingredients. Pour 1 tablespoon of mixture over each onion. Sprinkle with paprika. Bake covered for 45 minutes.

YIELD: 12 servings.

AUSTRIAN SPINACH SOUFFLE

6	tablespoons butter
8	tablespoons flour
2	teaspoons salt
½	teaspoon pepper
¼	teaspoon nutmeg
2	cups milk
2	cups grated cheddar cheese
2	10-ounce packages frozen spinach, well drained
6	eggs, separated

Preheat oven to 325°.
In a saucepan, melt butter and blend in flour and spices. Add milk, stir until blended and thick. Add cheese to mixture and stir until well blended. Stir in egg yolks and spinach. In a bowl, beat egg whites until stiff and fold into spinach mixture. In a 9x13x2-inch ovenproof casserole, pour the spinach mixture. Bake for 30 minutes. Cool and cut in squares. Reheat when needed. Can be made ahead.

YIELD: 12 servings.

SPECIAL SPINACH AU GRATIN

1	cup milk
2	tablespoons butter
2	tablespoons flour
1	8-ounce package jalapeno cheese (containing monterey jack)
2	10-ounce packages frozen spinach, cooked & drained
2	cans oyster pieces
1	14-ounce can artichokes, water packed halves, drained
1	can water chestnuts, sliced & drained
1½	cups grated cheddar cheese for garnish

Preheat oven to 350°.
In a small saucepan, blend milk, butter and flour. When mixture thickens, add the jalapeno cheese and stir constantly until cheese melts. In large mixing bowl, combine cooked spinach, oyster pieces, artichokes and chestnuts. To this add the cheese sauce. In a buttered 9x13x2-inch ovenproof casserole, pour the spinach and cheese sauce mixtures. Sprinkle with grated cheese. Bake 30 minutes.

YIELD: 8 to 12 servings.

SPINACH ITALIANO

2	pounds fresh spinach
3	tablespoons butter
1	clove garlic, chopped
3	tablespoons olive oil
	salt & pepper to taste
¼	teaspoon cayenne pepper
	grated parmesan to taste
1	tablespoon butter, melted

In a large saucepan, parboil spinach 30 seconds. Drain thoroughly and set aside. In a skillet, heat 3 tablespoons butter, garlic and oil. Add salt, pepper and cayenne pepper. Cook over low heat 5 minutes. In ovenproof baking casserole, put the spinach and the butter mixture. Sprinkle with parmesan cheese and the remaining 1 tablespoon butter. Brown under broiler until cheese is bubbly, 2 to 5 minutes.

YIELD: 4 to 6 servings.

SQUASH CASSEROLE

A great substitute for dressing at Thanksgiving.

1½-2 pounds yellow squash
    salt
1   package stuffing mix
      (we recommend
      Pepperidge Farm)
1   small can chopped pimientos
2   small onions, chopped
1   cup sour cream
1   10¾-ounce can cream of
      chicken soup
4   small carrots, grated
8   tablespoons butter or
      margarine

Preheat oven to 350°.
In a large saucepan, cook squash in boiling salted water and drain. Mash squash and mix with half bag of stuffing mix and pimientos, onions, sour cream, soup and carrots. Melt butter and mix with remaining stuffing mix and set aside. In a large ovenproof casserole, pour the squash mixture. Top with the buttered stuffing. Bake 30 minutes.

YIELD: 8 to 12 servings.

SQUASH AND HOMINY MEDLEY

2   pounds yellow squash
1   large onion, chopped
4   tablespoons butter
½   cup boiling water
2   cans hominy, drained
½   pound sharp cheese, grated
2   jalapeno peppers,
      seeded & chopped
1½ cups sour cream
1   teaspoon salt
    corn chips, crushed
      (we recommend Doritos)

Preheat oven to 325°.
In a large saucepan, cook squash, onion and butter over low heat until tender in boiling water. Add the hominy, half of grated cheese, jalapenos, sour cream and salt to the cooked squash and mix. In a greased ovenproof 3-quart casserole, pour the squash mixture. Top with remaining cheese and sprinkle with crushed corn chips. Bake 1 hour.

YIELD: 8 to 10 servings.

CALABACITAS CASSEROLE
(Mexican Squash Casserole)

4-5 calabacitas squash
1   onion, sliced
2-3 fresh tomatoes, chopped
8   tablespoons butter
1   8-ounce package mozzarella
      cheese, grated
    salt & pepper to taste

Preheat oven to 350°.
Wash and trim squash and slice crosswise, then cut wheels in half and place in large ovenproof casserole. Top with onion and tomatoes. Dot with butter. Top with grated cheese. Bake covered for 20 to 30 minutes until squash is crisp and tender. Remove cover and lightly brown cheese.

YIELD: 6 to 8 servings.

CALABAZA CON PUERCO
(Squash with Pork)

1½ pounds lean pork, cut into
    1-inch squares
2 tablespoons vegetable oil
1 pound calabaza (or squash),
    cut into 1-inch chunks
1 large onion, minced
2 cloves garlic, minced
1 16-ounce can tomatoes
1 cup whole kernel corn,
    fresh or canned, drained
1 teaspoon comino (cumin)
1 teaspoon salt
1 teaspoon black pepper
  hot cooked rice, optional

In a dutch oven, cook pork in hot oil until browned. Add remaining ingredients except rice. Cover. Simmer 30 to 40 minutes or until squash is tender. Serve over hot, cooked rice.

YIELD: 6 servings.

COUNTRY CLUB SQUASH

8 medium yellow squash
½ cup chopped onion
1 8-ounce carton sour cream
½ teaspoon salt
    (add more to taste)
¼ teaspoon pepper
¼ teaspoon basil
1 cup soft bread crumbs
½ cup grated medium-sharp
    cheddar cheese
⅓ cup butter or
    margarine, melted
½ teaspoon paprika
8 bacon slices,
    cooked & crumbled

Preheat oven to 300°.
Wash squash and trim off ends. In a large saucepan, cook squash and onion in boiling salted water until tender. Drain and coarsely mash. Combine squash, sour cream, salt, pepper and basil. In a greased 2-quart oven-proof casserole, pour the squash mixture. In a bowl, combine the bread crumbs, cheese, butter and paprika. Sprinkle over squash and top with bacon. Bake 30 minutes.

YIELD: 6 to 8 servings.

ZUCCHINI STUFFED WITH CRABMEAT

4-8 zucchini squash
2   tablespoons butter, melted
1   tablespoon flour
1   cup whipping cream
½   cup parmesan cheese
1   pound snow crabmeat, chopped
½   teaspoon salt
¼   teaspoon white pepper
2   green onions, chopped
¼   teaspoon paprika

Preheat oven to 350°.
Wash zucchini and split down middle end to end. Spoon out seeds, fiber and discard. Set aside zucchini. In a medium saucepan, combine butter and flour and cook 2 minutes. Add whipping cream and cook another 2 minutes. Add parmesan cheese stirring constantly and cook until all ingredients are smoothly blended. Add crabmeat, salt, pepper and green onions. Cook for 5 more minutes. Remove filling from heat and fill zucchini. In a large ovenproof casserole, place filled zucchini and sprinkle tops with paprika. Add half cup hot water to casserole and bake for 30 minutes or until zucchini are tender.
YIELD: 4 to 8 servings.

ZUCCHINI DELICIOUS

3   bacon slices, chopped
1   cup onion, chopped
3½ cups zucchini, sliced (or yellow squash)
2   tomatoes, sliced or 10-ounce can whole tomatoes
¾   teaspoon salt
⅛   teaspoon pepper
1   tablespoon picante sauce (optional)

In a large skillet, fry bacon slightly. Add onions and cook until tender. Add zucchini, tomatoes, salt, pepper and picante sauce. Cook covered until zucchini is tender and most of sauce absorbed about 20 to 25 minutes.
YIELD: 6 servings.

VARIATION: Add ½ teaspoon comino (cumin) to mixture, 1 cup grated cheddar cheese and ½ cup bread crumbs mixed with 2 tablespoons butter for topping.

BROILED ZUCCHINI

8   small zucchini squash
8   tablespoons butter
1   cup grated parmesan cheese

Preheat oven to broil or 550°.
Wash zucchini and cut off both ends. Cut each zucchini in half lengthwise. Using fork tines, draw deep grooves down the length of the cut surface. Spread butter over the cut surface and sprinkle with parmesan cheese on top. In a broiling pan, place the squash under broiler and watch carefully until cheese is browned. Squash will be crisp.
YIELD: 4 to 8 servings.

VARIATION: If a more cooked squash is preferred, parboil before broiling.

SPECIAL OCCASION VEGETABLE CASSEROLE

2   10-ounce packages frozen green beans
1   10-ounce package frozen lima beans
1   10-ounce package frozen green peas
1   medium onion, chopped
1   green pepper, chopped
½   pint whipping cream, whipped
1½ cups mayonnaise
1   8-ounce can grated parmesan cheese

Preheat oven to 350°.
Cook all vegetables as directed on package. Let cool. In a mixing bowl, combine onion, green pepper, whipping cream, mayonnaise and half the parmesan cheese. In a greased 8x12-inch ovenproof baking dish, place the cooked green beans, limas, and peas. Pour the sauce over the vegetables and sprinkle with an additional 4 ounces of parmesan cheese. Bake for 30 minutes until brown.

YIELD: 16 servings.

PINEAPPLE CASSEROLE

This favorite is served as a side dish with ham on Easter Sunday.

2   tablespoons flour
½   cup sugar
3   eggs, beaten
1   20-ounce can crushed pineapple, undrained
8   tablespoons butter or margarine, melted
6   bread slices (white or whole wheat), cubed

Preheat oven to 325°.
In a mixing bowl, mix flour and sugar. Add beaten eggs, pineapple, butter and blend. In a lightly greased 9x9-inch ovenproof baking dish, place the cubed bread in the bottom. Pour the pineapple mixture over the bread. Bake uncovered for 30 to 40 minutes. Serve warm in baking dish.

YIELD: 8 to 10 servings.

Recipe can be doubled using a 9x15-inch baking dish.

One of the most common varieties of cactus in South Texas is the "Prickly Pear." It is known for its sharp thorns, lovely blossoms and juicy apples. Jellies, relishes and sweet-wines are made from varying parts of the Prickly Pear. A similar form of cactus is served as a side dish in many Mexican homes.

CRANBERRIES IN CRUST

This cranberry side dish is delicious served with ham or turkey.

2	cups fresh cranberries
½	cup sugar
½	cup chopped nuts
2	eggs
1	cup sugar
1	cup flour
½	cup butter or margarine, melted
¼	cup shortening, melted

Preheat oven to 325°.
Grease a 10-inch pie plate. Spread cranberries over bottom of pie plate. Sprinkle with ½ cup sugar and nuts. In a bowl, beat eggs well and add 1 cup sugar gradually. Beat until mixed. Add flour, melted butter and shortening and beat well. Pour mixture over top of cranberries. Bake 60 minutes. Cut in wedges and serve with ham or turkey.

YIELD: 8 to 10 servings.

ZESTY FRUIT COMPOTE

1	8-ounce can pineapple chunks, drained
1	16-ounce can peach slices, drained
1	16-ounce can pear slices, drained
1	16-ounce jar maraschino cherries, drained
½	cup brown sugar, firmly packed
8	tablespoons butter
1½-2	tablespoons prepared mustard

Preheat oven to 325°.
In a 12x8x2-inch baking dish, combine drained fruit and set aside. In a small saucepan, combine brown sugar, butter and mustard. Cook over medium heat, stirring constantly until smooth. Pour over fruit and bake uncovered 20 minutes until thoroughly heated. Serve warm.

YIELD: 8 servings.

VARIATION: Add ⅓ cup coarsely chopped pecans, toasted.

ORANGE-PECAN BAKED APPLES

6	medium baking apples, cored
¼	cup orange marmalade
2	tablespoons finely chopped pecans
	ground cinnamon
	ground nutmeg

Preheat oven to 350°.
In a shallow baking dish, place apples and add water to cover bottom of dish. In a bowl, combine marmalade and pecans and mix well. Fill center of apples with marmalade mixture. Sprinkle with cinnamon and nutmeg. Bake 1 hour uncovered or until tender.

YIELD: 6 servings.

POTATO PANCAKES

Potatoes were a favorite of the early German settlers.   Potato pancakes topped with applesauce were served with homemade sausage.

6	medium potatoes
	ice water
3	eggs, beaten
1	small onion, grated
¾	cup all-purpose flour
2	teaspoons salt
	oil for frying

Peel potatoes, grate and put into a large bowl of ice water. Set aside. In another mixing bowl, add eggs, onion, flour and salt. Pour water from grated potatoes and place on paper towels, removing excess liquid from potatoes by pressing. Add potatoes to egg mixture and blend completely. In a large skillet, heat a small amount of oil over medium heat. Spoon a tablespoon of batter into pan and spread into round circles. Brown on one side and then on the other side. Remove from pan and drain on paper towels. Serve with hot applesauce and sausage.

YIELD: 12 pancakes.

BAKED FLORENTINE POTATOES
For Recipe Page - See Index.

FAST AND FANCY DUCHESS POTATOES

Mashed potatoes formed into fancy shapes can add elegance to a dinner.

2	cups firm mashed potatoes
3	egg yolks
3	tablespoons butter
2	tablespoons whipping cream
	salt, pepper & nutmeg to taste
½	cup grated swiss cheese for garnish

Warm the mashed potatoes. In a bowl, combine the warmed potatoes and the egg yolks. Add the butter, cream and seasoning to taste. Pipe warm mixture onto buttered and floured baking sheet. Sprinkle with cheese and refrigerate until needed.
Preheat oven to 400°.
Bake 30 minutes or until browned. Serve immediately.

YIELD: 8 to 10 servings.

SUPREME POTATO BAKE

6-8 medium potatoes
2   cups half & half cream
      or evaporated milk
8   tablespoons margarine
½   pound Velveeta cheese
1   tablespoon salt
½   pint sour cream
      bacon bits & chopped chives
      for garnish

Preheat oven to 350°.
Peel, boil and refrigerate potatoes overnight. The next day, grate potatoes. Combine milk, margarine, cheese and salt in saucepan. Heat until cheese and butter are completely melted. Pour into grated potatoes. Pour mixture into greased 9x13-inch baking dish. Bake 40 to 45 minutes. After baking, spread with sour cream and garnish with bacon and chives.

YIELD: 12 servings.

TWICE-BAKED POTATOES

6   large baking potatoes
¼   cup milk
6   tablespoons butter
1   egg
      salt & pepper to taste
1   cup shredded cheddar cheese
3   tablespoons finely chopped
      onion
3   tablespoons chopped green
      pepper
12 bacon slices, cooked
      & crumbled

Preheat oven to 425°.
Scrub potatoes. Bake 45 to 60 minutes or until done. Cut potatoes lengthwise and scoop out potato. Mash while hot and add milk, beaten egg and butter. Beat until fluffy. Season with salt and pepper. Spoon mixture into potato shells. Top each shell with cheddar cheese, onion, green pepper and crumbled bacon bits. Bake at 350° for 15 minutes or until cheese has melted.

YIELD: 12 servings.

SAN ANTONIO-STYLE VARIATION: Substitute 1 cup shredded monterey jack cheese for cheddar cheese and add 3 tablespoons chopped jalapeno peppers.

OVEN FRIED POTATOES

3   medium potatoes
¼   cup vegetable oil
1   tablespoon grated
      parmesan cheese
½   teaspoon salt
¼   teaspoon garlic powder
¼   teaspoon paprika
¼   teaspoon pepper

Preheat oven to 375°.
Scrub potatoes. Leaving skins on potatoes, cut into ⅛-inch wedges. Place wedges slightly overlapping in a single layer in a 9x13x2-inch baking dish. Combine oil, cheese, salt, garlic, paprika and pepper, stirring well. Brush potatoes with half of oil mixture. Bake uncovered for 45 minutes, basting occasionally with remaining oil mixture.

YIELD: 4 to 6 servings.

FIESTA POTATOES

3   tablespoons butter
3   medium baking potatoes,
        unpeeled, boiled & diced
1¼   cups grated monterey
        jack cheese
1¼   cups grated cheddar cheese
⅔   cup diced tomatoes or
        1 medium tomato
2   tablespoons minced onion
2   tablespoons chopped
        green onion
     salt
½   cup diced avocado
½   cup sour cream

In a large skillet, melt butter over medium heat. Add diced potatoes and cook until browned and crisp, stirring frequently. Add cheeses, tomato and onion and stir until cheese melts. Season with salt. Gently mix in avocado. Spoon on plates. Top with sour cream and serve. Serve as a main dish or as an accompaniment to fried eggs, omelets or hamburgers.

YIELD: 4 servings.

FLUFFY POTATO CASSEROLE

2   cups mashed potatoes
1   8-ounce-package cream
        cheese, room temperature
1   small onion, finely chopped
2   eggs
2   tablespoons all-purpose flour
     salt & pepper to taste
2   2.8-ounce cans french
        fried onions

Preheat oven to 300°.
In a large mixing bowl, place the mashed potatoes and add the cream cheese, onions, eggs and flour. Beat at medium speed with electric mixer until mixture is well blended. Beat at high speed until light and fluffy. Add salt and pepper to taste. Spoon into a greased 9x9-inch baking dish. Bake uncovered for 25 minutes. Top with french fried onions and bake 10 more minutes.

YIELD: 6 to 8 servings.

If recipe is doubled, bake 1 hour in a 9x13-inch casserole and then add onions and bake 10 minutes. Cover with foil if onions start to brown too much.

NEW POTATOES WITH PARSLEY

2   pounds new potatoes
        (approximately 8
        3-inch potatoes)
     seasoned salt & pepper
        to taste
1½-2 cups medium white sauce
1½   tablespoons parsley,
        freshly snipped

Scrub potatoes well. Boil whole unpeeled potatoes until fork tender in salted boiling water or peel one circle around each potato for interest. Drain and set aside. Add fresh parsley and seasoning to heated white sauce. Pour sauce over potatoes. Serve immediately.

YIELD: 4 to 6 servings.

PRALINE SWEET POTATOES

3   cups mashed, cooked,
        fresh sweet potatoes
1   cup sugar
1   teaspoon vanilla
2   eggs, beaten
½-1 cup milk, depending on
        consistency of potato
4   tablespoons margarine,
        melted

 Topping

½-1 cup chopped pecans
½   cup flour
4   tablespoons butter
½   cup brown sugar

Preheat oven to 325°.
In a large bowl, mix sweet potatoes, sugar, vanilla, eggs, milk and margarine. In a greased 9x13x2-inch baking dish, place the sweet potato mixture. In a bowl, mix the pecans, flour, butter and brown sugar. Sprinkle over sweet potatoes. Bake for 35 minutes.
YIELD: 6 to 8 servings.

SWEET POTATO CASSEROLE

3   large sweet potatoes or
        40 ounces canned
        sweet potato
2   cups milk
4   eggs, well beaten
8   tablespoons butter or
        margarine, melted
1½ cups sugar
½   teaspoon ground cloves
½   teaspoon ground ginger
1   teaspoon ground cinnamon
½   teaspoon ground nutmeg
    crushed pineapple &
        miniature marshmallows,
        optional

Preheat oven to 350°.
Wash, peel and cook the sweet potatoes in boiling water until tender. If using canned sweet potatoes, drain. In a large bowl, mash the sweet potatoes and add butter, milk, eggs, sugar and spices blending thoroughly. In a greased 9x13x2-inch baking dish, pour the sweet potato mixture. Garnish with crushed pineapple and miniature marshmallows if desired. Bake 45 to 60 minutes.
YIELD: 10 to 12 servings.

VARIATION: Using scooped out orange shells, place sweet potato mixture in shell and garnish with marshmallows. Broil until slightly brown.

SWEET POTATO MEDLEY

1   16-ounce can apricot halves
1   16-ounce can whole sweet
     potatoes, drained &
     halved lengthwise
1¼ cups brown sugar
1½ tablespoons cornstarch
¼ teaspoon salt
⅛ teaspoon cinnamon
1   teaspoon grated orange peel
2   tablespoons butter
½ cup pecan halves

Preheat oven to 375°.
In a greased 6x9-inch glass baking dish, place sweet potatoes and apricots, reserving apricot juice (approximately 1 cup). Stir juice into combined brown sugar, cornstarch, salt, cinnamon and orange peel. Boil together 3 minutes. Add butter and pecans. Pour over potatoes and apricots. Bake uncovered for 30 minutes.

YIELD: 6 servings.

BARLEY PILAF

1½ cups pearl barley, dried
     water to cover
1   teaspoon salt
4   cups boiling water
6   tablespoons butter
1   clove garlic
3   green onions, thinly sliced
     including tops
1   10-ounce can consomme
⅓ cup minced parsley

Preheat oven to 350°.
In a saucepan, combine barley and enough water to cover and let stand 1 hour. Drain. Cook in boiling salted water about 25 minutes until tender. Drain and rinse in colander with cold water. In a skillet, brown butter. Saute garlic and green onions in browned butter. Add consomme and parsley, stirring until well mixed. In a large baking dish, mix cooked barley and butter sauce. Cover tightly. Bake 30 minutes.

YIELD: 4 to 6 servings.

EL MIRADOR RICE
(A Mexican Rice)

CURRIED RICE "BOMBAY"
For Recipe Page - See Index.

SPANISH RICE

½ cup bacon grease
1 cup long grain rice, uncooked
1 small bell pepper, chopped
1 celery stalk, diced
⅓ cup diced onion
1 8-ounce can tomato sauce
1 cup water
1 clove garlic, minced
  salt & pepper to taste

In a large skillet, heat bacon grease and add rice stirring until brown. Add bell pepper, celery, onion, tomato sauce and water. Stir until well mixed. Add salt, pepper and garlic. Simmer over low heat approximately 45 minutes. The bacon grease gives this dish a distinctive delicious flavor.

YIELD: 6 servings.

VARIATIONS:
For Mexican Rice: Add 1 teaspoon cumin and/or ½ teaspoon chili powder.
For Authentic Arroz Espanola: Add ⅛ teaspoon powdered saffron.

GREEN CHILE RICE

This rice is great with barbecue of any kind. Men especially like it.

¼ cup butter or margarine
1 cup chopped onion
4 cups freshly cooked
    white rice
2 cups sour cream
1 cup cream-style
    cottage cheese
1 large bay leaf, crumbled
½ teaspoon salt
⅛ teaspoon pepper
3 4-ounce cans green chiles,
    drained, halved
    lengthwise, leaving seeds
2 cups grated sharp
    natural cheddar cheese
  chopped parsley for garnish

Preheat oven to 375°.
In a large skillet, saute onion in hot butter until golden. Remove from heat and stir in hot rice, sour cream, cottage cheese, bay leaf, salt and pepper. Toss lightly to mix. In a greased 12x8x2-inch baking dish, layer half rice mixture in bottom and then half the chiles. Sprinkle half the cheese. Layer the remainder of the rice, remainder of chiles and the remainder of the cheese. Bake uncovered 25 minutes until bubbly and hot. Garnish with chopped parsley.

YIELD: 10 to 12 servings.

CHINESE FRIED RICE

Use two-day old rice to make this Chinese dish with leftover pork, chicken, shrimp, bacon, ham, turkey, crabmeat and/or lobster.

3-5 tablespoons oil
1   clove garlic
1   cup sliced pork or any above
       fresh meat, diced
½   cup ham, diced
½   cup celery, sliced diagonally
½   cup chinese cabbage,
       sliced diagonally
1   carrot, sliced thinly, optional
2   cups fresh bean sprouts or
       1 cup canned & drained
1   medium onion, diced
5-6 cups cooked rice, 2 days old,
       room temperature
2   eggs, beaten
2   green onions, sliced thinly
       soy sauce
       salt & Accent or MSG

In large skillet or wok, put a tablespoon oil and heat to hot. Add the garlic and pork or whatever raw meat is being used and stir fry 4 minutes. Add ham, celery, cabbage and carrot. Stir fry 4 more minutes. Remove all from skillet and set aside in large bowl. Add more oil to skillet and stir fry bean sprouts and onions until limp and almost translucent. Sprinkle with salt and remove from heat and add to meat mixture. Add more oil to skillet and stir fry cooked rice until hot and add meat mixture to skillet and continue to stir fry. Pour egg over fried rice in a circular motion. Stir and sprinkle with green onions. Serve immediately with favorite Chinese food.

YIELD:10 to 12 servings.

CELERY RICE PILAF WITH LEMON

An excellent rice dish to serve with all fish entrees!

1   small onion, chopped
1   small clove garlic,
       finely chopped
4   tablespoons margarine
       or butter
2   cups water
1   cup rice, uncooked
2   celery stalks, finely chopped
2   teaspoons instant chicken
       bouillon
2   teaspoons finely shredded
       lemon peel
½   teaspoon salt
¼   teaspoon dry mustard
⅛   teaspoon tabasco
2   tablespoons snipped parsley

In a skillet, melt margarine and cook onion and garlic until tender. Stir in water, rice, celery, chicken bouillon, lemon peel, salt, dry mustard and tabasco. Heat until boiling and cover. Simmer 14 minutes. Remove from heat. Add parsley and cover for 5 to 10 minutes.

YIELD: 6 servings.

WILD RICE CASSEROLE

1   cup grated cheddar cheese
1   cup chopped ripe olives
2   cups chopped canned
      tomatoes, undrained
1   cup mushrooms, drained
½   cup chopped onion
1   cup wild rice
½   cup oil (we
      recommend Wesson oil)
1   cup hot water
    salt & pepper to taste

Preheat oven to 350°.
In a large mixing bowl, add all ingredients except cheddar cheese and mix together. In a large greased baking dish, place mixture and top with grated cheese. Bake covered 45 to 75 minutes until rice is cooked.

YIELD: 6 to 8 servings.

PARMESAN RICE

3   tablespoons butter or
      margarine
⅔   cup rice
1⅔ cups chicken broth
¼   cup grated parmesan cheese
2   tablespoons chopped parsley
½   teaspoon salt
    pepper to taste

Preheat oven to 350°.
In a large skillet, melt butter over low heat and add rice. Cook until golden brown. Remove from heat. In a 1-quart baking casserole, place the rice mixture, chicken broth, parmesan, parsley, salt and pepper. Bake covered 50 minutes, checking at 30 minutes.

YIELD: 4 servings.

RICE AND MUSHROOMS

2   small onions, diced
8   tablespoons margarine or
      butter
5   large fresh mushrooms,
      sliced or 1 medium
      can mushrooms
1   cup raw rice
1   10-ounce can beef consomme
10 ounces water
1   clove garlic, pressed
    salt & pepper to taste

Preheat oven to 350°.
In a large skillet, brown onion in margarine. Add mushrooms and saute. Add rice, consomme, water, garlic, salt and pepper. In a greased shallow baking dish, pour rice mixture. Bake uncovered 30 minutes until rice is done. Add additional water if necessary.

YIELD: 4 servings.

BANDERA PARTY GRITS

"Cowboy Capital of the World" is the giant billboard visitors encounter when visiting Bandera 50 miles northwest of San Antonio in the Hill Country. It is named after Spanish General Bandera who defeated the Apache Indians responsible for raiding San Antonio of livestock in 1720. Translated from Spanish *"bandera"* means *"banner or flag."* Dude ranches and rodeos with real cowboys entertain hundreds of visitors each year who want to know all about Texas ranch life.

2	cups grits
8	cups water
16	ounces sharp cheddar cheese, grated
8	tablespoons butter
3	eggs, lightly beaten
1	teaspoon garlic salt
½	teaspoon tabasco
2	canned jalapeno peppers, seeded & chopped (optional)
2	tablespoons chopped pimientos (optional)

Preheat oven to 400°.
Cook grits in water according to directions on box. Place grits in a 9x13-inch baking dish and add cheese, butter and eggs. Season with garlic salt and tabasco. Add jalapenos and pimientos, if desired. Bake 30 minutes. Cut into squares and serve hot with ham or fried chicken.

YIELD: 20 servings.

SOPA DE FIDEO
(Vermicelli Medley)

6	tablespoons safflower oil
1	5½-ounce package fine vermicelli in bundles
1	tomato, chopped
1	small onion, chopped
½	bell pepper, chopped
1	clove garlic, minced
2	10¾-ounce cans beef broth, heated
	salt & pepper to taste

In a large deep pan, preferably with teflon coating with a lid, heat oil over moderate heat and add vermicelli. Keep tossing to brown quickly and evenly. As soon as it is a dark brown color, add tomato, onion, pepper and garlic. Lower heat but continue to stir to saute vegetables briefly. Turn heat to low and add hot broth and stir. Add salt and pepper to taste. Cover and cook until broth is absorbed. This takes a few minutes. Add more water if vermicelli becomes too dry. This is a good substitute for rice.

YIELD: 6 servings.

FETTUCINE ALFREDO

1   8-ounce package fettucine or
     medium wide noodles
1   teaspoon olive oil
1   teaspoon salt
     boiling water
½   cup butter or margarine,
     melted
1   clove garlic
¼   cup whipping cream
     black pepper to taste
1   cup grated parmesan cheese

In a large pot, cook noodles al dente in salted boiling water with olive oil to prevent sticking. Drain. In large skillet, melt butter and add garlic and simmer slightly. Add noodles and whipping cream and toss until coated. Add pepper and parmesan cheese and toss gently. Serve immediately.

YIELD: 4 servings.

Pasta Hints:
Two ounces uncooked pasta = one serving.
Al dente = firm to the tooth.

FETTUCINE WITH CHIVES

1   pound fettucine or medium
     wide noodles
1   teaspoon olive oil
1   teaspoon salt
     boiling water
6   tablespoons butter
½   pint sour cream
½   pint whipping cream
4   ounces grated parmesan cheese
2   tablespoons chives,
     finely chopped
     sprinkle of nutmeg
     salt & white pepper to taste

In a large pot, cook noodles al dente in salted boiling water with olive oil to prevent sticking. Strain in colander. In same pot melt butter and add noodles. Stir until mixed and add sour cream. Stir over low heat then add whipping cream. Cook slowly 5 minutes. Add parmesan cheese, nutmeg and half the chives and continue stirring until cheese is melted. Sprinkle remaining chives on top. Serve immediately.

YIELD: 8 servings.

FETTUCINE GIACOMO

1   pound fettucine or any
     narrow noodle or
     spinach noodle
1   teaspoon olive oil
1   teaspoon salt
     boiling water
6   tablespoons butter, melted
⅓   cup grated swiss cheese
⅓   cup grated parmesan cheese
     salt & white pepper to taste
⅛   teaspoon nutmeg
½   cup whipping cream, heated

In a large pot, cook noodles al dente in salted boiling water with olive oil to prevent sticking. Drain well. Add butter and grated cheeses. Toss lightly, adding salt, pepper and nutmeg. Add the heated cream and mix gently. Serve immediately. Additional grated cheese can be added to garnish when serving.

YIELD: 8 servings.

PASTA WITH PESTO SAUCE

1   pound pasta (we recommend 1½-inch shells)
1   teaspoon olive oil
1   teaspoon salt
    boiling water
1   cup chopped fresh basil leaves
¼   cup finely chopped parsley
½   teaspoon salt
½   teaspoon black pepper, coarsely ground
1   clove garlic, minced
1   tablespoon pinenuts or walnuts
¼   cup butter, melted
¼   cup olive oil (we recommend extra virgin)
½   cup parmesan cheese

In a large pot, cook pasta al dente in salted boiling water with 1 teaspoon olive oil to prevent sticking. Drain well. In a blender or food processor, add basil, salt, pepper, garlic, nuts, and half of oil. Blend and add remaining parsley, cheese, butter and oil. Blend until mixed and thick. Add to cooked pasta and mix thoroughly. Serve immediately.

YIELD: 12 servings.

LINGUINE WITH CLAM SAUCE

1   pound linguine pasta
1   teaspoon olive oil
1   teaspoon salt
    boiling water
¼   cup butter
2   cloves garlic, minced
2   tablespoons flour
2   6½-ounce cans clams, minced & reserve liquid
¼   cup dry white wine
¼   cup chopped parsley
½   teaspoon thyme
1   pint half & half cream
    salt & pepper to taste

In a large pot, cook pasta al dente in salted boiling water with olive oil to prevent sticking. Drain well and set aside. In a large skillet, melt butter and add garlic and cook 1 minute. Stir in flour and cook 2 minutes. Combine reserved clam juice and white wine and add enough half and half cream to make two cups of liquid. Add to flour mixture gradually and cook until sauce is slightly thickened. Add parsley, thyme, salt and pepper and simmer 10 minutes. Combine the pasta and the clam sauce and heat to serving temperature. Serve immediately.

YIELD: 6 to 8 servings.

MANICOTTI CREPES

1 tablespoon butter, melted
1 cup flour, sifted
1 cup milk
½ cup water
1 tablespoon sherry, optional
½ teaspoon salt
3 extra large eggs,
     slightly beaten
  marinara sauce
12 mozzarella cheese slices
  parmesan cheese

Marinara Sauce

3 tablespoons olive or
     vegetable oil
1 medium onion, chopped
2 cloves garlic, minced
1 28-ounce can plum tomatoes
1 6-ounce can tomato paste
1 8-ounce can tomato sauce
½ teaspoon basil
¼ teaspoon pepper
  salt to taste

Filling For Crepes

1 pound ricotta cheese
     (we recommend
     Poly O brand)
2 eggs, beaten
4 ounces mozzarella cheese,
     grated
1 tablespoon dried basil
¼ cup grated parmesan cheese
  salt to taste

For Crepes: In a medium bowl, stir flour smoothly into melted butter. Stir in milk gradually to avoid lumps. Add water and stir. Add sherry, salt and eggs. Mix well. Cover bowl and let stand at room temperature for 1 hour. In a 7-inch frying or crepe pan sprayed with a vegetable shortening and lightly coated with butter on medium heat, pour ¼ cup batter into pan. When edges begin to brown slightly, flip over and cook other side. When cooked, place each crepe between wax paper to prevent sticking. After cooking each crepe, wipe pan with buttered paper towel.

For Marinara Sauce: In a medium pot, heat oil and cook onions and garlic until tender. In a blender, place tomatoes, tomato paste and tomato sauce blending until smooth. Add tomato mixture to onion in pot and also add basil, salt and pepper. Simmer for 1 hour with top loosely covered.
Preheat oven to 350°.

For Filling: In a mixing bowl, combine ricotta cheese, beaten eggs, mozzarella cheese, basil, parmesan cheese and salt. Spoon 3 tablespoons of filling into each crepe. Roll and place seam side down in a greased 10x15-inch pan. Place a slice of mozzarella cheese on each crepe. Pour marinara sauce over all. Sprinkle with parmesan. Bake 30 minutes uncovered.

YIELD: 12 crepes.

RICOTTA PASTA

⅔ cup ricotta or cottage cheese
½ cup grated parmesan cheese
  salt & fresh ground pepper
  pinch of nutmeg
1 8-ounce package macaroni or
     favorite pasta
1 teaspoon olive oil
2 tablespoons butter, melted

Preheat oven to 350°.
In a mixing bowl, mix the ricotta and parmesan cheese together and add salt, pepper and nutmeg. In a large pot, cook macaroni al dente in salted boiling water with olive oil to prevent sticking. Drain well. In a hot buttered baking dish, place the macaroni and stir cheese mixture into pasta and add butter. Bake for 5 minutes.

YIELD: 6 servings.

PEACH PRESERVES

9 cups sliced peaches
¾ cup water
6 cups sugar

Wash peaches and soak in hot water. Remove skins and slice peaches. In a saucepan, combine peach slices, sugar and water. Boil peach syrup until thickened and spins threads. Skim off any foam if it forms on top of surface. Pour peach mixture into sterilized pint jars with seals. Fill to ½ inch from top.

YIELD: 4 to 5 pints.

SPICED PEACHES

¼ cup vinegar
⅓ cup sugar
3 cinnamon sticks
10 cloves
¼ teaspoon salt
2 tablespoons red cinnamon candy
1 1-pound 13-ounce can canned peach halves, drained
¼ cup brandy, optional

In a saucepan, combine vinegar, sugar, cinnamon, cloves, salt, candy and simmer for 10 minutes. Add peaches and bring to a boil and simmer 5 minutes. Remove from heat and stir in brandy. Cover and chill. Make 24 hours ahead.

YIELD: 4 to 5 pints.

FIG PRESERVES

9	cups figs
2	tablespoons baking soda
6	cups sugar
1	lemon, sliced
¼	cup water

Wash figs and soak in baking soda and enough water to cover for about 1 hour. The soda takes the fuzz off the figs. Drain and measure. In a large saucepan, place figs, sugar, lemon and ¼ cup water. Cook very slowly on low until the sugar is melted. Adjust to medium heat and cook until syrup thickens about 2 hours. Be careful not to scorch. Pour hot mixture into sterilized pint jars with seals.

YIELD: 4 to 5pints.

STRAWBERRY PRESERVES

1	heaping quart strawberries
1	cup water
4	cups sugar

Wash and hull strawberries before measuring. In a large saucepan, bring water to boil and add sugar gradually until a heavy syrup is formed. Add strawberries. Boil until strawberry mixture thickens. Pour into sterilized pint jars with seals. Never cook more than 1 quart of strawberries at a time.

YIELD: 3 pints.

JALAPENO JELLY

3	jalapeno peppers, fresh, canned or pickled
4	medium bell peppers
1	cup white vinegar
1	3-ounce jar pectin
5	cups sugar

In a food processor or blender, process jalapeno and bell peppers with vinegar until smooth. In a saucepan, combine sugar and pepper mixture, boil for 10 minutes. Remove from heat. Add pectin and boil for 1 minute. Fill jelly jars. Seal with parafin or tight fitting lids. Serve with crackers and cream cheese.

YIELD: 6 to 8 jelly jars.

PICKLED EGGS

2   cups cider vinegar
6   cloves garlic, minced
2   tablespoons pickling spice
1   medium onion, minced
6   eggs, hard boiled & shelled

In a heavy saucepan with a tight fitting cover, boil vinegar, garlic, pickling spice and onion for 10 minutes. Cool mixture and strain into a wide-mouthed glass jar with a screw lid or tight cork. Put in eggs and make sure vinegar mixture covers eggs. Seal jar and refrigerate for at least 2 weeks. For best results, pickle for 6 weeks. Vinegar mixture may be reused. Serve as a snack, with a buffet dish or with a salad.

YIELD: 6 pickled eggs.

PICKLED BLACK EYED PEAS

1   pound dried black eyed peas
2   cups Italian salad dressing
2   cups diced green pepper
1½ cups diced onion
1   cup finely chopped
        green onion
½   cup finely minced
        jalapeno peppers
1   2-ounce jar diced
        pimiento, drained
1   tablespoon finely
        chopped garlic
    salt to taste
    hot pepper sauce to taste
1   cup chopped parsley, optional

Soak peas overnight. Cook until just tender about 40 minutes. Do not overcook. Drain peas. In a large bowl, combine peas and salad dressing. Let peas cool. Add green pepper, onion, green onion, jalapenos, pimiento, garlic, salt, hot pepper sauce and parsley. Marinate overnight. Serve as a relish, on a bed of lettuce as a salad or can be stuffed in a tomato.

YIELD: 10 to 12 servings.

San Antonians are very fond of jalapeno peppers, known as "Texas Pickles." These extremely hot chiles are used for relishes, sauces, egg dishes, nachos, garnishes and in countless Mexican recipes. For those who like it hot, jalapenos can be eaten whole.

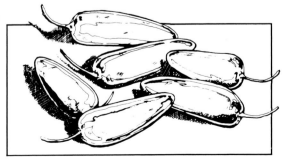

FRITTER BATTER

This batter is wonderful for vegetables, meat and fish!

2 cups vegetables, cut into
  1-inch pieces
1½ cups flour
1 teaspoon salt
¼ teaspoon pepper
1 tablespoon oil or butter
2 beaten eggs
¾ cup beer, flat
2 egg whites, stiffly beaten
  oil for frying

Use any large vegetables such as mushrooms, zucchini, cauliflower, okra, squash, broccoli, onion, green beans, asparagus or carrots. In a mixing bowl, add flour, salt, pepper, oil and eggs and blend well. Stir in beer gradually. Allow to rest covered in refrigerator 3 to 12 hours. Just before using, add stiffly beaten egg whites. (If in a hurry, whole eggs can be used but the mixture will be a little heavier. Use immediately.) Dip vegetable pieces in batter. Deep fry in oil until golden. Place on paper towels to drain. Serve immediately.
YIELD: 2 cups of fritters. 4 servings.

VARIATIONS: Use on meat and fish. Adjust frying time.

SALSA FRESCA

FRESH MEXICAN SALSA

CILANTRO CUMIN BUTTER

CHOW CHOW
For Recipe Page - See Index.

SEGUIN PICOSOS
(Hot Roasted Peanuts)

Seguin is the trading center for Guadalupe County, shipping large quantities of peanuts, cotton, corn, cattle and hogs. In 1839, it was named after Juan N. Seguin, who served in the Texas Army at the Battle of San Jacinto. It is located 35 miles east of San Antonio on the road to Houston. Peanuts are popular appetizers in San Antonio. These great *"beer nuts"* can be adjusted for their degree of *"hotness"* by adding more or less cayenne pepper. For a real *"Texas Gift,"* picosos are given in decorated tin containers. When stored in airtight containers, they will keep fresh for several weeks. Serve with beer or wine.

4	tablespoons vegetable oil
1	pound raw peanuts, shelled
1-2	tablespoons chili powder
¾	teaspoon paprika
2	teaspoons salt
½-1	teaspoon cayenne pepper

Preheat oven to 300°.

Place oil in a large, shallow baking pan. Add peanuts and toss to coat evenly with oil. Spread nuts in a single layer and bake for 30 minutes, stirring occasionally. Sift together remaining ingredients. Remove nuts from the oven after the 30 minutes. Sprinkle with seasoning mixture and toss well. Return to oven and continue to bake for 30 additional minutes. Drain on paper towels and allow to cool.

YIELD: 1 pound.

Nestled among 475 scenic acres joined by the San Antonio River, the four missions - Concepcion, Espada, San Jose and San Juan - are dedicated as the San Antonio Missions National Historical Park, commonly known as "The Mission Trail." It is a clearly marked path linking these missions. Most people travel the trail (city streets) by automobile. Some hearty souls travel it by bicycle or by foot. San Jose Mission is the largest of the four and features a true celebration for Sunday visitors. Mariachi Mass is celebrated every Sunday at the cathedral in San Jose Mission at noon. This tradition, begun many years ago, continues to inspire so many.

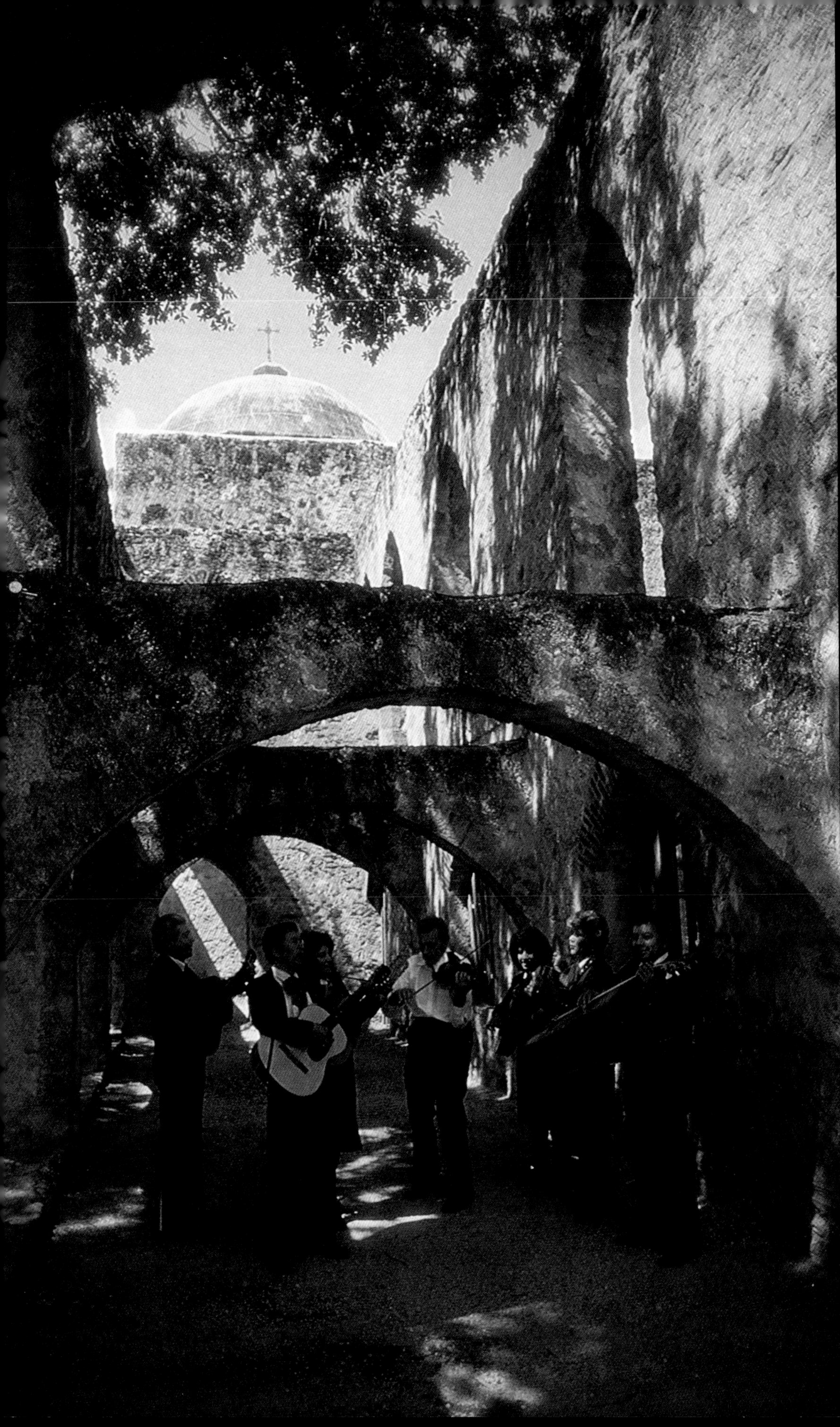

BREADS

HOMEMADE WHITE OR WHEAT BREAD

2¼ cups milk
¼ cup oil
1 ¼-ounce package dry yeast
2 teaspoons salt
¼ cup sugar
5¼-6½ cups flour

Heat milk and oil until warm. In a large bowl, combine milk and oil with yeast, salt, sugar and two cups flour and mix until well blended. Add the remaining flour, working it in until it is of a kneadable consistency. On a floured surface, knead for 10 minutes. Place in a greased bowl, cover and allow to rise until doubled in size. Punch down and shape into rolls, loaves or braids. Let rise again until doubled.

Preheat oven to 350°.

When ready to bake, place bread into greased pans and bake for 30 minutes, depending on the shape of the bread. For a golden brown, shiny crust, brush top of bread with egg yolk immediately before baking.

YIELD: 2 loaves.

VARIATION: **For Whole Wheat Bread:** *Use one-third part whole wheat flour to two-thirds parts white flour.*

FRENCH BREAD

2 ¼-ounce packages dry yeast
2½ cups warm water
1½ tablespoons sugar
2¼ teaspoons salt
6 cups flour, sifted
   butter
   cornmeal
1 egg white, room temperature
1 tablespoon water

In a small bowl, dissolve yeast in 1 cup warm water and set aside. In a large bowl, dissolve sugar and salt in remaining 1½ cups warm water. Add yeast mixture and flour and mix well. Punch the dough down, then punch down 5 more times at 10-minute intervals. Butter cookie sheets and sprinkle with cornmeal. Shake off excess cornmeal. Form dough into loaves on cookie sheets. Make 6 deep slashes in each. Combine egg white with 1 tablespoon water and brush loaves. Let rise for 1½ hours.

Preheat oven to 400°.

Bake 30 minutes.

YIELD: 4 loaves.

SWEDISH RYE BREAD

2	tablespoons grated orange rind
2	cups water
½	cup honey
2	teaspoons caraway seed
1	teaspoon anise seed
1	teaspoon fennel seed
2	tablespoons butter
2	¼-ounce packages dry yeast
¼	cup warm water
2	cups rye flour
2	teaspoons salt
4	cups flour

In a saucepan, combine the orange rind, water, honey, caraway seed, anise, fennel seed and butter. Boil for 5 minutes, then cool to lukewarm. In a large bowl, dissolve yeast in warm water. Add the cooled honey mixture. Stir in remaining ingredients. Knead dough until smooth. Cover and let rise until doubled in bulk. Divide into 2 loaves on a lightly floured board. Place in greased loaf pans and let rise until doubled.
Preheat oven to 350°.
Bake loaves for 60 minutes.

YIELD: 2 large loaves.

DILLY CASSEROLE BREAD

1	¼-ounce package dry yeast
¼	cup warm water
1	cup creamed cottage cheese
2	tablespoons sugar
1	tablespoon instant minced onion
1	tablespoon butter, softened
¼	teaspoon baking soda
2	teaspoons dill seed
1	teaspoon salt
1	egg, unbeaten
2¼-2½	cups flour

In a large bowl, dissolve the yeast in warm water. To the yeast, add the cottage cheese, sugar, onion, butter, baking soda, dill seed, salt and egg. Mix until well blended. Add the flour gradually to form a stiff dough, beating well after each addition. Cover and let rise in a warm place until doubled. Punch the dough down and turn into a well greased 8-inch casserole or loaf pan. Let rise 30 to 40 minutes more.
Preheat oven 350°.
Bake for 40 to 50 minutes. Bread will get very brown on top. Brush with softened butter and sprinkle with salt.

YIELD: 1 loaf.

San Antonio is famous for its summertime Brown Bag Days. People in the downtown area are treated to noontime concerts while enjoying picnic lunches in the park. The San Antonio Department of Parks & Recreation initiated this program at Travis Park. Several downtown parks are utilized today.

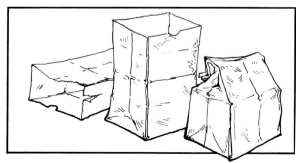

BOLILLOS
(Mexican Rolls or Little French Breads)

2 cups water
1½ tablespoons sugar
1 tablespoon salt
2 tablespoons butter
1 ¼-ounce package dry yeast
6 cups flour
1 teaspoon cornstarch dissolved in ½ cup water

In a saucepan, combine water, sugar, salt and butter. Heat to 110°. Pour into large bowl and stir in yeast until dissolved. Beat in 5 cups flour. Turn dough out onto board coated with remaining flour and knead 10 minutes. Place in greased bowl and turn dough to grease top. Cover bowl and let rise in warm place until it has doubled in size, about 1½ hours. Punch down and squeeze dough to release air bubbles. Turn onto a lightly floured board and divide into 16 equal pieces. Form each piece into a smooth ball by gently kneading. Shape into 4-inch long rolls and place on greased cookie sheets. Let rolls rise, covered, 35 minutes or until doubled in size.

Preheat oven to 375°.

Heat cornstarch and water to boiling. Cool slightly. Brush each roll with mixture and with sharp knife cut slash about ¾ inch deep and 2 inches long on top of each roll. Bake 35 to 40 minutes. Cool on wire racks.

YIELD: 16 rolls.

LA VILLITA ROLLS
For Recipe Page - See Index.

KERRVILLE RANCH YEAST BISCUITS

Located on the banks of the beautiful Guadalupe River 69 miles northwest of San Antonio, Kerrville attracted many German settlers from the surrounding area. It became the center of a thriving cattle business in 1869. Today Kerrville is one of the health and recreational centers of the Southwest and still retains a frontier atmosphere. Nearby is the famous Y O Ranch of approximately 700,000 acres, one of Texas' largest working ranches. Visitors can have a typical ranch lunch with the cowboys and take a tour of the ranch that also has a herd of Texas Longhorn cattle and exotic game.

1   ¼-ounce package dry yeast
¼   cup warm water
2½ cups flour
½   teaspoon baking soda
1   teaspoon baking powder
1   teaspoon salt
⅛   cup sugar
½   cup shortening
1   cup buttermilk

In a small bowl, dissolve the yeast in warm water and set aside. In a large bowl, mix the flour, baking soda, baking powder, salt and sugar and cut in the shortening. Stir in the buttermilk and yeast mixture and blend thoroughly. Refrigerate, covered, until ready to use.

Preheat oven to 400°.

When ready to bake, turn out dough onto a floured board and knead lightly. Roll out ¼-inch thick and cut with a 2-inch biscuit cutter. Place on a greased pan and allow to rise slightly. Bake for 12 to 15 minutes or until golden brown.

YIELD: 12 to 15 biscuits.

CRESCENT ROLLS

1½ ¼-ounce packages dry yeast
½   cup lukewarm water
1   cup milk, scalded
½   cup margarine or shortening
½   cup sugar
1   teaspoon salt
3   eggs, beaten
5-6 cups flour
    melted butter

In a large bowl, dissolve yeast in warm water and set aside. Scald milk and add margarine to melt. Add sugar, salt and well beaten eggs. Add this mixture to yeast and blend. Add enough flour to make a stiff dough. Let dough rest for a few hours covered in refrigerator before proceeding with rolls. May be kept at this point for 4 to 5 days, if needed. **When ready to prepare,** divide dough into 3 equal parts. Roll each part into 12-inch circles and cut into 12 pie shaped pieces. Beginning at the large end of each piece, roll dough into crescents. Place on greased sheet and let rise until doubled in bulk, about 2 hours.

Preheat oven to 375°.

Bake 12 to 15 minutes. Brush tops with melted butter when removing from oven.

YIELD: 36 rolls.

CINNAMON ROLLS

2 ¼-ounce packages dry yeast
1 teaspoon salt
½ cup sugar
1 egg
⅓ cup cooking oil
2 cups warm water
5 cups flour
½ cup butter, softened
½ cup sugar
1 tablespoon cinnamon
  Vanilla Glaze
2½ tablespoons half & half
    cream or milk
¼ teaspoon vanilla
1 tablespoon butter, softened
1½ cups powdered sugar
    pinch of salt

In a blender, put the yeast, salt, sugar, egg, oil and warm water and blend well. Place flour in a large mixing bowl, pour in yeast mixture and mix well. Cover and let rise to double. Punch down. (Dough may be refrigerated at this point until ready to use.) Working with half of the dough at a time, place dough on a floured board and roll to ½-inch thickness. Mix the butter, sugar and cinnamon and spread evenly on the dough. Roll the dough and slice into 1-inch pieces. Place in a well-greased round 9-inch cake pan. Let rise to double again.
Preheat oven to 350°.
Bake for 18 to 20 minutes. When done, remove from pan immediately. In a blender, add glaze ingredients and mix until thoroughly smooth. Spread with glaze when cool.

YIELD: 2 dozen rolls and 1 cup of glaze.

HONEY AS A NATURAL SWEETENER

Honey was the natural sweetener pioneers in Texas used. It was the only natural, unrefined sweetener available in large quantities for baked goods. The breads and cakes are tastier, moister and remain fresh for a longer period of time.

Follow this helpful chart when substituting "healthier" honey for sugar:

Yeast breads, quick breads, puddings and custards:
replace ounce for ounce.

Cookies, fruit breads, brownies and cakes:
replace ½ of the sugar amount with honey,
depending on the sweetness desired.

Replace 1 cup of sugar with 1 cup of honey:
reduce total liquid in recipe by ¼ cup.

Because honey causes browning,
reduce the baking temperature by 25 degrees.

Neutralize acidity of honey and improve the volume,
add ¼ teaspoon baking soda.
(If soda is already in the recipe, do not add extra soda.)

BUBBLE WREATH

1   ¼-ounce package dry yeast
3½-3¾ cups flour
1¼ cups milk
¼   cup sugar
¼   cup shortening
1   teaspoon salt
1   egg
2   tablespoons butter, melted
2   tablespoons light corn syrup
½   cup brown sugar
8   candied cherries, halved
¼   cup slivered almonds
     sugar
     cinnamon

In a large mixing bowl, combine the yeast and 2 cups flour and set aside. In a saucepan, combine the milk, sugar, shortening and salt and heat, stirring constantly until shortening is melted. Add this mixture to the flour mixture and mix well. Stir in the egg and beat with electric mixer on low speed for 30 seconds, scraping the sides of the bowl. Beat for an additional 3 minutes on high speed. By hand, stir in enough of the remaining flour to make a soft dough. Turn out onto a lightly floured surface and knead until smooth. Place the dough in a greased bowl, turning once to grease surface. Cover and let rise until double in size.

For Topping: Combine butter, corn syrup and brown sugar and mix until blended. Grease a 10-inch tube pan. Place cherry halves and almonds in bottom of pan. Spread bottom with the topping mixture. When dough has risen, punch down and shape into 48 small balls and roll each in a mixture of sugar and cinnamon. Place in layers in prepared pan. Let rise until double again.
Preheat oven to 400°.
Bake for 35 minutes. When done, invert pan immediately.

YIELD: 6 to 8 servings.

VARIATIONS:

For Monkey Bread: Roll balls of dough in melted butter and place in a greased 10-inch tube pan, omitting topping mixture. Let rise and bake as above.

Easy Bubble Wreath or Loaf

1   package frozen yeast
     parkerhouse rolls
½   cup chopped pecans
½   cup brown sugar
1   3⅝-ounce box regular
     butterscotch pudding mix
½   cup butter, melted

Set rolls out for 1 hour to thaw. Cut rolls in half and arrange in greased bundt pan. Sprinkle pecans on rolls. Combine sugar and pudding mix and sprinkle on top of rolls. Drizzle melted butter over all. Cover and let sit for 8 hours. Preheat oven to 325°.
Bake 35 to 40 minutes. When done, let sit for 5 minutes then turn out onto serving dish.

YIELD: 8 servings.

APPLE MUFFINS

2	cups flour
½	cup sugar
4	teaspoons baking powder
½	teaspoon salt
½	teaspoon cinnamon
1	egg, beaten
4	tablespoons butter, melted
1	cup milk
1	cup chopped, peeled apples
2	tablespoons sugar
½	teaspoon cinnamon

Preheat oven to 400°.

Sift together flour, sugar, baking powder, salt and cinnamon. In a mixing bowl, combine egg, butter and milk. Add dry ingredients and mix thoroughly. Fold in apples. Drop into well greased muffin pans. Combine sugar and cinnamon. Sprinkle on muffins. Bake 15 to 20 minutes.

YIELD: 12 to 15 muffins.

IRISH "CHEESECAKE" MUFFINS

These "cheesecake" muffins are commonly served with tea to guests in Irish homes.

Crust

4	cups flour
1½	cups shortening
¾	cup cold water

Filling

¾	cup raspberry or strawberry jam
1	cup butter or margarine, softened
1	cup sugar
2	cups flour
4	eggs

Preheat oven to 400°.

Place flour in a large mixing bowl. Cut in shortening and add enough water to make crust that is not sticky. Divide dough into 24 balls. On a floured board, roll crust balls into 3- to 4-inch rounds and line greased muffin tins. Place 1 to 2 teaspoons of jam in each muffin crust. Set aside. In a large mixing bowl, cream butter and sugar. Alternately add 1 cup flour and 2 eggs to creamed sugar until all flour and eggs have been added. Spoon batter over jam in tins. Bake 15 to 20 minutes. Serve warm or store in tightly closed tin. These muffins keep well.

YIELD: 24 muffins.

BLUEBERRY MUFFINS

½ cup butter or margarine,
      softened
1   cup sugar
2   eggs
2   cups flour
2   teaspoons baking powder
½   teaspoon salt
½   cup milk
1   teaspoon vanilla
½   12-ounce package frozen
      blueberries
2   tablespoons sugar

Preheat oven to 375°.
In a mixing bowl, cream the butter and sugar. Add the eggs one at a time, mixing well. Sift the dry ingredients and add alternately with the milk and vanilla. Fold in the blueberries. Grease muffin tins and fill to top with batter. Sprinkle tops with the remaining 2 tablespoons sugar. Bake 30 minutes. Cool 30 minutes before removing from pan.

YIELD: 12 large muffins.

BRAN MUFFINS

5   cups flour
5   teaspoons baking soda
2   teaspoons salt
2   cups boiling water
2   cups all-bran cereal
4   cups whole bran bud cereal
2   cups sugar
1   cup shortening
4   eggs, beaten
1   quart buttermilk

In a large mixing bowl, sift together the flour, soda and salt and set aside. Pour boiling water over the all-bran and bran bud cereal and set aside. In a mixing bowl, cream the sugar and shortening. To the flour mixture, blend in the creamed sugar mixture, eggs and buttermilk. Stir in the soaked bran and bran buds. Mix well and store in tightly covered container in the refrigerator. The mix will keep for 6 weeks.
Preheat oven to 400°.
When ready to bake, grease muffin tins and fill ⅔ full and bake 20 to 25 minutes.

YIELD: 5 dozen muffins.

DATE BAR MUFFINS

1   egg
1   cup milk
3   tablespoons vegetable oil
1   cup 100% bran cereal
      (we recommend Nabisco)
1   cup flour
2   teaspoons baking powder
½   teaspoon salt
¼   cup light brown sugar,
      firmly packed
1   cup chopped dates

Preheat oven to 400°.
In a mixing bowl, beat together egg, milk and oil. Stir in bran cereal and let stand for 5 minutes. In another bowl combine flour, baking powder and salt. Blend sugar and dates. Add bran mixture to flour mixture, stirring until combined. Do not over mix. Spoon batter into greased muffin tins, filling them ⅔ full. Bake 30 minutes.

YIELD: 12 muffins.

GRAHAM MUFFINS

1½ cups graham cracker crumbs
2 teaspoons baking powder
⅓ cup butter, melted
¼ cup dark corn syrup
1 egg, beaten
½ cup milk
½ cup chopped pecans
1 tablespoon flour

Preheat oven to 375°.
Combine cracker crumbs and baking powder in bowl. Combine butter, corn syrup, egg and milk and add to cracker mixture, stirring just enough to moisten. Stir in combined pecans and flour. Spoon batter into greased muffin tins filling ⅔ full and bake 20 minutes.

YIELD: 12 muffins.

SWEET POTATO MUFFINS

Guests will be delighted with this old southern recipe from a tavern in historic Williamsburg, Virginia.

½ cup butter, softened
1¼ cups sugar
2 eggs
1¼ cups canned sweet
   potatoes, mashed
1½ cups flour
2 teaspoons baking powder
¼ teaspoon salt
1 teaspoon cinnamon
¼ teaspoon nutmeg
1 cup milk
¼ cup chopped pecans
   or walnuts
½ cup raisins, chopped

Preheat oven to 400°.
In a mixing bowl, cream butter and sugar. Add eggs and mix well. Blend in sweet potatoes. Sift flour with baking powder, salt, cinnamon and nutmeg. Add alternately with milk. Do not over mix. Fold in nuts and raisins. Grease muffin tins and fill ⅔ full. Bake 25 minutes.

YIELD: 3 dozen muffins.

PLAIN AND FANCY MUFFINS

2 cups sifted flour
3 tablespoons sugar
2 teaspoons baking powder
½ teaspoon salt
1 egg, beaten
3 tablespoons butter, melted
1 cup milk

Preheat oven to 400°.
Sift together flour, sugar, baking powder and salt into mixing bowl. Combine egg, butter and milk and add to dry ingredients, stirring just enough to moisten. Spoon batter into greased muffin tins, filling ⅔ full. Bake 25 minutes.

YIELD: 12 muffins.

VARIATIONS: Add a drop of jam in center of each muffin or 1 cup of berries to the batter before baking.

FRENCH BREAKFAST PUFFS

½   cup sugar
⅓   cup shortening
1   egg
1½ cups sifted flour
1½ teaspoons baking powder
½   teaspoon salt
¼   teaspoon nutmeg
½   cup milk
½   cup sugar
1   teaspoon cinnamon
⅓   cup butter, melted

Preheat oven to 350°.
In a mixing bowl, cream together sugar, shortening and egg. Sift together flour, baking powder, salt and nutmeg and add to creamed mixture alternately with milk. Beat well after each addition. Fill 12 greased muffin tins ⅔ full and bake 20 to 25 minutes. Combine remaining sugar and cinnamon. Remove muffins from oven and dip in melted butter, then in cinnamon mixture until coated. Serve warm.

YIELD: 12 muffins.

STRAWBERRY BREAD

3   cups flour
2   cups sugar
3   teaspoons cinnamon
1   teaspoon baking soda
1   teaspoon salt
1¼ cups vegetable oil
4   eggs, beaten
2   10-ounce packages frozen
       strawberries, thawed
1¼ cups chopped pecans

Preheat oven to 350°.
In a large bowl, combine flour, sugar, cinnamon, baking soda and salt. Add oil and eggs and mix thoroughly by hand. Stir in strawberries and nuts. Pour batter into 2 greased and floured loaf pans and bake for 1 hour and 15 minutes or until done. The flavor improves if the bread is wrapped tightly and allowed to sit overnight before slicing.

YIELD: 2 loaves.

GRAPENUT BREAD

2   cups buttermilk
1   cup grapenut cereal
2   cups sugar
2   eggs
3½ cups flour, sifted
½   teaspoon salt
1   teaspoon baking soda
2   teaspoons baking powder

Preheat oven to 350°.
In a small bowl, combine buttermilk and grapenuts and allow to soak for 10 minutes. In a mixing bowl, cream sugar and eggs. Add milk mixture and dry ingredients and mix until blended. Pour into 2 greased loaf pans and bake for 1 hour or until done.

YIELD: 2 loaves.

TOMATO SOUP BREAD

2   tablespoons butter
1   cup sugar
1   egg
1½   cups flour
1   teaspoon baking soda
1   teaspoon cinnamon
½   teaspoon cloves
1   teaspoon nutmeg
¼   teaspoon salt
½   cup raisins
½   cup chopped nuts
1   10¾-ounce can tomato soup

Preheat oven to 350°.
In a mixing bowl, cream butter, sugar and egg and set aside. Sift together dry ingredients and add to creamed mixture. Stir in raisins, nuts and soup. Mix until well blended. Pour into greased loaf pan and bake for 1 hour or until done.

YIELD: 1 loaf.

SOUR CREAM BANANA NUT BREAD

¼   cup butter or margarine
1   cup sugar
2   eggs
1   teaspoon vanilla
1½   cups flour
1   teaspoon baking soda
⅛   teaspoon salt
1½   cups mashed bananas
½   cup sour cream
½   cup nuts (optional)

Preheat oven to 350°.
In a mixing bowl, cream butter and sugar. Add eggs and vanilla and beat for 1½ minutes. Combine flour, baking soda and salt and add to creamed mixture. Stir in bananas, sour cream and nuts and mix until well blended. Pour into greased and floured loaf pan. Bake 1 hour or until done. The sour cream makes this a moist bread.

YIELD: 1 loaf.

ZUCCHINI BREAD

3   eggs
1   cup oil
2   cups sugar
2   cups shredded raw zucchini
2   teaspoons vanilla
3   cups flour
1   teaspoon salt
1   teaspoon baking soda
3   teaspoons cinnamon
1   teaspoon baking powder
1½ cups nuts, chopped

Preheat oven to 325°.
In a mixing bowl, beat the eggs. Add oil, sugar, zucchini and vanilla and mix well. Combine dry ingredients, add to the egg mixture and mix until well blended. Stir in nuts. Pour into 2 greased loaf pans and bake for 1 hour.

YIELD: 2 loaves.

PUMPKIN BREAD

3   cups flour
3   cups sugar
3   teaspoons cinnamon
½   teaspoon allspice
1   teaspoon nutmeg
1   teaspoon baking powder
½   teaspoon baking soda
½   teaspoon salt
3   eggs
1   can pumpkin
3   teaspoons vanilla
1   cup salad oil
1   cup chopped nuts & raisins
      (optional)

Preheat oven to 350°.
In a large bowl, mix together flour, sugar, cinnamon, allspice, nutmeg, baking powder, baking soda and salt. Add eggs, pumpkin, vanilla, oil, nuts and raisins. Mix for 3 minutes with an electric mixer or until well blended. Grease and flour 3 one-pound coffee cans and fill to half full or use 2 greased and floured loaf pans. Bake 1 hour.

YIELD: 3 one-pound loaves.

BLUEBERRY LEMON BREAD

3   cups flour
4   teaspoons baking powder
1½   teaspoons salt
2   eggs
1   cup sugar
1   cup milk
3   tablespoons shortening,
         melted
1   teaspoon vanilla
1   teaspoon grated lemon rind
1   10-ounce package
         frozen blueberries,
         thawed & drained
         or 1 cup fresh blueberries
½   cup chopped walnuts
1   tablespoon flour

Preheat oven to 350°.
Sift together flour, baking powder and salt and set aside. In a mixing bowl, beat eggs well and gradually beat in sugar. Combine milk and shortening and add to egg mixture. Add vanilla and lemon and mix until well blended. Add dry ingredients and stir to blend. Combine berries, walnuts and 1 tablespoon flour and add to flour mixture. Pour into greased loaf pan. Bake 1 hour.

YIELD: 1 loaf.

OATMEAL RAISIN BREAD

2   cups whole wheat flour
2   cups rolled oats
2   cups buttermilk
1½   cups raisins
1   cup light brown sugar
3   eggs
2   tablespoons baking soda
2   tablespoons baking powder

Preheat oven to 350°.
Mix all the ingredients together thoroughly. Spoon into generously greased 9x5-inch loaf pan. Bake 1 hour or until inserted toothpick comes out clean. Remove from pan and cool on wire rack.

YIELD: 1 loaf.

JALAPENO CORNBREAD

TORTILLAS

SKY-HIGH BISCUITS
For Recipe Page - See Index.

CHEESE BISCUITS

2 cups sifted flour
3 teaspoons baking powder
1 teaspoon salt
⅓ cup shortening
¾ cup milk
½ cup grated cheese

Preheat oven to 450°.
In a mixing bowl, sift together flour, baking powder and salt. Using a pastry cutter, cut the shortening into the dry ingredients until the mixture has the texture of coarse meal. Slowly add the milk and cheese, mixing to form a smooth dough. Turn out onto a floured board and knead lightly. Roll out to ½-inch thickness and cut with a floured biscuit cutter. Place on an ungreased baking sheet 2 inches apart and bake 10 to 12 minutes.

YIELD: 1 dozen biscuits.

VARIATIONS: Add ⅓ cup fried, crumbled bacon or ⅓ cup finely diced ham to dough before kneading.

ONION CHEESE BREAD

½ cup chopped onion
2 tablespoons chopped parsley
2 tablespoons butter
1 egg
½ cup milk
1½ cups biscuit mix
1 cup cheddar cheese, grated
2 tablespoons butter, melted

Preheat oven to 400°.
In a small skillet, saute onions and parsley in butter and set aside. In a mixing bowl, combine egg and milk. Add onion mixture and blend in biscuit mix until just moist. Add cheese, reserving some for topping. Pour into 9x13-inch well-greased pan. Sprinkle remaining cheese and melted butter and bake 20 minutes. Slice in squares to serve.

YIELD: 12 to 15 servings.

SAUSAGE BREAD

This hearty bread is excellent for breakfast.

1 pound pork sausage
½ cup chopped onion
¼ cup parmesan cheese
½ cup grated swiss cheese
1 egg, beaten
¼ teaspoon tabasco sauce
1½ teaspoons salt
2 tablespoons chopped parsley
2 cups biscuit mix
⅔ cup milk
¼ cup mayonnaise

Preheat oven to 350°.
Cook sausage and onions until brown. Drain well and set aside to cool. In a mixing bowl, combine cheeses, egg, tabasco, salt and parsley and stir well. Add biscuit mix, milk and mayonnaise and stir until just blended. Pour into greased 9x5-inch loaf pan and bake 50 to 60 minutes.

YIELD: 1 loaf.

CORN FRITTERS

1 egg
½ cup milk
1 12-ounce can whole kernel corn, drained
1 tablespoon shortening, melted
1 cup flour
1 tablespoon sugar
½ teaspoon salt
1 teaspoon baking powder
shortening to fry

In a mixing bowl, combine egg and milk and mix until blended. Add corn and melted shortening. Sift dry ingredients together and add to egg mixture, stirring just enough to mix. Heat shortening for frying to 375°. Drop batter by teaspoons into shortening and fry for 4 to 5 minutes.

YIELD: 12 fritters.

ZUCCHINI FRITTERS

1 pound zucchini or 3 medium, unpeeled & grated
1 tablespoon fresh minced parsley
1 teaspoon fresh minced chives
1 cup buttermilk pancake mix
1 egg, beaten
¼ teaspoon salt
¼ teaspoon pepper
½ cup vegetable oil

In a large mixing bowl, combine zucchini, parsley, chives, buttermilk pancake mix, egg, salt and pepper. In a skillet with hot oil about 375°, drop tablespoonfuls of mixture into hot oil. Cook until golden brown, turning once. Drain on paper towels. Serve immediately!

YIELD: 1 dozen approximately.

KATY KORNETTES

These were made famous in the "Katy" railroad dining cars.

4 cups milk
½ cup butter
2 tablespoons sugar
1 teaspoon salt
3 cups yellow cornmeal

Preheat oven to 350°.
In a large saucepan, bring milk to boil and add butter, stirring until it melts. Add sugar, salt and cornmeal. Simmer for 5 minutes. Drop by teaspoonfuls onto greased cookie sheet and bake for 10 minutes or until golden.

YIELD: 6 dozen.

BEER PUFFS

These are perfect appetizers filled with crabmeat, chicken salad or meat filling!

1   cup beer
½   cup butter
1   cup flour
½   teaspoon salt
4   eggs

Preheat oven to 450°.

In a medium saucepan, combine beer and butter and bring to a boil. When butter has melted, add flour and salt all at once. Cook over lowheat, stirring until mixture leaves the sides of the pan. Remove from heat and beat in 1 egg at a time until dough is shiny. Drop by teaspoonfuls 1 inch apart on greased baking sheet. Bake 10 minutes and reduce heat to 350° and bake 10 more minutes or until brown and free from moisture. When cool, slice off top of puff and fill with choice of ingredients.

YIELD: 60 to 70 small puffs.

SPOON BREAD

3   cups milk
1   cup white cornmeal
1   teaspoon salt
1   teaspoon sugar
4   eggs, separated

Preheat oven to 350°.

In a large saucepan, combine milk, cornmeal, salt and sugar. Cook over medium heat until mixture becomes a thick mush, stirring constantly. Set aside and cool slightly. Beat four egg yolks and add to meal, mixing thoroughly. Beat egg whites until foamy and fold them into cornmeal mixture. Pour into greased 1½-quart casserole dish. Place casserole in a larger baking pan with 1 inch of water. Bake for 45 minutes to 1 hour. Best served at once with honey and butter.

YIELD: 1 loaf.

ORANGE ROLLS

2   tablespoons butter, melted
¼   cup sugar
1   teaspoon grated orange rind
3   tablespoons orange juice
1   10-ounce can flaky
        buttermilk biscuits

Preheat oven to 400°.
In a small bowl, combine butter, sugar, orange rind and orange juice and mix well. Grease 10 muffin cups. Put about 1 table-spoon orange mixture in each muffin cup. Place 1 biscuit in each cup. Bake 10 minutes. Invert biscuits immediately when done.

YIELD: 10 biscuits.

CARAMEL RING

1   tablespoon butter
½   cup orange marmalade
3   tablespoons chopped pecans
1   cup brown sugar, packed
½   teaspoon cinnamon
2   10-ounce cans flaky
        buttermilk biscuits
½   cup butter, melted

Preheat oven to 350°.
Grease bundt pan with butter. Spread orange marmalade in bottom of pan. Sprinkle with nuts. Combine brown sugar and cinnamon and set aside. Separate biscuits and dip into melted butter, then in sugar mixture. Stand biscuits on edge, spacing evenly in pan. Sprinkle with remaining sugar mixture and drizzle with remaining butter. Bake 30 minutes. Cool upright in pan for 5 minutes then invert on serving dish.

YIELD: 6 to 8 servings.

FROZEN BREAD DOUGH

Oh, the wonders of dough! Let your imagination just go! Let a loaf of frozen bread dough thaw and double in size. Roll the dough out to a 7x15-inch rectangle. Sprinkle with any of the following list of yummies. Fold in half and roll out again. Roll up, starting with the 7-inch side, sealing the ends. Place in well-greased loaf pan or cookie sheet. Cover and let rise again.
Preheat oven to 375°. Bake 30 to 35 minutes.

Ingredients
cinnamon, sugar & raisins
honey, butter & nutmeg
peanut butter & chocolate chips
raisins, grated orange peel & anise seeds
candied fruit, almonds & butter
dates, walnuts & grated lemon peel
wheat germ or quick rolled oats, softened in milk, raisins
jam or jelly with fruit chunks or marmalade & preserves
coconut, sugar, cinnamon & butter
brown sugar, cinnamon, butter & pecans

More Ingredients
walnuts, poppy seeds, honey & butter
parmesan cheese, worcestershire sauce, onions & parsley
browned hamburger, barbecue sauce & minced onion
crumbled fried bacon, minced onion & shredded cheese
pared shredded carrots, green pepper & onion
tuna, chopped mushrooms, shredded swiss cheese
dry onion soup mix & sour cream
cream cheese & browned spicy pork sausage

BEER BREAD

¼ cup butter
3 cups self-rising flour
2 tablespoons sugar
1 12-ounce can warm beer

Preheat oven to 350°.
In a loaf pan, melt butter and pour out. Save remaining butter after thoroughly greasing pan sides. In a large mixing bowl, combine flour, beer and sugar. Pour batter into loaf pan. Pour remaining butter over batter. Bake 1 hour.

YIELD: 1 loaf.

BREAD HERB TOPPING

½	teaspoon garlic salt
3	teaspoons parsley flakes
½	teaspoon oregano
2	tablespoons parmesan cheese
4	tablespoons sour cream
½	cup butter, softened
1	loaf french bread

In a small mixing bowl, mix together garlic, parsley, oregano, cheese, sour cream and butter. Cut the bread in half, lengthwise. Spread bread with butter mixture and wrap in foil. Let stand 30 minutes before heating. Preheat oven to 400°. When ready, heat for 10 to 15 minutes. Open top of foil the last few minutes of heating to crisp top of bread.

YIELD: 1 loaf.

HOT CHEESE AND GARLIC BREAD

½	cup butter, softened
½	teaspoon garlic salt
⅓	cup grated parmesan cheese
1	teaspoon worcestershire sauce
¼	teaspoon cayenne pepper or to taste
1	loaf french bread

Preheat oven to broil.
In a small mixing bowl, blend together butter, garlic, cheese, worcestershire and pepper. Slice french bread into thin slices. Butter both sides of each piece. Broil for 1 minute on each side. Great served with steak or Italian food.

YIELD: 1 loaf.

HERBED BREAD THINS

1	loaf french bread, cut into thin slices
1	clove garlic, crushed
½	cup butter, softened
1	teaspoon basil
½	teaspoon tarragon
½	teaspoon chervil
1	teaspoon chopped parsley vegetable oil

In a small mixing bowl, blend seasonings with butter to a smooth consistency and refrigerate overnight. The next day bring butter mixture to room temperature.
Preheat oven to 325°.
Brush each bread round with oil. Spread thinly with butter mixture and bake on cookie sheet until slightly brown and bubbly.

YIELD: 1 loaf sliced french bread.

BUNUELOS
(Fried Tortilla Pastries)

Christmas in San Antonio with foaming mugs of hot Mexican chocolate served with delicious bunuelos is traditional. Fried flour tortillas sprinkled with special spices such as cinnamon and sometimes anise are mouth-watering delicacies.

5	cups all-purpose flour
2	teaspoons baking powder
1	teaspoon salt
2	tablespoons sugar
4	tablespoons shortening (we recommend Crisco)
2	cups milk or water, hot
	oil for deep frying, 3 inches in frying pan
	cinnamon sugar

In a large mixing bowl, combine flour, baking powder, salt and sugar and mix thoroughly. Make a well in the flour mixture and add the hot milk or water and stir to combine ingredients. Add shortening to dough and mix. Knead dough and form a large ball. Cover with plastic wrap and let stand for 1 hour. On a floured surface, divide the dough into 30 balls about the size of ping pong balls. With a rolling pin, carefully roll out each ball into a round tortilla about 7 inches in diameter. This technique takes experience to achieve a perfectly round shaped tortilla but the flavor is just as good with an odd shaped one. (If smaller bunuelos are desired, roll out to whatever size needed. A 2-inch cookie cutter can be used for very small bunuelos!) In a large frying pan with at least 3 inches of hot oil, fry 1 tortilla at a time. Fry 1 side until crisp and turn and fry other side. Do not pour hot oil on top of frying tortilla or it will puff up too much. On a platter lined with paper towels, place hot bunuelos and drain. Sprinkle with cinnamon sugar. Serve bunuelos with a scoop of ice cream, use as a garnish for serving tropical fruit, drizzle with special Bunuelo Syrup for a delicious dessert or in the wintertime serve with hot cocoa!

YIELD: 30 7-inch bunuelos.

VARIATIONS:

For Quick Bunuelos: Deep fry commercially made flour tortillas and sprinkle with cinnamon sugar.

For Anise Bunuelos: Add ½ tablespoon anise seed to the basic ingredients for an even spicier treat.

For Bunuelo Syrup: In a saucepan, combine 1 cinnamon stick, 1 cup brown sugar and 2½ cups water. Bring to a gentle boil until syrup becomes thick and fine threads form when stirring with wooden spoon. For added flavor add ½ cup raisins and stir. Remove cinnamon stick before serving. Reheat syrup when ready to serve dessert bunuelos!

PAN DULCE
(Sweet Bread)

Pan Dulce are dome-shaped sweet rolls with a sugar topping of vanilla, chocolate or lemon etched into a shell design on top. Mexican neighborhood bakeries that are family owned and operated for two or three generations have fulfilled the baking needs of many San Antonians for a long time. Specializing in Pan Dulce, Bolillos, Reposteria, Empanadas and Bunuelos, their traditional flavorings include cinnamon, chocolate, anise and dried fruit.

Dough

1	tablespoon dry yeast
1	tablespoon sugar
¼	cup warm water
3⅔	cups white bread flour
1	teaspoon salt
⅓	cup sugar
2	tablespoons shortening
5	large eggs, beaten

Topping

¼	cup unsalted butter
¼	cup shortening
1	cup powdered sugar
1	cup all purpose flour
1	teaspoon vanilla
1	tablespoon lemon peel
1½	tablespoons granulated sugar
1½	tablespoons all purpose flour
1	tablespoon cocoa
⅛	teaspoon cinnamon

For Dough: In a small bowl, dissolve yeast and 1 tablespoon sugar in warm water. Let stand 6 to 8 minutes. In a large mixing bowl, combine 3 cups bread flour, salt, sugar and shortening and blend thoroughly. Add yeast mixture and 2 eggs. Mix completely. Add remaining eggs and mix. Add remaining bread flour and mix until the dough forms a loose, soft and elastic dough. It should be slightly sticky but firm enough to shape easily with buttered hands.

Butter work surface and top of dough. Shape dough into 4x6-inch rectangle, 1½ inches thick. Cut into 16 medium or 24 small squares. Cover lightly with plastic wrap for 1 to 1½ hours and let dough rise. Shape each dough square into a dome-shaped circle. On a lightly greased cookie sheet, place rolls 2 inches apart.

For Topping: In a food processor using a metal blade, add butter, shortening, powdered sugar, 1 cup flour and vanilla and process until smooth. Divide into 3 equal parts. Leave one part plain and shape into a log. With the second third, process in food processor with lemon peel and shape into a log. Process the remaining third with cocoa and cinnamon and shape into a log. Chill the 3 logs until ready to use.

Cut off 2 tablespoons of topping from log and flatten with palms into a circle. Place topping circle on top of dough circle. It should completely cover dough. Use a sharp knife to cut a crisscross or shell design on top. Let rolls rise again in a warm place for about 1 to 1½ hours.

Preheat oven to 350°.

Bake 12 to 15 minutes until lightly browned. Serve fresh from oven with Chocolate Mexicano or hot coffee.

YIELD: 16 medium or 24 small sweet breads.

CHURROS
(Spanish Fritters)

A popular, light and crisp Spanish pastry sold at fiestas or even at the shopping malls!

Cinnamon Sugar

1   cup granulated sugar
2   teaspoons cinnamon

Dough

1   cup water
2   tablespoons butter
2   tablespoons vegetable
    shortening
1   tablespoon sugar
½   teaspoon salt
½   cup white cornmeal
½   cup all purpose flour
2   large eggs, beaten
    peanut oil for deep frying

For Cinnamon Sugar: In a shallow bowl, combine sugar and cinnamon and mix thoroughly. Set aside.

For Dough: In a 3-quart saucepan, add water, butter, shortening, sugar and salt. Bring to a rolling boil. Remove from heat and stir in cornmeal and flour all at once. Return to low heat and stir vigorously with a spoon until a ball forms. Remove from heat. Place warm dough in a mixing bowl and add eggs. Blend until smooth and shiny.

In a deep skillet or dutch oven, place 3 inches of oil and heat to 375°. Place dough in a pastry bag fitted with a large star tip (#5 preferred). Pipe 8-inch strips of dough into hot oil and fry on both sides until browned and crisp. Drain on paper towels. Sprinkle with cinnamon mixture.

YIELD: 12 fritters.

VARIATION:
For Anise Flavor: Add ½ teaspoon anise oil to dough. For cocoa flavor, add 2 tablespoons unsweetened cocoa and 2 tablespoons more sugar when adding the eggs. Dust with powdered sugar instead of cinnamon.

Pan Dulce, Spanish for sweet bread, is a traditional favorite in thousands of San Antonio households. One of the city's greatest treats is to visit a Mexican bakery with all of its wonderful aromas and take home Pan Dulce.

BOHEMIAN COFFEE CAKE

Bohemian Coffee Cake and Kolaches are favorites anytime in San Antonio whether it be the Texas Folklife Festival or any gathering.

Dough

2	cups milk, scalded
2	¼-ounce packages dry yeast
¾	cup shortening
¼	cup butter
½	cup sugar
2	teaspoons salt
2	eggs, beaten
6	cups flour

Filling

4	cups dried apricots, finely chopped or mashed prunes
1½	cups sugar
1½	cups water
2	tablespoons lemon juice

For Dough: In a saucepan, heat the milk to scalding and cool to 110°. Sprinkle yeast over top and let stand.

In a mixing bowl, cream shortening, butter, sugar and salt until light and fluffy. Add eggs, yeast mixture and enough flour to make a soft dough mixture. On lightly floured board, knead until smooth. Place in a greased bowl. Cover and let rise until double in size.

For Filling: In a saucepan combine fruit, sugar, water and lemon juice. Cook slowly stirring constantly until thickened. Cool and set aside.

For Coffee Cake: On a greased cookie sheet, roll out ⅓ of dough into a 9x12-rectangle. Cut 3-inch slices, 2 inches apart, down both the 12-inch sides of the rectangle. Put ⅓ of the fruit filling down the uncut center of dough. Braid sides by folding side strips alternately over center so that each strip catches the previous strip. Let dough rise again. Preheat oven to 375°.

When double in size, bake 30 minutes.

YIELD: 12 to 15 servings.

*VARIATION: **For Kolaches***
Instead of rolling dough to a 9x13-inch rectangle, shape dough into small balls about 1½ inch in size and place on a greased cookie sheet and let rise again. Preheat oven to 375°.

When doubled in size, brush with melted butter. Make a deep hole in center of each ball and fill with apricot or prune filling. Bake for 15 minutes.

YIELD: 8 dozen.

TOFFEE COFFEE CAKE
For Recipe Page - See Index.

POPPY SEED COFFEE CAKE

3   cups flour
1½ teaspoons salt
3   eggs
1½ cups milk
1½ tablespoons vanilla
1½ tablespoons almond extract
1½ tablespoons poppy seeds
2   cups sugar
1½ teaspoons baking powder
1¼ cups oil

Glaze

½ cup orange juice
1½ cups powdered sugar
1   teaspoon vanilla
1   teaspoon butter extract
1   teaspoon almond extract

Preheat oven to 350°.
In a large bowl, combine all ingredients. Mix for 2 minutes. Pour mixture into a greased and floured loaf pan. Bake 1 hour. Let cool slightly. In a bowl, mix all of glaze ingredients. Glaze coffee cake.

YIELD: 12 servings.

RICH PINEAPPLE COFFEE CAKE

Your guests will want this moist, very rich coffee cake recipe!

1½ cups sugar
2   cups flour
1   teaspoon baking soda
½ teaspoon salt
2   eggs, beaten
2   cups crushed pineapple,
        slightly drained
½ cup brown sugar
½ cup chopped pecans

Topping

½ cup margarine
¾ cup sugar
1   cup evaporated milk
½ teaspoon vanilla

Preheat oven to 325°.
In a large mixing bowl, combine sugar, flour, soda, salt, eggs and pineapple. In a greased and floured 7x11-inch pan, pour mixture. In a separate bowl, mix brown sugar and pecans. Sprinkle over batter. Bake 30 minutes. Begin making topping about 10 minutes before cake is done. In a saucepan, mix together margarine, sugar and evaporated milk. Boil over medium low heat for 2 minutes. Stir in vanilla. Spoon over hot cake.

YIELD: 8 servings.

SOUR CREAM COFFEE CAKE

A quick, easy coffee cake with a wonderfully light texture!

½   cup butter
½   cup margarine
1¼   cups sugar
2   eggs, slightly beaten
1   cup sour cream
2   cups flour
½   teaspoon baking soda
1   teaspoon baking powder
1   teaspoon vanilla

Topping

6   tablespoons sugar
2   teaspoons cinnamon
½   cup nuts, chopped

Preheat oven to 350°.
In a large mixing bowl, cream butter, margarine, sugar, eggs and sour cream. In a separate bowl, combine flour, baking soda and baking powder and mix thoroughly. Gradually add flour mixture to butter mixture and blend thoroughly. Add vanilla. Grease and flour a bundt pan. In a small bowl, mix together the sugar, cinnamon and chopped nuts for the topping. Sprinkle half of topping in bottom of bundt pan. Pour half of cake batter over topping. Sprinkle remaining topping on batter layer. Pour remaining batter. Bake 45 to 55 minutes.

YIELD:10 to 12 servings.

VARIATION: Add 6 ounces of semi-sweet chocolate chips to batter.

FLORESVILLE COFFEE CAKE

Settled in 1832 by Spaniard Don Francisco Flores de Abrego, who established ranch headquarters in the area. In 1885, the Flores family donated the land for a township to be established on the San Antonio and Aransas Pass Railroad line. Famous Texan, John B. Connally, Governor of Texas 1963-1969, has a ranch in the Floresville area. Floresville is 29 miles southeast of San Antonio.

2½   cups sifted flour
1   cup brown sugar
¾   cup sugar
1   teaspoon cinnamon
½   teaspoon salt
¾   cup vegetable oil
1   teaspoon baking soda
1   teaspoon baking powder
1   cup buttermilk
1   egg, beaten
⅓   cup chopped pecans or
       walnuts

Preheat oven to 350°.
In a large mixing bowl, mix flour, brown sugar, sugar, cinnamon, salt and vegetable oil thoroughly. Remove ½ cup of flour mixture to use as topping and mix with pecans or walnuts and set aside. To remaining flour mixture, add baking soda, baking powder, beaten egg and buttermilk and thoroughly mix. In 2 greased and floured 6x10-inch baking pans, pour batter. Sprinkle on topping. Bake 20 to 30 minutes. May be frozen after baking.

YIELD: 10 to 12 servings.

DANISH PUFF

Crust

1 cup flour
8 tablespoons butter or
        margarine
2 tablespoons water

Puff

1 cup water
8 tablespoons butter or
        margarine
1 cup flour
2 teaspoons almond extract
3 eggs

Icing

3 ounces cream cheese
2 cups powdered sugar
2 tablespoons milk
1 teaspoon vanilla
½ cup chopped pecans

Preheat oven to 325°.
For Crust: In small bowl, cut butter into flour. Add water and blend with fork. Pat into large round on an ungreased cookie sheet. Set aside.
For Puff: In a saucepan, bring water and butter to a boil. Remove from heat and add flour and almond extract all at once. Beat until mixture leaves side of pan. Add eggs one at a time, beating by hand until each is well blended. Spread on top of crust. Bake 50 minutes. Cool completely.
For Icing: In a bowl, beat cream cheese until smooth. Add powdered sugar, vanilla and milk. Beat until smooth. Spread over puff and sprinkle with pecans.

YIELD: 12 servings.

COFFEE BREAKERS

¼ cup butter
⅓ cup brown sugar
1 teaspoon light corn syrup
⅓ cup chopped pecans
1 ¼-ounce package dry yeast
¾ cup warm water
2½ cups biscuit mix
2 tablespoons butter, melted
¼ cup brown sugar
1 teaspoon cinnamon

In a small saucepan, melt butter over medium heat and stir in ⅓ cup brown sugar and corn syrup. Bring to a full boil. Spread the butter mixture in a greased jelly roll pan and sprinkle with pecans. Set aside. In a large mixing bowl, dissolve yeast in warm water. Add biscuit mix and beat vigorously. Turn the dough onto a floured board and knead until smooth, about 20 times. Roll into a 12-inch square and brush with 2 tablespoons melted butter. Combine ¼ cup brown sugar and cinnamon. Sprinkle the center third of the dough with half of the mixture. Fold ⅓ over and sprinkle with remaining sugar mixture. Fold the remaining ⅓ over the other two layers. Cut with sharp knife, crosswise into strips about 1 inch wide. Grasp the ends of each strip and twist. Place in the prepared pan about 1½ inches apart and cover. Let rise in a warm place for one hour.
Preheat oven to 400°.
Bake for 15 to 20 minutes. Take out of oven and invert pan immediately.

YIELD: 12 twists.

The Tower of The Americas was designed and built to be the visual focal point for HemisFair '68, San Antonio's World's Fair. From high atop its 600-foot observation deck, visitors could see the entire fair, the city and the surrounding area. Today the tower serves as one of the newest symbols of San Antonio. At its base is The Institute of Texan Cultures, operated by The University of Texas. Each year in August, The Institute is host to The Texas Folklife Festival, a three-day feast of food, music, dancing and fun.

CHOCOLATE SIN

10 ounces semi-sweet chocolate,
     broken in small pieces
½ cup lightly salted butter,
     cut in 8 pieces
6 large eggs, separated,
     at room temperature
1 cup sugar, divided
2 teaspoons creme de cacao,
     coffee liqueur or
     dark rum
½ teaspoon vanilla
1½ cups whipping cream
3 tablespoons powdered sugar

Preheat oven to 375°.
Place oven rack in lower half of oven. In a small bowl, melt chocolate with butter and keep warm over a pan of warm tap water. In a large mixing bowl, beat egg yolks at high speed. Gradually add ¾ cup sugar. Beat until yolks are pale yellow and thick, 4 to 6 minutes. Add chocolate mixture to yolk mixture and beat until completely smooth. Add creme de cacao and vanilla and beat until blended. Set aside. In a medium mixing bowl at high speed, beat egg whites until soft peaks form. Gradually beat remaining ¼ cup sugar into egg whites, beating until stiff. Fold whites gently and thoroughly into chocolate mixture. In a buttered and floured 8-inch springform pan, pour batter and smooth top of cake. Bake 15 minutes. Reduce oven temperature to 350° and bake 15 minutes longer. Reduce temperature to 250° and bake 30 minutes more. (Total baking time is 1 hour.) Turn oven off and prop oven door open and allow cake to remain in oven for 30 minutes. Remove cake from oven and cover top with damp paper towel. Let stand 5 minutes. Remove towel and cool cake completely. It is normal for cake to crack and collapse. Press top of cake down lightly to smooth top. Remove springform pan and transfer cake to serving platter. Whip cream in chilled bowl on high speed until soft peaks form. Continue beating, gradually adding 2 tablespoons powdered sugar until stiff peaks form. Dust top of cake with remaining tablespoon powdered sugar. Serve cake at room temperature with whipped cream.

YIELD: 8 to 10 servings.

CREAMY CHOCOLATE FROSTING

1½ tablespoons butter, softened
3 ounces cream cheese, softened
1 teaspoon vanilla
3 cups powdered sugar
2 teaspoons cocoa
1-2 tablespoons milk

In a mixing bowl, cream butter, cheese, vanilla and 1 cup of powdered sugar until fluffy. Add remaining 2 cups powdered sugar, cocoa and milk and blend well.

DEVIL'S FOOD CAKE

½ cup hot water
1½ teaspoons baking soda
7 tablespoons cocoa
½ teaspoon red food coloring
1 cup shortening
2½ cups sugar
5 eggs
1 teaspoon salt
2½ cups flour
1 cup buttermilk
2 teaspoons vanilla

Preheat oven to 350°.
In a bowl, add soda, cocoa and food coloring to hot water. Mix well, cool and set aside. In a large mixing bowl, combine shortening, sugar, eggs and salt. Beat at medium-high speed for about 4 minutes. Fold cool cocoa mixture by hand into sugar mixture stirring gently. Add flour alternately with buttermilk, beginning and ending with flour. Add vanilla. In 3 greased and floured 9-inch cake pans, pour the batter. Bake 20 to 25 minutes until toothpick inserted in center comes out clean. Do not overcook. Frost with Chocolate Fudge or Colonnade Icing.

YIELD: 10 to 12 servings.

CHOCOLATE FUDGE ICING

¾ cup butter
2 ounces unsweetened chocolate
⅓ cup white corn syrup
3 cups sugar
¼ teaspoon salt
¾ cup half & half cream
2 teaspoons vanilla

In a heavy saucepan, mix butter, chocolate, corn syrup, sugar, salt and cream. Bring to boil over medium high heat and cook to soft ball stage of 238° on candy thermometer. Remove from heat, add vanilla and cool 5 minutes. Using electric mixer, beat well until almost stiff. If it becomes too stiff, add hot cream until spreadable.

COLONNADE ICING

3⅓ cups sugar
¾ cup water
4½ tablespoons white corn syrup
4-5 egg whites, stiffly beaten
⅓ cup powdered sugar
½ ounce unsweetened chocolate, melted, optional

In a heavy saucepan, mix sugar, water and corn syrup. Cook to soft ball stage of 238° on candy thermometer. While icing is cooking, beat egg whites until stiff but not dry. Slowly add hot mixture to egg whites, beating thoroughly with mixer on high speed until icing is like thick cream. Add powdered sugar. This never-fail icing is soft on inside and crusty on outside. If desired, drizzle melted chocolate over icing.

CHOCOLATE COLA CAKE

½   cup margarine
½   cup shortening
3   tablespoons cocoa
1   cup miniature marshmallows
1   cup Coca-Cola
2   eggs
2   cups sugar
2   cups flour
1   teaspoon baking soda
½   teaspoon salt
½   cup buttermilk
1   teaspoon vanilla

Preheat oven to 350°.
In a heavy saucepan, bring margarine, shortening, cocoa, marshmallows and cola to a boil. Stir until marshmallows melt and set aside. In a large mixing bowl, cream eggs and sugar. In a separate bowl, combine flour, soda and salt. Add to eggs and sugar alternately with buttermilk. Add vanilla and hot mixture together stirring by hand until blended. In a greased and floured 9x13-inch pan, pour batter. Bake 25 to 35 minutes.

YIELD: 12 servings.

CHOCOLATE COLA FROSTING

½   cup margarine
1   cup miniature marshmallows
3   tablespoons cocoa
6   tablespoons Coca-Cola
1   1-pound box powdered sugar
1   cup chopped pecans
1   teaspoon vanilla

In a heavy saucepan, bring margarine, marshmallows, cocoa and cola to a boil stirring until marshmallows are melted. Remove from heat and add powdered sugar, pecans and vanilla. Spread over cooled cake.

CHOCTAW PUMPKIN CAKE

An unusual combination of pumpkin and chocolate makes a truly delicious cake of American Indian origin.

2   cups flour
2   cups sugar
1   teaspoon salt
2   teaspoons baking soda
2   teaspoons cinnamon
1   tablespoon cocoa
1½ cups pumpkin
1½ cups salad oil
4   eggs, slightly beaten
1   teaspoon vanilla

Preheat oven to 350°.
In a large mixing bowl, combine flour, sugar, salt, baking soda, cinnamon and cocoa. Add pumpkin, oil, eggs and vanilla and blend well. In a greased and floured ring mold or bundt pan, pour batter. Bake 40 to 50 minutes. Frost with Creamy Chocolate Frosting.

YIELD: 15 servings.

LEMON SNOWBALL CAKE

A beautiful snow-capped lemon cloud!

2 ¼-ounce envelopes
   unflavored gelatin
4 tablespoons cold water
1 cup boiling water
1 cup sugar
   dash of salt
1 12-ounce can frozen orange
   juice concentrate, thawed
2 tablespoons lemon juice
   grated peel of 1 lemon
1½ pints whipping cream,
   divided
1 baked angel food cake, torn
   into 1-inch pieces
4 tablespoons powdered sugar
1 4-ounce package shredded
   coconut
   green garden leaves, such as
   mint, for garnish
   strawberries, optional

Line a large 12-cup bowl with 2 pieces of waxed paper overlapping to cover the entire bowl. Each piece should extend over opposite edges of bowl so that all edges are covered; paper will be wrinkled. Set bowl aside. In a large bowl, sprinkle gelatin over cold water and let stand for 5 minutes until softened. Add boiling water, stirring until gelatin is dissolved. Stir in sugar, salt, orange juice concentrate, lemon juice and grated peel. Refrigerate 30 to 60 minutes, stirring occasionally until partially set and mixture mounds when dropped from a spoon. In a large bowl, whip 1 pint of whipping cream until it forms soft peaks. Fold gelatin mixture into whipped cream. Into the waxed paper-lined bowl, spoon a small amount of lemon cream. Scatter cake pieces over lemon cream. Continue to alternate lemon mixture and cake pieces until all is used. Cover with plastic wrap and refrigerate 1 or 2 days. Cake may also be frozen, thawing overnight in refrigerator before unmolding. Before serving, invert bowl onto serving plate. Carefully remove bowl and waxed paper from cake. In a small bowl, whip remaining ½ pint of whipping cream with powdered sugar. Frost top and sides of molded cake with whipped cream. Sprinkle with coconut. For garnish, surround cake with leaves and fresh strawberries. Keep refrigerated.
YIELD: 16 servings.

ALMOND BUTTERCREAM FROSTING

⅓ cup butter, softened
   pinch of salt
3 cups sifted powdered sugar
2 tablespoons milk
¼- ½ teaspoon almond flavoring
½ teaspoon vanilla
½ cup pecans, toasted &
   lightly salted

In a bowl, cream butter, salt and 1 cup powdered sugar until fluffy. Add remaining 2 cups powdered sugar, milk, almond and vanilla flavorings. Blend well.

HEAVENLY STRAWBERRY ANGEL CAKE

This wonderful cake makes a beautiful presentation!

1   freshly baked 10-inch angel
      food cake
1   14-ounce can sweetened
      condensed milk
⅓   cup lemon juice
1   teaspoon almond extract
½   pint whipping cream,
      whipped
2   pints fresh strawberries

In a medium sized bowl, combine condensed milk, lemon juice and almond extract and blend well. Fold in whipped cream and chill about 10 minutes. Turn cake upside down. Cut a 1-inch slice from top and set aside. To make a tunnel for filling, cut around cake 1 inch from center and 1 inch from outer edge, leaving a 1-inch base. Scoop out tunnel with a fork and reserve cake pieces. Into a medium bowl, pour only 1½ cups of chilled mixture and stir in half of cake pieces. (Use other half for eating.) Slice and gently fold in 1½ pints of strawberries. Lightly spoon mixture into tunnel. Place cake layer cut from top over filling and press on gently. Use remaining chilled mixture to frost sides and top of cake. Place in freezer for about 2 hours. At serving time, garnish with remaining strawberries. Refrigerate after serving.

YIELD: 12 servings.

POTEET STRAWBERRY CAKE

In April, Poteet has a gigantic celebration called the "Strawberry Festival." Lush, plump and blushing strawberries are grown in and around this area located 26 miles south of San Antonio in the sandy soil. More than 150,000 people attend the festival to sample strawberry delicacies.

2¼ cups flour
1½ cups sugar
3   teaspoons baking powder
1   teaspoon salt
1   3-ounce package strawberry
      gelatin
¾   cup vegetable oil
4   eggs
1   10-ounce package frozen,
      sliced, sweetened
      strawberries, thawed or
      1 pint fresh sliced
      strawberries mixed with
      ½ cup sugar
1   cup chopped nuts, optional

Preheat oven to 350°.

In a large mixing bowl, combine flour, sugar, baking powder, salt, gelatin, oil, eggs and strawberries. Beat with mixer at medium high speed for 2 to 3 minutes until well blended. Fold in nuts. In two greased and floured 9-inch round cake pans, pour the batter and bake 30 to 40 minutes. If using bundt pan, bake 55 to 65 minutes. Test center of cake with toothpick to check for doneness. Cool 10 minutes before removing from pans. Frost cake with sweetened whipped cream or Strawberry Buttercream Icing or Colonnade Icing.

YIELD: 12 to 16 servings.

STRAWBERRY BUTTERCREAM ICING

⅓   cup butter, softened
3   cups sifted powdered sugar
3-4 tablespoons crushed fresh or
     frozen strawberries
¼- ½ cup chopped pecans,
     optional
¼- ½ cup shredded coconut,
     optional

In a mixing bowl, combine butter, powdered sugar, strawberries, pecans and coconut and blend until spreadable.

"PEA PICKIN'" CAKE

This cake is so easy that one can make it and still have lots of time to pick peas in the garden!

1   18¼-ounce package yellow
     cake mix (we recommend
     Duncan Hines)
1   6¼-ounce can mandarin
     oranges, undrained
½   cup vegetable oil
4   eggs, slightly beaten

Preheat oven to 325°.
In a large mixing bowl, blend cake mix, oranges and juice, oil and eggs with electric mixer.   Beat for 2 minutes on medium speed. In 3 greased and floured 9-inch cake pans, pour batter and bake 25 to 30 minutes.   When cake layers are cool, spread Pineapple Frosting between layers, on top and on sides of cake.   Refrigerate.

YIELD: 10 to 12 servings.

PINEAPPLE FROSTING

1   20-ounce can crushed pine-
     apple in heavy syrup,
     undrained
1   2¾-ounce package instant
     vanilla pudding
1   9-ounce carton whipped
     topping

In a medium bowl, mix undrained, crushed pineapple and pudding until thick.   Fold in whipped topping.

POPPY SEED CAKE

This is an unusual custard filled layered cake, loved by young and old alike.

2 ounces poppy seeds
1 18-ounce package white
cake mix

Vanilla Custard Filling

1 cup sugar
¼ teaspoon salt
3 tablespoons cornstarch
2 cups milk
4 egg yolks, slightly beaten
½ teaspoon vanilla

In a bowl, soak poppy seeds in liquid called for on cake mix box for 1 to 3 hours. Using poppy seed liquid, prepare cake according to directions on package for a 2-layer cake. Bake as directed. Cool.

For Vanilla Custard Filling: In a medium saucepan, mix sugar, salt and cornstarch. Add milk and cook until mixture begins to thicken, stirring constantly. Spoon some of custard into slightly beaten egg yolks. Pour egg yolk mixture into custard and cook about 10 minutes more. Add vanilla and cool completely.

To Assemble Cake: Place custard between layers, securing with toothpicks if necessary. Frost top and sides of cake with Almond Buttercream Frosting. Arrange pecans decoratively on top of cake. Keep refrigerated.

YIELD: 12 servings.

PINEAPPLE UPSIDE DOWN CAKE

A beautiful, prize-winning cake for really special occasions. Try baking two cakes and stack them with Caramel or Penuche Icing between layers.

½ cup butter
1 cup brown sugar
1 20-ounce can sliced pineapple
10- 15 large whole pecans, halved
3-4 eggs, separated
1 cup sugar
⅓ cup pineapple juice
1 cup flour
1 teaspoon baking powder
⅛ teaspoon salt

In a 10- or 12-inch black iron skillet, melt butter. Spread brown sugar evenly over butter and arrange pineapple slices on top, reserving juice for batter. Place pecan halves attractively around the pineapple. Set aside. Preheat oven to 375°.

Beat egg yolks until frothy and add sugar beating until creamy. Add pineapple juice to egg mixture. In a separate bowl, sift flour, baking powder and salt. Add to creamed mixture. Beat egg whites until stiff peaks form. Fold whites into creamed mixture. Pour batter over pineapple in skillet. Bake 25 to 45 minutes or until toothpick inserted in center of cake comes out clean. Remove from pan immediately by inverting onto a large cake plate. Serve warm.

YIELD: 8 to 10 servings.

SOAKY COCONUT POUND CAKE

2   cups sugar
1   cup shortening (we
        recommend Crisco)
        or margarine
    pinch of salt
5   eggs
2   teaspoons coconut flavoring
2   cups flour
1½ teaspoons baking powder
½   cup milk
1   3½-ounce can coconut
        (we recommend
        Angel Flake)

Topping

1   cup sugar
2   teaspoons coconut flavoring
½   cup water

Preheat oven to 325°.
In a large mixing bowl, cream together the sugar, shortening and salt. Add eggs, one at a time and coconut flavoring. In a separate bowl, sift together flour and baking powder. Add milk to cream mixture and mix well. Add flour mixture to cream mixture and fold in coconut. In a greased and floured tube or bundt pan, bake 1 hour.
For Topping: About 10 minutes before cake is done, in a saucepan, combine sugar, coconut flavoring and water and bring to a boil for 1 minute. Pour over cake immediately out of oven and let sit 30 minutes before removing from pan.
YIELD: 12 to 15 servings.

PENUCHE ICING

½   cup butter
1   cup brown sugar
¼   cup milk
1¾-2 cups sifted powdered sugar

In a saucepan, melt butter and stir in brown sugar. Boil and stir over low heat for 2 minutes. Stir in milk. Bring to boil, stirring constantly. Remove from heat and cool to lukewarm, 120°. Gradually stir in powdered sugar. If desired, place pan in ice water and stir until thick enough to spread.

The State Tree of Texas is the Pecan. This native fruit is used by South Texas cooks in the making of candies, and, of course, Pecan pie. Pecans are also very tasty by themselves, plain or dry roasted.

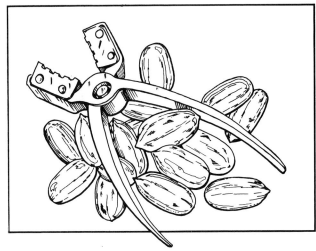

MOCHA RUM TORTE

2 eggs
¼ teaspoon salt
1 cup sugar
1 teaspoon rum
1 tablespoon butter
½ cup milk
1 cup flour
1 teaspoon baking powder
   favorite jam
½ pint whipping cream,
      whipped & sweetened

Coffee Syrup

½ cup strong coffee
½ cup sugar
1 tablespoon rum

Cream Filling

⅓ cup sugar
¼ cup flour
1 cup milk
1 egg yolk, slightly beaten

Preheat oven to 350°.

In a large mixing bowl, beat eggs with salt, sugar and rum with an electric mixer until very thick and fluffy. In a saucepan, heat butter with milk until scalded and beat into egg mixture. Add flour and baking powder and continue beating well. Into a buttered and floured 9-inch springform pan, pour batter and bake 30 minutes. While cake is cooling, prepare Coffee Syrup and Cream Filling. **For Coffee Syrup:** In a saucepan, boil coffee with sugar for 5 minutes and add rum. **For Cream Filling:** In a saucepan, combine sugar, flour and milk and whisk until smooth. Cook, stirring until thickened. In a separate bowl, add a little of hot mixture to beaten egg yolk and stir. Add egg mixture to hot milk mixture in saucepan and stir until thick. Chill until ready to use.

To Assemble Mocha Rum Torte: When cake is cool, slice in half to make 2 layers. Spoon half of coffee syrup over cake layer. Top with cream filling. Place second cake layer on top of filling. Spoon remaining coffee syrup over top. Spread favorite jam on top. Cover top and side of cake with sweetened whipped cream.

YIELD: 8 to 10 servings.

PRUNE CAKE

2 cups sugar
1 cup margarine or butter
3 eggs
1 teaspoon baking soda
1 cup buttermilk
1 cup cooked, chopped prunes
2 cups flour
1 teaspoon salt
1 teaspoon nutmeg
1 teaspoon cinnamon
1 teaspoon cloves
1 teaspoon allspice
1 cup pecans
   whipped cream, optional

Preheat oven to 300°.

In a large mixing bowl, cream sugar and margarine. Add eggs 1 at a time. In a separate bowl, combine baking soda with buttermilk and blend. Add to creamed mixture with cooked, chopped prunes. In a separate bowl, sift together flour, salt, nutmeg, cinnamon, cloves and allspice, mixing thoroughly. Add to creamed mixture and fold in pecans. In a greased and floured tube or bundt pan, pour batter. Bake 1 hour. Top each serving with whipped cream.

YIELD: 12 servings.

CRANBERRY CAKE WITH HOT BUTTER SAUCE

2 tablespoons butter, melted
1 cup sugar
1 teaspoon vanilla
2 cups sifted cake flour
3 teaspoons baking powder
½ teaspoon salt
1 cup milk
2 cups raw cranberries

Hot Butter Sauce

½ cup butter
1 cup sugar
½ cup half & half cream

Preheat oven to 400°.
In a large mixing bowl, cream butter and sugar with electric mixer and add vanilla. In a separate bowl, sift together flour, baking powder and salt. Add flour mixture and milk alternately to butter mixture and mix thoroughly. Fold in cranberries. In a greased and floured 8- or 9-inch square pan, pour batter. Bake 30 to 35 minutes. While cake is hot, cut into squares and top with hot butter sauce. Delicious!
For Hot Butter Sauce: In a medium saucepan, melt butter and blend in sugar. Stir in cream and simmer 3 to 4 minutes, stirring occasionally.

YIELD: 8 to 10 servings.

CHOCOLATE POTATO CAKE

1 cup butter, softened
2 cups sugar
1 teaspoon vanilla
1 cup cooked, mashed white potatoes, cooked just before baking cake
4 eggs, beaten
2½ cups flour
½ cup cocoa
1 tablespoon baking powder
1 teaspoon cinnamon
½ teaspoon nutmeg
½ teaspoon allspice
½ cup milk
1 cup chopped pecans, floured

Preheat oven to 350°.
In a large mixing bowl, cream butter and sugar until light and fluffy. Add vanilla and mix in mashed potatoes and beaten eggs. In a separate large bowl, sift together flour, cocoa, baking powder, cinnamon, nutmeg and allspice, mixing thoroughly. Stir in milk to potato mixture and mix thoroughly. Add flour mixture gradually until blended completely. Stir in pecans. In a greased and floured tube pan, pour batter. Bake 50 to 60 minutes. Sprinkle with powdered sugar or frost with Penuche Icing.

YIELD: 16 to 20 servings.

OATMEAL SPICE CAKE

Good, old-fashioned cake with a delicious icing!

1¼ cups boiling water
1   cup oatmeal
½   cup butter
1   cup white sugar
1   cup brown sugar
2   eggs, slightly beaten
1½ cups flour
1   teaspoon cinnamon
1   teaspoon baking soda
½   teaspoon salt
¼   teaspoon nutmeg
1   teaspoon vanilla

Preheat oven to 350°.
In a heat-proof bowl, pour boiling water over oatmeal and let stand for 20 minutes. In a large mixing bowl, cream butter and sugars. Add beaten eggs and mix thoroughly. Gradually add oatmeal and blend completely. In a separate bowl, mix flour, cinnamon, baking soda, salt and nutmeg thoroughly. Gradually combine flour mixture to oatmeal mixture in large mixing bowl. When blended add vanilla. In a greased and floured 9x13-inch baking dish, pour batter. Bake 35 to 40 minutes. Frost with Caramel Topping or Broiled Pecan Icing.

YIELD: 12 to 15 servings.

CARAMEL TOPPING

6   tablespoons butter
½   cup milk
⅔   cup brown sugar
1   cup coconut
½   cup powdered sugar, sifted
1   teaspoon vanilla

In a small saucepan, combine butter, milk, brown sugar and coconut. Bring to a full boil for 2 minutes. Remove from heat and add powdered sugar and vanilla. Spread over warm cake.

BROILED PECAN ICING

¼   cup canned milk
1   cup coconut
1   cup chopped pecans
¾   cup sugar
½   cup butter
1   teaspoon vanilla

In a saucepan, combine all ingredients and bring to a boil. Spread on top of cake while hot. Broil in oven until brown.

BUTTERMILK POUND CAKE

1 cup butter, softened
    (substitute margarine or
    ½ butter & ½ margarine)
2 cups sugar
4 eggs, separated
1 teaspoon salt
½ teaspoon baking soda
1 cup buttermilk
3 cups sifted flour
1 teaspoon vanilla
1 teaspoon almond extract
1 teaspoon lemon extract

Preheat oven to 325°.

In a large mixing bowl, cream butter and sugar. Add egg yolks 1 at a time. Add salt to creamed mixture and stir well. In a separate bowl, add soda to buttermilk and mix well. Gradually add buttermilk and flour to creamed mixture. Add vanilla, almond and lemon extracts to mixture. In a small mixing bowl, beat egg whites until stiff but not dry. Gently fold whites into batter. In a greased and floured 10-inch tube pan, pour batter. Bake 1 hour and 15 minutes until golden brown. Frost with Vanilla Glaze.

YIELD: 16 to 20 servings.

VANILLA GLAZE

1½ cups sifted powdered sugar
1 tablespoon soft butter
¼ teaspoon vanilla
⅛ teaspoon salt
2½ tablespoons half & half
    cream or milk

In a small bowl, blend powdered sugar, butter, vanilla, salt and half and half cream.

DATE NUT TORTE

1 cup chopped dates
1 teaspoon baking soda
1¼ cups boiling water
¾ cup shortening
1 cup sugar
2 eggs, beaten
1¼ cups plus 2 tablespoons flour
¾ teaspoon baking soda
½ teaspoon salt
6 ounces chocolate chips
½ cup chopped nuts
¼ cup sugar
    whipped cream, optional

Preheat oven to 350°.

In a small bowl, add dates and soda to boiling water and set aside. In a large mixing bowl, cream shortening and sugar. Add eggs, date mixture, flour, soda and salt, thoroughly mixing. In a greased and floured 9x13-inch baking pan, pour batter. In a small bowl, mix chocolate chips, nuts and sugar. Sprinkle over top of cake batter. Bake 25 to 30 minutes. Serve topped with whipped cream.

YIELD: 12 servings.

FRESH APPLE CRUNCH CAKE

A very rich cake, crunchy outside while moist and chewy inside.

2   cups flour
1½ teaspoons salt
1   teaspoon nutmeg
1   teaspoon cinnamon
1   teaspoon soda
1¼ cups oil
2   eggs
2   cups sugar
2   cups fresh apples,
       peeled & sliced
1   cup chopped nuts
1   teaspoon vanilla
⅓   cup brandy

Glaze (optional)

1½ cups sugar
½   cup sherry

Preheat oven to 350°.
In a large bowl, sift together flour, salt, nutmeg, cinnamon and soda. In another large bowl, mix oil, eggs and sugar. Gradually add flour mixture to egg mixture and mix well. Add apples, nuts, vanilla and brandy and mix thoroughly. The batter will be very stiff, almost like a cookie dough. In a lightly greased 9x13-inch baking dish, spread batter. Bake 40 to 45 minutes.
For Glaze: In a small saucepan, bring sugar and sherry to boil. Pour over warm cake.
YIELD: 12 to 15 servings.

EASY CHOCOLATE YULE LOG

¼   cup butter
1   cup chopped pecans
1⅓ cups flaked coconut
1   15½-ounce can sweetened
        condensed milk
3   eggs
1   cup sugar
⅓   cup cocoa
⅔   cup flour
¼   teaspoon salt
¼   teaspoon baking soda
⅓   cup water
1   teaspoon vanilla
       powdered sugar

Preheat oven to 350°.
Line a 15x10-inch jelly roll pan with foil. Melt butter in jelly roll pan. Sprinkle nuts and coconut evenly in pan. Drizzle with condensed milk and set aside. In a mixing bowl, beat eggs on high speed for 2 minutes until fluffy. Gradually add sugar and continue beating for 2 minutes. Add cocoa, flour and remaining ingredients. Blend 1 minute at low speed. Pour evenly into pan. Bake for 20 to 25 minutes until cake springs back when touched. Do not overcook. While cake is in pan, sprinkle with powdered sugar. Cover with a large clean towel. Invert pan so cake will turn out onto towel. Remove foil. Roll up cake immediately and re-cover with foil. When cool, place on a serving platter and frost with favorite chocolate icing. Frost both ends, as well as a few lengthwise swirls to resemble bark on a log. If desired, place holiday greenery on platter for color.
YIELD: 8 to 10 servings.

ITALIAN CREAM CHEESE CAKE

½   cup margarine
1   cup shortening
2   cups sugar
5   egg yolks
2   cups flour
1   teaspoon baking soda
1   cup buttermilk
1   teaspoon vanilla
1   cup coconut
1   cup chopped pecans or
     other nuts
5   egg whites, stiffly beaten

Preheat oven to 350°.
In a large mixing bowl, cream margarine and shortening. Add sugar and beat until mixture is smooth. Add egg yolks and beat well. In a separate bowl, combine flour and soda and mix thoroughly. Add to creamed mixture alternately with buttermilk. Stir in vanilla. Add coconut and chopped nuts. Fold in stiffly beaten egg whites. Into 3 greased and floured 8-inch cake pans, pour the batter. Bake 45 minutes.
     YIELD: 16 to 20 servings.

Frosting

1   8-ounce package cream
     cheese, softened
¼   cup margarine
1   16-ounce package
     powdered sugar
1   teaspoon vanilla
     chopped pecans

In a bowl, beat cream cheese and margarine. Add sugar and vanilla. Frost each layer of cake and stack. Frost top and sprinkle with pecans.

EASY "BRIDE'S" BARS

Even new brides can make this easy cake with lots of variations!

1   box cake mix
2   eggs, for chewy bars or
     3 eggs, for cake bars
1   21-ounce can pie filling
½   cup chopped nuts, optional

   Frosting

2   cups powdered sugar
1   8-ounce package cream
     cheese, softened
3   tablespoons cocoa

Preheat oven to 350°.
In a large mixing bowl, combine cake mix, eggs, pie filling and nuts. On a greased jelly roll pan, spread mixture. Bake 30 minutes.
For Frosting: Combine ingredients in bowl and spread over cool cake. Cut into bars or squares.
     YIELD: 12 to 15 servings.

VARIATIONS:
Chocolate cake mix and cherry pie filling.
Spice cake mix and apple pie filling.
Banana cake mix and blueberry filling.
Chocolate or strawberry cake mix and strawberry pie filling.

SOUTH TEXAS CARROT CAKE

2   cups all purpose flour
2   cups sugar
1   teaspoon baking powder
¼   teaspoon baking soda
¼   teaspoon salt
1   teaspoon cinnamon
4   eggs
1   cup vegetable oil
2   cups grated carrots

Preheat oven to 375°.
In a large bowl, combine flour, sugar, baking powder, baking soda, salt and cinnamon. In another large bowl, combine eggs and oil and beat thoroughly. Fold in dry ingredients and grated carrots. Spoon batter into 3 greased and floured 9-inch cake pans. Bake 25 minutes. Cake layers will be thin. Cool 10 minutes in pans and remove cakes from pans and cool. Frost with Coconut Cream Cheese Frosting between the layers, on top and sides of cake.

YIELD: 12 to 15 servings.

COCONUT CREAM CHEESE FROSTING

½   cup butter, softened
1   8-ounce package cream
       cheese, softened
1   16-ounce box powdered sugar
2   teaspoons vanilla
1   cup chopped pecans
1   cup flaked coconut

In a small bowl, combine butter and cream cheese. Cream until light and fluffy. Add sugar and vanilla. Mix well. Stir in pecans and coconut.

ORANGY DATE CAKE

A wonderful orange and date cake for holiday celebrations!

1   cup butter, softened
2   cups sugar
4   eggs, beaten
4   cups sifted flour
1   teaspoon baking soda
½   teaspoon salt
1½ cups buttermilk
1   tablespoon grated orange rind
1   8-ounce package dates,
        chopped
1   cup chopped pecans

Glaze

1   cup orange juice
2   cups sugar

Preheat oven to 325°.

In a large mixing bowl, cream together butter and sugar. Add beaten eggs and mix well. In a separate bowl, sift together flour, soda and salt. Add flour mixture and buttermilk alternately to creamed mixture. Add orange rind, dates and pecans and blend thoroughly. In a greased and floured tube or bundt pan, pour batter. Bake 1½ hours.

YIELD: 15 to 20 servings.

For Glaze: In a small saucepan, dissolve sugar with orange juice and heat over low heat. Do not boil.

When cake is done and before removing from pan, punch many holes with an icepick or skewer all the way to bottom of pan. Pour hot glaze over hot cake. If cake has not pulled away from sides of pan, loosen with knife so some of glaze runs down sides and center of cake. Let cake stand in pan for several hours before removing.

Bunuelos are round, crisp, tortilla-like pastries sprinkled liberally with cinnamon sugar. They are a favorite South Texas treat, especially when served with a scoop of ice cream, a cup of hot cocoa or a serving of tropical fruit. Bunuelos are popular during holiday times but are available year round.

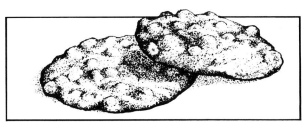

NO FAIL PIE CRUST

1 egg, beaten
5 tablespoons water
1 tablespoon vinegar
3 cups all-purpose flour
1 teaspoon salt
1 teaspoon sugar
1   cups shortening

In small bowl, combine egg, water and vinegar. In larger bowl sift together flour, salt and sugar. Cut shortening into flour mixture until it looks like cornmeal. Pour in liquid mixture, blend until all flour is moistened and is easy to roll into ball. Divide into 2 or 3 parts, depending on size of pie pan. Roll out on lightly floured surface. Use according to pie directions. This dough will keep in refrigerator for up to 2 weeks if well wrapped. Preheat oven 450°.
For A Baked Pie Shell: Thoroughly prick dough in pie plate and bake for 8 to 10 minutes.

YIELD: 2-crust pie or 2 pie shells.

BUTTERMILK PIE

½ cup butter, softened
2 cups sugar
3½ tablespoons flour
3 eggs
1 teaspoon vanilla
¼ teaspoon nutmeg
   dash allspice
   dash ginger
   juice & rind of one lemon
1 cup buttermilk
1 10-inch pie shell, unbaked

Preheat oven 250° to 275°.
In a mixing bowl, cream butter and sugar. Add flour, eggs, vanilla and spices, mixing well. Blend lemon juice and rind into mixture and add buttermilk. Fill pie shell and bake for 1½ to 2 hours or until knife inserted comes out clean.

YIELD: 6 to 8 servings.

PECAN PIE

1¼ cups white Karo syrup
1 cup brown sugar
4 tablespoons butter
4 eggs
1 teaspoon vanilla
1½ cups pecans, chopped
1 9-inch pie crust, unbaked

Preheat oven to 350°.
Bring Karo syrup and brown sugar to boil in medium saucepan. Add butter. Remove from heat and beat in eggs. Add vanilla and pecans. Pour into 9-inch unbaked pie crust and bake for 45 minutes.

YIELD: 8 servings.

APRICOT STRUDEL

2 cups flour
½ teaspoon salt
1 cup butter
1 cup sour cream
1 18-ounce jar apricot preserves
1 3½-ounce can coconut
2-3 tablespoons confectioners
    sugar

Preheat oven to 350°.
In a large bowl, blend flour and salt. Cut in butter until mixture is crumbly. Blend in sour cream. Chill mixture for about 1 hour in refrigerator. When dough is firm enough to roll out like a pie crust, remove from refrigerator and divide in half. Roll out ½ of dough on well-floured surface to make a rectangle approximately 11x13-inches. In a small bowl, mix preserves with coconut and spread half of this mixture on rectangle of dough, spreading to within ½ inch of edge. Starting with long edge, roll dough tightly like a jelly roll. Seal edge with water and place onto greased cookie sheet. Repeat procedure with other half of dough and remaining apricot preserves. Bake for 50 minutes. Slice immediately and sprinkle with confectioners sugar.

YIELD: 8 to 10 slices.

FRESH BLUEBERRY CREAM PIE

1 cup sour cream
2 tablespoons all-purpose flour
¾ cup sugar
1 teaspoon vanilla extract
¼ teaspoon salt
1 egg, beaten
2½ cups fresh blueberries
1 9-inch pastry shell, unbaked
3 tablespoons all-purpose flour
3 tablespoons butter, softened
3 tablespoons pecans or
    walnuts, chopped

Preheat oven to 400°.
In a large bowl, combine sour cream, flour, sugar, vanilla, salt and egg. Beat 5 minutes at medium speed with an electric mixer or until smooth. Fold in blueberries. Pour filling into unbaked pastry shell. Bake for 25 minutes. In a small bowl, combine 3 tablespoons flour, butter and chopped nuts, stirring well. Sprinkle over top of pie. Bake for 10 minutes. Chill before serving.

YIELD: 8 servings.

STRAWBERRY GLAZE PIE

4   cups fresh strawberries
1   cup water
1   cup sugar
3   tablespoons cornstarch
     few drops red food coloring
½   pint heavy cream, whipped
2   tablespoons sugar
1   9-inch pie shell, baked
     whipped cream for garnish

In a small saucepan, simmer 1 cup sliced strawberries and ⅔ cup water for 3 minutes. Pour mixture into strainer and use a spoon to squeeze juice out of strawberries. Discard mashed strawberries. Return juice to saucepan and set aside. In a small bowl, mix 1 cup sugar with cornstarch. Add ⅓ cup water and mix until smooth. Add to strained juice and boil, stirring constantly until thick and clear. Add coloring and cool. Place remaining 3 cups of strawberries (whole or halved) into cooled pie shell. Cover with cooled glaze and chill until firm. Garnish with sweetened whipped cream.

YIELD: 8 servings.

MARGERY FULTON'S CHOCOLATE CANDY BAR PIE

Crust

1⅓ cups grated coconut
2   tablespoons butter

Filling

2   tablespoons water
1   teaspoon instant coffee
1   8-ounce milk chocolate bar
     with almonds
4   cups Cool Whip

Preheat oven to 350°.
For Crust: Melt butter and mix with coconut and press into 8-inch pie pan. Bake crust until golden. Cool thoroughly.
For Filling: Dissolve coffee in water. Add chocolate and stir over low heat until melted. Cool to lukewarm. Fold in Cool Whip. Pour into cooled pie crust. Freeze several hours. Top with chocolate curls and toasted almonds.

YIELD: 6 to 8 servings.

LEMON CHESS PIE

2   cups sugar
1   tablespoon flour
1   tablespoon cornmeal
4   eggs, beaten
¼   cup butter, melted
¼   cup milk
¼   cup lemon juice
     peel of 1 lemon, grated
1   9-inch pie shell, unbaked

Preheat oven to 450°.
In a large bowl, toss sugar, flour and cornmeal with fork. Add remaining ingredients and mix well. Pour into unbaked pie shell and bake for 10 minutes. Reduce heat to 350° and bake 30 minutes more.

YIELD: 8 servings.

CARAMEL PIE

1¼ cups graham cracker crumbs
¼ cup sugar
¼ cup butter
1 14-ounce can sweetened
   condensed milk
1 banana, sliced
   whipped cream
½ cup pecans

Preheat oven to 375°.
Mix graham cracker crumbs, sugar and butter and press into bottom and sides of 9-inch pie pan. Bake for 8 minutes and cool.
To Caramelize Milk: Pour sweetened condensed milk into top of double boiler and place over boiling water. Simmer over low heat 15 minutes to 1 hour or until milk is thick and light caramel colored. Stir to smooth, then cool.
Place banana slices in pie shell, sprinkle with pecans and spread caramelized milk on top. Chill thoroughly and cover with whipped cream. Sprinkle with nuts and serve cold.
YIELD: 8 to 10 servings.

VANILLA COFFEE CHIFFON PIE

1 package unflavored gelatin
½ cup cold water
⅔ cup sugar
⅛ teaspoon salt
3 large eggs, separated
⅓ cup coffee liqueur (Kahlua)
1 tablespoon pure vanilla
   extract
1 cup whipping cream,
   whipped
1 9-inch pastry shell, baked
   (or chocolate cookie
   crumb crust)
½ cup whipping cream,
   whipped
   chocolate curls for garnish

In a small saucepan, soften gelatin in water for 5 minutes. Add ⅓ cup sugar, salt and egg yolks and blend well. Cook over low heat, stirring constantly until gelatin dissolves and mixture thickens. Remove from heat and stir in coffee liqueur and vanilla extract. Refrigerate until mixture thickens to consistency of unbeaten egg whites, about 30 minutes. In a large bowl, beat egg whites with electric mixer until soft peaks form. Gradually beat in ⅓ cup sugar, continue beating until stiff, but not dry. Gently fold beaten egg whites into gelatin mixture. Fold in 1 cup stiffly beaten whipped cream. Turn into pie shell. Refrigerate until thoroughly chilled, about 6 hours. To garnish, fold 1 tablespoon sugar into remaining whipped cream, dollop a ring of whipped cream in center of pie and top with chocolate curls.
YIELD: 8 to 10 servings.

GILMER SWEET POTATO PIE

This recipe comes from Gilmer, the Sweet Potato Capital of Texas, and is traditionally served at the Texas Folklife Festival. The annual Gilmer celebration is called "The Yamboree."

2	cups yams, cooked & mashed
2	eggs
¼	teaspoon salt
¾	cup milk
1	cup sugar
¼	cup butter, melted
1	teaspoon vanilla
1	10-inch unbaked pie shell
1	teaspoon cinnamon, optional
½	teaspoon allspice, optional

Preheat oven to 350°.
In a large bowl, mix all ingredients well. (If desired, add cinnamon and allspice.) Pour into unbaked 10-inch pie shell. Bake for 1 hour.

YIELD: 6 to 8 servings.

PUMPKIN PIE WITH BRANDY

9-inch Almond Pastry

1	cup all-purpose flour, sifted
½	teaspoon salt
⅓	cup shortening
¾	cup toasted almonds, finely chopped
2	tablespoons ice water

Pumpkin Filling

1	cup canned pumpkin
1	cup evaporated milk, undiluted
1	cup light brown sugar, firmly packed
3	eggs, slightly beaten
¼	cup brandy
1	teaspoon pumpkin pie spice (or 1 teaspoon nutmeg, ½ teaspoon ginger & ½ teaspoon mace)
¾	teaspoon salt
	whipping cream, whipped

For Almond Pastry: In a medium bowl, sift flour and salt. Cut in shortening with pastry blender or 2 knives until mixture is like coarse cornmeal. Stir in almonds. Sprinkle ice water gradually over mixture, tossing with a fork. Shape into ball; roll between sheets of waxed paper into an 11-inch circle. Refrigerate until ready to use. Fit pastry into a 9-inch pie plate. If it is crumbly, press gently against pie plate to repair breaks. Form neat rim around edge of pie plate; do not crimp.
Preheat oven to 400°.
For Filling: Combine pumpkin, milk and sugar in a large bowl, blending until well mixed. Stir in eggs, brandy, pumpkin pie spice and salt. Mix well. Pour filling into prepared pie shell. Bake for 50 to 55 minutes or until tip of a sharp knife inserted in center comes out clean. Cool on wire rack. Just before serving, garnish pie with 6 to 8 rosettes of whipped cream.

YIELD: 8 servings.

RAISIN-PECAN PIE

This old southern recipe was contributed by a distant relative of Stephen F. Austin, known as the "Father of Texas." Austin was responsible for bringing 300 families from the United States to establish a colony on the Brazos River in the 1820's.

1	8-inch pie crust, unbaked
2	eggs, room temperature
1	cup sugar
1	teaspoon cinnamon
¼	teaspoon ground cloves
1	cup pecans, whole or broken pieces
½	cup seedless raisins
4	tablespoons butter, melted
2	tablespoons vinegar
	whipped cream, sweetened or unsweetened for garnish

Preheat oven to 400°.
Line an 8-inch pie plate with pastry and refrigerate. Separate eggs. Put yolks in bowl and beat until light and fluffy. In a separate bowl, sift together sugar, cinnamon and cloves. Gradually beat this mixture into egg yolks. Add pecans, raisins and melted butter, beating at low speed. In separate bowl, beat egg whites until stiff. Using a spatula, fold whites into nut batter, adding them alternately with vinegar. Pour into pie shell and bake for 10 minutes. Reduce oven heat to 350° and bake 20 minutes longer. Let cool. Serve with whipped cream.

YIELD: 6 servings.

CARIBBEAN FUDGE PIE

¼	cup butter
¾	cup brown sugar, packed
3	eggs
1	12-ounce package semi-sweet chocolate pieces, melted
2	teaspoons instant coffee powder
1	teaspoon vanilla extract or rum extract
¼	cup flour
1	cup broken walnuts or pecans
1	9-inch pie shell, unbaked
½	cup walnut or pecan halves for decoration
	whipped cream

Preheat oven to 375°.
In a large bowl, cream butter and sugar. Beat in eggs 1 at a time. Add melted chocolate, instant coffee and extract. Stir in flour and broken nuts. Turn into unbaked pie shell. Bake for 25 minutes. Cool. May top pie with more nut halves and whipped cream if desired. Because this is a very rich pie, smaller slices should be served.

YIELD: 10 to 12 servings.

SOUR CREAM APPLE PIE

2   tablespoons flour
⅛   teaspoon salt
¾   cup sugar
1   egg, slightly beaten
1   cup sour cream
½   teaspoon vanilla
2   cups finely grated apples
       (or substitute pears)
1   9-inch pie crust, unbaked

 Topping

⅓   cup sugar
⅓   cup flour
1   teaspoon cinnamon
¼   cup butter, softened

Preheat oven to 425°.
In a large bowl, mix flour, salt and sugar. Add egg, vanilla and sour cream. Mix well with spoon. Add apples, mix well and be sure that all apples are coated with ingredients. Pour into unbaked 9-inch pie shell. Bake for 15 minutes and then lower temperature to 350° and bake for 30 additional minutes.
For Topping: In a small bowl, combine all of the topping ingredients. Using a fork, cream butter into other ingredients. After pie has baked for 45 minutes, sprinkle topping mixture over pie. Finally, return to oven and bake for 10 minutes at 425°. Serve hot with ice cream or cold. Freezes well before baking.

YIELD: 8 servings.

PINEAPPLE MERINGUE PIE

1   cup sugar
6   tablespoons flour
⅛   teaspoon salt
1½   cups milk
4   egg yolks
2   tablespoons butter, melted
1   tablespoon lemon juice
1   cup canned, crushed
       pineapple, well drained
1   9-inch baked pie shell
4   egg whites
¼   teaspoon salt
½   cup sugar

Combine sugar, flour and salt in the top of a double boiler. Slowly stir in milk, beaten egg yolks, butter and lemon juice. Cook over medium heat, stirring constantly until the mixture thickens. Fold in crushed pineapple and spoon mixture into baked pie shell.
Preheat oven to 350°.
In a small mixing bowl, combine egg whites and ¼ teaspoon salt. Beat with electric mixer on high speed until frothy. Continue beating, adding ½ cup sugar a little at a time, until stiff peaks form. Spoon meringue over filling and bake for 15 to 20 minutes or until meringue begins to brown. Remove from oven and allow to cool slightly before serving.

YIELD: 6 to 8 servings.

HILL COUNTRY PEACH COBBLER
For Recipe Page - See Index.

CHOCOLATE MOUSSE PIE

Crust

3	cups chocolate wafer crumbs
½	cup unsalted butter, melted

Filling

1	pound semi-sweet chocolate
2	eggs
4	egg yolks
2	cups whipping cream
6	tablespoons powdered sugar
4	egg whites, room temperature

Chocolate Leaves

8	ounces semi-sweet chocolate
1	tablespoon vegetable shortening
	camellia or other waxy leaves (optional)
2	cups whipping cream
	sugar

For Crust: Combine crumbs and butter in a mixing bowl. Press on bottom and completely up sides of 10-inch springform pan. Refrigerate 30 minutes.

For Filling: Soften chocolate in double boiler over simmering water. Let cool to lukewarm temperature of 95°. Add whole eggs and mix well. Add yolks and mix until thoroughly blended. Whip cream with powdered sugar until soft peaks form. Beat egg whites until stiff but not dry. Stir a little cream and white into chocolate mixture to lighten. Fold in remaining cream and whites until completely incorporated. Turn into crust and chill at least 6 hours or preferably overnight.

For Leaves: Melt chocolate and shortening in double boiler. Using spoon, generously coat underside of leaves. Chill or freeze until firm. Whip remaining 2 cups whipping cream with sugar to taste until quite stiff. Loosen crust on all sides using sharp knife. Remove springform pan. Spread all but about ½ cup cream over top of mousse. Pipe remaining cream into rosettes in center of pie. Separate chocolate from leaves, starting at stem end of leaf. Arrange in overlapping pattern around rosettes. Cut pie into wedges with thin sharp knife.

YIELD: 10 servings.

VINEGAR PIE

1½	cups sugar
½	cup butter, melted
3	eggs
2	tablespoons distilled white vinegar
1	teaspoon vanilla
1	9-inch pie crust, unbaked

Preheat oven to 325°.

In a medium bowl, whisk sugar and butter until well blended. Fold in eggs, vinegar and vanilla and whisk until thoroughly combined, about 2 minutes. Pour mixture into pie crust. Bake for 50 minutes or until the filling is golden brown and sharp knife inserted in center filling is withdrawn clean. Serve warm or at room temperature.

YIELD: 6 to 8 servings.

LEMON AMBROSIA PIE

Coconut crust makes this an unusual pie!

1	teaspoon salt
1	cup flour
⅓	cup shortening
1	3½-ounce can flaked coconut, toasted & cooled
3	tablespoons or more milk
1⅓	cups sugar
6	tablespoons cornstarch
1½	cups boiling water
2	eggs, separated
2	tablespoons butter
1	teaspoon grated lemon rind
⅓	cup lemon juice
1	teaspoon vanilla extract
1	¼-ounce envelope unflavored gelatin
¼	cup cold water
1	cup half & half cream

Preheat oven to 400°.

For crust, in a mixing bowl, combine ½ teaspoon salt, flour and cut in shortening. Add ½ cup coconut. Blend in 3 tablespoons milk or more if necessary to make a dough that will form a ball. Roll out dough between 2 sheets waxed paper to fit a 9-inch pie pan. Bake for 10 to 12 minutes. Cool.

For Filling: In the top of a double boiler, combine ½ teaspoon salt, sugar and cornstarch. Gradually stir in boiling water. Cook over direct heat stirring constantly until smooth and thickened. Put over boiling water and cook, covered, for 10 minutes. Stir small amount into beaten egg yolks. Add balance of egg yolk mixture to sugar mixture in double boiler and cook for 2 minutes, stirring constantly. Add butter, lemon rind, juice and vanilla. Take out 1 cup filling and set aside. Soften gelatin in cold water and stir into remaining filling. When dissolved, stir in cream. Chill until thickened and fold in stiffly beaten egg whites. Pour into pie shell. Chill until firm. Spread reserved filling on pie. Top with remaining coconut. Chill.

YIELD: 8 to 10 servings.

BOHEMIAN APPLE NUT DESSERT

2	pie crusts, 8x12-inch or 9x13-inch rectangles
3	pounds or 7 cups Jonathan apples, sliced & chopped
3	tablespoons lemon juice
3	tablespoons melted shortening
3	tablespoons flour
3	teaspoons cinnamon
2	cups sugar
½	cup whipping cream
2	cups pecans, finely chopped

Preheat oven to 350°.

Cover bottom of 8x12-inch rectangular baking dish with unbaked pie crust. The pie will be thinner but acceptable in a 9x13-inch pan. In a large mixing bowl, combine apples, lemon juice, shortening, flour, cinnamon, sugar, whipping cream and pecans. Place mixture over bottom crust. Cover mixture with top crust. Slit top so steam can escape. Bake for 60 minutes and brown. Cool and serve with ice cream.

YIELD: 12 to 15 servings.

BAKLAVA

An authentic Lebanese recipe handed down from generation to generation.

1   pound filo or pastry leaves,
        available in frozen foods
1   pound unsalted butter
2   pounds ground nuts
½- ¾ cups sugar

Simple Syrup

1   cup sugar
1   cup water
     juice of 1 lemon
1   tablespoon orange flower
        water, available in liquor
        store (or 1 table-
        spoon honey)

Preheat oven to 300°.
In a buttered 9x13-inch baking dish, layer half of the filo leaves on the bottom of pan. Using pastry brush, butter each layer making sure the dough goes to edge of pan.   In a bowl, add ground nuts and sugar, mixing thoroughly. Add orange flower water to nuts. Place a layer of the nut mixture on the filo leaves. Place another layer of filo leaves on top of the nut mixture. Using a sharp knife, score filo leaves completely through pan. Prepare simple syrup before Baklava is baked. In a saucepan, add sugar and water boiling until barely thick. Add lemon juice and orange flower water. Pour syrup over all of pastry. Bake 50 to 60 minutes until barely golden brown.

YIELD: 12 to 15 servings.

RHUBARB STRAWBERRY COBBLER

Filling

2   cups sugar
5   tablespoons cornstarch
4   cups sliced rhubarb,
        fresh or frozen
4   cups sliced strawberries,
        fresh or frozen
¼   cup butter, melted

Pastry

⅔   cup shortening
2   cups flour
2   tablespoons sugar
     pinch of salt
4-5 tablespoons ice water
3   tablespoons butter, melted
2   tablespoons sugar

Preheat oven to 400°.
For Filling: In a bowl, blend sugar and cornstarch. Toss with rhubarb and strawberries. Add melted butter. Mix well and set aside.
For Pastry: In a large mixing bowl, cut shortening into flour until mixture is consistency of coarse cornmeal. Add sugar and salt. Gradually add ice water and mix until dough holds its shape. Roll out on a floured board and cut into 5, 1x13-inch strips and 7, 1x9-inch strips. In a buttered 9x13-inch baking dish, pour filling. Crisscross dough strips over filling. Brush dough with melted butter and sprinkle with sugar. Bake 30 minutes or until crust is browned.

YIELD: 10 to 12 servings.

*VARIATION: **Peach Cobbler***
Substitute 8 cups fresh or frozen peaches. Use 2 to 2½ cups sugar and add ½ teaspoon almond extract. Follow above directions and bake at 400° for 40 to 45 minutes.

CARMELITAS

36 light caramels
5   tablespoons evaporated milk
1   cup flour
1   cup rolled oats
¾   cup brown sugar
½   teaspoon soda
¼   teaspoon salt
¾   cup melted butter
6   ounces chocolate chips
¾   cup chopped pecans

Preheat oven to 350°.
In a small saucepan, heat caramels and evaporated milk until mixture is smooth and creamy. Remove from heat and set aside. In mixing bowl, combine flour, oats, brown sugar, soda, salt and butter. Press half of mixture into greased 8x12-inch baking pan. Bake 10 minutes. Sprinkle chocolate chips and pecans over cooked oatmeal mixture. Cover with caramel mixture. Top with remaining oatmeal mixture. Return pan to oven. Bake for an additional 15 minutes. Cool in refrigerator for 2 hours before cutting. Cut into bars and store in refrigerator or at room temperature.

YIELD: 4 dozen 1½-inch bars.

CREME DE MENTHE BROWNIES
For Recipe Page - See Index.

SAN ANTONIO'S BEST BROWNIES

Brownies are very fudgy and chewy. San Antonio pecans make these truly delicious brownies!

1   cup sweet butter
    (unsalted) or margarine
4   1-ounce squares unsweetened
    chocolate
4   eggs
2   cups sugar
1   teaspoon vanilla extract
½   cup unsifted flour
1   cup chopped pecans or
    walnuts
    powdered sugar, optional

Preheat oven to 350°.
In top of a double boiler, completely melt butter and chocolate over boiling water. Set aside and cool at room temperature. In a large mixing bowl, beat eggs and sugar thoroughly until very thick and well blended. Add vanilla and gently fold in chocolate mixture, blending thoroughly. Add sifted flour to chocolate batter and fold gently until well blended. Fold in pecans. In a greased and floured 9x12-inch baking pan, pour batter and spread evenly in pan. Bake 25 minutes until center is set. Do not overbake. Cool for 1 hour before cutting. Dust with powdered sugar if desired before serving.

YIELD: 30 bars.

MARBLED CHEESE BROWNIES

1   6-ounce package semi-sweet
    chocolate pieces
6   tablespoons butter or
    margarine
⅓   cup honey
2   eggs, beaten
1   teaspoon vanilla
½   cup all-purpose flour
½   teaspoon baking powder

Cheese Filling

1   8-ounce package cream
    cheese, softened
½   cup sugar
1   egg, beaten
    dash of salt
½   cup chopped pecans
    (or other nuts)

Preheat oven to 350°.

In a saucepan over low heat, melt chocolate and butter, stirring constantly. Cool. In a large mixing bowl, gradually add honey to beaten eggs. Blend in chocolate mixture and vanilla until completely mixed. In a separate bowl, combine flour and baking powder and mix thoroughly. Add flour mixture gradually to chocolate mixture and stir until dry ingredients are moist. In a greased 9x9-inch baking pan, pour half of the batter. Bake 10 minutes.

For Cheese Filling: In a mixing bowl, cream together cream cheese and sugar. Add beaten egg, salt and chopped pecans. Pour cheese filling over partially baked batter. Carefully spoon remaining brownie batter over filling and swirl slightly with cheese filling. Bake 30 to 35 minutes. Cool. Cut into bars.

YIELD: 24 marbled brownies.

MILKY WAY SQUARES

1   box German chocolate
    cake mix
½   cup evaporated milk
½   cup margarine, melted
2   eggs, beaten
1   15-ounce package vanilla
    caramels (we
    recommend Kraft)
⅓   cup evaporated milk
1   12-ounce package chocolate
    chips

Preheat oven to 350°.

In a large mixing bowl, combine cake mix, ½ cup evaporated milk, margarine and eggs and blend thoroughly. Divide in half. In a greased and floured 9x13-inch baking pan, spread half of batter. Bake 5 minutes. In a small saucepan, carefully melt caramels and ⅓ cup of evaporated milk. Spread caramel filling very gently over baked crust. Sprinkle with chocolate chips. Spread the remaining batter over the chocolate chip and caramel layer. Bake for an additional 20 minutes. Cool in refrigerator for two hours before cutting.

YIELD: 20 to 25 squares.

FUDGE NUT BARS

1 cup butter or margarine
2 cups light brown sugar
2 eggs, beaten
2 teaspoons vanilla
2½ cups sifted flour
1 teaspoon baking soda
1 teaspoon salt
3 cups quick cooking
   rolled oats
1 12-ounce package semi-sweet
   chocolate pieces
1 cup sweetened condensed
   milk
2 tablespoons butter or
   margarine
½ teaspoon salt
1 cup chopped pecans or
   other nuts
2 teaspoons vanilla

Preheat oven to 350°.

In a large mixing bowl, cream 1 cup butter and brown sugar. Blend in beaten eggs and 2 teaspoons vanilla. In a separate bowl, combine flour, baking soda and 1 teaspoon salt. Stir in rolled oats and mix thoroughly. Combine and blend flour mixture with creamed mixture and set aside cookie dough. In a saucepan over boiling water, melt chocolate pieces with condensed milk, 2 tablespoons butter and ½ teaspoon salt. Stir until smooth. Remove from heat and stir in pecans and 2 teaspoons vanilla. In a greased jelly roll pan or cookie sheet, spread ⅔ of cookie dough in bottom of pan. Cover dough with fudge filling. Dot with remainder of cookie dough and swirl over fudge filling. Bake 25 to 30 minutes until lightly browned. Cut into 2x1-inch bars. Cool in pan on racks.

YIELD: 6 dozen bars.

CINNAMON BARS

Great with coffee or as a cookie!

1 cup butter (no substitutes)
¾ cup sugar
2 cups flour
1 egg, separated
3 teaspoons cinnamon
1 teaspoon vanilla
1 cup chopped pecans

Preheat oven to 350°.

In a large mixing bowl, cream butter and sugar. Gradually add flour and mix. Add egg yolk, cinnamon and vanilla and blend thoroughly. Mixture will be stiff and sticky. Beat egg white very slightly and set aside. Grease hands with butter. In a jelly roll pan or cookie sheet greased with butter, pat cookie mixture over surface of pan. Spread reserved egg white over cookie mixture. Sprinkle pecans evenly over surface and press into dough. Bake 20 minutes until top is golden. Remove and slice immediately into bars. Freezes well.

YIELD: 54 bars, 1½ to 2 inch.

HONEY SPICE BARS

¾ cup corn oil (we recommend Mazola)
¼ cup honey
1 cup sugar
2 cups flour
1 teaspoon soda
1½ teaspoons cinnamon
½ teaspoon cloves
1½ teaspoons salt
1 egg, beaten
1 cup pecans or walnuts, broken into small pieces
1 cup golden raisins, optional

Glaze
1 cup powdered sugar
1 tablespoon water
2 tablespoons mayonnaise
1 teaspoon vanilla

Preheat oven to 350°.
In a large mixing bowl, combine oil, honey and sugar and blend thoroughly. In a separate bowl, mix flour, soda, cinnamon, cloves and salt. Add flour mixture to oil mixture. Blend thoroughly and add egg and pecans. In a greased 10x15-inch cookie sheet, pat cookie mixture. Bake 18 minutes.
For Glaze: Combine in a mixing bowl, powdered sugar, water, mayonnaise and vanilla and mix well. Spread over cookie mixture as soon as it comes out of the oven. Cut while slightly warm and remove from pan.

YIELD: 54 bars, 1½ to 2 inches.

LEMON SQUARES

1 cup flour
½ cup butter
¼ cup powdered sugar
2 eggs, beaten
1 cup sugar
½ teaspoon baking powder
2 tablespoons lemon juice & rind
2 tablespoons flour

Frosting
1½ cups powdered sugar
2 tablespoons butter
1 tablespoon milk
1 teaspoon vanilla

Preheat oven to 350°.
In a bowl, mix 1 cup flour, ½ cup butter and ¼ cup powdered sugar and pat into an 8x8-inch pan. Bake 20 minutes. In a large mixing bowl, combine beaten eggs, 1 cup sugar, ½ teaspoon baking powder, 2 tablespoons lemon juice and rind and 2 tablespoons flour and mix thoroughly. Pour over crust. Bake 25 minutes. Cool.
For Frosting: In a small bowl, blend 1½ cups powdered sugar, 2 tablespoons butter, 1 tablespoon milk and 1 teaspoon vanilla. Spread over bars and cut.

YIELD: 20 large bars.

SAUCEPAN SCOTCHIES

½   cup butter or margarine
1½ cups brown sugar
2   eggs
1   teaspoon vanilla
1½ cups flour
2   teaspoons baking powder
1   cup chopped pecans or nuts

Preheat oven to 350°.
In a saucepan, melt butter and remove from heat. Add sugar and blend. Add eggs, 1 at a time and beat well. Add vanilla, flour and baking powder and blend thoroughly. Add nuts. In a greased 9x13-inch baking pan, pour batter. Bake 30 minutes. Do not over-bake or scotchies will be too crisp when cool. Cool in pan. Cut into squares.

YIELD: 20 large squares.

MINCEMEAT BARS

1   tablespoon butter, melted
1½ cups brown sugar
2   eggs, beaten
2   tablespoons molasses
1   teaspoon vanilla
2   cups flour
½   teaspoon salt
½   teaspoon baking soda
1   teaspoon cinnamon
1   teaspoon ground cloves
3   tablespoons hot water
¼   cup sliced almonds
¼   cup raisins
1   9-ounce package mincemeat

Icing

1½ cups powdered sugar
3   tablespoons hot milk
½   teaspoon vanilla
½   teaspoon almond extract

Preheat oven to 400°.
In a large mixing bowl, cream butter, brown sugar, eggs, molasses and vanilla until well blended. In a separate bowl, sift flour, salt, baking soda, cinnamon and cloves, mixing to-gether. Add to creamed mixture and blend thoroughly. Stir in hot water, sliced almonds, raisins and mincemeat. In two greased 9x13-inch baking pans, spread batter. Bake 12 to 15 minutes.
For Icing: In a bowl, mix powdered sugar, hot milk, vanilla and almond extract to-gether. Spread over mincemeat immediate-ly after coming out of oven.

YIELD: 30 bars.

TEXAS RANGER COOKIES

A nutritious, delicious granola cookie named after the famous Texas Rangers! In 1823, Stephen F. Austin personally financed 10 men to protect his small colony. Later small companies of soldiers organized by Sam Houston in defense of the frontier were known as the Texas Rangers. Capt. Jack Hays was the best known frontier defender. In 1935, the famed Texas Rangers merged with the state highway patrol.

½   cup granulated sugar
½   cup brown sugar
½   cup shortening
        (or butter flavored)
1   egg, beaten
½   teaspoon vanilla
1   cup flour
¼   teaspoon baking powder
¼   teaspoon salt
½   teaspoon baking soda
2   cups granola
1   cup raisins or coconut
        or chocolate chips or
        chopped pecans, optional

Preheat oven to 350°.
In a mixing bowl, cream sugars, shortening, egg and vanilla. In a separate bowl, sift together flour, baking powder, salt and baking soda. Add to sugar mixture and blend thoroughly. Stir in granola and blend completely. (Add raisins and pecans, if desired.) On a greased cookie sheet, drop a teaspoon of dough at a time. Bake 10 to 15 minutes until cookies are set but not hard.
                              YIELD: 4 to 5 dozen.

DISAPPEARING OATMEAL COOKIES

These oatmeal cookies are so good and nutritious that they will disappear before you know it! Thus the name.

1½ cups flour
½   teaspoon baking soda
1   teaspoon cinnamon
½   teaspoon salt
1   egg, well beaten
1   cup sugar
½   cup butter, melted
½   cup shortening
1   tablespoon molasses
¼   cup milk
1¾ cups oatmeal
1   cup raisins
1   cup pecans or nuts

Preheat oven to 350°.
In a large mixing bowl, sift flour, baking soda, cinnamon and salt together. Stir in the remainder of the ingredients. On a greased cookie sheet, drop a teaspoon of the dough on the sheet one at a time. Bake for about 12 minutes until the cookie edges are brown.
                              YIELD: 5-6 dozen.

VARIATION: One cup of grated carrots can be added.

GINGERBREAD MEN OR GINGERSNAPS

A wonderful way to let children be creative and make special homemade gifts for teachers, relatives and friends at Christmas! Decorate the gingerbread men with faces and clothes. Wrap in plastic wrap and hang on the Christmas tree with colorful ribbons or give as gifts. A delicious project children will remember and pass on to their children!

¾ cup shortening
1 cup brown sugar
¼ cup molasses
1 egg
2¼ cups all purpose flour, sifted
2 teaspoons baking soda
½ teaspoon salt
1 teaspoon ginger
1 teaspoon cinnamon
½ teaspoon cloves

Icing For Gingerbread Men

½ cup butter
3½ cups powdered sugar
    salt, a few grains
4-5 tablespoons cream,
    milk or hot water
1½ teaspoons vanilla
    assorted colors of food
        coloring

Preheat oven to 350°.

In a large mixing bowl, cream together shortening, brown sugar, molasses and egg until light and fluffy. Sift together dry ingredients. Stir into molasses mixture until blended.

For Gingerbread Men: Refrigerate dough in freezer until firm about 1 hour. Roll out between floured sheets of wax paper. Refrigerate in freezer until dough is thoroughly chilled. Use gingerbread man cookie cutter for cutting approximately 30 cookies. Bake for 10 minutes. Let cool about 5 minutes and remove from pan. When cool, decorate with colored icing.

For Icing: Cream butter and sugar, stirring until well blended. Add a few grains of salt. Stir in the cream. Add just enough to give a good spreading consistency. Beat until fluffy. Add vanilla. Place in small dishes and add food coloring. Leave 1 bowl with plain white icing. Let icing thicken about 2 hours. Decorate cookies creatively.

YIELD: 30 gingerbread men.

For Gingersnaps: Form into small balls. Roll in granulated sugar and place 2 inches apart on greased cookie sheet. Bake about 10 minutes. Remove from pan immediately.

YIELD: 5 dozen gingersnaps.

COCONUT MACAROONS

1⅓ cups flaked coconut
⅓ cup sugar
2 tablespoons flour
½ teaspoon salt
2 egg whites
½ teaspoon almond extract

Preheat oven to 325°.
In a mixing bowl, combine coconut, sugar, flour and salt. In a separate bowl, beat egg whites until stiff peaks form and add almond extract, folding carefully. Gently fold egg white mixture into coconut mixture. On a greased cookie sheet, drop cookie dough a teaspoon at a time. Bake 16 to 18 minutes until top and edges are lightly browned. Watch carefully. Do not overcook!
YIELD: 18 cookies.

CANDY COOKIES

This is a quick and easy no-bake favorite!

2 cups sugar
½ cup milk
5 tablespoons cocoa, heaping
8 tablespoons butter or margarine
½ cup peanut butter, crunchy
1 teaspoon vanilla
3 cups 1-minute oatmeal

In a saucepan, combine sugar, milk, cocoa and butter. Cook over top of stove until mixture boils. Remove from heat. Add peanut butter, vanilla and oatmeal. On a cookie sheet with wax paper on top, drop by teaspoon and let cool. Do not bake.
YIELD: 5 to 6 dozen cookies.

CASHEW CRUNCH COOKIES

1 cup butter
¾ cup brown sugar
½ cup granulated sugar
1 egg, beaten
1 teaspoon vanilla
2¼ cups all-purpose flour
½ teaspoon soda
½ teaspoon cream of tartar
1½ cups finely chopped cashews, unsalted

Preheat oven to 350°.
In a large mixing bowl, cream butter, brown sugar and granulated sugar. Add egg and vanilla to creamed mixture. In a separate bowl, combine flour, soda and cream of tartar and mix thoroughly. Stir in cashews. Add flour mixture to creamed mixture and blend together. Onto a lightly greased cookie sheet, drop cookie dough by rounded teaspoons. Bake 12 to 15 minutes.
YIELD: 70 cookies.

DA TEES

8	tablespoons margarine
1	cup brown sugar
1	8- to 10-ounce package dates, chopped
2	cups Rice Krispies, lightly crushed
1	cup chopped pecans
½	cup flaked coconut
	powdered sugar

In a cast iron skillet, melt margarine, brown sugar and dates. Cook over moderate heat until well blended. Remove from heat and add crushed Rice Krispies, pecans and coconut and mix thoroughly. With hands, shape mixture into round balls or finger shapes. Roll in powdered sugar.

YIELD: 5 dozen.

PECAN SAND TARTS

These are similar to the locally popular Mexican Wedding Cookies!

1	cup butter, softened
½	cup granulated sugar
2	teaspoons vanilla
2	cups flour
2	cups pecans, finely chopped
	powdered sugar

In a mixing bowl, cream butter, sugar and vanilla. Add flour to creamed mixture. Sprinkle pecans on mixture and stir until blended completely. Chill in refrigerator for 1 hour.
Preheat oven to 275°.
Form into tiny crescents or half moon shapes and place on ungreased cookie sheet. Bake 30 to 45 minutes until lightly browned. Remove carefully and cool slightly. Roll in powdered sugar or use a paper bag to dust cookies. Store in airtight can. Do not freeze.

YIELD: 65 cookies.

WALK-TO-SCHOOL COOKIES

2	cups butter or margarine
1	cup granulated sugar
4	cups flour
1	teaspoon vanilla
1	cup pecans, finely chopped
	powdered sugar

In a mixing bowl, combine all ingredients and mix well. Pat into several long rolls and wrap tightly in wax paper. Place in refrigerator to chill several hours.
Preheat oven to 325°.
Slice and bake on ungreased cookie sheet for about 12 minutes. Cookies should not be brown all over but only slightly around the rim. When cold, sprinkle cookies with powdered sugar. Store in tightly covered cookie tin. These cookies store well.

YIELD: 6 dozen.

"BRAGGIN BEST" SUGAR COOKIES

1 cup margarine
1 cup vegetable oil
1 cup granulated sugar
1 cup powdered sugar
2 eggs, beaten
1 teaspoon vanilla
4 cups flour
1 teaspoon cream of tartar
1 teaspoon baking soda
1 teaspoon salt

Preheat oven to 350°.
In a large mixing bowl, cream margarine, vegetable oil and sugars. Add eggs and vanilla and beat well. In a separate bowl, sift flour, cream of tartar, baking soda and salt together and mix thoroughly. Add flour mixture to creamed mixture and blend completely. Chill cookie dough at least 30 minutes. When thoroughly chilled, shape dough into walnut size balls or smaller. On a lightly greased baking sheet, arrange balls of dough. Using a glass with a flat bottom, dip glass into granulated sugar and flatten each ball. Return to sugar to dip glass bottom again and repeat procedure on next dough ball. Bake 10 to 12 minutes until cookies have a brown rim.

YIELD: 8 dozen.

VARIATION: At Christmas time, use colored sugar to flatten cookies. For different Christmas shapes, roll chilled dough into a ¼-inch thick layer and use cookie cutters. Bake and frost!

CANDY POCKETS

36 miniature Reese's chocolate peanut butter cup candies
1 14-ounce package refrigerated Pillsbury Slice & Bake Peanut Butter Cookies

Preheat oven to 350°.
Spray miniature muffin tins with Pam. Chill peanut butter cups and remove wrappings. Slice cookies 1 inch thick and then quarter each slice. Drop a quarter slice in each muffin cup. Bake 8 to 10 minutes. Remove from oven and immediately push a peanut butter cup into each cookie-filled muffin cup. Cookie will rise and puff out of each muffin tin. (When the peanut butter cup presses into the baked cookie dough, the cookie goes down and nestles around the candy, making a perfect tart.) Let pan cool, then refrigerate until shine leaves the chocolate and becomes dull as before. When cool, remove each tart with tip of knife.

YIELD: 36 cookies.

VARIATION:
Using Chocolate Caramel Rolo's: Substitute 36 Rolo's for the peanut butter candy and use the same amount of Sugar Cookie dough. Follow the same instructions.

BUTTERSCOTCH CHEESECAKE BARS

1   12-ounce package
      butterscotch morsels
⅓   cup butter
2   cups graham cracker crumbs
1   cup chopped nuts
1   8-ounce package cream
      cheese, softened
1   14-ounce can sweetened
      condensed milk
      (Eagle Brand)
1   teaspoon vanilla
1   egg

Preheat oven to 350°.

In a medium saucepan, melt butterscotch morsels and butter. Stir in graham cracker crumbs and nuts. In a greased 9x13-inch baking pan, press half of mixture firmly on-to bottom. In a large mixing bowl, beat cheese until fluffy and add condensed milk, vanilla and egg. Mix well and pour on top of butterscotch layer. Top with remaining butterscotch crumb mixture. Bake 25 to 30 minutes. Cool to room temperature. Chill before cutting into bars. Refrigerate.

YIELD: 35 bars.

FRUIT CAKE COOKIES

1½ cups flour
½   teaspoon cinnamon
½   teaspoon nutmeg
½   teaspoon ground cloves
4   ounces candied cherries,
      finely chopped
4   ounces candied pineapple,
      finely chopped
8   ounces pitted dates,
      finely chopped
4   ounces raisins, finely chopped
3   cups broken pecans
¼   cup butter
½   cup brown sugar
2   eggs, slightly beaten
⅓   cup brandy or rum
2   tablespoons milk
1½ teaspoons soda

Preheat oven to 300°.

In a large mixing bowl, combine flour, cinnamon, nutmeg and cloves. Measure ¾ cup flour mixture, pecans and mix with candied fruit and nuts and set aside. Reserve remaining flour mixture for batter. In another large mixing bowl, cream butter and sugar. Add eggs and brandy. Dissolve soda in milk and add to creamed mixture. Add reserved flour mixture to creamed mixture and blend thoroughly. Add fruit and pecans to batter and mix well. Batter will be very stiff. Fill miniature muffin liners in a miniature muffin tin by teaspoonfuls. Bake 20 minutes. Cool on wire rack. Store in airtight container to "ripen." Recipe should be made at least 1 week before serving.

YIELD: 80 cookies.

PEANUT BUTTER AND JELLY SWIRLS

⅓- ½ cup grape jam
½ cup peanuts, chopped
½ cup raisins, chopped, optional

Cookie Dough

½ cup shortening
½ cup sugar
½ cup brown sugar
1 egg
½ cup peanut butter
1 teaspoon vanilla
½ teaspoon baking soda
½ teaspoon salt
2 cups flour, sifted

In a large mixing bowl, combine all of the cookie dough ingredients and mix thoroughly. Spread cookie dough on a piece of wax paper on a 9x13-inch baking sheet. On top of cookie dough spread jam and sprinkle with nuts and raisins. Roll into a log and wrap in more wax paper. Refrigerate 8 hours or overnight.

Preheat oven to 375°.

Cut dough roll in to ¼-inch slices. Bake for 10 to 12 minutes.

YIELD: 3 dozen.

CHEESECAKES

One of San Antonio's favorite desserts is the versatile cheesecake. A popular way to serve one is with fresh strawberries from Poteet, Texas, a small town on the outskirts of our city that produces giant, juicy strawberries! Cheesecake is a popular favorite because of its rich flavor, but also because it can be made ahead of time and frozen. Cheesecakes with fresh fruit, liqueurs or avocados are served in San Antonio.

QUICK AND EASY CHEESECAKE

Graham Cracker Crust

1¾ cups graham cracker crumbs
⅓ cup margarine or butter, softened
¼ cup sugar or brown sugar

Cheesecake

3 8-ounce packages cream cheese, softened
2 teaspoons vanilla
3 eggs
1 cup sour cream
1 cup sugar

Preheat oven to 350°.
In a bowl, combine graham cracker crumbs, sugar and margarine. Into an 8-inch spring-form pan, press crust mixture. In a blender, place cream cheese and blend. Add vanilla, eggs and sour cream and blend. Add sugar and blend. Pour into prepared springform pan. Bake 60 minutes until cheesecake is firm in center. Turn off oven. Leave door slightly open and leave in oven for 1 hour. Cool in pan. Chill for several hours or overnight.

YIELD: 8 to 10 slices.

VARIATIONS:

Grand Marnier Cheesecake: *Add ½ cup Grand Marnier Liqueur and 1 teaspoon grated lemon rind to batter before baking.*

Amaretto Cheesecake: *Add ½ cup Amaretto Liqueur to batter. When cool dust top of cake with powdered sugar and slivered almonds.*

Strawberry Cheesecake: *In a bowl add 1 pint fresh strawberries, 1 tablespoon Kirsch liqueur and 1 tablespoon brown sugar. Mix and let sit for at least 2 hours for strawberries to absorb liquid. Pour over top of cheesecake before serving.*

Pineapple Cheesecake: *In a bowl add an 8-ounce can of crushed pineapple, shredded coconut and cherries, with 2 tablespoons of brown sugar and 2 tablespoons of lemon juice. Let stand for at least 1 hour. Pour over cheesecake.*

Peach Cheesecake: *Combine 1 pint of fresh peaches, 2 tablespoons of brown sugar, 2 tablespoons of lemon juice and Texas pecans. Let stand for at least 1 hour. Pour over cheesecake.*

TEXAS PRALINE CHEESECAKE

1 cup graham cracker crumbs
3 tablespoons sugar
3 tablespoons margarine, melted
3 8-ounce packages cream cheese
1¼ cups brown sugar, packed
2 tablespoons all purpose flour
3 eggs
1½ teaspoons vanilla
½ cup finely chopped pecans for garnish
  maple syrup

Preheat oven to 350°.
In a bowl, combine crumbs, sugar and margarine. Press into 9-inch springform pan. Bake 10 minutes. Remove from oven. Increase oven temperature to 450°. In a mixing bowl, combine softened cream cheese, brown sugar and flour. Mix at medium speed with an electric mixer until well blended. Add eggs, one at a time, mixing well after each addition. Blend in vanilla. Pour mixture over crust. Bake at 450° for 10 minutes. Reduce oven temperature to 250° and continue baking 30 minutes. Loosen cake from rim of pan. Chill. Brush with maple syrup and garnish with pecan halves if desired.

YIELD: 8 to 10 slices.

PECAN CHEESECAKE
For Recipe Page - See Index.

AVOCADO CHEESECAKE

Crust
1¾ cups graham cracker crumbs
⅓ cup margarine or butter, softened
¼ cup sugar

Avocado Filling
1 avocado, halved & peeled
1 8-ounce package cream cheese, softened
½ cup sour cream
3-4 strips lemon peel
1 3¾-ounce package instant vanilla pudding mix

Preheat oven to 350°.
In a bowl, combine graham cracker crumbs, margarine and sugar. Into a 9-inch springform pan, press crust mixture. Bake 7 to 10 minutes.
For Filling: In a blender place avocado, cream cheese, sour cream and lemon peel and blend until smooth. Add pudding mix and blend until mixed. Pour batter into prepared crust. Chill several hours before serving.

YIELD: 8 to 10 slices.

CHOCOLATE SWIRL CHEESECAKE

1	6-ounce package semi-sweet chocolate morsels (we recommend Nestle's)
½	cup sugar
1¼	cups graham cracker crumbs
2	tablespoons sugar
¼	cup margarine, melted
2	8-ounce packages cream cheese, softened
¾	cup sugar
½	cup sour cream
1	teaspoon vanilla extract
4	eggs

Preheat oven to 325°.

In a double boiler, combine chocolate morsels and ½ cup sugar. Heat until morsels melt and mixture is smooth. Remove from heat and set aside. In a small bowl, combine graham cracker crumbs, 2 tablespoons sugar and melted margarine. Mix well and pat firmly into a 9-inch springform pan covering bottom and about 1½ inches up sides. In a large bowl, beat cream cheese until light and creamy. Gradually beat in ¾ cup sugar. Mix in sour cream and vanilla. Add eggs, one at a time, beating well after each. Divide batter in half. Stir melted chocolate into half the batter and pour into crumb-lined pan. Cover with plain batter. With a knife, swirl plain batter to give marbled effect. Bake for 50 minutes. Refrigerate until ready to serve. For thinner cheesecake, use a 10-inch spring-form pan.

YIELD: 12 servings.

SPECIAL CRUST FOR CHEESECAKES

1	cup sifted all purpose flour
¼	cup sugar
1	teaspoon grated lemon peel
½	teaspoon vanilla extract
1	egg yolk
¼	cup soft butter or margarine

In small bowl, combine flour, sugar, lemon peel and vanilla. Make a well in center. Add egg yolk and butter. With fingertips, mix until dough leaves side of bowl. Form into a ball. Wrap in waxed paper. Refrigerate 1 hour.

Preheat oven to 400°.

Lightly grease bottom and inside of a 9-inch springform pan. Remove side. Take ⅓ of dough from refrigerator. Roll out directly on bottom of springform pan. Trim dough even with edge. Bake 8 to 10 minutes until golden. Cool. Divide remaining dough into 3 parts. On a lightly floured surface, roll each part into a strip 2½ inches wide. Press strips to side of springform pan, joining ends of strips to line inside completely. Trim dough so it comes only ¾ up side. Refrigerate side. When ready to add cheesecake filling, assemble bottom and side of springform pan. Bake according to directions on cheesecake filling.

YIELD: 1 cheesecake crust.

DELICATESSEN CHEESECAKE

A crustless cheesecake brought to Texas from the old delicatessens of New York. It can be made several days in advance.

16	ounces cream cheese
16	ounces cottage cheese
1½	cups sugar
4	eggs, beaten
3	tablespoons all purpose flour
3	tablespoons cornstarch
1½	tablespoons lemon juice
1	teaspoon vanilla
½	cup melted butter, cooled
1	pint sour cream

Preheat oven to 325°.
In a food processor, beat cream cheese, cottage cheese and sugar until creamy and very smooth. Add eggs to creamed mixture and beat at slow speed. Beat in flour, cornstarch, lemon and vanilla. Add melted butter and sour cream, mixing thoroughly. In a greased springform pan, pour mixture. **In a gas oven,** bake for 80 minutes until edges are light brown. Turn off oven and leave cake until oven is cold. **In an electric oven,** bake for 60 minutes. Turn off oven and leave cake until oven is cold. Chill cheesecake thoroughly before serving.

YIELD: 10 servings.

FROSTY STRAWBERRY SQUARES

1	cup all purpose flour, sifted
¼	cup brown sugar
½	cup chopped nuts
½	cup butter, softened
2	egg whites
2	tablespoons lemon juice
1	cup sugar
2	cups of fresh strawberries, sliced (substitute 10-ounce package frozen strawberries with ⅔ cup sugar)
1	cup whipped cream or Cool Whip

Preheat oven to 350°.
In a bowl, stir together flour, brown sugar, nuts and butter. In a shallow baking dish, spread crust mixture evenly on bottom. Bake 20 minutes. While baking, stir occasionally so nut mixture will not stick to dish. In a greased 9x13-inch baking dish, sprinkle ⅔ of nut mixture. In a large mixing bowl, combine egg whites, sugar, strawberries, lemon juice and beat with an electric beater on high speed to stiff peak stage, about 10 minutes. Fold in whipped cream. Spoon strawberry mixture over nut mixture in baking dish. Sprinkle remaining nut mixture on top. Freeze 6 hours or overnight. Slice and garnish with a fresh strawberry.

YIELD: 10 to 12 servings.

BANANA MERINGUES
For Recipe Page - See Index.

SAN ANTONIO RIVER MUD

Crust

2   cups all purpose flour
1   cup chopped pecans
1   cup butter or margarine, melted

Filling

1¼ cups whipping cream
4   ounces cream cheese, softened
½   cup sifted powdered sugar
2   3¾-ounce packages instant chocolate fudge pudding mix
2½ cups milk
1   banana, thinly sliced
1   cup whipping cream
½   cup toasted chopped pecans
½   cup toasted flaked coconut

Preheat oven to 350°.

In a bowl, combine flour, chopped pecans and butter. Pat into a 9x13-inch baking dish. Bake in lower ⅓ rack of oven, about 25 minutes. Let completely cool.

For Filling: In a mixing bowl, beat 1¼ cups whipping cream with cream cheese and sugar until thoroughly blended. Spread over cooled crust. Cover and chill. Whisk pudding mix with milk until thickened. Spread pudding over cream cheese layer. Chill. Thinly slice bananas and arrange over pudding. Whip remaining cream and fold in pecans. Spread over bananas. Sprinkle with toasted coconut. Chill thoroughly before serving.

YIELD: 10 to 12 servings.

VARIATION: Substitute lemon pudding for the chocolate fudge. Substitute Pistachio pudding and fresh sliced strawberries for the chocolate fudge and bananas.

GRAHAM CRACKER GREEK DESSERT

1   pound butter
16 ounces powdered sugar
4   egg yolks
1½ teaspoons vanilla
4   tablespoons cocoa
2½ pounds graham crackers
3   cups strong cold coffee
½   pound slivered almonds

In a large bowl, cream together butter and sugar. Add yolks, vanilla and cocoa. Add more chocolate if so desired. Dip each cracker quickly into cold coffee and lay on wax paper covered cookie sheet. Spread thinly with chocolate mix. Add another layer of dipped crackers and spread with chocolate mixture. Do this until it is 6 or 7 layers high. Ice top and side with chocolate. Sprinkle with almonds. Can make small loaves by using 4 sectioned graham crackers as the length. To freeze, wrap in waxed paper.

YIELD: 20 to 25 servings.

GRAND MARNIER SOUFFLE

An impressive restaurant favorite to serve guests at home. Have ready to pop into oven when serving main course. Only takes 20 minutes to bake!

2	cups milk
8	tablespoons sugar
1	pinch salt
8	tablespoons sifted all purpose flour
¼	cup cold milk
8	ounces Grand Marnier Liqueur
12	egg yolks, beaten
2	tablespoons butter, softened
16	egg whites, stiffly beaten powdered sugar for garnish

Preheat oven to 350°.
In a saucepan, bring milk, sugar and salt to a boil. Blend flour with a little cold milk and add to mixture. Add Grand Marnier. Cook, stirring for 2 or 3 minutes. Remove from heat and mix in egg yolks and butter. Butter and sugar coat 6 to 8 small souffle dishes or ramekins. Quickly fold in stiffly beaten egg whites to flour mixture. Pour into souffle dishes, smoothing surface. Bake 20 minutes until golden brown. Remove from oven. Sprinkle with powdered sugar. Serve immediately!

YIELD: 6 to 8 servings.

VARIATIONS: Serve with hot vanilla custard, English Bird's Eye Custard or raspberry custard.

NEW BRAUNFELS SCHAUM TORTE

German immigrants led by Prince Carl of Solms Braunfels established a community known as New Braunfels 33 miles northeast of San Antonio. It has retained much of its charming, old world German influence today. A famous "Wurstfest" with dancing, food and fun is held in October. Visitors enjoy tubing down the river where the Comal and Guadalupe Rivers meet. Shop at Gruene, Texas, and have lunch in the historic old Grist Mill restored as a thriving restaurant. This traditional German meringue is served at Christmas!

6	egg whites
2	cups sugar
½	teaspoon salt
1	tablespoon vinegar
1	teaspoon vanilla vanilla ice cream
½	pint whipping cream, whipped & sweetened
1	pint frozen strawberries, pre-sweetened & sliced fresh strawberries, halved & slightly sweetened

Preheat oven to 300°.
In a mixing bowl, beat egg whites about 5 minutes to stiff peak stage. Change to medium speed and add sugar, salt, vinegar and vanilla. Beat to stiff peaks. In a well buttered springform pan lined with brown paper, spread the egg white mixture. Bake about 50 minutes.
To Assemble Schaum Torte: Place meringue on bottom of large platter, next place layer of frozen strawberries, layer of vanilla ice cream, layer of whipped cream and on top of the holiday torte in a special design, the halved fresh strawberries.

YIELD: 8 to 10 servings.

FREDERICKSBURG PEACH ICE CREAM

½   cup sugar
4   cups sliced fresh peaches
6   eggs
1   cup sugar
1   14-ounce can sweetened
      condensed milk
1   13-ounce can evaporated milk
1   pint whipping cream
1   tablespoon vanilla
      whole milk

Sprinkle ½ cup sugar over peaches. Beat eggs, add 1 cup sugar, canned milks, cream and mix well. Stir in peaches and vanilla. Pour into ice cream freezer. Use whole milk to fill freezer. Follow freezer directions.

YIELD: 1 gallon.

VARIATION: Homemade Vanilla Ice Cream

5   pints whipping cream
1   13-ounce can evaporated milk
5   large eggs
2½ cups sugar
      half & half cream and milk to
      fill electric ice cream
      freezer can ⅔ full
2   teaspoons vanilla

In a double boiler, make custard by scalding whipping cream and evaporated milk. In a mixing bowl, beat eggs with sugar and slowly add to custard. Continue to heat until mixture coats spoon. Chill thoroughly in refrigerator. When ready to freeze, add enough milk and half and half cream to fill electric ice cream freezer only ⅔ full, leaving room for ice cream to expand. Add vanilla. Add equal layers of chipped ice and ice cream salt, packing ice cream freezer well to start and then adding as needed until motor shuts off.

YIELD: 1 gallon.

FRIED ICE CREAM

HOT FUDGE SAUCE

For Recipe Page - See Index.

YOGURT ICE

1   cup milk
1   7-ounce jar marshmallow
      creme (we
      recommend Kraft)
2   8-ounce containers fruit
      flavored yogurt
1   pint fresh strawberries,
      sliced or fruit of
      choice to garnish

In a mixing bowl, gradually add milk to marshmallow creme, beating with wire whisk until well blended. Stir in yogurt. Into a 9x5-inch loaf pan, pour mixture. Cover and freeze until firm. To serve, remove from freezer for 10 minutes prior to serving. Cover with fresh fruit. Slice and serve.

YIELD: 6 servings.

APRICOT DREAM DESSERT

An elegant meringue base with a delicate apricot filling topped with whipped cream!

4 eggs, separated
1 teaspoon ice water
¼ teaspoon cream of tartar
1 cup sugar
6 tablespoons lemon juice
1 14-ounce can sweetened condensed milk
1 17-ounce can apricot halves, drained & mashed
1 teaspoon vanilla
8 ounces whipping cream, whipped

Preheat oven to 275°.

In a mixing bowl, beat egg whites, ice water and cream of tartar until foamy. Gradually add sugar and beat until stiff. Into a greased 9x13-inch baking pan, spread the mixture. Bake for 1 hour and cool. In a separate bowl, beat egg yolks and stir in lemon juice. Add sweetened condensed milk, beating constantly. Stir in apricots and vanilla. Spread over cooled meringue base. Chill several hours or until firm. Spread whipped cream over top. Cut into squares.

YIELD: 15 servings.

BREAD PUDDING WITH WHISKEY SAUCE

½ pound French bread
¼ cup pecans, toasted
4 ounces butter or margarine, melted

Custard Mix

8 large eggs
1 teaspoon salt
2 cups sugar
1 teaspoon vanilla
5½ cups milk

Whiskey Sauce

8 ounces butter or margarine
2 cups powdered sugar
2 large eggs
1 ounce whiskey

Preheat oven to 350°.

For custard: In a mixing bowl, blend eggs, salt and sugar with wire whisk. Add vanilla and milk. Blend and strain. Break French bread into medium pieces. In a 9x13-inch baking dish, add bread pieces and sprinkle with pecans and pour melted butter over bread. Pour custard mix over bread pieces. For custard to bake properly, create a double boiler effect. Bake 30 to 35 minutes in a pan with 1 inch of water. Test with knife to make sure pudding is cooked.

For Whiskey Sauce: In a saucepan, melt butter and whip in powdered sugar. Fold in eggs and add whiskey. Serve warm over bread pudding.

YIELD: 12 to 16 servings.

AMARETTO ORANGES

4-5 large naval oranges,
   peeled & thinly
   sliced into rounds
¼   cup Amaretto liqueur
1 - 1½ pints lemon, grapefruit or
   melon sorbet or sherbet
   fresh mint leaves,
   optional garnish

In a bowl, place orange slices and sprinkle with liqueur. Refrigerate until serving time. Drain slices and arrange in overlapping fan pattern on dessert plates. Using 2 tablespoons, scoop sorbet into 6 to 8 egg-shaped mounds and set each on plate at base of fan pattern. Garnish with leaves and serve immediately.

YIELD: 6 to 8 servings.

TROPICAL PINEAPPLE DELIGHT

1   package pie crust stick or
   1 frozen pie crust
1   8-ounce can crushed
   pineapple, drained
1   tablespoon flour
½   cup margarine, softened
1   8-ounce package cream
   cheese, softened
½   cup sugar
½   cup brown sugar
2   teaspoons vanilla
¼   teaspoon salt
¼   teaspoon cinnamon
¼   teaspoon nutmeg
3   eggs
1   cup whipping cream,
   whipped

Preheat oven to 350°.
Make a 9-inch pie crust according to package directions. In a bowl, toss pineapple and flour. In another bowl, cream margarine and cream cheese. Slowly add sugars, continuing to beat until mixture is light and fluffy. Add vanilla, salt, cinnamon and nutmeg. Beat in eggs, one at a time. Fold in pineapple. Pour into pastry shell. Bake 40 minutes. Cool and serve with whipped cream.

YIELD: 8 servings.

ROMANOFF SAUCE

Serve over any fresh fruit especially plump, juicy strawberries!

2   cups sour cream
⅔   cup brown sugar
½   teaspoon nutmeg
1   teaspoon cinnamon
¼   ounce brandy

In a large mixing bowl, combine all ingredients together at low speed with an electric mixer for 15 to 20 minutes. This mixture grows in size as it mixes.

YIELD: 3 cups or 15 servings.

PEANUT BUSTER DESSERT

Kids of every age will love it!

1   pound Oreo cookies, crushed
½   cup butter, softened
½   gallon French vanilla ice cream
Sauce
1   13-ounce can evaporated milk
       (we recommend Carnation)
½   cup butter
2   squares semi-sweet chocolate
Topping
       Spanish peanuts
       whipped cream

In a bowl, mix crushed cookies and softened butter together. Pat into two 9x13-inch baking pans. Chill. Soften and spread French vanilla ice cream on crust and refreeze.
For Sauce: In a heavy saucepan, cook evaporated milk, butter and chocolate squares until melted and mixture thickens, about 45 minutes. Cool. Spread over ice cream and sprinkle with peanuts and refeeze. Serve with whipped cream topping.

YIELD: 20 servings.

DATE TORTE

½   pound powdered sugar
6   egg yolks, beaten
6   egg whites, stiffly beaten
½   pound dates, finely chopped
6   tablespoons cracker meal
       (we recommend Nabisco)
2   teaspoons baking powder
1   cup chopped pecans
1   pint whipping cream,
       whipped until stiff
       maraschino cherries for
       garnish, drained & halved

Preheat oven to 350°.
In a mixing bowl, combine powdered sugar, egg yolks, dates, cracker meal, baking powder and pecans. Add stiffly beaten egg whites. Into two greased 8-inch layer pans, pour batter. Bake 30 minutes. Remove from oven and cool. On a cake plate, make a mound of torte mixture by breaking cake into pieces with hands and alternating layers with generous amounts of whipped cream. Form into a rounded "cake" or torte which will be totally iced on top and sides with whipped cream. Decorate all over with cherries. Chill for several hours before serving.

YIELD: 10 to 12 servings.

QUICK FRUIT TORTE

1   roll sugar cookie dough (we
       recommend Pillsbury)
1   8-ounce package cream cheese
¼   cup sugar
1   teaspoon vanilla
2   tablespoons milk
       fresh fruit or canned fruit

Preheat oven to 350°.
Pat dough on a pizza pan. Bake until golden. Remove from oven and cool. In a bowl, beat cream cheese, milk, vanilla and sugar until fluffy. Spread on cooled cookie dough. Top with favorite fresh fruit in season. (May even substitute canned fruit.)

YIELD: 6 servings.

APPLE GOODIE

Bottom Layer

3   heaping cups chopped apples

Middle Layer

½   cup sugar
½   teaspoon salt
½   teaspoon cinnamon
½   teaspoon nutmeg
1   teaspoon all purpose flour
2   tablespoons hot water

Top Layer

½   cup all purpose flour
½   cup rolled oats
½   cup brown sugar, packed
¼   teaspoon baking soda
¼   teaspoon baking powder
½   cup butter or oleo, melted

Preheat oven to 350°.
Put chopped apples in a buttered 9x9-inch pan. In a bowl, mix together ingredients in middle layer and add hot water last. Pour mixture over apples. In another bowl, mix together ingredients for top layer and crumble on top. Bake 45 minutes and then increase temperature to 400° for 10 minutes. Great with vanilla ice cream.

YIELD: 8 to 10 servings.

ITALIAN BISCUIT TORTONI

¾   cup crispy macaroons
¾   cup half & half cream
¼   cup sugar
    pinch of salt
1   cup whipping cream
½   teaspoon vanilla
¼   teaspoon almond extract

Roll macaroons until finely crushed. Add ½ cup crumbs to half and half cream. Add sugar and salt. Stir until well mixed and let soak 1 hour. Beat whipping cream until thick and gradually beat in macaroon mixture. Add vanilla and almond extract. Fill paper cups in muffin tins with mixture. Sprinkle rest of macaroons on top. Place in freezer for 3 hours or until ready to serve.

YIELD: 12 servings.

VARIATION:
For Chocolate Tortoni: Add 6 ounces chocolate bits with flavorings.

FLAN
(Caramel Custard)

BAKED CUSTARD

CANARY ISLANDER DONUTS

REPUBLIC OF TEXAS TRIFLE
For Recipe Page - See Index.

HINTS FOR COOKED CANDIES

Use only copper or glass bowls when beating egg whites for candy.

Always use an accurate candy thermometer when exact temperatures are required.

Substitution of ingredients in candy recipes is risky and should be avoided.

To avoid crystallizing problems:

Grease sides of pans or bowls before assembling recipes which contain butter or margarine.

Stir in sugar thoroughly before heating mixture. Do not scrape the sides of pan once sugar mixture boils.

Remember any agitation of the pan during cooling will cause crystallization.

Cover pan until time sugar mixture begins to boil. Steam will melt any sugar remaining on sides of pan.

Never scrape away last of syrup when pouring into cooling pan or next mixing step.

APRICOT STICKS

1 pound apricots, washed & dried
1 whole orange, peel & all juice of ½ orange
2 cups sugar
1 pound chopped pecans small bowl powdered sugar

In a food processor, chop and grind apricots and orange. Add juice of orange. In a heavy saucepan, place fruit mixture and add sugar. Cook over low heat until mixture begins to thicken. Cool and add chopped pecans. Into a small bowl of powdered sugar, drop small amounts of mixture and roll well to desired size in palm of hands. Cool.

YIELD: Approximately 80 sticks.

CREAM CHEESE MINTS

2½ cups powdered sugar
3 ounces cream cheese
½ teaspoon flavoring

In a large mixing bowl, cut powdered sugar into cream cheese and flavoring with 2 knives or a pastry cutter (as for pie dough). Roll in balls about ¾ inch in diameter. Place one side in small amount of sugar. Press sugar side down in candy mold of roses or leaves. Unmold at once on waxed paper. (For a firmer mixture, add more powdered sugar.)

YIELD: 23 roses and 23 leaves.

Use food coloring if desired and flavor to correspond with color:
For White Mints: *Add peppermint flavoring. For wintergreen, add a touch of green or pink coloring. For lemon mints, add a touch of yellow food coloring.*
For Chocolate Mints: *Add 3 teaspoons cocoa and ½ teaspoon vanilla.*

DATE ROLL

3   cups sugar
1   cup evaporated milk
3   tablespoons margarine
3   tablespoons light corn syrup
1   cup chopped dates
1   cup chopped walnuts
1   teaspoon vanilla

In a medium saucepan, combine sugar, milk, margarine and corn syrup. Over medium heat, bring to boil and stir. Add dates to mixture. Boil to soft-ball stage of 238° on candy thermometer or until a little drop in cold water forms a soft ball. Remove from heat and add walnuts and vanilla. Beat by hand until thick. Turn out on board or waxed paper and shape into two rolls about 1¾ inches in diameter. Wrap in waxed paper. Place in refrigerator. When cooled, slice in ⅓-inch slices.

YIELD: 2½ pounds.

FESTIVE WHITE CONFETTI FUDGE

1½ pounds white chocolate
1   14-ounce can Eagle Brand
    Condensed Milk
1   teaspoon vanilla
⅛   teaspoon salt
1   cup chopped candied cherries
1   cup chopped nuts

In a heavy saucepan, melt white chocolate with condensed milk on medium low heat. Remove from heat and add vanilla, salt, cherries and nuts. Line an 8-inch square pan with wax paper and spread mixture evenly. Chill 2 to 3 hours until firm. Turn fudge onto a cutting board. Peel off paper, cut into squares and top with half a cherry.

YIELD: 16 pieces.

FUDGE

2   tablespoons flour
6   tablespoons cocoa
3   cups sugar
¾   cup half & half cream or
    Carnation evaporated
    milk
⅓   cup light corn syrup
    (we recommend Karo)
½   teaspoon salt
1   tablespoon butter
1   cup pecans
½   teaspoon vanilla

In a saucepan, combine flour, cocoa, sugar, cream, Karo syrup and salt. Cook to soft ball stage, 238°. Add butter and vanilla. Remove from heat and let stand 20 minutes. Beat and add pecans. Pour into a 9x9-inch pan.

YIELD: 4 to 5 pounds.

ENGLISH TOFFEE

½ cup margarine
1 cup sugar
½ cup butter
3 tablespoons water
1 6-ounce package chocolate chips or use less if desired
¾ cup chopped almonds, toasted, divided

In a 2-quart saucepan, combine margarine, butter, sugar and water. Cook to 300° or the hard-crack stage, stirring constantly. Do not overcook. Remove from heat. Stir in ½ cup almonds and immediately pour onto a buttered cookie sheet. Sprinkle with chocolate chips. After chips have melted, spread with spatula. Sprinkle with ¼ cup almonds. Chill to set chocolate. Break into pieces.

YIELD: 6 sheets.

PEANUT BUTTER CRUNCH

2 cups dark corn syrup (we recommend Karo)
2 cups sugar
1¼ pounds peanut butter
1 small box corn flakes

In a saucepan, cook syrup and sugar until boiling. Stir constantly. Do not overcook. Remove from heat. Add peanut butter and stir until dissolved. In a bowl with corn flakes, pour peanut butter mixture. In a buttered 10½x15½-inch pan, pour mixture. Press lightly with buttered hands. Let cool and cut in squares.

YIELD: 3½ pounds.

MICROWAVE PEANUT BRITTLE

1 cup raw unsalted peanuts
½ cup white corn syrup
1 cup sugar
⅛ teaspoon salt
1 teaspoon vanilla
1 teaspoon butter
1 teaspoon soda

In a 1½-quart heatproof glass bowl, combine peanuts, syrup, sugar and salt. Stir and blend. Microwave 8 minutes on high, stopping and stirring several times. Use wooden spoon for stirring. Add butter and vanilla. Microwave for an additional 2 minutes **without stirring.** Remove candy from oven and add soda. On a buttered cookie sheet, pour candy mixture. Cool. Break into small pieces.

YIELD: 15 to 20 pieces.

MEXICAN PRALINES
For Recipe Page - See Index.

PECANS

The state tree of Texas, the Pecan Tree, has provided a staple food item for inhabitants of the Texas region for centuries. Long before the Europeans set foot on Texas soil, the migration pattern of the Indians followed the pecan harvest.

Not only did the Indians grind the pecans into a meal for an ingredient in bread and soups, they used pecans as bartering items.

The settlers used pecans as a source of protein during the winter months after the Indians introduced them to their tasty staple.

Texas ranks second in the nation in pecan production, a multi-million dollar agricultural product.

DRY ROASTED PECANS

Drop pecan halves in boiling water for 3 minutes. Drain in colander. Put on cookie sheet, one layer deep. Roast at 300° for 25 to 30 minutes or until pecans are dried out. Do not overcook. Salt while hot.

Hint: To get pecans out of shell whole or in large pieces, soak for 2 hours in cold water, drain and let stand. Crack with a slight blow on the end. Pecans stay fresh for months if refrigerated in a moisture-proof bag or tin.

ROASTED PECANS

3 tablespoons butter or margarine
3-4 cups pecan halves
salt

Preheat oven to 350°.
In a shallow 11x15-inch baking pan, melt butter in oven. Remove pan and add pecans. Using hands, gently rub both sides of pecans with butter. Sprinkle salt over pecans. Return pan of pecans to oven and bake 10 minutes. Stir and turn. Cook an additional 8 minutes. Do not overcook! Cool. Store in airtight container.

YIELD: 3 to 4 cups roasted pecans.

SPICED NUTS

1 cup sugar
½ teaspoon cinnamon
⅛ teaspoon cream of tartar
¼ cup boiling water
1½ cups pecan halves
½ teaspoon vanilla

In a saucepan, combine sugar, cinnamon, cream of tartar and boiling water. Stir constantly while boiling to soft-ball stage, 238°. Add pecans and let cool a few minutes. Add vanilla and stir until pecans are coated. Pour on waxed paper and separate.

YIELD: 2½ cups spiced nuts.

MINTED PECANS

2   cups sugar
     dash of salt
¾   cup evaporated milk
⅛   teaspoon green food coloring
1   tablespoon butter or
        margarine
1   tablespoon creme de menthe
4   cups pecan halves

In a medium saucepan, mix sugar, salt, evaporated milk, food coloring and butter. Cook over low heat and stir until sugar is dissolved. Cook over medium heat, stirring constantly until mixture comes to a full rolling boil. Continue cooking and stirring 7 additional minutes. Remove from heat and stir in flavoring and pecans. Stir to coat nuts well. Using 2 forks, quickly drop nuts onto foil. Cool. Store in airtight container.

YIELD: 2 pounds minted pecans.

TOASTED PECANS

2   egg whites
1   cup sugar
     dash of salt
4   tablespoons margarine or
        butter
1   pound pecan halves

Preheat oven to 325°.
In a large cookie sheet or jelly roll pan, toast pecan halves for 15 to 20 minutes. In a mixing bowl, beat egg whites, sugar and salt until stiff peaks form. Fold nuts into egg white mixture. In the same cookie sheet, melt butter and pour pecan mixture into pan. Bake for 30 minutes. Stir pecan mixture every 10 minutes until butter is gone.

YIELD: 1 pound toasted pecans.

SPECIAL OCCASION CHOCOLATE DELIGHT

3   8-ounce bars Hershey
        chocolate with almonds
⅓   cup coconut
⅓   cup marshmallows
¼   cup raisins
¼   cup pecans, walnuts or
        almonds

In a saucepan, melt chocolate bars. Add all ingredients, mixing well. Spoon into pan of choice. At Christmas time, use a tree cake pan. On Valentine's Day, use a heart-shaped cake pan.

YIELD: 16 pieces.

STRAWBERRY DIVINITY
For Recipe Page - See Index.

Imagine 100,000 colored lights strategically placed in the centuries-old trees gracing the Riverwalk. Add to this thousands of lighted candles along the banks. This is San Antonio at Christmas time. The season is steeped in tradition. The first lighting of the lights brings the city to a virtual standstill. One of the most special events of the season is Las Posadas, a Mexican tradition which depicts the moving story of Joseph and Mary trying to find lodging before the birth of Jesus.

Mary Alice Cisneros
(Mrs.Henry)

Mary Alice Cisneros is the wife of the Mayor of the City of San Antonio. As a student, she studied business administration at Our Lady of the Lake University and San Antonio College. Mrs. Cisneros has had a leadership role in community projects such as: Commission for Family and Children, Senior Community Services, Texas United Way, Southland Task Force. She received a scholarship to attend the Texas Leadership Conference. She is a member of the Mexican American Business and Professional Women and a member of the Committee for Southwest Craft Center.

CHILES RELLENOS
(Stuffed Peppers)

12 fresh chiles poblanos (or substitute bell peppers)

Picadillo

1½ pounds ground pork
1½ pounds lean ground chuck roast
½ onion, finely chopped
2 cloves garlic, finely chopped
1 tablespoon salt
¼ teaspoon black pepper
3 tablespoons shortening
1 cup raisins, finely chopped
1 cup pecans, chopped
2 carrots, finely chopped
1 medium tomato, boiled, peeled & strained
1 teaspoon sugar

Batter

6 eggs separated, room temperature
½ cup flour for dusting

Sauce

6 medium sized fresh tomatoes
½ onion, sliced
1 chicken bouillon cube
3 cloves garlic
salt & pepper to taste
shortening or oil for deep frying
1 tablespoon oil

Preheat oven to broil.
Fresh chiles need to be roasted and peeled to remove the rough outer skins and improve the flavor. Make a slit in each chile to avoid "explosions" during the roasting. Place chiles on a cookie sheet and set under the broiler 4 to 6 inches from the heat source. Watch closely during the broiling. The chiles will blister and burn slightly in the roasting process. Turn chiles from time to time for even roasting. When chiles are roasted, place in a plastic bag and seal. **Let stand about 20 minutes.** The burned skin will flake off very easily, and the flesh will become a little more cooked with the steam in the bag. Make a slit in the side of each chili carefully removing the seeds and veins. Be careful to leave the top of the chili around the base of the stem intact.

For The Picadillo (*meat for stuffing chiles*): In a large dutch oven, brown the pork and beef in shortening. Add onion, garlic, salt and pepper and cook for 5 minutes. Add raisins, pecans, carrots, tomato and sugar. Cover and cook until done. Set aside for stuffing chiles.

For Batter: In a mixing bowl beat egg whites with an electric mixer until soft peaks form. Fold in beaten egg yolks. Set aside for stuffing chiles.

Recipe instructions continue on Page 343.

To Assemble Chiles Rellenos: Stuff peppers with equal portions of meat stuffing holding the opening so as not to lose any of the meat. Dust each chile with flour. Dip chile in egg batter making sure entire chile is coated. Repeat the procedure with all 12 chiles. Place on a cookie sheet.

For Frying: In a skillet or dutch oven, place enough shortening or oil to deep fry chiles. Fry until golden brown and place on paper towels to drain.

For Sauce: In a blender place tomatoes, onion, chicken bouillon cube, garlic, salt and pepper. Blend until smooth. In a large saucepan with oil, heat tomato mixture and bring to the boil and simmer about 5 minutes. To serve chiles rellenos, place on plate and pour a large spoonful of sauce over chile.

YIELD: 12 chiles rellenos.

The famous "Rose Window," sculptured on the exterior wall of the church sacristy of San Jose Mission, has fascinated visitors to the mission for generations. Known as the "Queen of the Missions," San Jose is part of the State and National Historic Site called the "Mission Trail." Built between 1768 and 1782, the entire mission compound has been restored including the outer wall with Indian dwellings, granary and workshops. The old nearby flour mill used by the mission was the first in Texas. The Spanish priests converted the pagan Indians to Christianity and utilized their labor to construct beautiful mission edifices and dig a complex water system. The acequia system made possible the cultivation of the land outside the mission walls. Visitors can view remnants of the aqueduct system today.

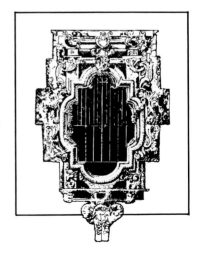

Barbara Bush
(Mrs. George)

Barbara Bush is the wife of the Vice President of the United States. In 1974, while her husband was serving as the Chief U.S. Liaison to Peking, Mrs. Bush learned much about China and has lectured to numerous groups on the subject. She is also a director of Reading Is Fundamental (R.I.F.).

LEMON CHICKEN
Rich, but wonderful!

Rub 6 chicken breasts (bones removed) with lemon, salt, pepper and a little flour.

Saute in butter for 7 minutes on each side. Remove from heat and put chicken in baking dish.

Mix together in saute pan:

2	tablespoons vermouth
1	cup heavy whipping cream
2	tablespoons lemon juice
1	little lemon, grated

Deglaze the saute pan, scraping in all the ingredients. Strain the sauce over the chicken breasts.

Sprinkle parmesan cheese over the top and brown lightly under the broiler for a few minutes.

YIELD: 6 servings.

Linda Gale White
(Mrs. Mark)

Linda Gale White is the wife of the Governor of the State of Texas. She is a member of Houston Junior Forum, a teacher by profession and a concerned community volunteer.

SMOTHERED QUAIL

6	tablespoons butter, divided
1	medium onion, finely chopped
½	pound fresh mushrooms, sliced
1	tablespoon oil
8 - 12	quail breasts
½	cup dry white wine or vermouth
1	cup light cream (half & half cream)
1	10¾-ounce can cream of mushroom soup

Melt 3 tablespoons butter and saute onion and mushrooms until tender. Remove from pan. Melt 3 tablespoons butter and oil; saute birds until brown. Remove from pan, pour off remaining fat. Add white wine or vermouth; scrape up particles on bottom of skillet. Add mushroom soup, onions, mushrooms and cream; stir until well blended. Return birds to pan, spooning sauce over them. Cover and simmer for 30 minutes. (Chicken breasts may be substituted.)

YIELD: 8 servings.

CUCUMBER / SHRIMP BISQUE

1	quart buttermilk
1	tablespoon dijon mustard
1½	pounds cooked shrimp, deveined, peeled & sliced
1½	pounds English cucumber, peeled & finely diced
1	tablespoon fresh dillweed, chopped
1	tablespoon chives, finely chopped

Mix the buttermilk and mustard. Fold in the shrimp, cucumber, dillweed and chives. Chill mixture at least four hours before serving.

YIELD: 6 servings.

Lady Bird Johnson
(Mrs. Lyndon B.)

Lady Bird Johnson is the widow of the 36th President of the United States. Her husband was born and reared 90 miles northwest of San Antonio in the Texas Hill Country. During Johnson's presidency, the L.B.J. Ranch on the banks of the Pedernales River near Stonewall, Texas, often was the center of world attention. The Texas White House, as it was known, is now part of the Lyndon Baines Johnson National Historic Park and administered by the National Park Service. Tourists visiting San Antonio take a day's tour of the ranch and birthplace to experience early pioneer life in Texas. The Johnsons introduced the world to Texas barbecues.

NOCHE SPECIALS

"Noche Specials announce to our guests that they are in the Southwest - a favorite snack with drinks in our part of the country." – Lady Bird Johnson.

15 corn tortillas
   oil for frying
1½ cups grated cheese
60 jalapeno pepper slices

Cut tortillas into quarters and fry in deep, hot fat until brown and crisp on both sides. Drain and put about 1 teaspoon of grated cheese and a slice of jalapeno pepper on each quarter. Place in hot oven until well heated and cheese begins to melt. Serve at once.
YIELD: 10 to 12 servings.

PEDERNALES RIVER CHILI

4 pounds chili meat, ¾-inch plate coarse ground round steak or well trimmed chuck roast
1 large onion, chopped
2 cloves garlic
1 teaspoon grand oregano
1 teaspoon comino seed
6 teaspoons chili powder, more if needed
1½ cups canned whole tomatoes
2-6 dashes liquid hot sauce
   salt to taste
2 cups hot water

In a large, heavy fry pan or dutch oven, place meat, onion and garlic. Cook until light-colored. Add oregano, comino seed, chili powder, tomatoes, hot pepper sauce, salt and hot water. Bring to boil, lower heat and simmer for 1 hour. Skim off fat during cooking.
YIELD: 6 to 8 servings.

Margaret Cousins

Margaret Cousins has been an editor and contributor to **Good Housekeeping,** **McCall's** and **Ladies' Home Journal** magazines. She is the author of numerous children's books. She resides in San Antonio where she is a former member of the San Antonio Advisory Riverwalk Commission.

Ms. Cousins has been named to the Texas Women's Hall of Fame for her contributions to the literary arts.

BAKED CUSTARD

4 eggs
¼ cup granulated sugar
¼ teaspoon salt
2½ cups milk
1 teaspoon vanilla flavoring
    nutmeg or shredded coconut

Preheat oven 300°.
Butter 6 custard cups or ramekins. Break eggs into large bowl and beat until foamy. Add sugar, salt and beat until thick and lemon-colored. Add milk and vanilla and beat thoroughly again. Pour into custard cups, about ½ inch from the top of the cups. Sprinkle nutmeg or shredded coconut on top of each one. Place custard cups in shallow baking pan. Pour hot water into the baking pan about ¾ inch from top of cups. Place pan on oven rack in oven. Bake for approximately 1 hour. Test custard for doneness by inserting a silver knife. If knife comes out clean, the custards are done. Remove from oven and hot water immediately and cool on a cake rack. Chill thoroughly in refrigerator. To serve, unmold custards by running a knife around the rims and upending on dessert plates. Top with sweetened whipped cream, fresh, frozen or canned or stewed dried fruits or berries or apple sauce. Also serve with chocolate sauce, caramel sauce and chopped pecans, maple syrup or amaretto.

YIELD: 6 servings.

Rosita Fernandez

Famous local performer and personality, "Rosita" has appeared in many Walt Disney productions and "The Alamo" with John Wayne.

RELLENO PARA PAVO
(Turkey Stuffing)

1	pound pork meat (excess fat removed)
	gizzard, liver, heart from turkey
	salt & pepper to taste
3	cinnamon sticks
¼	cup sugar
4	cups water
1	medium potato, cooked & diced
1	apple, diced
1	medium onion, chopped
2	sweet pickles, chopped
1	cup pecans, chopped
1	cup raisins
2	cups croutons
2-3	cooked egg yolks
1	tomato, mashed

Cook pork meat, gizzard, liver and heart in water with salt, pepper, cinnamon sticks and sugar. Drain and save broth. After meat is cooked, dice it into small pieces and add cooked potato, apple, onion, pickles, pecans, raisins and croutons, mashed egg yolks and tomato. Mix all ingredients well, if too dry add some broth. Stuff turkey.

YIELD: 20 servings.

VARIATION: Use leftover stuffing to make Chiles Rellenos.

GALLINA EN MOLE
(Chicken in Chili Sauce)

1	2-3 pound chicken, cut in pieces
1	cup mole paste (Dona Maria or Bueno Mole)
½	cup smooth peanut butter
3	bricks Mexican chocolate
	salt to taste
4	cups water

Cook chicken. Drain and save broth. In large pan, dissolve mole paste, peanut butter and chocolate on low heat. Add 2 cups of chicken broth. Mix well and add chicken pieces. Serve hot. Maybe frozen. Do not reheat in microwave.

YIELD: 4 to 6 servings.

Karen Haram

Express/News Food Editor Karen Haram is a world traveler, food expert and wife of an Air Force officer. A native of Illinois, Haram has been a food writer for over ten years.

HOT FUDGE SAUCE

"This recipe originally came from the Scottish Rite Dormitory at the University of Texas. For years, I looked for a hot fudge sauce that tasted as good as those sold commercially. When I found this recipe, what I found was one that tastes even better!"

1   stick sweet (unsalted) butter
1   5⅓-ounce can evaporated milk
2½ cups confectioners' sugar
6   1-ounce squares unsweetened chocolate
2   teaspoons vanilla extract

Put butter in double boiler over low heat. Add evaporated milk, confectioners' sugar and chocolate squares. Heat, stirring occasionally, until chocolate is completely melted, about 25 to 30 minutes. Remove sauce from heat and add vanilla, stirring vigorously. Serve sauce warm over scoops of ice cream or roll scoops of ice cream in coconut and freeze, then serve warmed sauce over these snowballs. Sauce will keep indefinitely in the refrigerator. To serve, reheat slowly in double boiler. This sauce is very thick. To thin, add light cream or evaporated milk. **Do not thin with water.** This sauce can easily be made 1 or 2 hours before serving. Just keep over very low heat in double boiler.

YIELD: 3 cups.

SPINACH SALAD

1   pound bag fresh spinach
3   hard-cooked eggs
10 slices bacon, crisply cooked & crumbled
1   can sliced water chestnuts, drained

Dressing
½   cup vegetable oil
1   small onion, finely chopped
¼   cup sugar
2   tablespoons catsup
2   tablespoons red wine vinegar
    salt to taste
2   tablespoons bottled Italian salad dressing
1   tablespoon worcestershire sauce

Thoroughly clean spinach, discarding stems. Tear into bite-sized pieces. Chop eggs and combine with spinach, bacon and water chestnuts. Combine all dressing ingredients in a jar. Shake thoroughly to combine well. Toss with spinach just before serving. Dressing can be made several hours ahead of time and left at room temperature until serving time.

YIELD: 8 servings.

Candy Erben Wagner

Cooking expert and author, Candy Erben Wagner is a member of San Antonio Junior Forum and has been a major influence on the writing of this cookbook. In her book, *Cooking Texas Style,* Wagner states: "Some aficionados say that authentic Fajitas must be grilled over a mesquite fire, but they are delectable regardless of the type of fire used as long as they are not overcooked. We cannot deny, though, that being out in the wideopen spaces under the stars around a pit fire of mesquite, its distinctive aroma filling the air and fajitas grilling, is a scenario beyond compare. But in this case, perhaps it is the atmosphere as well as the mesquite which prompts such absolutes!"

FAJITAS

1	cup dry red wine
½	cup oil
½	cup red wine vinegar
2	tablespoons worcestershire sauce
2	cloves garlic
1	teaspoon oregano
½	teaspoon basil
1	teaspoon whole peppercorns
2½	pounds skirt steak
12	flour tortillas
1	onion, thinly sliced

Combine wine, oil, vinegar, worcestershire sauce, garlic, oregano, basil and peppercorns in a large, nonmetallic bowl. Add steak and toss well. Marinate 24-48 hours in the refrigerator. Toss several times during marination.

Grill steaks over a very hot fire, 4-6 inches from heat, 3-4 minutes per side. Do not overcook.

Cut steaks in thin strips across the grain. Warm tortillas. To serve, place a portion of the meat strips down the center of each tortilla. Top with salsa and sliced onions and fold in half or overlap the edges.

YIELD: 4-6 servings.

FRESH MEXICAN SALSA

1	cup chopped tomato
¼	cup chopped onion
1	tablespoon fresh coriander or cilantro, finely chopped
2-3	fresh serrano peppers, minced
½	teaspoon salt
2-4	tablespoons water

Combine tomato, onion, coriander and peppers. Add salt and mix well. Add 2-4 tablespoons water, depending on juiciness of tomatoes. This sauce is best used immediately. However, it can be made up to 3 hours ahead if need be.

YIELD: 1½-2 cups.

COOKING TEXAS STYLE
by Candy Wagner & Sandra Marquez
The University of Texas Press, 1983

Nancy Parker

Food Demonstrator and Party Consultant, Nancy Parker, is well known for the Nancy Parker Cooking School in Greenville, Texas.

BROCHETTES OF SHRIMP AND ZUCCHINI

24 medium shrimp, uncooked
24 medium mushroom caps
5 slices bacon, cut in
    1-inch squares
24 1¼-inch slices unpeeled
    zucchini
    salt & fresh coarsely
    ground pepper
3 tablespoon fresh lemon juice

Garlic Butter

1 stick butter
1 medium shallot
3 large cloves garlic
2 tablespoons chopped parsley
1 teaspoon freshly
    ground pepper
½ teaspoon salt
1 tablespoon lemon juice
¼ teaspoon basil & marjoram
    garnish with chopped parsley

Mince garlic and shallot in processor with steel knife, add butter and remaining ingredients from garlic butter. Place butter in a piece of foil and make a roll. (Double this recipe and freeze some for later use.) This butter is good over steaks, chicken or pork ribs.

Peel shrimp. Alternate on a skewer: shrimp, mushroom, bacon, zucchini. Brush with garlic butter.

Preheat oven to broil.

Cook brochettes, 6 inches away from heat for 3 minutes on each side. Brush each side with garlic butter. Sprinkle with lemon juice and garnish with chopped parsley. Serve with buttered rice, broiled tomatoes and crusty French bread.

YIELD: 4 servings.

Adele's Catering

Junior Forum members Yolanda Wright and Lucille Hooker own and operate Adele's Catering and have turned their fascination for entertaining into creative catering.

BEARNAISE SAUCE

Blender Hollandaise Sauce

1   cup butter
2   egg yolks
2   tablespoons lemon juice
½   teaspoon salt
¼   teaspoon tabasco

Bearnaise Sauce

¼   cup white wine
2   tablespoons tarragon vinegar
2-4 tablespoons fresh chopped tarragon
2   tablespoons chopped shallots
¼   teaspoon pepper
     Blender Hollandaise Sauce

Make Blender Hollandaise Sauce first. In a small saucepan, heat butter until very hot but not brown. Set aside. In a blender, add egg yolks, lemon juice, salt and tabasco. Put cover on blender and turn on low speed. Immediately remove cover and while on, pour hot butter in a steady stream. Turn off and set blender in 2 inches of hot water. If sauce becomes too thick, add 1 tablespoon hot water and blend. Set aside.

For Bearnaise Sauce: In a small saucepan, combine white wine, tarragon vinegar, fresh tarragon, shallots and pepper. Bring to a boil and cook rapidly until liquid is reduced. Pour mixture into blender with Hollandaise Sauce and stir. Serve over steaks or fish.

YIELD: 10 servings.

Catering by Don Strange

Specializing in the Tastes of Texas, be it Mexican, German or seafood from the Gulf, Don Strange's goal is to show off the variety of Texas foods across the country. At his ranch near Welfare, Texas, he can hold barbecues that are so authentic in both surroundings and food that visitors to the state feel like they have "really been to Texas!"

BARBECUED BRISKET

2   9-pound pieces of brisket of beef
1   teaspoon salt
1   teaspoon pepper
1   teaspoon paprika
2   cups catsup
1   tablespoon sweet relish
1   tablespoon margarine
½   teaspoon liquid smoke
1   tablespoon worcestershire sauce
    salt, pepper & paprika to taste

Mix salt, pepper and paprika together and sprinkle on brisket. Cook slowly over charcoals for six hours. To make sauce, bring catsup, relish, margarine, liquid smoke and worcestershire sauce to a boil. Add salt, pepper and paprika to taste. Use as a sauce on the brisket after it is cooked.

YIELD: 18 to 20 servings.

BONELESS PORK LOIN WITH TANGY SAUCE

4   pounds pork loin, boneless
3   tablespoons garlic salt
3   tablespoons chili powder
1   cup apple jelly
1   cup catsup
2   tablespoons cider vinegar
2   teaspoons chili powder

Preheat oven 350°.
Mix garlic salt and chili powder together and rub on pork. Put pork in roasting pan and cook 2 hours, uncovered. Prepare sauce by taking apple jelly, catsup, cider vinegar and chili powder and bring to a boil in a saucepan. Drizzle sauce over pork 20 minutes before meat is done. Excess sauce can be served along side the pork loin. Drippings can also be added to the sauce.

YIELD: 8 to 10 servings.

Catering by Rosemary

Uniquely decorated, colorful food areas with special themes is the trademark of Rosemary Kowalski, President of Catering by Rosemary. One of her special party themes is "Six Flags Over Texas" featuring cuisine from France, Spain, Mexico, Texas, the Confederacy and the United States. Artistically displayed flags and beautifully decorated food booths add to the festivity of the event. From large fiesta convention parties to small intimate dinners, the cuisine is prepared and served exquisitely.

CRAB AND AVOCADO ENCHILADAS

¼ cup finely chopped onion
¼ cup chopped ripe olives
¼ cup fresh mushrooms, sliced
2 tablespoons butter
10 ounces crabmeat (fresh, canned or frozen)
1 ripe avocado, mashed
1 ripe avocado, sliced (for garnish)
1½ cups sour cream, divided
½ teaspoon salt
   dash of pepper
   crushed red pepper flakes to taste, optional
1 dozen tortillas
   hot vegetable oil
1 cup grated cheddar cheese
½ cup sliced ripe olives

Preheat oven to 350°.
Saute onion, chopped olives and mushrooms in butter. Remove from heat and stir in crabmeat, mashed avocado mixed with 1 cup sour cream, salt, pepper and red pepper. Dip each tortilla in hot oil and drain on absorbent paper. Fill each tortilla with some of the crab mixture, roll and place seam side down in a buttered 9x11-inch casserole. Cover with remaining sour cream and sprinkle with cheese and sliced olives. Bake for 20 minutes and serve immediately topped with fresh avocado slices. This type of dish does not hold for any length of time. The moisture from the seafood makes the tortillas crack; the flavor is good but the appearance is not the same.

YIELD: 6 servings.

Celebration Savvy

Entertaining creatively is what Dorothy Berend and Debbie Schueneman feel they do best and Celebration Savvy allows them to do just that. Their goal is to make the host's event as relaxed and enjoyable as possible; hence, their motto "Leave the party to us!"

BOURBON CASHEW STUDDED HAM

Ham

5-6 pound cooked ham
1   cup bourbon
1   cup packed brown sugar
¼   teaspoon ground cloves
15- 20 whole cashews

Stuffing

1½ cups herb stuffing mix
        (we recommend
        Pepperidge Farm)
8   tablespoons butter, melted
3   tablespoons prepared mustard
3   eggs
¾   cup parsley, minced

Preheat oven to 325°.
In a saucepan, combine bourbon, sugar and cloves. Simmer mixture for 5 minutes. In a medium bowl, mix stuffing ingredients together. Make holes in top of ham with apple corer at 2-inch intervals. Save ham pieces for another use. Stuff holes in ham with one cashew then stuffing mix and one cashew on top. Spread rest of stuffing on top of ham. In a 9x13-inch glass baking dish, place ham and pour bourbon sauce on top. Bake uncovered for 1½ hours until crust is golden brown. Baste with bourbon sauce while ham is cooking.

YIELD: 20 to 25 servings.

BANANA MERINGUES

Meringues

4   egg whites
¼   cup + 3 tablespoons sugar
½   cup powdered sugar
2   tablespoons cornstarch

Filling

1¼ cups whipping cream
¼   cup powdered sugar
1   tablespoon cocoa powder,
        sifted
6   bananas

Topping

1   12-ounce package semi-sweet
        chocolate chips
2   teaspoons Kahlua

Preheat oven to 250°.
For Meringues: In a small mixing bowl, beat egg whites until stiff. Slowly add sugar beating constantly. Sift powdered sugar and cornstarch onto whites and gently fold in. Prepare 2 greased cookie sheets. Spoon meringue into pastry tube with large star tip squeezing onto cookie sheets in banana shapes. Bake 3 to 4 hours.

For Filling: In a small mixing bowl, whip cream with powdered sugar until stiff. Stir in cocoa powder gently. Top meringues with dollops of whipped cream. Top cream with banana halves. In a saucepan, melt chocolate chips and Kahlua. Drizzle topping over bananas.

YIELD: 12 banana meringues.

Fresh Horizons Creative Catering

True to its name, Fresh Horizons Creative Catering is noted for its exclusive use of fresh fruits and vegetables and unique methods of preparing foods. Specializing in cooking on location, Caryn Hasslocher Johnson prepares American and regional style cuisines with great gusto!

PECAN CHEESECAKE

This delicious cheesecake using San Antonio pecans is a **no bake** recipe.

Crust

1	cup Graham cracker crumbs
2	teaspoons of sugar
2	teaspoons of cinnamon
¼	cup margarine, chilled

Filling

3	8-ounce packages cream cheese, softened
¾	cup sugar
1	cup pecans, chopped
2	tablespoons vanilla

For Crust: Combine the crackers crumbs with the sugar, cinnamon and margarine. Press into a 9-inch springform pan.

For Filling: In a food processor with a whipping attachment, beat cheese and sugar for 10 minutes until smooth. Add vanilla and stir in pecans. Pour into 9-inch springform pan with cracker crumb crust. Chill overnight.

YIELD: 10 to 12 servings.

Royal Catering

Bill Stephens' Royal Catering prides itself in its ability to create special occasions that accomplish the goals of clients, whether a promotional banquet for thousands or a simple get together with friends. Western barbecues to haute cuisine menus, plus decorations and entertainment with a royal flair, go together to make magic events.

HOT ARTICHOKE DIP

1   cup artichoke hearts
1   cup mayonnaise
1   cup grated parmesan cheese
1   tablespoon chopped chives
½   teaspoon paprika
1   8-inch ovenproof casserole
1   pound melba toast

Preheat oven to 350°.
Blend artichoke hearts in food processor. Add mayonnaise, parmesan cheese, chives and blend all ingredients well. Spoon into casserole and sprinkle top with paprika. Place in oven about 20 minutes until top is brown. Serve with melba toast. Can be made a day ahead. Cover tightly and refrigerate until needed.

YIELD: 8 to 10 servings.

Simply Delicious

Dana Di Castro and Junior Forum members Margie Weiss and Beverly Zaiontz own and operate an American gourmet carry-home and delicatessen located in Villita del Sol in Alamo Heights.

BROCCOLI CROWN WITH CHERRY TOMATOES

An elegant souffle-like broccoli ring filled with colorful cherry tomatoes.

2	pounds fresh broccoli
1	small onion, chopped
6	tablespoons margarine or butter, divided
4	tablespoons all-purpose flour
1	teaspoon seasoned salt
1	cup milk
3	eggs
½	cup mayonnaise or salad dressing
¼	cup fresh parsley, chopped
2	cups cherry tomatoes
½	teaspoon leaf marjoram, crumbled

Clean broccoli and chop stems and flowers. This will make approximately 4 cups. In a medium saucepan, cook in a small amount of boiling water for 10 minutes until crispy and drain. In a medium saucepan, saute onion in 4 tablespoons margarine until soft. Stir in flour and seasoned salt. Cook, stirring constantly, just until bubbly. Stir in milk. Continue cooking and stirring until sauce thickens and boils 1 minute. In a small bowl, beat eggs slightly. Stir in a generous ½ cup of hot sauce. Quickly stir back into remaining sauce in pan. Cook and stir constantly over medium heat for 3 minutes or until mixture thickens again. Remove from heat. Stir in mayonnaise and parsley. Fold into drained broccoli. Spoon into a well-greased 5-cup ring mold. Set mold in a baking pan. Place on a shelf in the oven. Pour boiling water into pan to a depth of about 1 inch. Bake in moderate oven of 350° for 30 minutes or until set.

For The Cherry Tomatoes: Wash and remove stems. In a small frying pan, melt 2 tablespoons margarine with crumbled marjoram and stir in tomatoes. Cook for 5 minutes or just until heated.

Remove broccoli crown from pan of water. Let ring stand several minutes, then loosen around edge with a knife. Invert onto serving platter. Fill center with herb butter tomatoes.

YIELD: 6 servings.

Club Josef

Josef Freed started Josef's University Club in 1962. Today his daughter, Jennifer Langley, operates Club Josef, a private club located in the Olmos Tower near Alamo Stadium specializing in intercontinental cuisine. The view of the city lights at night is beautiful from this hilltop location.

STEAK TARTARE A LA JOSEF

9	ounces ground sirloin
1	dash Lea & Perrins worcestershire sauce
1	dash tabasco sauce
1	teaspoon dijon mustard
1	teaspoon ketchup
1	dash brandy
1	teaspoon olive oil
1	wedge of lemon
1	egg yolk
1	teaspoon capers
2	tablespoons chopped onions
2	or 3 anchovy filets
2	tablespoons chopped hard-boiled egg

Grind 9 ounces sirloin. Separate 1 egg, reserving the yolk. Chop anchovies into bits. Combine beef, egg yolk, anchovies, dijon mustard, capers, onions and chopped boiled egg in large bowl. Add dash of brandy, dash of worcestershire, dash of tabasco, ketchup and olive oil. Squeeze lemon wedge over mixture and grind fresh pepper to taste. Blend all ingredients and mix well. Serve on a cold plate and garnish with chopped fresh parsley. Excellent with fresh rye or pumpernickel bread.

YIELD: 1 to 2 servings.

MANGO SAUCE

2	fresh mangos
1	tablespoon confectioners' sugar
½	teaspoon granulated sugar
1	can sliced mangos
½	scoop mango ice cream (substitute vanilla)

Peel fresh mangos, cut into quarters and place in blender along with both sugars. Drain off about ⅓ of juice from canned mangos. Add remaining ⅔'s can juice and canned mangos to blender with mango ice cream. Blend thoroughly to make sauce. Serve on top of ice cream.

YIELD: 8 servings.

Jennifer and Gregory Langley

Dominion Country Club

Officially opened in May 1985, the Dominion Country Club has become one of San Antonio's most exclusive clubs. Featuring an 18-hole golf course and 13 tennis courts, the club offers seven dining areas ranging from the very formal Wine Room, to the casual Cabana at the Swim Center.

MEDALLIONS AU POIVRE
(Tenderloins on Pepper Sauce)

This dish is quick and easy to prepare and the taste excellent! Never do in advance. The recipe is considered a dish of the "Original French Kitchen."

4	4-ounce beef tenderloins
1	tablespoon vegetable oil
1	teaspoon salt & white pepper, ground
1	tablespoon black pepper, cracked
1	tablespoon fresh butter, unsalted
1	tablespoon shallots, chopped
1	tablespoon parsley, chopped
¼	cup brandy
1	cup heavy cream
½	cup demi-glace, instant

Preheat oil in a 8-inch skillet. Prepare meat by seasoning on both sides with salt and white pepper. Press fresh, cracked black pepper on one side of each tenderloin. Place cracked pepper side down in skillet. (Pores close immediately and pepper remains on meat). When meat is cooked to preference, drain grease. Add fresh butter to meat and continue heating. Saute shallots and rest of cracked pepper with meat for approximately 30 seconds. Just before adding brandy, add parsley. (This prevents the burning of the parsley.) Add brandy and flame the meat for a couple of seconds. Remove the meat. Add demi-glace and heavy cream with salt and white pepper. Let it boil and reduce until the sauce is thick and smooth.

For Medium Cooked Tenderloins: Drain the grease when medium rare and begin adding other ingredients. Any kind of pasta is a perfect side dish.

YIELD: 2 servings.

Beda Steiner, Chef

Oak Hills Country Club

Majestic old oak trees cover the prestigious private country club hosting the Texas Open Golf Tournament for many years. Located near the South Texas Medical Center, the club has an extraordinary reputation for gourmet cuisine.

CURRIED RICE "BOMBAY"

10	ounces or 2 cups converted rice
½	cup onion, finely chopped
½	cup celery, finely chopped
3	tablespoons butter or margarine
4	cups chicken stock
2	teaspoons curry powder
½	teaspoon salt or to taste

Melt butter in a 2-quart sauce pan over medium heat. Add onion and celery. Saute until onion appears glossy. Add curry powder. Stir frequently. After 4 minutes, add rice and stir until it is coated with all ingredients in pan. Saute for 5 minutes, and add chicken stock. Simmer until liquid is absorbed by the rice at medium to low heat. Take pan off the heat and let sit covered until ready to serve. Before serving fluff rice with fork.

Paul Rossmeier, Executive Chef

YIELD: 8 servings.

DEMI-GLACE OR BROWN SAUCE

2	pounds veal bones, cut in small pieces
1	carrot, cut in chunks
1	onion, not peeled, cut in chunks
1	stalk celery, cut in chunks
½	teaspoon whole rosemary
½	teaspoon whole thyme
½	teaspoon whole marjoram
¼	teaspoon whole peppercorns
½	cup tomato paste

Place all ingredients in a roasting pan and roast until dark brown, stirring occasionally in a hot oven. When brown, add water. Boil for about 3 hours, strain and put liquid into saucepan and discard bones. Bring to a boil and thicken with 2 cups red wine mixed with 1½ cups flour. Let simmer for 1 hour and strain. Adjust seasoning with salt and white pepper. Cooking time is approximately 4½ hours. This sauce is used with Schnitzel A La San Antonio and Acapulco Chicken With Lemon Butter Sauce.

YIELD: 2 to 3 quarts.

VARIATION: Brown Sauce or Packaged Demi Glace of good quality can be substituted.

Paul Rossmeier, Executive Chef

Plaza Club

An exclusive private club located atop the Frost Bank Tower near San Fernando Cathedral in downtown San Antonio, the Plaza Club has a panoramic view of the city. Specializing in Continental and American cuisine, it is a popular location for private parties.

LOBSTER BISQUE

3½ cups rich fish stock
½ cup brandy or cognac
6 tablespoons butter
4 tablespoons flour
2 teaspoons tomato paste
 salt & white pepper
1-1 ½ pound boiled lobster
6 tablespoons unsalted butter
1 cup heavy cream
2 teaspoons minced parsley

Melt 6 tablespoons butter over low heat. Add flour, tomato paste and a pinch of white pepper and cook, stirring constantly for 3 to 5 minutes, not allowing flour to brown. Add fish stock and brandy and stir over medium heat until it comes to a boil. Simmer 15 minutes. In the meantime, shell the lobster, set the tail meat aside and grind the claw and knuckle meat until very fine in a food processor using the stainless steel cutting blade. Add 6 tablespoons unsalted butter and grind again. Strain through a fine mesh strainer. Set aside. Add heavy cream to fish stock mixture and simmer for 5 more minutes. Use this time to dice the reserved lobster meat to garnish the soup bowls. Just before serving, warm fish stock mixture and add lobster butter a little at a time. Pour into warmed soup bowls and add diced lobster meat and garnish with minced parsley.

Henry B. Rebmann III, Executive Chef

YIELD: Approximately 5 cups.

The Crockett Hotel

BREAST OF CHICKEN "AMERICAN BOUNTY"

Located at the back door of the Alamo is the newly renovated Crockett Hotel, named after Davy Crockett, one of the most famous heroes in the Battle of the Alamo. The restaurant known as **Lela B's** is a small, intimately formal dining room open only for dinner and songtime with waiters that burst into song at the drop of a napkin. American cuisine, from roast duck Minnesota Lakes style to rack of lamb, is its specialty.

2	8-ounce boneless chicken breasts
1	shallot
4	ounces chopped mushrooms
2	ounces bay shrimp, chopped
1	celery stalk, finely diced
1	carrot, finely diced
1	teaspoon chopped parsley
	salt & pepper to taste
	dijon mustard
	fresh chives, chopped
1	teaspoon flour
1	teaspoon butter
1	cup heavy cream
¼	cup white wine

William H. Fontes, Executive Chef

Preheat oven to 400°.
Combine shallot, mushrooms, shrimp, celery, carrot and parsley. Saute until all the mushroom liquid is cooked off and dry. Allow to cool. Spread this mixture over chicken breast and roll. Secure chicken with picks. Bake for approximately 20 minutes.

For The Sauce: Make a roux with the flour and butter. Add cream to roux stirring until smooth. Add white wine and reduce to thicker consistency. Add dijon mustard and chives. Salt and pepper to taste.

To Serve: Put sauce underneath slice of chicken and fan chicken breast over sauce. Serve with wild rice and fresh seasonal vegetables.

YIELD: 2 servings.

Four Seasons Hotel

Go for the surroundings as well as the food. The Four Seasons Hotel has a knack for understated class and its dining room is no exception. Located at the corner of South Alamo and Durango, the beautifully landscaped courtyard is your picturesque view while dining on coho salmon or roast lamb. American and Continental menus are rotated periodically.

BLACKENED RIVER TROUT WITH CAYENNE AND PAPRIKA

2   trout, deboned
2   lemons
½   cup butter, clarified
1   tablespoon paprika
¼   tablespoon cayenne pepper
    salt & pepper to taste

Salt and pepper the trout. Squeeze lemon on the fish. Sprinkle cayenne on fish. Mix clarified butter and paprika together. Brush mixture on fish until red. Heat heavy skillet until very hot. Drop fish flesh down in skillet until it turns charcoal black on the outside. Remove from pan; place in another pan and finish in oven. (Finish according to preference. Some prefer it burnt outside and uncooked inside.) Brush on more butter and lemon prior to serving. Broccoli, cauliflower and potatoes are a nice accompaniment for this gourmet fish dish.

YIELD: 2 servings.

VARIATION: Try with red snapper or other fish fillets.

Hilton Palacio Del Rio

Built in 1968 during HemisFair when Texan Lyndon B. Johnson was President of the United States, this Hilton on the river was erected by H.B. Zachry in approximately 60 days and made world history. The beautiful Spanish Colonial hotel has one of the prime locations on the river. The ticket office for river boat rides is directly across from the hotel.

SAUTEED VEAL CHOPS PALERMO

4   veal chops, ½-inch thick with cornerbone removed(so chops can be pounded flat to ¼-inch thick)

2   teaspoons fresh rosemary, finely chopped

4   cloves garlic, 3 finely chopped, reserve 1 clove

2   teaspoons fresh basil, finely chopped

1   cup flour

2   eggs, beaten well

1   cup bread crumbs

4   tablespoons olive oil

4   tablespoons clarified butter
   salt & pepper to taste

8   ounces good Italian tomato sauce

Flatten veal chops. Combine rosemary, garlic, basil, salt, pepper and bread crumbs. Press the chops into the flour to coat evenly. Dip them into the eggs. Press into the bread crumb mixture. Put olive oil, butter and garlic clove into a shallow saute pan. Begin heating. When the garlic is brown, remove it and discard. The pan is now ready to saute the chops. Saute the chops 2 to 3 minutes on each side until the crust is golden brown. Veal does not need to be well done. Medium done is suggested. Transfer veal to paper towels to drain and serve promptly. Serve the Italian tomato sauce on the side with two fresh steamed vegetables and risotto or pasta.

YIELD: 4 servings.

Louis Spost, Executive Chef

The Gunter Hotel

One of the oldest and finest hotels in San Antonio is located in the heart of the downtown area on Houston Street near the renovated Majestic Theatre. The Cafe Suisse restaurant with its delicious pastries, is popular with theatergoers before and after Majestic roadshows.

CHICKEN CASA DE MOROS

Tarragon Butter

3   ounces unsalted butter
      room temperature
½   ounce dried tarragon
      pinch white pepper
2   drops tabasco

Chicken

2   7-ounce boneless chicken
      breasts, *skin on*
3   ounces tarragon butter
      flour for dusting
      salt & pepper mix
2   ounces dry white wine
3   ounces brandy
      (Cognac preferred)
2   ounces fresh mushrooms,
      sliced
1   cup heavy cream
2   ounces shallots,
      finely chopped

Mix all ingredients from tarragon butter together. Stuff each chicken breast with 1½ ounces tarragon butter under the skin. Dust breasts with flour and saute in clarified butter until golden brown on both sides. Put shallots in pan and saute for 1 minute. Add wine to deglaze pan and reduce by ½ its volume. Add brandy and flame. Add mushrooms and heavy cream. Reduce cream mixture by ⅓ its volume. Serve chicken breasts on favorite bed of rice and pour sauce over. Serve immediately.

YIELD: 2 servings.

Mark Weber, Executive Chef

ACAPULCO CHICKEN
WITH LEMON BUTTER SAUCE

Chicken Breasts

2 7-ounce boneless breasts of chicken, *skin off*
   flour for dusting
   egg wash with fresh chives & lime juice
3 ounces clarified butter
4 slices tomato, ¼-inch thick
6 wedges avocados
2 slices monterey jack cheese (2 ounces each)

Lemon Butter

2 teaspoons fresh parsley, chopped
4 tablespoons unsalted butter, room temperature
   juice of 1 lemon
   pinch salt & pepper mix
4 tablespoons heavy cream
4 tablespoons demi-glace sauce

Heat pan with butter in it. Season chicken with salt and pepper mix. Dust with flour. Dip in egg wash and saute until golden brown on each side. Take out and let drain. Place 2 tomato slices on breasts and 3 wedges of avocado on tomato and top with monterey jack cheese. Place in oven until cheese is melted. Meanwhile make lemon butter sauce. In saute pan on medium high, heat heavy cream and lemon juice. Reduce to approximately ½ its volume. Add demi-glace sauce. Mix well. Add butter into sauce away from heat and whip butter into sauce very well until sauce is smooth. Adjust seasonings. Add fresh parsley. Serve over chicken breasts immediately.

YIELD: 2 servings.

Mark Weber, Executive Chef

Hyatt Regency San Antonio

Located on the Riverwalk at the Paseo del Alamo, the Hyatt Regency San Antonio is where the San Antonio River flows through the lobby from a series of water cascades. It is one of the most unique hotel lobbies in the world!

BEEF WELLINGTONS WITH PUFF PASTRY

**Puff Pastry (available at
  most grocery stores)**

2   cups bread flour
½   teaspoon salt
½   pound unsalted butter,
       cut into small
       bits & chilled
6-8 tablespoons cold water

**Wellington Filling
  (Duxelle of Mushroom)**

12   ounces fresh mushrooms,
       finely chopped
2   tablespoons fresh butter
2   tablespoons shallots,
       finely chopped
2   ounces white wine
3   ounces pate de fois gras
       (available in gourmet section)

Egg Wash

1   egg (beat with water &
       brush on pastry)
2   tablespoons water
4   6-ounce filet mignons
       clarified butter or oil

To Form Dough: Mix flour and salt in mixing bowl. Add butter and cut it into flour quickly (before it can soften) using 2 knives. This should only take 2 to 3 minutes; do not overwork. Add half of the water and with a fork, quickly blend into flour and butter mixture. Add just enough of remaining water to form the dough into a firm ball. Wrap dough in plastic wrap and refrigerate for 3 hours.

To Roll Out Puff Pastry: Place dough on a cool, floured surface and smack it flat with a rolling pin. Be sure both sides of pastry are floured well. Roll out pastry rapidly into a rectangle about 12 inches long and 6 inches wide. Fold the 2 short ends to meet each other in center, then fold again to align folded edges with each other. Following the direction of the fold lines, roll dough into a rectangle again and repeat the folding process. Refrigerate for at least 30 minutes. Repeat this process 3 more times before using dough.

For Wellington Filling: In a food processor, finely chop fresh mushrooms. Heat a heavy skillet and add butter and shallots. Add mushrooms and white wine. With skillet on medium heat, reduce until no liquid is left. Be careful not to burn the mixture near the end. Allow to cool, then stir in pate de fois gras.

For Filet Mignon: In a heavy skillet, season and sear off the 4 filets at high heat in clarified butter or oil. Seal them completely, but leave the meat rare inside. Refrigerate until completely cool.

Recipe instruction continued on Page 369.

Assembling The Wellingtons: Roll dough out to 10x10-inch square, dividing dough into 4 five-inch squares. Place egg wash on edges of each square to hold together during baking. Place a cooled filet on each square of puff pastry. Divide Wellington filling among the 4 filets, spreading it evenly over top surface of filet. Wrap filet in puff pastry by folding edges over each other so pastry is completely sealed. Turn the Wellington over so unbroken surface is now on top. (Can be stored covered, in refrigerator, for up to 2 days.)

Preheat oven to 400°.

Bake until light golden brown. The longer it bakes, the darker the puff pastry and the more well done the meat. Serve with a madeira sauce or by itself.

YIELD: 4 servings.

Bruce R. Bartz, Executive Sous Chef

La Mansion del Norte Hotel

In the **San Angel** restaurant, sample the *Paella* and the cheese blintzes, or drop by on a Sunday for an elaborate brunch. This Spanish Colonial hotel with a beautiful inner courtyard is located near North Star Mall and the San Antonio International Airport.

RED SNAPPER SOUP

2   tablespoons butter
2   tablespoons flour
6   cups beef stock
6   cups fish stock
28 ounces catsup
        (we recommend Heinz)
1   28-ounce can peeled
        tomatoes, finely diced
1½ medium onions, diced
2½ green bell peppers, diced
¼   cup celery, diced
¼   teaspoon white pepper
2½ pounds flaky fish
        (cod or haddock)
1½ pounds red snapper
3   ounces sherry

In large soup pan, melt butter. Saute onions and celery until lightly golden brown about 5 to 10 minutes. Add flour to the pan to make a roux or thick sauce. **Cook slowly** together for several minutes. (This step of cooking the flour eliminates the raw, pasty uncooked flour taste in some sauces.) After mixture has become bubbly and even in consistency, add beef stock, fish stock, catsup and tomato. Bring to a boil and allow broth to thicken. Add both fish and green peppers. Return to boil. Finish the soup by adding the sherry. Adjust seasoning to taste.

YIELD: 10 to 15 servings.

James Ertelt, Executive Chef

GERMAN STYLE MUSTARD STEAK

2   4-ounce beef medallions,
        tenderloin
3   tablespoons shallots, minced
3   ounces seasoned flour,
        to dust meat
1½-2 ounces clarified butter
1   ounce cognac to flame
4   teaspoons German mustard
5½ tablespoons heavy cream
        salt & pepper to taste

Take two medallions and push the minced shallots into the meat. Dust with seasoned flour. Heat clarified butter and add medallions. Saute to desired doneness. When cooking completed, add cognac and flame. Take meat from pan and keep warm. Add mustard and heavy cream in same pan and reduce to desired consistency. Re-season sauce with salt and pepper to taste. Place meat on plate. Pour sauce over meat. Garnish with vegetables and serve.

YIELD: 2 servings.

Brad Kelm, Executive Sous Chef

La Mansion del Rio

The 1852 Spanish Colonial building that houses La Mansion del Rio has housed a boys' boarding school and St. Mary's University Law School and is now a unique hotel on the banks of the San Antonio River downtown. In **Las Canarias** restaurant, named after the Canary Islanders that first settled San Antonio, cuisine from Spain and the Continent are featured in a romantic river setting with a Spanish flair.

GRILLED DUCK BREAST WITH HONEY PORT SAUCE AND FRESH RASPBERRIES

2   Long Island duck breasts cut
      in half, boneless
½   cup ruby port wine
1   cup heavy cream
1   tablespoons honey
½   pint raspberries,
      fresh or frozen

Combine port, cream and honey in a saucepan and reduce by ⅓ volume and hold. Place the duck breasts, skin down in a very hot skillet and sear to remove excess fat. (This can be done ahead of time.) Place duck breasts, skin down, on a grill preferably mesquite. Give a good char on both sides but meat should still be pink (for medium preference). Cut breast on the bias about 7 slices and place on 2 ounces of sauce. Garnish with fresh berries.

Clay Alexander Summers, Executive Chef   YIELD: 4 servings.

POACHED SALMON WITH OYSTER BEURRE BLANC AND SORREL

1   7-ounce salmon filet
5   oysters
½   ounce lemon juice
2   ounces cream
4   ounces fish stock
1   ounce white wine
1   ounce butter
¼   teaspoon caviar
      sorrel leaves

Poach the salmon in fish stock, white wine, lemon juice with oysters. When it boils, remove oysters. Remove salmon when slightly underdone. Reduce liquids for a few seconds. Add cream and reduce liquid until thick and finish sauce by adding the butter. Separately steam the sorrel leaves on parchment paper. Turn the sorrel on the plate and place the salmon on the sorrel and add sauce. Garnish with oysters crowned with caviar.

YIELD: 1 serving.

Clay Alexander Summers, Executive Chef

Marriott Hotels

River taxis serve the visitors at the San Antonio Marriott Hotel on the River-walk which is located near the Convention Center and Hemisfair Plaza. The **Cactus Flower** restaurant with a Spanish flair provides a perfect view of river gardens, waterfalls and activities on the Riverwalk.

FRIED ICE CREAM

Topping

1   cup corn flakes
1   cup coconut
1   cup brown sugar
1   egg
2   tablespoons milk
4   large scoops vanilla ice cream

Kahlua-Fudge Sauce

½   ounce kahlua
4   ounces hot fudge sauce

Garnish

   whipped cream
   chocolate shavings

Crush corn flakes. Mix with coconut and brown sugar and toast in oven. Scoop vanilla ice cream with large scooper. Make sure scoops are well shaped. Freeze scoops. Combine eggs with milk and beat for egg-wash. Dip in eggwash and roll topping to coat well. Freeze again. When ready to serve, place scoop in fry basket and dip into hot oil for approximately 1 second. Remove immediately. Serve with kahlua hot fudge sauce in a bowl or lipped dish. Garnish with freshly whipped cream and chocolate shavings.

YIELD: 4 servings.

Thimothy Penn, Executive Chef

The Bayous

John Cace, owner of the Bayous, is from a family of East Texas restauranteurs. Many of his Creole style recipes were his grandmother's, and he is continuing the tradition of family involvement by having three of his specialties named for his children - Redfish Rachel, Crab Andrew and Nathan's Pecan Surprise.

CRAYFISH BIENVILLE

1 onion
1 clove garlic
1 stalk celery
1 stick butter
1 pound crayfish with fat
  tabasco sauce to taste
1 tablespoon lemon juice
1 tablespoon worcestershire
    sauce
1 small can mushrooms,
    drained
1 tablespoon cooking sherry
2 tablespoons flour
½ cup bouillon
½ pound parmesan cheese,
    grated
  bread crumbs
  chopped parsley
  paprika

Preheat oven to 375°.
Chop onions with garlic and celery and wilt in butter. Add crayfish and saute 5 minutes more. Season to taste with tabasco sauce and add lemon juice, worcestershire sauce, mushrooms, sherry, flour and bouillon. Place mixture in casserole dish and cover liberally with parmesan cheese. Sprinkle with breadcrumbs, parsley and paprika. Bake for 10 to 15 minutes or until bread crumbs are brown. This entree is nice served with baked potato and tossed green salad.

YIELD: 4 servings.

John and Linda Cace

Cappy's

Cappy Lawton, owner of 1776, Inc., has several famous local restaurants. He is a community-oriented San Antonio native who knows what attracts business to his restaurants - pleasant surroundings, changing art displays and great menus. *Cappy's* on Broadway in Alamo Heights was an old lumberyard that has been renovated into a classy fern/collectibles restaurant. *Mama's* is known for its Avocado Beanburgers and Curly French Fries.

PASTA FRESCA

½   cup butter
1   garlic clove, minced
1   pound mushrooms, sliced
½   pound Canadian bacon, julienned
2   tablespoons flour
¼   cup white wine
1   pint whipping cream
1   cup artichoke hearts
¼   cup parmesan cheese
¼   cup sour cream
1   10-ounce bag spinach noodles, cooked

Melt butter in saucepan. Saute mushrooms until brown. Add garlic. Remove from pan. Saute ham until lightly browned. Add flour and wine. Reduce down for 5 minutes. Add mushrooms, artichoke hearts, sour cream, cream, and parmesan cheese. Heat thoroughly. Do not boil. Toss in cooked noodles.

YIELD: 8 servings.

Cappy Lawton

REDFISH IN LEMON-CAPER-DILL BUTTER

Sauce
⅔   cup capers, small size
1   pound butter
¼   cup white wine
2   teaspoons fresh dill
1   tablespoon worcestershire
2-3 tablespoons lemon juice

Fillets
4   8-ounce fillets of redfish seasoned flour
2   eggs
1   cup beer
1   cup milk
¼   cup clarified butter
¼   cup vegetable oil

Strain the capers and rinse with water. Allow to drain well. In a skillet, heat the butter until the solids turn a golden brown color. Immediately pour browned butter into another container. Deglaze the skillet with white wine and then add to browned butter. Add the fresh dill, worcestershire, lemon juice and capers.

Combine eggs, beer and milk in a pan and mix well. Dust fish fillets in seasoned flour, then dip into batter mixture. Return to flour and dust again. Tap off excess flour. Heat oil and butter in a skillet over medium heat. Add redfish and saute, turning carefully, until fish is cooked. Transfer to serving plate and top with sauce. Garnish with lemon wedges.

YIELD: 4 servings.

Cappy Lawton

Crumpets

Classical music and polished service help make Crumpets a favorite Alamo Heights restaurant. Delicious entrees ranging from quail in brown sauce to redfish with a variety of sauces, along with a dessert case filled with sumptuous pastries, bring many repeat customers.

CHICKEN CHASSEUR

2   pounds chicken breasts, boned
    salt & pepper to taste
    flour to cover chicken
1   tablespoon olive oil
2   tablespoons butter
½   cup scallions
¼   pound mushrooms, sliced
    thyme to taste
    white cooking wine
    chicken stock
½   cup tomatoes, peeled & quartered
    parsley, chopped

Add salt and pepper to flour and dredge the boned chicken. Brown in skillet with butter and oil until tender. Transfer chicken with a slotted spoon to dish and keep warm. Add chopped scallions, mushrooms and tomatoes. Saute. Add white wine to deglaze pan and add chicken stock. Season with salt, pepper and thyme to taste. Cook 5 minutes uncovered or until thickened. Serve sauce over chicken. Sprinkle with parsley.

       YIELD: 4 to 6 servings.

Francois Maeder

Crystal Baking Co.

Shades of Victorian atmosphere, with an antique bar and beautiful stained glass, is the nostaglia created at Crystal Baking Co. on Loop 410. Gourmet lunches are the favorite of local businessmen with piping hot french rolls and seafood chowder!

CHEESE WITH SPINACH PUFFS

Filling

8   ounces feta cheese
8   ounces cottage cheese
1   ounce grated parmesan cheese
2   teaspoons tabasco
3   eggs, beaten
2   ounces spinach,
        chopped coarsely

Pastry

6   ounces butter, melted
1   pound filo or pastry leaves
        found in frozen foods

Preheat oven to 350°.
Mix all ingredients of filling very well together and set aside. Brush cookie sheet with butter. Cut filo into lengthwise ⅓'s. Cover ⅔'s with a smooth damp towel to retain moisture. Filo dries out quickly so work with speed. Brush top strip of filo with butter. Place a tablespoon of filling on the end of the strip. Fold lower corner over the filling to make a triangle. Then fold upper corner straight to the left to make the next triangle. Continue folding from side to side until the entire strip is used and forms a triangle. Place on cookie sheet, one inch from the edge. Repeat until all filo strips are filled. Bake for 15 minutes or until golden brown. Serve hot. Can be frozen. To reheat, place on cookie sheet. Bake, uncovered about 15 minutes.
    YIELD: 50 triangular-shaped appetizers.

Tom Tasos Tsirigotis

SEAFOOD CREPES

Crepes Batter

2   cups flour
3   cups milk
½   cup clarified butter
1   teaspoon salt
6   eggs

Seafood Filling

8   ounces trout
8   ounces shrimp
3   ounces scallops
3   ounces crabmeat
3   tablespoons flour
1½ ounces butter
½   tablespoon chicken base
⅓   cup half-and-half cream
1   ounce pimiento red peppers
½   teaspoon seasoning salt
1   ounce shallots
6   ounces fresh mushrooms

Cheese Sauce

1   pint milk
1½ ounces butter
1½ ounces flour
1   teaspoon chicken base
1   ounce swiss cheese
1   ounce cheddar cheese
    salt & pepper to taste

For Crepe Batter: Put salt in bowl. Break in eggs and beat with wire whisk. Add flour and mix well. Add milk and butter and beat. The batter should be the consistency of thick cream. Cook crepes in crepe pan or skillet. Makes approximately 30.

For Seafood Filling: Melt butter, add flour and stir. Add seasoning salt, hot half-and-half cream and chicken base. Boil trout and shrimp separately for 5 minutes to cook. Saute mushrooms, shallots and scallops. Drain both mixtures and add to liquid mixture. Finally, add crabmeat and red peppers and mix well. Spoon 1 ounce of seafood mixture into each crepe shell. Cover with cheese sauce and serve.

For Cheese Sauce: Melt butter, add flour and cook for 2 to 3 minutes without browning. Add chicken base and scalded milk. Mix well with wire whip until thickened. Add cheese and stir until melted. Pour over crepes.

YIELD: 30 servings.

Tom Tasos Tsirigotis

Ernesto's

Ernesto's started as Ernesto's Seafood Corner, a very casual restaurant serving its specialties on paper plates. It has evolved into *Ernesto's,* an elegant restaurant specializing in Mexican food and seafood. Many patrons never look at a menu. They ask Ernesto to select what is especially good that day!

SOPA ANAUACHALLI
(Tortilla Soup)

2   quarts chicken broth
    fresh onion, chopped
    fresh tomato, chopped
    dried chicken base or
    bouillon to taste
10 thin corn tortillas,
        cut into thin strips
¼   pound butter
8   ounces Mexican or monterey
        jack cheese, grated
1   medium avocado, diced
4   teaspoons sour cream
½   teaspoon chopped cilantro
        (coriander)

Make a good chicken broth with your favorite recipe, adding some chopped fresh onion, tomatoes and chicken base.

Fry tortilla strips in butter until crisp. To serve soup, pour chicken broth in bowl. Add one handful of fried tortilla strips. Next add the cheese, then the avocado, then the sour cream and cilantro. Serve very hot.

YIELD: 4 to 6 servings.

Ernesto Torres

Grey Moss Inn

Candelight dining before a crackling fireplace or a patio table under a leafy umbrella of ancient oak trees are the trademarks of the charming Grey Moss Inn in the hill country overlooking San Antonio. For half a century diners have enjoyed the beautiful drive on historic Scenic Loop Road to Boerne to this delightful inn.

GREY MOSS INN FRENCH APPLE PIE

5 apples, peeled & thinly sliced
2 tablespoons lemon juice
½ cup chopped pecans
¼ cup golden raisins
½ cup brown sugar
¼ cup white sugar
½ teaspoon cinnamon
⅛ teaspoon nutmeg
2 tablespoons flour
1 unbaked 9-inch pie crust
    & 1 top crust

Preheat oven to 350°.
In a large bowl, sprinkle lemon juice over apple slices and stir gently. Add pecans and raisins. In a small bowl, mix the sugars, spices and flour. Pour spice mixture over apples. Stir gently. Pour apples into pie pan lined with crust. Dot with butter. Roll out top crust and place over apples. Slice small vent slits in top crust. Brush crust lightly with a little milk. Dust lightly with sugar. Bake for 45 minutes to 1 hour until crust is golden.

YIELD: 8 servings.

Jerry and Mary Martin

El Jarro de Arturo Restaurants

Step back into the atmosphere of old Mexico and watch fresh tortillas being made before your eyes. Enjoy a hot Quesadilla while making selections from the extensive menu. Famous for their catering, Art and Sandy Cerna are experts on Mexican cuisine.

GREEN ENCHILADAS

Chicken Filling

4   chicken breasts
    water to cover
2   cups chicken broth
2   cups canned tomatoes,
       mashed
½   cup diced onions
1   teaspoon salt
1   teaspoon granulated garlic

Green Sauce

4   pounds tomatillo tomatoes,
       peeled & washed
½   cup diced onions
¼   cup oil
1   teaspoon salt
1   teaspoon chopped garlic

Enchiladas

15 corn tortillas
    hot oil
    sour cream

To Prepare Chicken Filling: Boil chicken breasts in water until tender. Cool chicken and shred. Using water in which chicken was boiled to equal 2 cups of stock or 2 cups of chicken broth, place in pan. Add tomatoes, onions, salt and garlic. Add chicken and boil for 10 minutes or until mixture is reduced and proper consistency for enchilada filling.

To Prepare Green Sauce: Boil the tomatillos in a small amount of water until tender and blend. In skillet, saute onions in oil. Add puree of tomatillos, salt and garlic.
Preheat oven to 375°.

To Assemble Enchiladas: Pass tortillas in hot oil, stuff with chicken filling which has been strained to get rid of excess juices and cover with tomatillo sauce. Place in oven until hot. Add a dab of sour cream on top before serving.

YIELD: 6 to 8 servings.

Arthur and Sandra Cerna

SHRIMP CEVICHE

2   pounds raw shrimp
1   cup lime juice
1   cup diced tomato
½   cup diced onion
1   teaspoon chopped cilantro
         (coriander)
1   teaspoon chopped olives
2   cups V-8 juice
1   teaspoon tabasco sauce
4-5   avocados, cut in half

Marinate shrimp in lime juice for 3 hours. Remove juice and add tomato, onion, cilantro, olives, V-8 juice and tabasco sauce. Chill for 2 hours. Serve over avocado half.

YIELD: 8 to 10 servings.

Arthur and Sandra Cerna

Little Rhein Steakhouse

Popular with symphony goers, the Little Rhein Steakhouse is a dining delight on the Paseo del Rio. Walls adorned with old momentos express a colorful past from 1847 - the oldest building on the Riverwalk. The bar came from an old local saloon. Dining on the river terrace is picturesque while enjoying steaks or seafood.

LITTLE RHEIN CHICKEN

1 piece breast of chicken, flattened
pepper to taste
1 fresh asparagus spear
1 slice longhorn cheese
1 slice summer sausage
buttermilk
cracker crumbs

Preheat oven to 350°.
Flatten chicken breast and season with pepper. Stuff with the asparagus, longhorn cheese and summer sausage. Roll up and close with toothpicks to hold chicken. Dip in buttermilk and then cracker crumbs. Repeat twice. Bake in oven for 15 minutes. Deep fry for 3 to 5 minutes.

YIELD: 1 serving.

Frank Phelps

Luigi's Restaurant

Roman columns and red drapes set the atmosphere for one of San Antonio's finest gourmet Italian restaurants located near North Star Mall. Luigi and his sons, Raymond and Domenico, specialize in Northern Italian cuisine including fresh seafood dishes, veal and a wine list with over 150 selections. Desserts prepared daily include cannoli and Italian fruit tarts.

SALTIMBOCCA ALLA LUIGI

2-3 small medallions of veal, pounded ¼-inch thick (approximately 5 ounces)

3 ounces precooked sliced mushrooms

2 slices prosciutto ham

3 ounces fresh spinach, blanched

3 ounces butter

1 pinch of sage
flour, to lightly flour veal
salt & pepper to taste

Marsala Sauce

3 tablespoons sweet marsala

3 tablespoons dry white wine

3 tablespoons water

Pound veal with flat side of meat cleaver between 2 pieces of waxpaper. Slice and precook mushrooms by sauteing in oil, salt and pepper over low heat for 15 minutes. To blanch spinach, wash well and place in hot water for 2 minutes until slightly wilted.

For Marsala Sauce: Mix the marsala, white wine and water in a suitable container. Place 2 medium sized-skillets over medium heat. Add 2 ounces butter to the first pan and 1 ounce butter to the second. In the first skillet, add the spinach and spread evenly across the heating surface. In the second, place the lightly floured veal, add salt, pepper and sage seasonings. As soon as one side is cooked to a golden brown, turn veal over. Immediately place the prosciutto ham over the veal, then add the sliced mushrooms. Wait for the other side of the veal to brown and then add the marsala sauce.

For Serving: First place the spinach on the plate. Next spread the veal across the spinach and follow with the prosciutto ham. Spoon out the mushrooms evenly over the dish and cover with the remaining marsala sauce.

YIELD: 1 serving.

Luigi Ciccarelli

Los Patios

On the banks of Salado Creek are three restaurants nestled in a tree-studded garden nursery setting. The beautiful, lush *Los Patios* restaurants are the Gazebo, the Hacienda and the Brazier. They are noted for their delicious food and picturesque scenery which can be enjoyed while watching ducks and geese on the banks of the creek. This is a lovely spot for parties and weddings or just for meandering among the galleries and boutiques.

LOS PATIOS CHEESE SOUP

¼   cup butter or margarine
½   onion, chopped
5   stalks celery, chopped with
      some leaves minced
2   carrots, minced
2   10¾-ounce cans chicken
      broth (sometimes
      salty-substitute water
      for half of amount)
3   10¾-ounce cans Heinz
      Potato Soup
8   ounces yellow cheese, grated
      a few parsley flakes & chives
      white pepper to taste
3   tablespoons cooking sherry

Melt butter over low heat and saute onions, celery and carrots. Add chicken broth, cover and simmer for 30 minutes. Add potato soup and bring to boil. Then add cheese, parsley, chives and white pepper. Simmer 15 minutes. Add sherry and stir. Can be refrigerated and reheated.

YIELD: 10 cups.

SHRIMP SALAD

Serve chilled on a bed of lettuce leaves.

1   pound cooked, peeled &
      deveined shrimp
1⅓ cups chopped celery
      white pepper
      celery salt
½   cup mayonnaise
¼   teaspoon salt
1   teaspoon lemon juice

Combine shrimp, celery, white pepper and celery salt. In separate bowl, combine mayonnaise, salt and lemon juice. Add to shrimp mixture and serve chilled, mounded on leaf lettuce. Adjust seasonings to taste.

YIELD: 6 servings.

Maggie's

Open 24 hours a day, Maggie's is a popular restaurant on San Antonio's north-side. It has something for almost everyone. It features breakfast buffets, lunches and dinner with special nightly entertainment.

MAGGIE'S ITALIAN OMELET

2	large bell peppers, chopped in ½-inch cubes
1	large onion, sliced thin in ½-inch strips
1	clove fresh garlic, minced
¼	cup olive oil
⅛	teaspoon oregano
¼	teaspoon basil leaves
1	bay leaf
¼	teaspoon rosemary
⅛	teaspoon white pepper
¼	teaspoon salt
¼	teaspoon Accent or MSG
2	8-ounce cans whole peeled tomatoes
1	6-ounce can tomato sauce
1	small can sliced mushrooms
¼	cup white wine
½	cup water

Saute onions, bell peppers and garlic together in olive oil until tender, about 4 minutes. Strain tomatoes and blend in food processor. In a saucepan add the tomatoes, tomato sauce, onions, bell peppers, garlic, water and spices. Bring to a boil and simmer for 30 minutes. Add mushrooms and cook for an additional 15 minutes. Remove bay leaf. Remove from heat and add white wine. This sauce makes enough for 6 to 8 omelets. Additional sauce will keep in refrigerator for several days or it may be frozen. Make cheddar cheese omelets and ladle sauce over them. Sprinkle with grated mozzarella cheese and place under oven broiler briefly to melt cheese. *Never put omelet in microwave!*

YIELD: Omelet sauce for 6 to 8 servings.

Meatball's

Fresh, handmade pastas and sausages and moderate prices are the keys to Meatball's success, feels owner Jerry Jungmann. These three family owned and operated restaurants have received excellent reviews from state and local restaurant critics, and the authentic family recipes seem to insure their continued success.

ITALIAN VEAL ROLLS

Serve the veal rolls on a bed of linguine with garlic butter dusted with grated parmesan cheese!

½   pound unflavored bacon
1   pound boneless chicken
      breast
1   10-ounce package frozen
      chopped spinach
¼   cup grated parmesan cheese
3   cloves garlic, finely chopped
2   teaspoons salt
1   teaspoon ground black pepper
2   pounds veal leg sirloin,
      cut ¼-inch thick
½   cup unflavored bread crumbs,
      divided into 2 equal parts
2   eggs, beaten
2   tablespoons milk

Fry bacon in heavy skillet until very crisp. Remove bacon and crush. Set aside. Reserve half of bacon fat in skillet and fry chicken, about 5 minutes per side. Remove chicken, drain and cut up into small pieces. Cook spinach according to package directions and drain very well.

Preheat oven to 350°.
Make egg-milk mixture by beating 2 eggs with 2 tablespoons of milk. Divide into 2 equal parts. Combine bacon, chicken, spinach, parmesan cheese, garlic, half of the bread crumbs, salt, pepper and half of the egg-milk mixture. Mix very well and set aside. Cut veal into 6 equal pieces and pound out to about ⅛-inch thickness. Spread each piece of veal with mixture, dividing equally. Roll up veal, jelly-roll fashion, pressing edges to seal. Dip each veal roll in the other half of the egg-milk mixture and roll in the second half of the bread crumbs until lightly coated. Place veal rolls in shallow baking pan and bake for 45 minutes. Serve simply and easily with just lemon wedges and parsley.

YIELD: 6 servings.

Jim, Larry and Jerry Jungmann

El Mirador Restaurant

A famous Mexican restaurant near the historic King William area is well known for its soup. Caldo Xochitl is a famous soup from El Mirador which has appeared in national gourmet magazines. It has a fragrant combination of chicken, garlic, herbs and spices served over El Mirador Rice. "Xochitl" translated from Mexican Nahuatl means "little flower." It is also the name of a beautiful garden in Cuernavaca, Mexico.

CALDO XOCHITL

4-5 cloves garlic, minced

1 tablespoon dried oregano

¼ teaspoon ground cloves

2½ quarts water

1 2½-3-pound frying chicken

1 tablespoon chicken stock base

1 tablespoon salt

1 tablespoon ground cumin

1 teaspoon freshly ground pepper

3 bay leaves

1 sprig fresh basil

2 cups sliced zucchini

1½ cups quartered & sliced carrots

1½ cups diced green bell pepper

1½ cups diced celery

1 medium onion, sliced

1 17-ounce can garbanzo beans, drained

Garnish

El Mirador Rice

1 bunch green onions, chopped

½ bunch fresh cilantro (leaves only), chopped

1-2 fresh jalapeno chiles, chopped

2 firm tomatoes, cubed

1 avocado, seeded & cubed

Mix garlic, oregano and cloves to a paste. Bring water to boil in large pot. When water is boiling, add chicken, salt and pepper and simmer for a few minutes. Skim off foam and add chicken stock base, cumin, bay leaves, basil and garlic paste. Let chicken simmer until cooked, about 45 minutes to 1 hour. Remove chicken and set aside to cool. Add zucchini, carrots, bell pepper, onion and beans to pot and bring to boil. Reduce heat and simmer until tender, about 15 minutes.

Meanwhile, remove skin and bones from chicken; shred meat. When vegetables are tender, add meat to soup and heat through.

For Each Serving: Place ¼ cup El Mirador Rice in soup bowl. Pour soup over the rice and top with onion, cilantro, chiles, tomatoes and avocado.

YIELD: 12 servings.

Julian Trevino

EL MIRADOR RICE

¾ cup long-grain rice
    lemon juice
2   tablespoons oil
2   medium tomatoes, chopped
2   medium green bell peppers,
       chopped
1   clove garlic, minced
1   tablespoon chicken stock base
1   cup hot water
1   teaspoon ground cumin
¼   teaspoon salt
    freshly ground pepper

Cover rice with hot water. Add squeeze of lemon juice and let soak for 5 minutes. Drain thoroughly in colander.

Heat oil in large skillet. Add rice and saute until golden. Drain off any excess fat. Stir in tomatoes, peppers and garlic and saute 5 minutes. Add chicken base dissolved in water and seasonings. Reduce heat, cover and simmer 15 minutes. *Do not remove lid while rice is cooking.* Fluff with fork.

YIELD: 12 servings.

Julian Trevino

Old San Francisco Steak House

"The girl in the red velvet swing" and the "big block of cheese" are two popular descriptions of the famous Old San Francisco Steak House. Built in Victorian Barbary Coast decor, it is famous for prime rib, aged heavy beef steaks and lobster tails. It lives up to its motto "A good Steak! A good time!"

CANDY CRUNCH CAKE

¾   cup sugar
½   teaspoon instant coffee
2   tablespoons light corn syrup
2   tablespoons water
1½ teaspoons sifted baking soda
1   angel food cake
    Cool Whip topping
    slivered almonds, toasted

In saucepan, mix sugar with coffee, corn syrup and water. Cook to the hard crack stage, 285° on candy thermometer. Remove from heat and add soda all at once. Stir vigorously, but only until mixture blends and pulls away from pan. Quickly pour onto a piece of foil paper. Do not spread or stir. Let it cool and harden. Then crush it into crumbs.

Cut an angel food cake into 2 layers. Mix some of the powdered parts of candy into Cool Whip. Spread over first layer of cake. Add some of the larger pieces of candy. Add second layer of cake. Spread with more Cool Whip. Add generous amounts of candy and toasted slivered almonds. Refrigerate until ready to serve. It is tastier if it is put together a couple of hours before it is to be served. It will not be as good the second day as it gets weepy and the candy softens.

YIELD: 6 to 8 servings.

Paesano's Restaurant

Paesano's is famous for "Shrimp Paesano" and house salads with special garlic dressing. This well-known Italian restaurant is near the historic old San Pedro Park.

EGGPLANT PARMIGIANA

1   eggplant, sliced into ½-inch thick slices
    flour
½   cup oil
1   cup grated parmesan cheese
3   tablespoons chopped basil
½   pound mozzarella cheese, thinly sliced

#1 Tomato Sauce

2   tablespoons oil
½   onion, finely chopped
1   clove garlic, crushed
1   celery stalk with leaves, chopped
4   ripe tomatoes, peeled, seeded, mashed & chopped
4   sprigs fresh basil or ½ teaspoon dried
4   sprigs fresh parsley
    salt & pepper
    pinch of sugar

For #1 Tomato Sauce: Heat oil in saucepan over medium heat; add onion, garlic and celery. Cook until onion is soft. Add tomatoes, basil and parsley. Season to taste with salt, pepper and sugar. Simmer 45 minutes. Stir occasionally. Pour mixture into blender and mix for 30 seconds at low speed. **Makes 3 cups.**

Preheat oven to 450°.
Salt eggplant and drain off water. Flour slices. Heat oil in large frying pan over high heat, then brown slices quickly on both sides. Arrange slices in a lightly oiled baking dish in 3 layers. Cover each layer with **#1 Tomato Sauce**, parmesan cheese, chopped basil and finally the sliced mozzarella cheese. Place dish in a hot oven about 8 minutes or until dish is bubbly and top of mozzarella is lightly browned.

YIELD: 6 servings.

Joseph Cosniac

La Paloma del Rio

With Aztec surroundings and balconies overlooking the Riverwalk, La Paloma del Rio captures the essence of Mexican cuisine and atmosphere unique in San Antonio. A great place for river watching.

FLAN
(Caramel Custard)

⅓   cup sugar
2   eggs
1   13-ounce can evaporated milk
      (1⅔ cups)
¼   cup sugar
1   teaspoon vanilla
      dash salt

Preheat oven to 350°.
In a small skillet, stir in ⅓ cup sugar over medium heat until sugar melts and becomes golden brown. Quickly pour caramelized sugar into a 3-cup ring mold, tilting mold to coat bottom and sides. In a bowl, beat eggs and stir in milk, ¼ cup sugar, vanilla and salt. Pour in mixture into caramel coated mold. Set mold in baking pan on oven rack. Pour hot water around mold in pan to a dept of 1 inch. Bake uncovered 50 to 55 minutes or until a knife inserted halfway between center and edge comes out clean. Chill. Carefully loosen custard from sides and center. Invert on a platter.

Roger Flores

YIELD: 8 servings.

CHOCOLATE MEXICANO
(Mexican Hot Chocolate)

6   cups milk
¼   cup sugar
3   1-ounce squares unsweetened
      chocolate, cut up
1   teaspoon ground cinnamon
¼   teaspoon salt
2   eggs, beaten
2   teaspoons vanilla
      cinnamon sticks, optional

In a saucepan, combine milk, sugar, chocolate, ground cinnamon and salt. Heat and stir until chocolate melts and milk is very hot. Gradually stir 1 cup of the hot mixture into eggs and return to saucepan. Cook 2 to 3 minutes more over low heat. Remove from heat. Add vanilla and beat with rotary beater or "molinilo" until mixture is well combined. Pour into mugs. Garnish with cinnamon sticks.

YIELD: Six 8-ounce servings.

Roger Flores

"The Copper Kitchen" at the Southwest Craft Center

On the banks of the San Antonio River in the original home of the Ursuline Academy and Convent is the Southwest Craft Center. It represents the French influence of early San Antonio. The old, distinguished site was established by Bishop John Odin in 1851. The craft center today is dedicated to professional education in the arts and the stimulation of interest and appreciation of craftsmen. It also provides an attractive cultural center for the city. The beautiful grounds are settings for intimate parties, outdoor weddings and an annual Fiesta Arts Fair, at which Junior Forum members volunteer. The Copper Kitchen is open for delicious lunches.

HERB SALAD DRESSING

1½ teaspoons salt
1   teaspoon oregano
1   teaspoon ground black pepper
1   teaspoon dillweed
6   tablespoons chopped parsley
2   tablespoons dijon mustard
2   tablespoons sugar
3   minced garlic cloves
½   cup vinegar
¾   cup salad oil

Combine all ingredients in blender. Blend until smooth. Serve on top of salad greens.
YIELD: 8 to 10 ounces salad dressing.

This old clock tower tops the original Ursuline Academy and Convent on the banks of the San Antonio River. These historic buildings house the Southwest Craft Center, a prominent institution of art education and preservation of artistic skills.

INDEX

A

Acapulco Chicken with Lemon
    Butter Sauce 367
Adele's Catering 352
Aguacate Fritos (Fried Avocados)48
Alamo Pecan Cheese Ball 17
Almond Buttercream Frosting . . 289
Amaretto Cheesecakes 324
Amaretto Oranges 332
Ambrosia Cake 49
Angel Food Cake, Mocha 43
Anticuchos (Marinated Beef
    Cubes on a Stick) 34

APPETIZERS

DIPS

Artichoke, Hot (Royal Catering)
    357
Avocado 53
Bean, Prairie Fire 56
Beef, Chipped 56
Black Bean, Yucatan 57
Chili Con Queso (Peppers with
    Cheese) 58
Chorizo Con Queso (Sausage
    with Cheese Dip) 57
Crab, Coastal 69
Guacamole (Avocado Mixture) . 4
Hot Sauce, Mexican Army . . . 75
Meat, Mexican 52
Oyster, Smoked 54
Picadillo, Sweet (Minced Meat
    Mixture) 63
Picante Sauce (Hot Sauce) . . . 75
Pico de Gallo 6
Salsa Fresca (Fresh Sauce) . . . 75
San Antonio 55

FINGER FOODS

Aguacate Fritos 48
Avocados 53
Nachos (Toasted Chips) 52
Anticuchos (Marinated Beef
    Cubes on a Stick) 34
Ceviche (Marinated Fish) 4
Cheese Sticks 65
Chicken Puffs 58
Chicken Wings, Sweet & Sour 59
Chiles Rellenos, Mary Alice
    Cisneros 342-343
Corn Baskets, Mexican 73
Crabbies 68
Eggs, Caviar Stuffed 61
Eggs, Shy Poke 64
Empanadas (Meat Pies) 64
English Olive Appetizers 62
Flautas de Pollo (Chicken
    Flutes) 71
Jalapeno Cheese Squares 59
Jalapeno Peppers, Stuffed 7
Jalapenos, Party Fried 59
Mushrooms Parmigiana 67
Mushrooms, Marinated 66
Mushrooms, Oyster Stuffed . . 66
Mushrooms, Stuffed 66
Noche Specials 346
Olive Twists 61
Peppers, Stuffed, Mary Alice
    Cisneros 342-343
Potato Skins, Cheesy 71
Puffs, Cheese with Spinach
    (Crystal Baking Co.) 376
Quesadillas (Cheese Tortillas)73
Sausage Crescent Nuggets . . . 74
Shrimp Ceviche 380
Shrimp Congiglia 60
Shrimp in Dill Mayonnaise . . 60
Snow Peas, Stuffed 63
Tomatoes, Stuffed Cherry . . . 62
Tostadas (Toasted Chips) 10
Turkey Bites, Bacon 74

SPREADS

Beer Cheese 65
Brie, Baked 62
Caponata (Eggplant Relish) . . 40
Caviar Pie 61
Cheddar Log 72
Cheese Ball, Alamo Pecan . . . 17
Cheese Spread, Cinnamon
    Strawberry 24
Chicken Liver Pate 64
Corned Beef in Rye 68
Salmon Ball 72
Salmon Mousse 60
Seafood Cocktail Spread 69
Shrimp Mold 70
Shrimp Pate 70
Spinach Dip/Pumpernickel . . 67
Swiss Cheese Spread 65
Apple Crunch Cake, Fresh 298
Apple Goodie 334
Apple Muffins 264
Apple Nut Dessert, Bohemian . 310
Apple Pie, Grey Moss Inn 379
Apple Pie, Sour Cream 308
Apples, Orange-Pecan Baked . . 238
Apricot Dream Dessert 331
Apricot Salad, Congealed 112
Apricot Sticks 335
Apricot Strudel 303
Arneson River Theater 7
Arroz con Pollo Espanola 173
Artichoke Casserole, Egg and . 211
Artichoke Dip, Hot
    (Royal Catering) 357
Artichoke Dip, Hot 54
Artichoke Mushroom Velvet . . 222
Artichoke Soup with Lemon & Dill
    88
Artichoke Soup 88
Artichoke Spinach Delight 222
Asparagus Brunch Con Queso . 210
Asparagus Parmesan, Fried . . . 40
Asparagus, Holiday 223
Asparagus, Orange Butter for . 223
Asparagus, Sweet and Sour . . . 223
Aunt Dixie's Pea Salad 118
Avocado Cheesecake 325
Avocado Cream Soup, Sherried . 89
Avocado Dip 53
Avocado Mixture (Guacamole) . 4
Avocado Sauce, Chicken with . 172
Avocados 53
Avocados, Fried (Marriott Hotels)48

B

Baked Beans, Aunt Bessie's Sweet
    and Sour 225
Baklava 311
Banana Meringues (Celebration
    Savvy) 355
Banana Nut Bread, Sour Cream . 268
Band, Army, Ft. Sam Houston . . 19
Bandera Party Grits 247
Barbecue - San Antonio Style . . 8
Barbecue Sauce, Chuckwagon . 134
Barbecue Sauce, Pappy Skrap's . 11
Barbecue, history 132
Barbecued Steaks 133
Barbecuing, Techniques for . . . 132
Barley Pilaf 243
Bars, Easy "Brides" 299
Basting Sauce 134

BATTERS

English Fish Batter 202
Fritter Batter 254

Battle of Flowers Parade 86-87
Bayous, The 373
Bean Dip, Prairie Fire 56
Beans, Chili 144
Beans, Cowboy 12
Bearnaise Sauce 352
Beef and Brew Take Along 16
Beef and Dumplings 151
Beef and Mushroom Salad . . . 128
Beef Burgundy 153
Beef Cubes on a Stick, Marinated
    (Antichuchos) 34
Beef Dip, Chipped 56
Beef Filling, Mexican Mashed
    (Machacado) 149
Beef Flutes (Roast Beef Flautas)148
Beef Jerky 139
Beef Spaghetti Casserole 159
Beef Stroganov 153
Beef Wellingtons with Puff Pastry
    (Hyatt Regency San Antonio)
    368
Beef with Snow Peas, Oriental . 151
Beefy Pasta Florentine 159
Beer Bread 275
Beer Cheese 65

BEVERAGES

ALCOHOLIC

Bloody Marys, Overnight 18
Bourbon Cloud 82
Chablis Surprise 81
Coffee, Mexican 80
Daiquiris, Bananas (Variation)83
Daiquiris, Strawberry 83
Eggnog, Yuletide 78
Green Lizards 83
Julep, Jungle 83
Liqueur, Coffee 80
Liqueur, Irish Cream 80
Magnolias 23
Margarita 81
Margaritas, Frozen 81
Pina Colada a la Alamo 82
Punch, Champagne 77
Punch, Cranberry Holiday . . . 76
Punch, Luling Watermelon
    Wine 78
Punch, Whiskey Sour 84
Rum Mix, Hot Buttered 84
Sangria 36
Tequila Sunrise 31
Texas Sunshine 81
Tumbleweeds, Texas 84

NON-ALCOHOLIC

Eggnog, Chocolate 79
Chocolate Mexicano 390
Chocolate Mix, Hot 85
Cider for a Crowd, Hot 76
Orange Jubilees 82
Punch, Big Red 77
Punch, Coffee 77
Punch, Holiday Hot 76
Punch, Yellow Rose 79
Tea, Almond 78
Tea, Spiced (variation) 76
Tea, Texas Sun 79
Biscuits, Sky-High 17
Black Bean Dip, Yucatan 57
Black Eyed Peas, Pickled 253
Bloody Marys, Overnight 18
Blueberry Cream Pie, Fresh . . . 303
Blueberry Lemon Bread 270
Blueberry Muffins 265
Bluebonnets 157
Bohemian Coffee Cake 280
Bolillos (Mexican Rolls) 260
Bolognese Sauce 187

Booberry Salad............111
Botica Guadalupana...........29
Bourbon Cloud...............82
Bran Muffins...............265
Bread Dough, Frozen.........275
Bread Herb Topping..........276
Bread Pudding with Whiskey
    Sauce....................331
Bread Thins, Herbed.........276

BREADS
  BISCUITS
    Cheese.................271
    Sky-High................17
    Yeast, Kerrville Ranch.....261
  COFFEE CAKES
    Bohemian................280
    Coffee Breakers..........283
    Floresville..............282
    Pineapple, Rich..........281
    Poppy Seed.............281
    Puff, Danish............283
    Sour Cream..............282
    Toffee...................25
  MUFFINS
    Apple..................264
    Blueberry..............265
    Bran...................265
    Date Bar...............265
    Graham................266
    Irish "Cheesecake"......264
    Plain and Fancy.........266
    Puffs, French Breakfast....267
    Sweet Potato...........266
  QUICK BREADS
    Beer...................275
    Blueberry Lemon.........270
    Bread Dough, Frozen......275
    Caramel Ring............274
    Corn Fritters............272
    Cornbread, Jalapeno.......13
    Doughnuts, Canary Islander..36
    Grapenut...............267
    Katy Kornettes..........272
    Oatmeal Raisin..........270
    Onion Cheese...........271
    Puffs, Beer.............273
    Pumpkin...............269
    Sausage................271
    Sour Cream Banana Nut....268
    Spoon.................273
    Strawberry.............267
    Tomato Soup............268
    Tortillas, Flour...........6
    Zucchini...............269
    Zucchini Fritters.........272
  ROLLS
    Bolillos (Mexican Rolls).....260
    Cinnamon..............262
    Crescent...............261
    Orange................274
    La Villita...............43
  SWEET BREADS
    Bunuelos)..........277, 301
    Churros (Spanish Fritters)..279
    Kolaches...............280
    Pan Dulce (Sweet Bread)...278
  TOPPINGS
    Bread Herb Topping......276
    Bread Thins, Herbed......276
    Cheese & Garlic Bread, Hot.276
  YEAST BREADS
    Bubble Wreath, Easy......263
    Bubble Wreath..........263
    Dilly Casserole..........259
    French.................258
    Monkey................263
    Swedish Rye............259
    White or Wheat..........258
Breakfast Casserole, Mexican..209
Breakfast Pizza.............216
Brie, Baked.................62
Brisket in Beer.............135

Brisket in Soy Sauce.........136
Brisket Sauce..............136
Brisket, Barbecued..........353
Brisket, Barbecued..........133
Brisket, Oven Baked Barbecued135
Broccoli Crown with
    Cherry Tomatoes........358
Broccoli Molded Salad........119
Broccoli Salad Supreme.......119
Broccoli with Mushrooms,
    Chinese Stir-Fry........224
Broccoli, Ritz Cheese........224
Brown Bag Days.............259
Brown or Demi-Glace Sauce...361
Brownies, Creme de Menthe....18
Brownies, Marbled Cheese.....313
Brownies, San Antonio's Best...312
Brunch Pie................213
Bubble Wreath or Loaf, Easy...263
Bubble Wreath.............263
Bunuelos................277, 301
Burrito, Fried (Chimichangas)..142
Bush, Barbara.............344
Butter, Cilantro Cumin........47
Buttermilk Pie..............302
Buttermilk Pound Cake.......297
Butterscotch Cheesecake Bars..322

C

Cabbage and Apples, Red......226
Cabbage Casserole, Layered....226
Cabbage Chowder.............89
Cabbage, Castroville.........227
Cactus....................237
Cajun Coo Bee Yon (Court
    Bouillon)................203
Cakes - See Sweets
Calabacitas Casserole (Mexican
    Squash Casserole).........234
Calabaza con Puerco (Squash with
    Pork)..................235
Caldo de Pollo (Mexican Chicken
    Soup)...................37
Caldo Xochitl (El Mirador
    Restaurant)..............386
Canary Islanders.......36, 50, 201
Candies, Hints for...........335
Candy Cookies.............319
Candy Crunch Cake.........388
Candy Pockets.............321
Caponata (Eggplant Relish).....40
Cappy's...............49, 374
Caramel Pie...............305
Caramel Ring..............274
Caramel Topping............296
Caribbean Fudge Pie.........307
Carmelitas.................312
Carne Guisada (Stewed Meat)..145
Carrot Cake, South Texas.....300
Carrots Lyonnaise............228
Carrots with Horseradish Glaze.227
Carrots, Lemon Basil........228
Cascarones.................31
Cashew Crunch Cookies.......319
Castroville Stuffed Cabbage....227
Catering by Don Strange.....353
Catering by Rosemary........354
Cauliflower and Bacon Salad...120
Cauliflower and Broccoli Salad.120
Caviar Pie..................61
Celebration Savvy...........355
CELEBRITIES
  Adele's Catering
    Bearnaise Sauce........352
  Bayous, The
    Crayfish Bienville......373

  Bush, Barbara
    Lemon Chicken.......344
  Cappy's
    Ambrosia Cake.........49
    Pasta Fresca..........374
    Redfish in Lemon-Caper-Dill
      Butter................374
  Catering by Don Strange
    Barbecued Brisket......353
    Boneless Pork Loin Tangy
      Sauce................353
  Catering by Rosemary
    Crab & Avocado
      Enchiladas............354
  Celebration Savvy
    Banana Meringues......355
    Bourbon Cashew Studded
      Ham..................355
  Chez Ardid
    Noisettes de Porc aux
      Pruneaux (Pork Tenderloin)
     46
  Cisneros, Mary Alice
    Chiles Rellenos (Stuffed
      Peppers)..........342-343
  Club Josef
    Steak Tartare a la Josef.359
    Mango Sauce..........359
  Copper Kitchen, The, (S.W.
    Craft Center)
    Herb Salad Dressing....391
  Cousins, Margaret
    Baked Custard.........347
  Crockett Hotel, The
    Breast of Chicken "American
      Bounty"..............363
  Crumpets
    Chicken Chasseur......375
  Crystal Baking Co.
    Cheese w/Spinach Puffs.376
    Seafood Crepes........377
  Dominion Country Club
    Medallions au Poivre...360
  Ernesto's
    Sopa Anauachalli (Tortilla
      Soup).................378
  Fernandez, Rosita
    Gallina en Mole (Chicken in
      Chili Sauce)...........348
    Relleno Para Pavo (Turkey
      Stuffing).............348
  Four Seasons Hotel
    Blackened River Trout with
      Cayenne and Pepper...364
  Fresh Horizons Creative
    Catering
    Pecan Cheesecake......356
  Grey Moss Inn
    French Apple Pie......379
  Gunter Hotel, The
    Acapulco Chicken with
      Lemon Butter Sauce....367
    Chicken Casa de Moros.366
  Haram, Karen
    Pasta in Cream Sauce...47
    Hot Fudge Sauce.......349
    Spinach Salad.........349
  Hilton Palacio del Rio
    Sauteed Veal Chops
      Palermo..............365
  Hyatt Regency San Antonio
    Beef Wellingtons with Puff
      Pastry.............368-369
  Jarro de Arturo Restaurants, El
    Green Enchiladas......380
    Shrimp Ceviche.......380
  Johnson, Lady Bird
    Noche Specials........346
    Pedernales River Chili..346
  La Mansion del Norte Hotel
    Red Snapper Soup......370
    German Style Mustard
      Steak................370

La Mansion del Rio
  Cilantro Cumin Butter...47
  Grilled Duck Breast with
    Honey Port Sauce......371
  Poached Salmon with
    Oyster Beurre Blanc and
    Sorrel.................371
Little Rhein Steakhouse
  Little Rhein Chicken....381
Los Patios
  Los Patios Cheese Soup.383
  Shrimp Salad.........383
Luigi's Restaurant
  Saltimbocca alla Luigi...382
Maggie's
  Maggie's Italian Omelet.384
Marriott Hotels
  Aguacate Fritos (Fried
    Avocados).............48
  Fried Ice Cream.......372
Meatballs
  Italian Veal Rolls......385
Mirador Restaurant, El
  Caldo Xochitl.........386
  El Mirador Rice.......387
Oak Hills Country Club
  Curried Rice 'Bombay,'.361
  Demi-Glace or Brown Sauce
   361
  Schnitzel a la "San Antonio"
   46
Old San Francisco Steak House
  Candy Crunch Cake 388
Paesano's Restaurant
  Eggplant Parmigiana....389
Paloma del Rio, La
  Chocolate Mexicano....390
  Flan (Caramel Custard).390
Parker, Nancy
  Brochettes of Shrimp and
    Zucchini..............351
Plaza Club
  Lobster Bisque.........362
Royal Catering
  Hot Artichoke Dip......357
Simply Delicious
  Baked Florentine Potatoes48
  Broccoli Crown with Cherry
    Tomatoes.............358
Wagner, Candy Erben
  Fajitas................350
  Fresh Mexican Salsa....350
White, Linda Gale
  Smothered Quail.......345
  Cucumber/Shrimp Bisq.345
Celery and Corn..............228
Ceviche (Marinated Seafood).4, 380
Chablis Surprise.............81
Chalupas, Beef.............143
Champagne Chicken w/ Shrimp189
Chapeau Rouge (Red Hat).....188
Cheddar Log.................72
Cheese and Garlic Bread, Hot..276
Cheese Ball, Alamo Pecan......17
Cheese Biscuits.............271
Cheese Casserole, Herbed
  Egg and...............212
Cheese Date Pastry...........23
Cheese Soup, 1886...........90
Cheese Soup, Los Patios......383
Cheese Spread, Cinnamon
  Strawberry.............24
Cheese Sticks...............65
Cheese with Spinach Puffs.....376
Cheesecake Bars, Butterscotch..322
Cheesecakes.................324
Cheesecakes, Special Crust for.326
Cherry Tomatoes, Broccoli Crown
  with..................358
Cherry Tomatoes, Stuffed......62
Chez Ardid..................46

Chicken "American Bounty,"
  Breast of.................363
Chicken a la King............190
Chicken Amandine, Hot......193
Chicken Almond Crepes......190
Chicken and Corn Tortilla
  Casserole (Chilaquiles).....28
Chicken Aspic, Molded.......124
Chicken Bar-B-Q, Lemon-Garlic.178
Chicken Breasts, Jap. Mandarin192
Chicken Canneloni...........187
Chicken Cantonese...........124
Chicken Casa De Moros......366
Chicken Chasseur...........375
Chicken Delight, East Indian...191
Chicken Divan, Classic.......183
Chicken Divan, Easy.........183
Chicken Fajitas...........141, 174
Chicken Fiorentina...........185
Chicken Flutes (Flautas de Pollo)
 71
Chicken Fricassee with Paprika188
Chicken Fried Steak..........138
Chicken in Chili Sauce.......348
Chicken Kiev, Fiesta.........172
Chicken Liver Pate...........64
Chicken Mexicana...........171
Chicken Ole'................171
Chicken Omelet, Florentine....208
Chicken Paprika.............179
Chicken Pasta Salad, Hot.....121
Chicken Pot Pie.............182
Chicken Pot Pie, Easy........182
Chicken Puffs...............58
Chicken Rice-A-Roni, Oriental..125
Chicken Roll-Ups, Imperial....181
Chicken Salad, Aloha.........123
Chicken Salad, Chinese.......123
Chicken Salad, Curried Rice &.125
Chicken Salad, Hot..........122
Chicken Salad, Picante.......122
Chicken Soup, Cheesy........90
Chicken Spaghetti...........186
Chicken Strips..............184
Chicken Strips, Marinated
  (Chicken Fajitas).........174
Chicken Stuffed with Crab.....175
Chicken Taco Filling.........173
Chicken Washington.........181
Chicken Wellington..........180
Chicken Wings, Sweet and Sour.59
Chicken with Avocado Sauce...172
Chicken with Lemon Butter
  Sauce, Acapulco.........367
Chicken w/Shrimp, Champagne189
Chicken, Apricot............178
Chicken, Artichoke..........179
Chicken, Barbecued..........133
Chicken, Busy Day El Rancho..176
Chicken, El Rancho..........176
Chicken, Forty Clove Garlic...185
Chicken, Ginger Nectarine....193
Chicken, Healthy............177
Chicken, Lemon............344
Chicken, Little Rhein........381
Chicken, Peruvian Baked.....175
Chicken, Prairie Chili........177
Chicken, Red Hat (Chapeau
  Rouge).................188
Chicken, Szechwan..........192
Chilaquiles, Chicken.........28
Chiles en Frio (Cold Peppers)..229
Chiles Rellenos..........342-343
Chili Con Queso.............58
Chili.......................144

Chili, Pedernales River........346
Chimichangas (Fried Burrito)..142
Chips, Toasted (Nachos).......52
Chips, Toasted (Tostadas).......10
Chocolate Candy Bar Pie.....304
Chocolate Cola Cake.........288
Chocolate Cola Frosting......288
Chocolate Delight, Sp. Occasion339
Chocolate Frosting, Creamy....286
Chocolate Fudge Icing........287
Chocolate Mexicano..........390
Chocolate Mix, Hot..........85
Chocolate Mousse Pie........309
Chocolate Potato Cake.......295
Chocolate Sin...............286
Chocolate Swirl Cheesecake....326
Chocolate Yulelog, Easy......298
Choctaw Pumpkin Cake......288
Chorizo Con Papas...........30
Chorizo Con Queso..........57
Chow Chow.................13
Churros (Spanish Fritters).....279
Cider for a Crowd, Hot.......76
Cilantro.....................89
Cinnamon Bars.............314
Cinnamon Rolls.............262
Cisneros, Henry.............ix
Cisneros, Mary Alice......342-343
Clock Tower, S.W. Craft Center.391
Club Josef..................359
Coconut Cr: Cheese Frosting...300
Coconut Macaroons..........319
Coconut Pound Cake, Soaky...293
Coffee Breakers.............283
Coffee, Mexican.............80
Cointreau Marinade, Fresh Fruit
  Salad with..............107
Cold Peppers (Chiles en Frio)..229
Cole Slaw..................117
Coleslaw, 24 Hour...........117
Colonnade Icing.............287
Commander's House..........41
Convention Center......130-131
Cookies, Mexican (Reposteria)...30
Cookies, Walk-To-School......320
Copper Kitchen, The.........391
Coquilles St. Jacques..........41
Corn Baskets, Mexican........73
Corn Casserole, Hondo.......230
Corn Chowder w/Ham & Thyme91
Corn Chowder, Easy.........91
Corn Fritters...............272
Corn Pudding, Mexican.......229
Corn Salad.................120
Corn, Creamed Cheese.......230
Cornbread, Jalapeno..........13
Corned Beef in Rye...........68
Corned Beef................140
Costumes, early settlers......35
Court Bouillon (Cajun)......203
Cousins, Margaret...........347
Cowboy Beans...............12
Crab.......................199
Crab & Avocado Enchiladas....354
Crab Dip, Coastal............69
Crab Soup..................92
Crab, Chicken Stuffed with....175
Crab, Shrimp and Artichokes au
  Gratin.................205
Crabbies....................68
Crabmeat Salad.............127
Crabmeat, Zucchini Stuffed w/.236
Cranberries in Crust.........238
Cranberry Cake.............295

Cranberry Cream Cheese Salad.113
Crayfish Bienville (The Bayous)373
Cream Gravy..............138
Creme Dijon..............136
Crepe Filling and Chicken a la
     King..............190
Crepes, Manicotti..........250
Crepes, Seafood...........377
Crescent Rolls............261
Crockett Hotel............363
Crumpets..............375
Crust for Cheesecakes........326
Crystal Baking Co........376, 377
Cucumber Soup, Easy Cream of.92
Cucumber/Shrimp Bisque.....345
Cucumbers, Sour Cream......117
Curried Rice "Bombay".......361
Curried Rice & Chicken Salad..125
Custard, Baked............347
Custard, Caramel (Flan).......390

D

Da Tees.................320
Daiquiris, Bananas (Variation)...83
Daiquiris, Strawberry.........83
Date Bar Muffins..........265
Date Nut Torte............297
Date Roll................336
Date Torte...............333
Delicatessen Cheesecake......327
Devil's Food Cake..........287
Dilly Casserole Bread........259
Divinity, Strawberry.........19
Dominion Country Club......360
Doughnuts, Canary Islander....36
Dove or Quail, Tim's Grilled...168
Doves a la San Antonio.......170
Duck Breast with Honey Port
     Sauce, Grilled...........371

E

Egg and Artichoke Casserole...211
Egg & Cheese Casserole, Herbed212
Eggnog, Chocolate.............79
Eggnog, Yuletide.............78
Eggplant Parmigiana.........389
Eggplant Pie..............231
Eggplant Relish (Caponata).....40
Eggs with Poblano Peppers.....28
Eggs, Caviar Stuffed...........61
Eggs, Make Ahead Baked.....214
Eggs, Pickled.............253
Eggs, Shy Poke.............64
El Mercado.............23, 27
Empanadas (Meat Pies).......64
Enchilada Casserole..........146
Enchilada Casserole, Very Easy..146
Enchiladas, Cheese.........217
Enchiladas, Crab and Avocado..354
Enchiladas, Green..........380
English Olive Appetizers.......62
Ernesto's................378

ETHNIC DISHES
ENGLISH
     Beef Wellingtons..........368
     English Fish Batter........202
     Lamb, Roast Leg of.......162
     Mint Sauce, Grandad's......162
     Trifle, Republic of Texas.....42
FRENCH
     Chapeau Rogue (Red Hat)..188
     Chicken Chasseur.........375
     Coquilles St. Jacques (Scallops &
          Mushrooms in Wine Sauce) 41
     Crayfish Bienville.........373
     French Apple Pie.........379

French Bread............258
Fricassee de Poulet Paprika.188
Jambalaya...............34
Souffle, Grand Marnier....329
GERMAN
German Style Mustard Steak370
Konigsberger Klopse
     (German Meatballs)....154
Potato Pancakes..........239
Sausage and Kraut.......165
Schitzel a la "San Antonio"...46
Torte, New Braunfels Schaum
     (German Meringue)....329
ITALIAN
Beefy Spaghetti Casserole...159
Bolognese Sauce..........187
Chicken Spaghetti........186
Chicken Canneloni........187
Eggplant Parmigiana......389
Fettucine Giacomo........248
Fettucine Alfredo.........248
Fettucine with Chives......248
Italian Meatballs w/Sauce...158
Italian Cream Cheese Cake.299
Italian Spaghetti Sauce, Easy158
Lasagna with Tiny Meatballs157
Linguine with Clam Sauce..249
Manicotti Crepes.........250
Omelet, Maggie's Italian....384
Pasta Fresca............374
Pasta with Pesto Sauce....249
Pasta Timbale...........129
Pasta Salad, Garden......116
Pollo alla Fiorentina......185
Pork Chops, Italian Spiced..165
Pork Chops, Italian........164
Ricotta Pasta............250
Saltimbocca alla Luigi.....382
Shrimp Congiglia.........60
Spinach Italiano.........233
Tortoni, Italian Biscuit....334
Veal Chops Palermo, Sauteed365
Veal Rolls, Italian.........385
Veal Scaloppine, Easy.....160
MEXICAN
Aguacate Fritos.............48
Anticuchos................34
Asparagus Brunch........210
Avocado Dip.............53
Avocados 53
Bean Dip, Prairie Fire.......56
Beans, Chili............144
Black Bean Dip, Yucatan....57
Bolillos 260
Breakfast Casserole, Mex....209
Calabacitas Casserole.......234
Calabaza Con Puerco......235
Caldo de Pollo............37
Caldo Xochitl............386
Carne Guisada...........145
Ceviche 4
Chalupas, Beef............143
Chicken Casa de Maros.....366
Chicken Fajitas...........174
Chicken Mexicana.........171
Chicken Ole.............171
Chicken Taco Filling.......173
Chicken with Lemon Butter
     Sauce, Acapulco........367
Chilaquiles, Chicken........28
Chiles en Frio...........229
Chiles Rellenos.......342-343
Chili 144
Chili, Pedernales River....346
Chili Con Queso...........58
Chimichangas 142
Chocolate Mexicano........390
Chorizo Con Papas.........30
Chorizo Con Queso........57
Cilantro Cumin Butter......47
Coffee, Mexican..........80
Corn Baskets, Mexican.....73
Corn Pudding, Mexican....229

Cornbread, Jalapeno......13
Empanadas 64
Enchilada Casserole.......146
Enchiladas, Cheese........217
Enchiladas, Crab & Avocado354
Enchiladas, Green........380
Fajitas.................5
Fajitas Cooking Techniques.141
Flan (La Paloma del Rio)...390
Flautas de Pollo..........71
Frijoles 225
Gallina en Mole..........348
Gazpacho, Chunky........99
Gazpacho, Smooth and Easy.99
Guacamole...............4
Huevos Poblanos..........28
Jalapeno Jelly............252
Jalapeno Peppers, Stuffed....7
Jalapenos, Cheese Squares...59
Jalapenos, Party Fried......59
Macaroni Salad, Fiesta.....115
Machacado 149
Margarita 81
Margaritas, Frozen........81
Meat Dip, Mexican........52
Mexican Army Hot Sauce....75
Mexican Brunch..........26
Mexican Chowder........100
Migas 209
Nachos 52
Noche Specials..........346
Pan Dulce..............278
Picante Sauce............75
Piccadillo, Sweet..........63
Pico de Gallo..............6
Picosos, Seguin..........255
Pina Colada a la Alamo.....82
Pralines, Mexican..........7
Quesadillas 73
Quiche, Jalapeno.........213
Relleno Para Pavo
     (Turkey Stuffing).......348
Reposteria 30
Rice, El Mirador..........387
Rice, Green Chili..........244
Roast Beef Flautas........148
Salsa Fresca.............75
San Antonio Dip..........55
Shrimp Ceviche..........380
Shrimp Salad, Mexican.....126
Sopa Anauachalli
     (Tortilla Soup)........378
Shy Poke Eggs............64
Taco Avocado...........145
Taco Salad..............114
Tamale Casserole........148
Tamale Soup, Mexican....101
Tequila Sunrise..........31
Tortilla Casserole.........147
Tortilla Bake, Easy........147
Tortilla Soup, Easy.......100
Tortillas, Flour............6
Tostadas 10
Vegetables, Spicy Mexican
     Pickled...............29
SPANISH
Arroz con Pollo Espanola...173
Bunuelos 277
Churros 279
Doughnuts, Canary Islander..36
Paella 201
Rice, Spanish............244
Sangria 36
Sole, Senoritas..........199
Sopa de Fideo...........247

F

Fajitas (Candy Erben Wagner).350
Fajitas (Marinated Skirt Steak)....5
Fajitas Cooking Techniques....141
Fajitas Marinades, Additional...141
Fernandez, Rosita.........5, 345

Fettucine Alfredo............248
Fettucine Giacomo............248
Fettucine with Chives........248
Fiesta Buffet..................3
Fiesta Noche del Rio...........7
Fig Preserves................252
Fish Batter, English.........202
Fish, Marinated (Ceviche)......4
Flamencos.....................7
Flan (Caramel Custard).......390
Flautas de Pollo (Chicken Flutes)71
Floresville Coffee Cake.......282
Folklife Festival.............33
Four Seasons Hotel...........364
Fredericksburg Peach Ice Cream.330
French Bread.................258
Fresh Horizons Creative
    Catering.................356
Fricassee de Poulet au Paprika
    (Chicken Fricassee Paprika)188
Frijoles (Pinto Beans)........225
Fritter Batter...............254
Fritters, Spanish (Churros).....279
Fritters, Zucchini...........272
Fruit Cake Cookies...........322
Fruit Compote, Zesty.........238
Fruit Salad with Cointreau
    Marinade, Fresh..........107
Fruit Salad with Variations,Hot.109
Fruit Salad,On the Go Friendly.106
Ft. Sam Houston, Army Band...19
Fudge Nut Bars...............314
Fudge Pie, Caribbean.........307
Fudge Sauce, Hot.............349
Fudge........................336
Fudge, Festive White Confetti..336

G

Gallina en Mole (Chicken in
    Chili Sauce).............348
Garlic Bread, Hot Cheese &...276
Gazpacho, Chunky.............99
Gazpacho, Smooth and Easy....99
Gilmer Sweet Potato Pie......306
Gingerbread Men..............318
Gingersnaps (Variation)......318
Gourmet Celebration..........45
Graham Cracker Greek Dessert.328
Graham Muffins...............266
Grand Marnier Cheesecakes...324
Grapenut Bread...............267
Greek Salad, Marinated.......115
Green Bean Bundles...........231
Green Beans, Bacon Fried.....231
Green Beans, Savory..........230
Green Lizards.................83
Green Salad, Layered.........116
Grey Moss Inn, Fr. Apple Pie.379
Grits, Bandera Party.........247
Guacamole (Avocado Mixture)...4
Gunter Hotel, The........366, 367

H

Ham Carvonara...............164
Ham Slices, Stuffed..........167
Ham Strata..................211
Ham, Bourbon Cashew Studded.355
Haram, Karen............47, 349
Hens with Herbs, Rock Cornish170
Herb Salad Dressing..........391
Hilly Dilly Salad............118
Hilton Palacio del Rio.......365
Hondo Corn Casserole........230
Honey as a Natural Sweetener.262
Honey Lemon Dressing.......102

Honey Port Sauce, Grilled Duck
    Breast with.............371
Honey Spice Bars.............315
Hot Sauce, Mexican Army......75
Huevos Poblanos (Eggs with
    Poblano Peppers).........28
Hyatt Regency San Antonio...368

I

Ice Cream, Fredericksburg
    Peach...................330
Ice Cream, Fried (Marriott
    Hotels).................372
Ice Cream, Homemade Vanilla.330
Imperial Sauce for Seafood.....198
Institute of Texan Cultures
    ....32, 284-285
Irish "Cheesecake" Muffins.....264
Italian Cream Cheese Cake....299
Italian Meatballs with Sausage
    Sauce...................158
Italian Spaghetti Sauce, Easy...158

J

Jalapenos....................253
Jalapeno Cheese Squares......59
Jalapeno Jelly...............252
Jalapeno Peppers, Stuffed......7
Jalapenos, Party Fried........59
Jambalaya....................34
Japanese Tea Gardens........21
Jarro de Arturo Restaurants, El.380
Johnson, Lady Bird..........346
Julep, Jungle................83

K

KaffeeKlatsch................21
Katy Kornettes..............272
Kerrville Ranch Biscuits......261
King William Cocktail Buffet....39
King William Fair............39
King William Historic District...39
Kolaches....................280
Konigsberger Klopse (Meatballs)154

L

La Mansion del Norte Hotel....370
La Mansion del Rio........47, 371
La Villita....................43
Lamb Kebobs San Antonio Style163
Lamb with Grandad's Mint
    Sauce, Roast Leg of.......162
Las Posadas on the river...340-341
Lasagna with Tiny Meatballs...157
Lemon Ambrosia Pie..........310
Lemon Butter Sauce..........367
Lemon Chess Pie.............304
Lemon Snowball Cake.........289
Lemon Soup...................93
Lemon Squares...............315
Lemon-Caper-Dill Butter......374
Lentil Soup..................93
Lentil Soup, Cream of.........93
Lettuce Salad, Mandarin......106
Linguine with Clam Sauce....249
Liqueur, Coffee..............80
Liqueur, Irish Cream.........80
Little Rhein Steakhouse......381
Livestock Show and Rodeo......11
Loaf, Fancy Layered..........22
Lobster Bisque (Plaza Club)....362
Locro De Papas (Ecuadorian
    Potato Soup).............95
Los Patios..................383
Luigi's Restaurant..........382

Luling Watermelon Wine Punch.78

M

Macaroni Salad, Fiesta.......115
Machacado (Beef Filling).....149
Maggie's....................384
Magnolias....................23

MAIN DISHES
  BEEF
Barbecue, history...........132
Barbecued Steaks............133
Barbecuing, Techniques for.132
Beef and Brew Take Along...16
Beef and Dumplings..........151
Beef Burgundy...............153
Beef Jerky..................139
Beef Spaghetti Casserole....159
Beef Stroganov..............153
Beef Wellingtons with Puff
    Pastry..................368
Beef w/Snow Peas, Oriental.151
Beefy Pasta Florentine.....159
Brisket in Beer.............135
Brisket in Soy Sauce........136
Brisket, Barbecued.....133, 353
Brisket, Oven Barbecued....135
Carne Guisada (Stewed Meat) 145
Chalupas, Beef.............143
Chili.......................144
Chili, Pedernales River.....346
Chimichangas (Burrito).....142
Corned Beef.................140
Enchilada Casserole........146
Fajitas (Candy Wagner).....350
Fajitas (Marinated Skirt Steak).5
Fajitas Cooking Techniques.141
Italian Meatballs with Sauce.158
Italian Spaghetti Sauce, Easy158
Konigsberger Klopse........154
Lasagna with Tiny Meatballs157
Machacado (Beef Filling)...149
Medallions Au Poivre
    (Tenderloins Pepper
    Sauce).................360
Ribs, Barbecued............133
Roast Beef Flautas (Flutes)..148
Roast, Rock Salt............139
Round in Red Wine, Eye of.150
Sauerbraten.................35
Steak Diane.................150
Steak Tartare a la Josef....359
Steak, German Style Mustard370
Steak, Pepper...............137
Steaks, Chicken Fried.......138
Steaks, Chili Cheese........137
Stew with Wine, Beef......156
Stew, Alamo City...........155
Stew, Easy Oven Meat......155
Taco Avocado Pie...........145
Tamale Casserole...........148
Tenderloin, Marinated......152
Tortilla Bake, Easy........147
Tortilla Casserole.........147
  EGGS & CHEESE
Chorizo Con Papas (Sausage
    with Potatoes)...........30
Huevos Poblanos (Eggs with
    Poblano Peppers)........28
Omelet, Elegant Oven.......24
Omelet, Maggie's Italian....384
Asparagus Brunch..........210
Breakfast Casserole, Mex...209
Breakfast Pizza............216
Brunch Pie, Quick........213

Egg & Artichoke Casserole..211
Egg & Cheese Casserole....212
Eggs, Make Ahead Baked...214
Enchiladas, Cheese........217
Ham Strata................211
Migas (Tortilla Crumbs)....209
Omelet, Florentine Chicken.208
Omelet, The Perfect.......207
Prairie Casserole.........210
Quiche Lorraine Tarts.....216
Quiche, Gourmet Crab......218
Quiche, Jalapeno..........213
Quiche, Magic Crustless....215
Sausage Brunch Squares....212
Sausage Quiche............214
Swiss Pie.................219

GAME
Dove or Quail, Tim's Grilled168
Doves a la San Antonio.....170
Duck Breast with Honey Port
    Sauce, Grilled.........371
Hens w/Herbs, Rock Cornish 170
Quail in Sherry...........168
Quail, Smothered..........345
Venison Backstrap.........169
Venison Guisada...........169
Venison Stroganoff........169

LAMB
Lamb Kebobs...............163
Lamb with Grandad's Mint
    Sauce, Roast Leg of.....162

PORK
Ham Carvonara.............164
Ham Slices, Stuffed.......167
Ham, Bourbon Cashew.....355
Noisettes de Porc Aux
    Pruneaux (Pork Tenderloin
    with Prunes)...........46
Pork Chops, Creole........164
Pork Chops, Italian Spiced.165
Pork Chops, Italian.......164
Pork Loin with Tangy Sauce,
    Boneless..............353
Pork Roast in Vermouth....166
Pork Roll-Ups, Baked......166
Pork Tenderloin with Prunes.46
Sausage and Kraut.........165
Sausage, Barbecued........133
Spareribs, Barbecued......165

POULTRY
Arroz con Pollo Espanola
    (Sp. Rice with Chicken).173
Champagne Chicken with
    Shrimp................189
Chapeau Rouge (Red Hat)..188
Chicken "American Bounty,"
    Breast of.............363
Chicken a la King w/Filling.190
Chicken Almandine, Hot...193
Chicken Almond Crepes....190
Chicken Barbecue,
    Lemon-Garlic..........178
Chicken Breasts, Japanese
    Mandarin..............192
Chicken Canneloni.........187
Chicken Casa De Moros....366
Chicken Chasseur..........375
Chicken Delight, East Indian.191
Chicken Divan, Classic.....183
Chicken Divan, Easy.......183
Chicken Fajitas (Marinated
    Chicken Strips).......174
Chicken in Chili Sauce
    (Gallina en Mole)......348
Chicken Kiev, Fiesta......172
Chicken Mexicana.........171
Chicken Ole'..............171
Chicken Paprika...........179
Chicken Pot Pie...........182
Chicken Pot Pie, Easy.....182
Chicken Roll-Ups, Imperial.181
Chicken Spaghetti.........186
Chicken Strips............184

Chicken Stuffed with Crab..175
Chicken Taco Filling.......173
Chicken Washington.......181
Chicken Wellington........180
Chicken w/Avocado Sauce..172
Chicken with Lemon Butter
    Sauce, Acapulco.......367
Chicken, Apricot..........178
Chicken, Artichoke........179
Chicken, Barbecued........133
Chicken, El Rancho........176
Chicken, Forty Clove Garlic.185
Chicken, Ginger Nectarine.193
Chicken, Healthy..........177
Chicken, Lemon...........344
Chicken, Little Rhein......381
Chicken, Peruvian Baked...175
Chicken, Prairie Chili.....177
Chicken, Szechwan........192
Chilaquiles, Chicken.......28
Enchiladas, Green.........380
Fricassee de Poulet au Paprika
    (Chicken Paprika).....188
Gallina en Mole (Chicken in
    Chili Sauce)..........348
Moo Goo Gai Pan.........191
Pollo alla Fiorentina
    (Chicken Fiorentina)....185
Turkey Creole.............194
Turkey in Cheese Sauce....194

SEAFOOD
Cajun Coo Bee Yon (Court
    Bouillon).............203
Coquilles St. Jacques (Scallops
    and Mushrooms)........41
Crab, Shrimp & Artichokes.205
Crayfish Bienville.........373
Enchiladas, Crab & Avocado354
Jambalaya.................34
Oyster Stew a la Burt......200
Paella....................201
Redfish in Lemon-Caper-Dill.374
Salmon Souffle Torte.......197
Salmon with Oyster Beurre
    Blanc and Sorrel.......371
Seafood Casserole.........204
Seafood Crepes............377
Senoritas' Sole...........199
Shellfish in Paprika.......206
Shrimp and Zucchini.......351
Shrimp Steamed in Beer....196
Shrimp Victoria Gourmet...204
Shrimp, Tejas Garlic.......195
Trout Amandine...........196
Trout with Cayenne, Blackened
    River.................364

VEAL
Saltimbocca alla Luigi.....382
Schnitzel a la San Antonio...46
Veal Chops Palermo.......365
Veal Chops, Apple Brandy.160
Veal Rolls, Italian........385
Veal Scaloppine, Easy.....160
Veal with Paprika, Lemon..161
Mango Mousse, Tropical.......31
Mango Sauce................359
Manicotti Crepes............250
Margarita...................81
Margaritas, Frozen...........81

MARINADES
24 Hour Meat..............138
Chicken Fajitas.........141, 174
Fajitas (Candy Wagner).....350
Fajitas....................141
Fresh Fruit Salad w/Cointreau 107
San Antonio...........5, 141
Market Square.........23, 27
Marriott Hotels............48
Fried Ice Cream............372
Meat Dip, Mexican.........52
Meat Mixture (Picadillo)....63
Meat, Stewed (Carne Guisada)..145

Meatballs, German........154
Meatball's................382
Medallions Au Poivre......360
Melon Boat, Lively........108
Melon Boat, Spicy.........108
Meringue, German.........329
Mexican Brunch............26
Mexican Chowder..........100
Mexican Cookies (Reposteria)...30
Migas (Tortilla Crumbs)......209
Military...............14, 86-87
Milky Way Squares..........313
Mincemeat Bars..........316
Mint Sauce, Grandad's.....162
Mints, Cream Cheese.......335
Mirador Restaurant, El....386, 387
Mission San Jose..........256-257
Molcajete..................71
Monkey Bread..............263
Moo Goo Gai Pan............191
Mushroom Soup............94
Mushrooms in Sour Cream....232
Mushrooms Parmigiana, Stuffed.67
Mushrooms, Marinated......66
Mushrooms, Oyster Stuffed....66
Mushrooms, Stuffed........66

N
Nachos (Toasted Chips)........52
Navy Bean Soup..............94
New Braunfels Torte Schaum..329
Night in Old San Antonio
    (N.I.O.S.A.)...........220-221
Noche Specials.............346
Noisettes de Porc Aux Pruneaux.46
Nuts, Spiced................338

O
Oak Hills Country Club....46, 361
Oatmeal Cookies, Disappearing.317
Oatmeal Raisin Bread........270
Oatmeal Spice Cake.........296
Oil Well...................219
Old San Francisco Steak House.388
Olive Twists................61
Omelet, Elegant Oven........24
Omelet, Florentine Chicken....208
Omelet, Maggie's Italian......384
Omelet, The Perfect.........207
Onion Cheese Bread.........271
Onion Soup, French..........95
Onions, Baked..............232
Onions, Glazed.............232
Orange Jubilees............82
Orange Pineapple Congeal.....110
Orange Rolls...............274
Orange Butter..............223
Orangy Date Cake...........301
Oyster Dip, Smoked.........54
Oyster Stew a la Burt.........200
Oyster Stuffed Mushrooms......66

P
Paella....................201
Paesano's Restaurant........389
Paloma del Rio, La........390
Pan Dulce (Sweet Bread).....278
Pancakes, Flour (Flour Tortillas)..6
Parker, Nancy.............351
Paseo del Rio...............7
Pasta Fresca (Cappy's).......374
Pasta in Cream Sauce.........47
Pasta Salad, Garden.........116
Pasta Timbale.............129

Pasta with Pesto Sauce.......249
Pasta, Ricotta...............250
Pea Pickin Cake.............291
Peach Cheesecake...........324
Peach Cobbler (Variation).....311
Peach Cobbler, Hill Country....12
Peach Preserves..............251
Peaches, Spiced..............251
Peanut Brittle, Microwave.....337
Peanut Buster Dessert........333
Peanut Butter & Jelly Swirls...323
Peanut Butter Crunch.........337
Peanuts, Hot Roasted.........255
Pecan Cheesecake............356
Pecan Icing, Broiled..........296
Pecan Pie....................302
Pecan Sand Tarts.............320
Pecans, Dry Roasted..........338
Pecans, history of.......293, 338
Pecans, Minted...............339
Pecans, Roasted.............338
Pecans, Toasted.............339
Penuche Icing...............293
Peppers with Cheese..........58
Peppers, Stuffed (Chiles).....342
Pesto Sauce, Pasta with.......249
Picadillo, Sweet.............63
Picante Sauce (Hot Sauce)......75
Picnic in the Park............15
Pico de Gallo (Chopped tomato)..6
Pie Crust, No Fail...........302
Pina Colada a la Alamo........82
Pineapple and Coconut Drink...82
Pineapple Casserole..........237
Pineapple Cheesecake.........324
Pineapple Coffee Cake, Rich...281
Pineapple Delight, Tropical....332
Pineapple Frosting...........291
Pineapple Meringue Pie......308
Pineapple Upside Down Cake..292
Pinto Beans (Frijoles)........225
Piquant Herb Sauce..........152
Plain and Fancy Muffins......266
Plaza Club..................362
Plum Sauce..................184
Pollo alla Fiorentina.........185
Poppy Seed Cake.............292
Poppy Seed Coffee Cake.......281
Poppy Seed Dressing, Lime....102
Pork Chops, Creole...........164
Pork Chops, Italian Spiced.....165
Pork Chops, Italian..........164
Pork Loin with Tangy Sauce...353
Pork Roast in Vermouth.......166
Pork Roll-Ups, Baked.........166
Pork Tenderloin with Prunes....46
Potato Bake, Supreme........240
Potato Casserole, Fluffy......241
Potato Pancakes.............239
Potato Salad with Sour Cream..105
Potato Salad, Old-Fashioned....10
Potato Skins, Cheesy.........71
Potato Soup, Ecuadorian.......95
Potatoes with Parsley, New....241
Potatoes, Baked Florentine.....48
Potatoes, Fast Duchess.......239
Potatoes, Fiesta.............241
Potatoes, Oven Fried.........240
Potatoes, Twice-Baked........240
Poteet Strawberry Cake.......290
Prairie Casserole............210
Praline Cheesecake, Texas....325
Pralines, Mexican............7
Prune Cake.................294

Puff Pastry..................368
Puff, Danish................283
Puffs, Beer.................273
Puffs, Cheese with Spinach....376
Puffs, Chicken..............58
Puffs, French Breakfast.....267
Pumpkin Bread.............269
Pumpkin Pie with Brandy....306
Punch, Big Red.............77
Punch, Champagne.........77
Punch, Coffee..............77
Punch, Cranberry Holiday......76
Punch, Holiday Hot.........76
Punch, Watermelon Wine.....78
Punch, Spanish Red Wine.....36
Punch, Whiskey Sour.........84
Punch, Yellow Rose.........79
Purple Plum Salad..........111

Q

Quail in Sherry..............168
Quail, Smothered............345
Quesadillas 73
Quiche Lorraine Tarts........216
Quiche, Gourmet Crab.......218
Quiche, Jalapeno............213
Quiche, Magic Crustless......215
Quilting 37

R

Raisin-Pecan Pie.............307
Raspberry Salad.............110
Red Snapper Soup...........370
Redfish in Lemon-Caper-Dill
    Butter 374
Reinee Dressing............103
Relleno Para Pavo (Turkey
    Stuffing) 348
Reposteria (Mexican Cookies)...30
Republic of Texas............42
Rhubarb Strawberry Cobbler...311
Ribs, Barbecued............133
Rice "Bombay," Curried......361
Rice and Artichoke Salad.....125
Rice and Mushrooms.........246
Rice Casserole, Wild.........246
Rice Pilaf with Lemon, Celery..245
Rice Salad with Eggplant......121
Rice with Chicken, Spanish....173
Rice, Chinese Fried Rice......245
Rice, El Mirador.............387
Rice, Green Chili............244
Rice, Parmesan..............246
Rice,Spanish 244
River Parade................1
River, San Antonio
    ....1, 20, 44, 340, 341
Roast (Sauerbraten)...........35
Roast Beef Flautas (Flutes).....148
Roast, Rock Salt............139
Rolls, La Villita.............43
Rolls, Mexican..............260
Romanoff Sauce............332
Round in Red Wine, Eye of....150
Royal Catering..............357
Rum Mix, Hot Buttered.......84

S

Salad Seasoning Mix, Super....105
Salad, Vermicelli.............16
SALADS
  CHICKEN
    Chicken Aspic, Molded.....124
    Chicken Cantonese......124
    Chicken Rice-A-Roni.......125

Chicken Salad, Aloha......123
Chicken Salad, Chinese.....123
Chicken Salad, Curried Rice
    and.....................125
Chicken Salad, Hot.......122
Chicken Salad, Picante.....122
DRESSINGS
Herb Salad Dressing.......391
Honey Lemon Dressing.....102
Poppy Seed Dressing, Lime.102
Reinee Dressing...........103
Salad Seasoning Mix, Super.105
Sesame Dressing...........123
Spinach Salad Dressing.....102
Tomato Vinaigrette........103
Vegetable Marinade, Fresh..104
FRUIT
Apricot Salad, Congealed...112
Booberry Salad...........111
Cranberry Cream Cheese
    Salad 113
Fruit Salad with Cointreau
    Marinade, Fresh........107
Fruit Salad with Variations,
    Hot....................109
Fruit Salad, On the Go
    Friendly................106
Lettuce Salad, Mandarin....106
Mango Mousse, Tropical.....31
Melon Boat, Lively.........108
Melon Boat, Spicy.........108
Orange Pineapple Congealed
    Salad 110
Purple Plum Salad.........111
Raspberry Salad..........110
Strawberry Nut Salad......112
Yogurt Fruit Low-Cal Salad..107
MEAT
Beef and Mushroom Salad..128
Taco Salad.................114
PASTA
Chicken Pasta Salad, Hot...121
Fiesta Macaroni Salad......115
Garden Pasta Salad........116
Pasta Timbale.............129
Vermicelli Salad...........16
SEAFOOD
Crabmeat Salad............127
Mexican Shrimp Salad.....126
Shrimp Salad..............383
Shrimp Salad Mold.........126
Shrimp Souffle Salad.......127
Tuna-Avocado Salad, Molded.28
VEGETABLE
Aunt Dixie's Pea Salad......118
Broccoli Molded Salad......119
Broccoli Salad Supreme.....119
Cauliflower & Bacon Salad...120
Cauliflower & Broccoli Salad120
Cole Slaw.................117
Coleslaw, 24 Hour.........117
Corn Salad...............120
Cucumbers, Sour Cream....117
Greek Salad, Marinated.....115
Green Salad, Layered......116
Hilly Dilly Salad..........118
Pea Salad, Aunt Dixie's......118
Potato Salad w/Sour Cream.105
Potato Salad, Old-Fashioned..10
Rice and Artichoke Salad...125
Rice Salad with Eggplants...121
Spinach Salad.............349
Vegetable Salad, Marinated.118
Western Salad.............114
Salmon Ball.................72
Salmon Mousse.............60
Salmon Souffle Torte.........197
Salmon with Oyster Beurre Blanc
    and Sorrel, Poached.......371
Salsa (Sauce), Fresh Mex......350
Salsa Fresca (Fresh Sauce).....75
Saltimbocca alla Luigi........382

San Antonio River Mud.......328
San Antonio River1, 20, 44, 340-341
San Antonio Zoo..........17, 21
San Fernando Cathedral..25, 50-51
Sandwich, Special Sunday......113

SANDWICHES
    Loaf, Fancy Layered.......22
    Sandwich, Special Sunday...113
Sangria (Spanish Red Wine Punch) 36
Saucepan Scotchies..........316

SAUCES
    Asparagus, Orange Butter...223
    Barbecue, Chuckwagon....134
    Barbecue, Pappy Skrap's....11
    Basting..................134
    Bearnaise................352
    Bolognese................187
    Brisket..................136
    Brown or Demi-Glace......361
    Butter, Cilantro Cumin.....47
    Cream Gravy.............138
    Creme Dijon.............136
    Fudge, Hot..............349
    Honey Port, Grilled
       Duck Breast with......371
    Imperial Sauce for Seafood..198
    Lemon Butter, Acapulco
       Chicken...............367
    Lemon-Caper-Dill Butter,
       Redfish in............374
    Mango...................359
    Mint, Grandad's.........162
    Pesto, Pasta with.........249
    Piquant Herb............152
    Plum....................184
    Romanoff...............332
    Salsa, Fresh Mex.........350
    Sauce, Fresh (Salsa Fresca)...75
    Sauce, Hot (Picante Sauce)...75
    Sauce, Italian Spaghetti.....158
    Sauce, Italian Meatballs w/.158
    Sauce, Mexican Army Hot...75
    Sauce, Seafood, Imperial....198
    Tangy, Pork Loin with.....353
Sauerbraten...................35
Sausage and Kraut...........165
Sausage Bread...............271
Sausage Brunch Squares......212
Sausage Crescent Nuggets......74
Sausage Quiche..............214
Sausage with Cheese Dip.....57
Sausage with Potatoes.........30
Sausage, Barbecued..........133
Scallops and Mushrooms......41
Schnitzel a la "San Antonio"...46
Seafood Casserole............204
Seafood Cocktail Spread.......69
Seafood Crepes..............377
Seguin Picosos (Peanuts).....255
Senoritas' Sole..............199
Sesame Dressing (Variation)..123
Shellfish in Paprika..........206
Shishkebobs.................141
    San Antonio Marinade......5
Shrimp......................205
Shrimp & Zucchini, Brochettes.351
Shrimp Ceviche.............380
Shrimp Congiglia.............60
Shrimp in Dill Mayonnaise....60
Shrimp Mold.................70
Shrimp Pate..................70
Shrimp Salad................383
Shrimp Salad Mold...........126
Shrimp Salad, Mexican.......126
Shrimp Souffle Salad.........127
Shrimp Steamed in Beer......196
Shrimp Victoria Gourmet.....204
Shrimp, Tejas Garlic.........195

SIDE DISHES
FRUIT
Apples, Orange-Pecan Baked238
Cranberries in Crust.......238
Fruit Compote, Zesty.......238
Pineapple Casserole.......237
PASTA
Fettucine Alfredo..........248
Fettucine Giacomo.........248
Fettucine with Chives.....248
Linguine with Clam Sauce..249
Manicotti Crepes..........250
Pasta Fresca..............374
Pasta in Cream Sauce......47
Pasta with Pesto Sauce....249
Pasta, Ricotta.............250
Sopa de Fideo (Vermicelli)..247
POTATOES
Baked Florentine Potatoes...48
Fancy Duchess Potatoes....239
Fiesta Potatoes............241
Oven Fried Potatoes.......240
Potato Bake, Supreme......240
Potato Casserole, Fluffy...241
Potato Pancakes...........239
Potatoes with Parsley, New.241
Twice-Baked Potatoes......240
Sweet Potato Casserole....242
Sweet Potato Medley......243
Sweet Potatoes...........242
POTPOURRI
Black Eyed Peas, Pickled...253
Chow Chow...............13
Eggs, Pickled.............253
Fig Preserves.............252
Grits, Bandera Party.......247
Jalapeno Jelly............252
Peach Preserves..........251
Peaches, Spiced..........251
Peanuts, Hot Roasted......255
Relleno Para Pavo.........348
Salsa (Sauce), Fresh.......350
Strawberry Preserves......252
Turkey Stuffing...........348
Yorkshire Pudding, Peg's....162
RICE
Chinese Fried Rice........245
El Mirador Rice...........387
Green Chili Rice..........244
Parmesan Rice...........246
Pilaf w/Lemon, Celery....245
Spanish Rice.............244
Rice "Bombay," Curried....361
Rice and Mushrooms......246
Rice Casserole, Wild......246
VEGETABLES
Artichoke Mushroom Velvet222
Artichoke Spinach Delight..222
Asparagus Parmesan, Fried..40
Asparagus, Holiday.......223
Asparagus, Sweet and Sour..223
Avocados, Fried..........48
Baked Beans, Aunt Bessie's..225
Beans, Chili.............144
Beans, Cowboy...........12
Broccoli Crown with Cherry
    Tomatoes.............358
Broccoli with Mushrooms...224
Broccoli, Ritz Cheese.....224
Cabbage and Apples, Red..226
Cabbage Casserole, Layered.226
Cabbage, Castroville.......227
Calabacitas Casserole......234
Calabaza con Puerco.......235
Carrots Lyonnaise.........228
Carrots with Horseradish...227
Carrots, Lemon Basil......228
Celery and Corn..........228
Chiles en Frio (Peppers)...229
Corn Casserole, Hondo....230
Corn Pudding, Mexican....229
Corn, Creamed Cheese....230
Eggplant Parmigiana......389

Eggplant Pie..............231
Frijoles (Pinto Beans).....225
Green Bean Bundles.......231
Green Beans, Bacon Fried..231
Green Beans, Savory......230
Mushrooms in Sour Cream..232
Onions, Baked............232
Onions, Glazed...........232
Spinach Au Gratin, Special..233
Spinach Italiano..........233
Spinach Souffle, Austrian...233
Squash & Hominy Medley..234
Squash Casserole.........234
Squash, Country Club.....235
Sweet Potato Medley......243
Tomatoes, Stuffed........226
Vegetable Casserole, Special.237
Vegetables, Spicy Mex......29
Zucchini Delicious.........236
Zucchini Stuffed with Crab..236
Zucchini, Broiled.........236
Simply Delicious.........48, 358
Snow Peas, Stuffed........63
Sole, Young Ladies' (Senoritas).199
Sopa Anauachalli.........378
Sopa de Fideo.............247
Sorrel, Poached Salmon with
    Oyster Beurre Blanc and...371
Souffle, Grand Marnier......329
SOUPS
    Artichoke, w/Lemon & Dill..88
    Artichoke................88
    Avocado Cream, Sherried....89
    Cabbage Chowder........89
    Caldo de Pollo...........37
    Caldo Xochitl............386
    Cheese, 1886............90
    Cheese, Los Patios........383
    Chicken, Cheesy.........90
    Corn Chowder w/Ham....91
    Corn Chowder, Easy......91
    Crab....................92
    Cucumber, Easy, Cream....92
    Cucumber/Shrimp Bisque..345
    Gazpacho, Chunky........99
    Gazpacho, Smooth & Easy...99
    Lemon..................93
    Lentil...................93
    Lentil, Cream of.........93
    Lobster Bisque..........362
    Locro De Papas..........95
    Mexican Chowder........100
    Mushroom..............94
    Navy Bean.............94
    Onion, French...........95
    Red Snapper...........370
    Sopa Anauachalli (Tortilla)..378
    Spinach Bisque..........96
    Squash, Cold............96
    Steak, Cattlemen's.......97
    Tamale, Mexican........101
    Tortilla Soups.......100, 378
    Vegetable Beef..........97
    Zucchini................98
Sour Cream Banana Nut Bread.268
Sour Cream Coffee Cake......282
Southwest Craft Center......391
Spareribs, Barbecued.........165
Spinach Au Gratin, Special.....233
Spinach Bisque..............96
Spinach Dip in Pumpernickel...67
Spinach Italiano............233
Spinach Puffs, Cheese with....376
Spinach Salad..............349
Spinach Salad Dressing......102
Spinach Souffle, Austrian......233
Spoon Bread................273
Squash and Hominy Medley...234
Squash Casserole............234
Squash Casserole, Mexican....234

Squash Soup, Cold............96
Squash with Pork............235
Squash, Country Club........235
Starving Artist Show..........20
Steak Diane.................150
Steak Soup, Cattlemen's.......97
Steak Tartare a la Josef......359
Steak, German Style Mustard...370
Steak, Marinated Skirt (Fajitas)...5
Steak, Pepper...............137
Steaks, Chicken Fried........138
Steaks, Chili Cheese.........137
Stew with Wine, Beef........156
Stew, Alamo City............155
Stew, Easy Oven Meat........155
Strawberry Angel Cake.......290
Strawberry Bread............267
Strawberry Buttercream Icing..291
Strawberry Cake, Poteet.....290
Strawberry Cheesecakes......324
Strawberry Glaze Pie........304
Strawberry Nut Salad........112
Strawberry Preserves........252
Strawberry Squares, Frosty...327
Sugar Cookies, "Braggin Best"...321
S.W. Craft Center............391
Swedish Rye Bread..........259
Sweet Bread (Pan Dulce).....278
Sweet Potato Casserole.......242
Sweet Potato Medley.........243
Sweet Potato Muffins........266
Sweet Potato Pie, Gilmer.....306
Sweet Potatoes..............242

SWEETS
CAKES
Ambrosia....................49
Angel Food, Mocha..........43
Apple Crunch, Fresh........298
Bars, Easy "Brides".........299
Buttermilk Pound...........297
Candy Crunch...............388
Carrot, South Texas.........300
Chocolate Cola..............288
Chocolate Potato............295
Chocolate Sin...............286
Chocolate Yulelog, Easy....298
Choctaw Pumpkin...........288
Coconut Pound, Soaky......293
Cranberry, Hot Butter Sauce295
Date Nut Torte.............297
Devil's Food...............287
Italian Cream Cheese......299
Lemon Snowball............289
Oatmeal Spice.............296
Orangy Date...............301
Pea Pickin.................291
Pineapple Upside Down....292
Poppy Seed................292
Prune.....................294
Strawberry Angel..........290
Strawberry, Poteet........290
Torte, Mocha Rum........294
CANDIES
Apricot Sticks.............335
Candies, Hints for.........335
Chocolate Delight, Special
    Occasion...............339
Date Roll.................336
Divinity, Strawberry.......19
Fudge.....................336
Fudge, Festive White Confetti
   336
Mints, Cream Cheese.....335
Nuts, Spiced.............338
Peanut Brittle, Microwave..337
Peanut Butter Crunch.....337
Pecans, Dry Roasted......338
Pecans, history of.........338
Pecans, Minted............339

Pecans, Roasted...........338
Pecans, Toasted...........339
Pralines, Mexican............7
Toffee, English............337
CHEESECAKES
Amaretto..................324
Avocado...................325
Cheesecakes..............324
Chocolate Swirl...........326
Crust for Cheesecakes.....326
Delicatessen..............327
Grand Marnier............324
Peach.....................324
Pecan.....................356
Pineapple.................324
Praline, Texas............325
Strawberry................324
COOKIES
Brownies, Creme de Menthe.18
Brownies, Marbled Cheese..313
Brownies, San Antonio's Best312
Butterscotch Cheesecake...322
Candy....................319
Candy Pockets............321
Carmelitas................312
Cashew Crunch............319
Cinnamon Bars............314
Coconut Macaroons........319
Cookies, Mexican..........30
Cookies, Walk-To-School....320
Da Tees...................320
Fruit Cake Cookies........322
Fudge Nut Bars............314
Gingerbread Men..........318
Gingersnaps (Variation)....318
Honey Spice Bars.........315
Lemon Squares............315
Milky Way Squares........313
Mincemeat Bars...........316
Oatmeal, Disappearing.....317
Peanut Butter & Jelly Swirls323
Pecan Sand Tarts.........320
Reposteria (Mexican).......30
Saucepan Scotchies.......316
Sugar, "Braggin Best".....321
Texas Ranger.............317
DESSERTS
Amaretto Oranges.........332
Apple Goodie..............334
Apricot Dream Dessert....331
Banana Meringues.........355
Bread Pudding w/Sauce....331
Custard, Baked............347
Custard, Caramel (Flan)....390
Date Torte................333
Flan (Caramel Custard).....390
Graham Cracker Greek.....328
Ice Cream, Fredericksburg
    Peach..................330
Ice Cream, Fried..........372
Ice Cream, Homemade Van.330
New Braunfels Schaum Torte
    (German Meringue)....329
Peanut Buster Dessert.....333
Pineapple Delight, Tropical.332
San Antonio River Mud....328
Souffle, Grand Marnier....329
Strawberry Squares, Frosty..327
Torte, Quick Fruit........333
Tortoni, Italian Biscuit....334
Trifle, Republic of Texas....42
Tumbleweed Dessert.......84
Yogurt Ice................330
FROSTINGS
Almond Buttercream.......289
Caramel..................296
Chocolate Cola............288
Chocolate, Creamy........286
Chocolate Fudge..........287
Coconut Cream Cheese....300
Colonnade................287
Pecan, Broiled............296
Penuche..................293

Pineapple.................291
Strawberry Buttercream....291
Vanilla Glaze.............297
PASTRIES
Apple Nut Dessert........310
Apple Pie, Grey Moss Inn..379
Apple Pie, Sour Cream.....308
Apricot Strudel...........303
Baklava..................311
Blueberry Cream Pie......303
Buttermilk Pie............302
Caramel Pie..............304
Caribbean Fudge Pie......307
Cheese Date Pastry........23
Chocolate Candy Bar Pie,
    Margery Fulton's......304
Chocolate Mousse Pie.....309
Lemon Ambrosia Pie......310
Lemon Chess Pie..........304
Peach Cobbler............311
Peach Cobbler, Hill Country.12
Pecan Pie................302
Pie Crust, No Fail.........302
Pineapple Meringue Pie....308
Pumpkin Pie with Brandy..306
Raisin-Pecan Pie..........307
Rhubarb Strawberry Cobbler311
Strawberry Glaze Pie......304
Sweet Potato Pie, Gilmer..306
Torte, Fruit..............333
Vanilla Coffee Chiffon Pie..305
Vinegar Pie..............309
Swiss Cheese Spread..........65
Swiss Pie....................219

T

Taco Avocado Pie.............145
Taco Salad..................114
Tamale Casserole.............148
Tamale Soup, Mexican........101
Tangy Sauce, Pork Loin with...353
Tea, Almond.................78
Tea, Spiced (variation).........76
Tea, Texas Sun...............79
Tejas Garlic Shrimp...........195
Tenderloin, Marinated.........152
Tequila Sunrise...............31
Texas Folklife Festival.........32
Texas Ranger Cookies........317
Texas Sunshine...............81
Toffee Coffee Cake...........25
Toffee, English..............337
Tomato Salad for fajitas.........6
Tomato Soup Bread..........268
Tomato Vinaigrette Marinade..103
Tomatoes, Stuffed Cherry......62
Tomatoes, Stuffed............226
Torte, Mocha Rum...........294
Torte, New Baunfels Schaum...329
Torte, Quick Fruit............333
Tortilla Bake, Easy...........147
Tortilla Casserole............147
Tortilla Crumbs, Fried (Migas).209
Tortilla Pastries, (Bunuelos)....277
Tortilla Soups............100, 378
Tortillas, Cheese Filled........73
Tortillas, Flour................6
Tortoni, Italian Biscuit........334
Tostadas (Toasted Chips).......10
Tower of the Americas....284-285
Trifle, Republic of Texas.......42
Tree of Life.................149
Trout Amandine.............196
Trout with Cayenne & Paprika,
    Blackened River..........364
Tumbleweed Dessert.........84
Tumbleweeds,Texas..........84
Tuna-Avocado Salad, Molded...128

Turkey Bites, Bacon..........74
Turkey Creole...............194
Turkey in Swiss Cheese Sauce.194
Turkey Stuffing (Relleno Para
    Pavo), Rosita Fernandez....348
Turnovers or Meat Pies........64

V

Vanilla Coffee Chiffon Pie.....305
Vanilla Glaze.................297
Vaquero.....................13
Veal Chops Palermo, Sauteed..365
Veal Chops, Apple Brandy.....160
Veal Rolls, Italian............385
Veal Scaloppine, Easy.......160
Veal with Paprika, Lemon.....161
Vegetable Beef Soup..........97
Vegetable Casserole, Special...237
Vegetable Marinade, Fresh.....104
Vegetable Salad, Marinated....118
Vegetables, Marinated........141
    San Antonio Marinade.....5
Vegetables, Mexican Pickled....29
Venison Backstrap...........169
Venison Guisada.............169
Venison Stroganoff...........169
Vermicelli Medley...........247
Vinegar Pie.................309

W

Wagner, Candy Erben........350
Western Salad...............114
Wheat or White Bread........258
White or Wheat Bread........258
White, Linda Gale...........345
Windmill...................195

Y

Yeast Biscuits, Kerrville Ranch.261
Yogurt Fruit Low-Cal Salad.....107
Yogurt Ice..................330
Yorkshire Pudding, Peg's.......163

Z

Zoo, San Antonio..........17, 21
Zucchini Bread..............269
Zucchini Delicious...........236
Zucchini Fritters............272
Zucchini Soup...............98
Zucchini Stuffed with Crab...236
Zucchini, Brochettes of Shrimp.351
Zucchini, Broiled...........236

PARTY MENUS

FIESTA BUFFET.............3
Ceviche.....................4
Guacamole..................4
Fajitas......................5
Pico de Gallo.................6
Flour Tortillas................6
Mexican Pralines.............7
Stuffed Jalapeno Peppers........7
**BARBECUE SAN ANTONIO
    STYLE.................8**
Tostadas...................10
Old Fashioned Potato Salad.....10
Pappy Skrap's Barbecue Sauce...11
Cowboy Beans...............12

Hill Country Peach Cobbler.....12
Jalapeno Cornbread...........13
Chow Chow..................13
PICNIC IN THE PARK.......15
Vermicelli Salad..............16
Beef and Brew Take Along......16
SkyHigh Biscuits.............17
Alamo Pecan Cheese Ball......17
Overnight Bloody Marys.......18
Creme de Menthe Brownies....18
Strawberry Divinity...........19
KAFFEEKLATSCH..........21
Fancy Layered Loaf...........22
Cheese Date Pastry...........23
Magnolias..................23
Elegant Oven Omelet.........24
Cinnamon Strawberry Cheese
    Spread..................24
Toffee Coffee Cake...........25
MEXICAN BRUNCH........26
Huevos Poblanos............28
Chicken Chilaquiles...........28
Spicy Mexican Pickled Vegetables
   29
Chorizo Con Papas...........30
Mexican Cookies.............30
Tequila Sunrise..............31
Tropical Mango Mousse.......31
FOLKLIFE FESTIVAL.......33
Anticuchos..................34
Jambalaya..................34
Sauerbraten.................35
Canary Islander Doughnuts....36
Sangria.....................36
Caldo de Pollo..............37
**KING WILLIAM COCKTAIL
    BUFFET...............39**
Caponata...................40
Fried Asparagus Parmesan......40
Coquilles St. Jacques.........41
Republic of Texas Trifle.......42
La Villita Rolls..............43
Mocha Angel Food Cake.......43
GOURMET CELEBRATION....45
Noisettes de Porc aux Pruneaux.46
Schnitzel a la "San Antonio".....46
Cilantro Cumin Butter.........47
Pasta in Cream Sauce.........47
Baked Florentine Potatoes......48
Aguacate Fritos..............48
Ambrosia Cake..............49

DIVIDER PAGES

River Parade...................1
San Fernando Cathedral..25, 50-51
"Battle of Flowers" Parade....86-87
Convention Center........130-131
"Night in Old San Antonio"
    (N.I.O.S.A.)...........220-221
Mission San Jose.........256-257
Institute of Texan Cultures/Tower
    ....32, 284-285
"Las Posadas" on the River..340-341

CULTURAL NOTES

Avocados....................53
Arnesen River Theater.........7
Battle of Flowers Parade.....86-87

Bandera....................247
Bluebonnets................157
Botica Guadalupana..........29
Brown Bag Days.............259
Bunuelos...................301
Cactus.....................237
Canary Islanders.......36, 50, 201
Cascarones..................31
Castroville..................227
Cilantro....................89
Cisneros, Henry..............iv
Clock Tower, S.W. Craft Center
   391
Commander's House..........41
Convention Center........130-131
Costumes early settlers.........35
Crab.......................199
Fiesta Noche del Rio..........52
Flamencos...................2, 7
Floresville..................282
Fredericksburg (Hill Country)...12
Ft. Sam Houston, 5th Army Band
   19
Gilmer.....................306
Hondo.....................230
Institute of Texan Cultures
    ....32, 284-285
Jalapenos..................253
Japanese Tea Gardens........21
Kerrville...................261
King William Historic District...39
King William Fair............392
Las Posadas............340-341
La Villita...................43
Livestock Show and Rodeo.....11
Longhorns..................133
Luling......................78
Mariachis...............256-257
Market Square.............23, 27
Mercado, El...............23, 27
Military influence........14, 86-87
Mission San Jose.........256-257
"Mission Trail"..............256
Molcajete...................71
New Braunfels.............329
"Night In Old San Antonio"
    N.I.O.S.A............220-221
Oil Wells...................219
Pan Dulce..................279
Paseo Del Rio................5
Peaches...................109
Pecans................293, 338
Poteet.....................290
Quilting....................37
Republic of Texas............42
River Parade...................1
Rosita (Rosita Fernandez)...5, 348
San Antonio Zoo.........17, 21
San Antonio River
    ....1, 20, 44, 340-341
San Fernando Cathedral..25, 50-51
Shrimp....................205
Southwest Craft Center.......391
Starving Artist Show..........20
Texas Folklife Festival.........32
Tower of the Americas.20, 284-285
Tree of Life.................149
Vaquero...................13
Windmills..................195

ORDER FORM

Celebrate San Antonio
San Antonio Junior Forum
P.O. Box 791186
San Antonio, Texas 78279-1186
Phone: (512) 349-6367

Please send _____ copies of cookbook . . . . . . at $ 21.95 ea. $ _____

Postage & Handling . . . . at $ 2.50 ea. $ _____

Gift wrap with enclosure card . . . . at $ 2.00 ea. $ _____

from: _____

Texas residents add 7.50% Sales Tax . . . . at $ 1.65 ea. $ _____

Enclosed is my check ☐ . . . . TOTAL $ _____

Please charge to   ☐ VISA   ☐ MASTERCARD

    Card Number _____

    Expiration date _____ Interbank Number _____

    Signature of card holder _____

Name _____

Street _____

City _____ State _____ Zip _____

CSA-88-3

Ship to *(If other than name and address above):*

Name _____

Street _____

City _____ State _____ Zip _____

Make checks payable to: **Celebrate San Antonio**